MW01097121

365 Special Goat Cheese Recipes

(365 Special Goat Cheese Recipes - Volume 1)

Fannie Sims

Copyright: Published in the United States by Fannie Sims/ © FANNIE SIMS

Published on December, 07 2020

All rights reserved. No part of this publication may be reproduced, stored in retrieval system, copied in any form or by any means, electronic, mechanical, photocopying, recording or otherwise transmitted without written permission from the publisher. Please do not participate in or encourage piracy of this material in any way. You must not circulate this book in any format. FANNIE SIMS does not control or direct users' actions and is not responsible for the information or content shared, harm and/or actions of the book readers.

In accordance with the U.S. Copyright Act of 1976, the scanning, uploading and electronic sharing of any part of this book without the permission of the publisher constitute unlawful piracy and theft of the author's intellectual property. If you would like to use material from the book (other than just simply for reviewing the book), prior permission must be obtained by contacting the author at author@shellfishrecipes.com

Thank you for your support of the author's rights.

Content

365 Awesome Goat Cheese Recipes

***

1. Fresh Radish Baguette With Genoa Salami

Serving: Makes 8-10 servings | Prep: | Cook: |Ready in:

Ingredients

- 5 radishes (your favorite variety, rinsed, trimmed, and thinly sliced)
- 1 fresh baguette
- 1 cup soft goat cheese
- 1/4 pound Genoa salami (thinly sliced)
- 2 teaspoons celery seeds
- sea salt and freshly ground black pepper

Direction

- Preheat oven to 400 degrees. Slice baguette in half and place on baking sheet. Toast in oven for 10 minutes, until it just starts to crisp up and brown. Smear all the goat cheese over the 2 baguette halves. Sprinkle sea salt, pepper and celery seeds over the cheese. Next, push the radish pieces into the cheese, covering the bread. On top of all the ingredients, fold the salami slices in half over the whole loaf. That's it! Simple and delicious.

2. Grilled Corn And Summer Squash Quesadillas

Serving: Serves 2 | Prep: 0hours5mins | Cook: 0hours20mins |Ready in:

Ingredients

- 2 ears of corn, husks and silks removed
- 4 flour tortillas
- 1 heaping cup shredded pepper jack cheese
- 1 medium summer squash or zucchini, sliced into 1/4 inch-thick rounds
- 4 ounces goat cheese
- Freshly ground pepper
- Tomatillo salsa (homemade or store-bought), for serving

Direction

- If you have a real live grill, fire that baby up (also I'm coming over). Place the corn directly on the grill grates and cook, turning occasionally, until lightly charred on all sides, about 8 to 10 minutes.
- If you have a gas stove, turn one burner to medium-high. Working one ear at a time, place the corn directly on the grate or coils (you can also hold the corn aloft in the flame with tongs, if you'd prefer). Cook, turning occasionally, until lightly charred on all sides, about 4 to 6 minutes. Some kernels may pop as they cook. For either grilling method, when cool enough to handle, cut the kernels off the cobs.
- Top two of the tortillas with the goat cheese, spread into an even layer. Set aside. Heat a drizzle of olive oil in a pan over medium heat. Add one plain tortilla; top with an even sprinkling of cheese and grilled corn. Add the sliced zucchini, shingling the pieces as necessary, in a single layer. Sprinkle with more cheese and a few turns of black pepper. Top with a goat cheese's tortilla, cheese side down.
- Cook about 2 minutes on the first side, or until the cheese is beginning to melt. Carefully flip and continue to cook, about 5 minutes, or until golden brown. Transfer to a cutting board and slice into wedges. Repeat with the remaining tortillas. Serve with salsa.

- If your pan isn't big enough to fit one flat tortilla, make 4 folded-over quesadillas instead of 2 two-layer ones. Pile up the filling on one half of the tortilla, then fold the other side over the filling. Cook about 6 minutes per side, or until golden brown and the cheese is melted. Slice into wedges.

3. Wintry Spinach, Beetroot And Pumpkin Salad With Caramelized Goat Cheese

Serving: Serves 2 | Prep: | Cook: |Ready in:

Ingredients

- For the dressing
- 1/8 cup olive oil
- 1/8 cup white wine vinegar
- 1 teaspoon honey
- 1 teaspoon mustard
- 1 teaspoon finely grated onion
- salt and pepper to taste
- For the salad
- 1 bag baby leaf spinach
- 1/2 small pumpkin, hokkaido or alike
- 1 apple
- 3 precooked red beets
- 1 thik slice of creamy goat cheese
- 1 tablespoon honey
- 2 handfuls walnuts

Direction

- Wash the pumpkin, remove seeds and cut into bite-sized cubes. Steam or cook in little water until tender (about 10 minutes). Put the goat cheese on an oven-proof dish, drizzle the honey over it and pop it in the oven for about 10-15 minutes at 300°F.
- In the meantime, whisk together the dressing. Wash and dry the spinach leaves (I don't care to stem them, but do if you like!), core and cut the apple in cubes. Quarter the beets and slice

them thinly. Arrange spinach on two plates. Take the warm pumpkin pieces, apples and beets and divide equally over the spinach. Drizzle the dressing on top. Take the goat cheese out of the oven when it turns soft and the honey begins to caramelize. Divide on the two plates. Crumble a handful of walnuts over each salad.
- Enjoy with a peace of ciabatta on the side!

4. "Modern" Potato Gratin

Serving: Makes 1 dish | Prep: | Cook: |Ready in:

Ingredients

- 500g potatoes
- 350g sweet potatoes
- 200g parsnip
- 320 milliliters 10% cream
- 320 milliliters low-fat cream (5%) or milk
- 50g firm or soft goat cheese
- 50g gouda cheese
- salt and pepper
- dried or fresh Coriander
- dried or fresh Rosmary

Direction

- Peel the potatoes, sweet potatoes and parsnip. Cut into slices (I like them thin)
- Spread them out (in layers) in an oven dish and season each layer. Also add some coriander and rosemary.
- Grate the Gouda cheese and crumble/grate the goat cheese. In bowl, whisk together cream and cheese. Pour over the vegetables
- Bake in the oven at 350F for 60-90 minutes

5. 'Georgia Caprese' Salad

Serving: Serves 4 | Prep: | Cook: |Ready in:

Ingredients

- 2   Peaches, firm but ripe
- 3 ounces goat cheese, sliced in disks
- 1 handful arugula
- 2-3 teaspoons balsamic vinegar
- 2-3 teaspoons good quality, fruity olive oil
- 12-16   Basil leaves (depending on the size)

Direction

- Slice the peaches, you should be able to get 6 - 8 slices out of each peach. Slice the goat cheese, I find this to be the easiest by placing it in the freezer for 10-15 minutes and using waxed dental floss for the slicing rather than a knife.
- Divide the arugula between 4 salad plates. Then layer the salad in a stack alternating peaches, basil, and goat cheese. I aim for 3 layers of peaches and basil and one two layers of the cheese. If you have large basil leaves most likely just one per layer will be needed, if they are small ones from your yard then 2-3 per layer. Drizzle each salad with oil and vinegar.

6. Acacia Honey, Strawberry & Goat Cheese Gelato

Serving: Serves makes 1 quart | Prep: | Cook: | Ready in:

Ingredients

- 5   egg yolks (organic & free range if possible)
- 3/4 cup honey (Acacia)
- 2 cups (whole) goat's milk
- 6 ounces soft goat cheese (fresh)
- 1/2 teaspoon vanilla extract
- 1/2   basket strawberries (sliced in thirds)

Direction

- In a stand mixer with the whisk attachment or in a medium blow using a hand-held mixer, beat the egg yolks and honey together until

pale yellow and satiny, about 2 minutes. Set aside.

- In a large saucepan, mix the milk and goat cheese together over medium heat, stirring constantly, just until hot (be careful not to boil). Slowly pour one-half cup of the warm milk mixture into the egg mixture, whisking constantly. Whisk in an additional one-half cup of the milk mixture to fully temper the yolks. Pour the egg mixture back into the saucepan and cook over medium heat, stirring constantly, until the mixture coats the back of a spoon, about 5 minutes.
- Pour the mixture into a medium bowl set over an ice bath. Allow the mixture to chill completely, 10 to 15 minutes. Stir in the vanilla.
- Freeze in an ice cream maker according to manufacturer's directions 25 minutes. Add sliced strawberries and continue to freeze in ice cream maker an additional 5 to 10 minutes. Spread the gelato evenly into a container with a lid; cover the surface with plastic wrap and then cover with the lid. Freeze it until completely set, at least 5 hours, preferable overnight.

7. Adult Fruit Salad

Serving: Serves 2 | Prep: | Cook: | Ready in:

Ingredients

- 1 cup of fresh cherries, pitted and halved
- 2 cups of strawberries, thinly sliced
- 3   oranges, segmented
- 1/4 cup of unsalted pistachios, chopped
- 100 grams of goat cheese
- 4 tablespoons of cream
- 1/4 cup of balsamic reduction
- 5 tablespoons of elderflower cordial

Direction

- If you have never made balsamic reduction before, it is super easy to make. You don't need a fancy bottle of balsamic vinegar; just get a cheap one, since it's going to reduce a lot. Pour 250ml of balsamic vinegar into a pan. Reduce over medium-low heat until it has reduced to about 1/3 of a cup. Don't let it get too thick though, as it will thicken as it cools down. If it gets too thick, you can always warm it up in the microwave for a few seconds to loosen it up. You can make this in advance and keep it in your pantry.
- Prepare all of your fruit.
- To make the whipped goat cheese, just place the goat cheese and cream in the food processor and pulse until smooth.
- To make the dressing, place the balsamic reduction and elderflower cordial in a pan. Let it simmer over med-low heat for about 1-2 minutes, until it is all mixed. Don't let it reduce too much, otherwise it will become a caramel and you won't be able to pour it.
- To plate up, pour some of the dressing on the plate. Then add the fruit. I formed quenelles with the whipped goat cheese. Finally, sprinkle some pistachios.

8. Almost Vegetarian Crêpe

Serving: Makes 4 crêpes | Prep: | Cook: | Ready in:

Ingredients

- Crêpes Salées (these measurements come from David Lebovitz's recipe for Buckwheat Crêpes, and yields about 20 crêpes)
- 2 cups milk
- 1 tablespoon sugar
- ¼ teaspoon sea salt
- 3 tablespoons melted, plus more for cooking
- ½ cup buckwheat flour
- ¾ cup white flour
- 3 eggs
- Crêpe Filling

- 2 sweet potatoes
- 1.5 tablespoons duck fat
- sea salt, freshly ground black pepper
- a bunch of asparagus
- a measure of olive oil
- 4 tablespoons of goat cheese
- ¼ cup of Marcona almonds, lightly crushed
- 1 tablespoon blood orange juice
- 3 tablespoons avocado oil
- 1 head of frisee, washed and dried
- balsamic cream

Direction

- Crêpes Salées (these measurements yield about 20 crêpes)
- In a large bowl, mix all the ingredients together. If you are letting it rest overnight, cover the bowl and move it to the refrigerator. (Bring it to room temperature before you start cooking.) If it will only sit for 2 hours or so, cover it and keep it at room temperature.
- When you are ready to make the crêpes, locate your widest, flattest non-stick pan. Using a paper towel, rub a thin sheen of butter all over the pan, and then set it over medium heat. (You can repeat this for every new crêpe, but it usually isn't necessary.)
- When the pan is hot, use a ladle to quickly drop a measure of the batter into the pan. Turn the pan in a wide circle, as quickly as you can, so that the batter distributes evenly and rapidly. You want as thin a pancake as possible. Don't worry if the first one is a disaster; it's part of the process. Save the disasters for yourself. You will get better with each crêpe.
- As the crêpes cook, pile them on a plate; you want to cook all of your crêpes before you start filling them.
- Crêpe Filling
- Prepare the vegetables: Preheat an oven to 400F. In a saucepan, melt the duck fat. Meanwhile, peel and dice both sweet potatoes. When the duck fat is melted, give the sweet potato cubes a bath, and add some salt and pepper for good measure.

- Wash and dry the asparagus, and then rub each spear down with olive oil, salt and pepper.
- Throw everything on a parchment paper-covered baking sheet, making sure not to crowd the vegetables. I used thick asparagus and cut my sweet potatoes small, so both vegetables cooked at the same rate, about 30 minutes. However, if your asparagus are thin, keep an eye on them, they may need to come out of the oven earlier than the sweet potato.
- Prepare the salad: In a small bowl, combine the blood orange juice with the avocado oil, and a little salt and pepper. Toss in the frisee and mix until it's covered in the dressing. Easy peasy.
- Prepare the crêpe: Heat each buckwheat crêpe in a non-stick skillet. Add the vegetables, and then sprinkle on the goat cheese and the almonds. Top with the salad, and a drizzle of the balsamic cream.

9. Alon Shaya's Whole Roasted Cauliflower And Whipped Goat Cheese

Serving: Serves 4 to 6 | Prep: 0hours10mins | Cook: 1hours0mins | Ready in:

Ingredients

- Roasted Cauliflower
- 1 head cauliflower, whole, stem trimmed and leaves removed
- 2 1/2 cups dry white wine
- 1/3 cup olive oil plus more for serving
- 1/4 cup kosher salt
- 3 tablespoons fresh lemon juice
- 2 tablespoons unsalted butter
- 1 tablespoon crushed red pepper flakes (or to taste)
- 1 tablespoon sugar
- 1 bay leaf
- 1 pinch Coarse sea salt (for serving)

- Whipped Goat Cheese
- 4 ounces fresh goat cheese
- 3 ounces cream cheese
- 3 ounces feta cheese
- 1/3 cup heavy cream
- 2 tablespoons olive oil plus more for serving

Direction

- Roasted Cauliflower
- Heat oven to 475° F. Bring wine, oil, salt, lemon juice, butter, red pepper flakes, sugar, bay leaf, and 8 cups water to a boil in a large pot.
- Carefully lower in cauliflower, reduce heat, and simmer, turning occasionally, until a knife easily inserts into center, 15 to 20 minutes.
- Using 2 slotted spoons or a mesh strainer or spider, transfer cauliflower to a rimmed baking sheet or roasting pan, draining well.
- Roast, rotating pan halfway through, until brown all over, 30 to 40 minutes.
- Transfer cauliflower to a plate. Drizzle with oil; sprinkle with sea salt. Serve with whipped goat cheese (recipe below).
- Whipped Goat Cheese
- Blend goat cheese, cream cheese, feta, cream, and 2 tablespoons olive oil in a food processor until smooth; season with sea salt.
- Transfer whipped goat cheese to a serving bowl and drizzle with olive oil.
- Note: Whipped goat cheese can be made one day ahead. Cover and chill in the refrigerator.

10. An Autumn Salad Of Figs And Toasted Goat Cheese

Serving: Serves 2 as an entreé, 4 as a side salad | Prep: | Cook: | Ready in:

Ingredients

- 8 1/2 inch slices of a plain goat cheese loge
- 1 organic egg white, slightly beaten
- 1 cup panko breadcrumbs

- 1/2 cup walnut pieces
- 1 tablespoon sherry vinegar, best quality
- 1/2 teaspoon Dijon mustard
- 3 tablespoons virgin olive oil, divided use
- 1 teaspoon organic honey
- kosher salt and ground black pepper
- 4 cups organic "baby" or field greens
- 8 organic figs
- 1 tablespoon organic, unsalted butter

Direction

- Coat each slice of cheese with some of the egg white mixture. Roll each one in the panko crumbs until coated. Set coated cheese slices aside on a rack and chill in the coldest part of your fridge while you prepare the rest of the salad.
- Heat a small skillet and add the walnuts. Cook until your nose reminds you to remove the skillet from the heat before they scorch. Set aside.
- Using a good-sized salad bowl, prepare your vinaigrette: add the vinegar, mustard, salt and pepper. Whisk to combine. Add the honey and 3 tablespoons of olive oil. Whisk together.
- Add the greens to the vinaigrette and toss. Stem and halve the figs. Add figs and toasted walnuts. Toss gently. Set aside.
- Using a medium-sized skillet, heat the butter and remaining tablespoon of oil over medium-high heat. You want this process to occur quickly in order not to melt the goat cheese! Add the goat cheese slices and cook until lightly browned on both sides.
- Serve the chilled greens on two plates. Top each portion with 2-4 slices of the toasted goat cheese, as desired.

11. Apricot Chutney Ham And Cheese With Spiced Caramel Crust

Serving: Serves 4 | Prep: | Cook: | Ready in:

Ingredients

- 1/2 cup apricot preserves
- 2 tablespoons cider vinegar
- 1 teaspoon fresh grated ginger
- 2 teaspoons ground cinnamon
- 2 tablespoons granulated sugar
- 8   slices sourdough bread
- 6 tablespoons butter, divided
- 8 ounces goat cheese
- 12   slices deli-style ham (preferably maple glazed)

Direction

- In a small bowl, mix the apricot preserves, vinegar and ginger. Set aside.
- In another small bowl, mix together sugar and cinnamon. Set aside.
- Butter one side of each of the slices of bread. Spread goat cheese on the other side. Spread about 2 tablespoons of apricot chutney on top of the goat cheese and then fold three slices of ham on top.
- Close up the sandwich. Sprinkle cinnamon sugar mix over the outside of the sandwich.
- Heat a large skillet over medium heat. Melt the remaining butter (about 1 tablespoon per sandwich) in the skillet. Working 2 sandwiches at a time, brown each one, about 3-5 minutes on each side, covering the pan in between flips. The outside should get golden brown and slightly gooey.
- Repeat for remaining two sandwiches, keeping the first sandwiches warm in a toaster oven set on low. Serve immediately.

12. Artichoke & Sun Dried Tomato Stuffed Mushrooms

Serving: Makes 16 | Prep: | Cook: | Ready in:

Ingredients

- 16   White Button Mushrooms-stems Removed

- 2 tablespoons Roasted Garlic Olive Oil
- 5 ounces Frozen Chopped Spinach-thawed And Water Squeezed Out
- 4 Sun-Dried Tomatoes-finely Diced
- 1/4 cup Marinated Artichoke Hearts, Roughly Chopped
- 4 ounces Goat Cheese
- 4 ounces Cream Cheese
- 2 tablespoons Grated Parmesan Cheese

Direction

- Preheat the oven to 350 degrees (F) and line a baking sheet with aluminum foil. Wipe mushroom caps clean with a damp paper towel.
- Heat 2 tbsp. of garlic olive oil in a medium pan over medium heat. Add spinach, sun-dried tomatoes and marinated artichoke hearts. Stir to combine and cook for 2-3 minutes. Remove the mixture from the pan and place it into a bowl. Add the goat cheese and cream cheese to the bowl and stir to combine. Mix well.
- Fill the mushroom caps with the mixture and place them on the cookie sheet. Sprinkle mushrooms with grated parmesan cheese. Bake for 20 minutes. Serve warm.

13. Artichoke, Asparagus, & Mushroom Pizza

Serving: Serves 2-4 | Prep: | Cook: | Ready in:

Ingredients

- 1 ball Your preferred pizza dough
- 14 ounces Cannellini beans
- 1 Garlic clove, smashed
- 2 tablespoons Olive oil, divided
- Water
- Salt, to taste
- 1/2 pound Asparagus, cut into 1 inch pieces
- 6-8 Cremini mushrooms, sliced
- 6 ounces jar of Marinated artichokes
- 4 ounces Goat cheese, crumbled

- Thyme, to garnish
- Red pepper flakes (optional)

Direction

- Heat oven to 450 degrees.
- Prepare the sauce. Drain cannellini beans and pour into a blender. Add garlic, 1 tbsp. olive oil, and 1 tbsp. water. Blend adding water one tbsp. at a time until smooth. It should be slightly thinner than dip. Add salt to taste. Set aside.
- Heat the remaining oil in a pan and add the asparagus. Sauté for a few minutes. Try not to cook all the way through. Move asparagus to a bowl. Now add the mushrooms to the pan. Let cook for a few minutes, and then add the marinated artichokes (not the liquid). Heat through and break up the artichokes with a wooden spoon. Remove from heat and combine with the asparagus.
- Dust a cookie sheet with corn meal. Stretch your pizza dough to fit, and par bake for 5 minutes.
- Remove dough from the oven and assemble the pizza. Spread the sauce. (You may have some sauce left over. It's great with lemon and pita chips.) Then, layer the vegetables and crumbled goat cheese. Top with a sprinkling of thyme and red pepper flakes to taste.
- Bake another 5-10 minutes. The cheese will not brown so keep an eye on the bottom of the dough for done-ness

14. Arugula Salad With Melon And Crispy Prosciutto

Serving: Serves 2 as a main course, 4-6 as a side | Prep: | Cook: | Ready in:

Ingredients

- For the dressing:
- 1 small shallot, minced
- 2 tablespoons sherry vinegar

- 1/4 cup extra virgin olive oil
- Salt and pepper
- For the salad:
- 3 ounces prosciutto (approximately 6 slices)
- 1 pint Padrón peppers (or use shishito peppers)
- Olive oil
- 5 ounces baby arugula
- 1/2 large cantaloupe or other orange-fleshed melon, cut into 3/4-inch pieces
- 1/3 cup sliced or slivered almonds, toasted
- 1/2 cup goat cheese, crumbled

Direction

- Preheat the oven to 375 degrees. Line a baking sheet with parchment paper and arrange the prosciutto in a single layer on top. Bake for 13-15 minutes, until crisp but not browned. Let cool on baking sheet.
- Meanwhile, make the dressing: put the minced shallot in the bottom of your salad bowl with the sherry vinegar, and let sit for 15 minutes. Whisk in the olive oil in a thin stream until blended and season to taste with salt and pepper.
- While the shallot is marinating, prepare the peppers: preheat a large skillet (not nonstick, preferably cast iron) over medium high heat for 5 minutes. Add enough olive oil to just coat the bottom, and add the peppers to the pan. Cook for 3-4 minutes depending on size (5-6 if you are using larger shishitos), tossing every 45-60 seconds to encourage blistering on all sides. Remove from heat, and once cool enough to handle, slice into ¾-inch rings, discarding the stems. Let cool completely.
- Add the arugula to the salad bowl and toss to coat with the dressing. Gently fold in the melon and peppers until well-distributed. Break the crispy prosciutto slices into bite-sized pieces, and scatter over the top of the salad along with the toasted almonds and goat cheese crumbles. Serve.

15. Arugula, Delicata, And Honeycrisp Salad

Serving: Serves 4 | Prep: | Cook: | Ready in:

Ingredients

- 2 delicata squash, scrubbed clean, seeds removed, sliced into rings or chunks
- 1 honeycrisp apple, cored and chopped
- 4-6 ounces baby arugula, washed
- 1/4 cup crumbled goat cheese
- 1 small clove of garlic, pressed or finely minced
- 1 tablespoon sherry vinegar
- 3 tablespoons olive oil
- 1/4 teaspoon Dijon mustard

Direction

- Salt the delicata squash and let sit for 15 minutes. Pat dry.
- In a large skillet, heat 1 tablespoon olive oil over medium heat. Add the delicata squash and cook until browned on all sides, about 15 minutes. The squash should be crisp on the outside and tender inside.
- Make the vinaigrette: mix the garlic, mustard, and vinegar. Whisk in 2 tablespoons of olive oil. Season with salt and pepper.
- Place the cooked squash on a plate. Drizzle with 2 teaspoons of vinaigrette. Toss the goat cheese, arugula, and apples with the vinaigrette and place on top of the squash. Add freshly ground black pepper if desired.

16. Arugula, Peach & Goat Cheese Salad With Cherry Dressing

Serving: Serves 4 | Prep: | Cook: | Ready in:

Ingredients

- For the dressing:
- 1/2 cup fresh or frozen cherries

- 2 tablespoons water
- 2 tablespoons mild flavored olive oil
- 1 tablespoon lemon juice
- salt and pepper to taste
- For the salad:
- 6 cups arugula leaves
- 2 peaches, pitted and sliced finely
- 4 shots fine slices of red onion
- 4 ounces goat cheese, crumbled
- 1 handful fresh basil leaves, finely sliced

Direction

- For the dressing:
- In a blender, combine the cherries and water until liquefied. Strain the cherries using a fine meshed strainer to remove the cherry pulp and keep the cherry juices in a bowl.
- Add the olive oil, lemon juice, salt and pepper; whisk to emulsify.
- For the salad:
- Divide the arugula between four plates. Top with finely sliced red onion and peach slices.
- Sprinkle the crumbled goat's cheese on top of the salads and drizzle liberally with cherry dressing.
- Garnish with sliced basil leaves and serve.

17. Arugula, Pear And Goat Cheese Salad With Pomegranate Vinaigrette

Serving: Serves 6 | Prep: 0hours15mins | Cook: 0hours0mins | Ready in:

Ingredients

- Vinaigrette
- 1 large shallot, halved and thinly sliced
- 1 tablespoon pomegranate molasses
- 2 tablespoons sherry or apple cider vinegar
- 1/2 teaspoon kosher salt
- 1/4 teaspoon black pepepr
- 1/3 cup extra virgin olive oil

- For the salad
- 4 cups arugula, lightly packed
- 4 cups romaine, torn into bite-sized pieces
- 2 ripe pears, cored and cut into 1/2" cubes
- 1/3 cup pomegranate seeds
- 3 ounces fresh goat cheese or feta, crumbled
- 1/4 cup pistachios, toasted and coarsely chopped

Direction

- In a small bowl combine the shallot, pomegranate molasses, vinegar, salt and pepper and whisk until the salt is dissolved.
- Whisk in the olive oil and let vinaigrette stand at room temperature until salad is assembled.
- Combine the arugula, romaine, pears and half of the pomegranate seeds in a large bowl.
- Crumble half of the goat cheese over the ingredients in the bowl (this works best if the cheese is very cold).
- Whisk the vinaigrette until uniform and add all but 2 tablespoons of it to the bowl.
- Gently toss the salad with your hands or salad tongs, coating the ingredients well with the vinaigrette. If the salad seems dry, add the vinaigrette in small increments until it is dressed to your liking.
- Crumble the remaining cheese over the salad and sprinkle the remaining pomegranate seeds and the pistachios over the top. Serve immediately.

18. Asparagus And Goat Cheese Frittata Over Salad With Chive Flower Vinaigrette

Serving: Serves 4-6 | Prep: | Cook: | Ready in:

Ingredients

- For the chive flower infused vinegar:
- 5-6 Chive flowers, stems removed
- 2 Garlic cloves, smashed

- 1/2 cup White wine or champagne vinegar
- For the frittata:
- 12-14 Thin asparagus spears, trimmed
- 2 tablespoons Olive oil
- 2 Spring garlic stalks, chopped
- 12 Eggs
- 1/2 cup Whole milk
- 1 teaspoon Salt
- 1/2 teaspoon Black pepper
- 3 tablespoons Chives, chopped
- 3½ ounces Goat cheese

Direction

- For the chive flower infused vinegar:
- In an 8 ounce canning jar, combine chive flowers and garlic cloves. Fill jar with vinegar, leaving about 1 inch space at the top. Use a spoon to press chive flowers against side of jar, breaking them up just a little. Cover top with parchment paper and then close with lid. Let sit in a cool, dry place for at least 1 week.
- For the frittata:
- Preheat oven to 350F.
- Bring a pot of heavily salted water to boil. Add asparagus and boil for 3 minutes. Transfer asparagus to a bowl and cover with ice water. Let cool completely.
- In a large bowl, whisk together eggs, milk, salt and pepper. Set aside.
- In a 10 inch cast iron skillet, heat olive oil over medium heat. Add the spring garlic and cook until fragrant, about 1 minute. Add egg mixture and chives and stir to distribute greens evenly. Cook for 5 minutes over medium heat, until edges start to set. Remove from heat and arrange asparagus spears, all pointing towards the center, in the eggs and dollop goat cheese around the entire pan. Transfer pan to oven and bake for 15-20 minutes, until center is just set. Make sure to watch as you don't want the eggs to overcook!
- To make the salad: While frittata is baking, prepare the salad. In a small bowl, whisk together 4 tbsp. olive oil and 4 tsp infused vinegar. Pour over 6 oz. greens and add salt and pepper to taste.

19. Asparagus And Leek Puff Pastry Tart

Serving: Serves 6-8 | Prep: | Cook: | Ready in:

Ingredients

- 2 frozen puff pastry sheets, thawed
- 1 bunch asparagus, trimmed
- 2 leeks, white and lt green part only, sliced
- 2 tablespoons butter
- asiago cheese, grated
- fontina cheese, grated
- goat cheese
- sea salt

Direction

- Preheat oven to 400
- Roll out the puff pastry sheets and fit together inside a jelly roll pan and roll the edges over. Make a diagonal slit all around the edge about 1 inch apart. Prick holes in bottom of puff pastry with a fork. In a medium saucepan, heat butter and add leek. Cook until caramelized and add a little salt.
- On the bottom of puff pastry, add fontina and asiago cheese and then add dollops of goat cheese. Toss asparagus in a little olive oil and salt.
- Begin at one end of pan and down the middle, lay the asparagus. Around the border spoon the cooked leeks.
- Put in oven and bake 20-25 minutes or until golden brown.

20. Asparagus With Goat Cheese And Pickled Red Onion

Serving: Serves 4 | Prep: | Cook: | Ready in:

Ingredients

- 1/2 small red onion
- 2 tablespoons fresh lemon juice
- 2 tablespoons rice wine vinegar
- 1 pound thin-stalk asparagus
- 2 tablespoons olive oil
- Sea salt and freshly ground pepper
- 2 ounces fresh goat cheese

Direction

- Place the onion on a flat surface and cut off the top. Peel away the dried outer layers. Cut into thin slices. Put in a small bowl and add the lemon juice and vinegar. Stir to combine. Let sit 30 minutes. Drain in a colander and set aside.
- Preheat the oven to 425°F.
- Put the asparagus on a baking sheet and pour the olive oil over the top. Toss to coat the asparagus. Sprinkle with salt and pepper. Spread the asparagus out into a single layer and bake just until tender, about 8 minutes for stalks less than 1/2-inch in diameter. Add 3 minutes for stalks more than 1/2-inch in diameter and 6 minutes for stalks 1-inch in diameter.
- Transfer the asparagus immediately to a cool plate to stop the cooking. Arrange the onions over the asparagus and crumble the goat cheese over the top of the onions.

21. Aviva's Breakfast Sandwich

Serving: Serves 1 | Prep: | Cook: | Ready in:

Ingredients

- 1 multi grain roll (Tomkat bakery rolls are used here)
- 1 egg
- 1/3 cup sauteed Swiss chard, chopped
- 1 tablespoon chopped sundried tomato
- 1 teaspoon black olive spread, or coursly chopped olives if you prefer
- 1 tablespoon soft goat cheese
- 1/2 handful chopped pea shoots
- 1 teaspoon softened unsalted butter

Direction

- Slice the multi grain roll in half and place in the toaster. While it is toasting mix goat cheese with olive and sundried tomato. Set aside.
- Poach or fry the egg. We fry more often than not, but poaching works too.
- After the roll is toasted, spread the cheese mixture on one side and the butter on the opposite side. Assemble the remaining ingredients in whatever order you like. Enjoy!

22. Avocado, Black Bean & Sweet Potato Chopped Salad

Serving: Serves 3 | Prep: | Cook: | Ready in:

Ingredients

- Dressing
- 1 cup loose packed cilantro
- 1/4 cup canola oil
- 2 tablespoons lime juice (juice of 1 lime)
- 1 teaspoon honey
- 1/2 teaspoon salt
- Salad
- 1 pound sweet potatoes, peeled and cut into small (approx 1/2") pieces
- 1 tablespoon canola oil
- 1 teaspoon ground chipotle chile powder
- 1/2 teaspoon salt
- 2 romaine hearts, chopped into bite sized pieces
- 1 15-oz can black beans, rinsed & drained
- 1 large avocado, chopped into bite sized pieces
- 3 ounces goat cheese, crumbled
- cilantro springs

- roasted pepitas (pumpkin seeds)
- thinly sliced red onion

Direction

- To make the dressing, combine all dressing ingredients in a blender or food processor and process until well blended.
- Preheat oven to 400 degrees.
- Toss sweet potatoes with the oil, chipotle chile powder, and salt until well coated. Spread potatoes in an even layer on a baking sheet and roast at 400 degrees until tender and beginning to brown on the edges, about 30 minutes.
- Place chopped romaine in a large bowl. Give your dressing a good stir, then pour over lettuce and toss to coat evenly. Divide lettuce evenly between plates. Top each with equal amounts of roasted sweet potatoes, black beans, chopped avocado, and crumbled goat cheese. Garnish with cilantro sprigs, pepitas, and thinly sliced red onion.

---

23. Baby Bella Asparagus Quiche With Goat Cheese

Serving: Serves 8 | Prep: | Cook: | Ready in:

Ingredients

- Baby Bella Asparagus Quiche with Goat Cheese
- 1 savory pie crust (recipe follows)
- 1 tablespoon butter
- 1 1/2 cups asparagus cut in 1 inch pieces
- 3 pieces bacon cooked and crumbled
- 2 1/2 cups baby bella (portabella) mushrooms thinly sliced
- 1 small shallot minced
- 4 large eggs slightly beaten
- 1 cup half & half
- 1/2 teaspoon salt
- 1/2 teaspoon fresh black pepper
- 1/2 cup gruyere cheese shredded

- 1/2 cup goat cheese
- Savory Pie Crust
- 1 1/4 cups unbleached all purpose flour
- 1/4 teaspoon salt
- 6 tablespoons unsalted butter cubed
- 2 tablespoons canola oil
- 1 1/2 teaspoons lemon juice

Direction

- Baby Bella Asparagus Quiche with Goat Cheese
- Prepare pie crust and line a 9 inch tart pan. Chill for 20 minutes.
- Cook asparagus in boiling salted water until just tender. Drain.
- Melt butter in a fry pan and sauté the mushrooms and shallot until mushrooms brown. Set aside to cool.
- In a large bowl combine eggs, half & half, cooked asparagus, cooked bacon, sautéed mushrooms and shallots, salt and pepper. Stir.
- Crumble the goat cheese and stir gently into egg mixture.
- Sprinkle the gruyere on the bottom of the tart pan.
- Pour the egg mixture gently into tart pan.
- Preheat oven to 375 degrees.
- Bake for 35 minutes or until browned on top and firm.
- Cool and let rest for 10 minutes.
- Savory Pie Crust
- Mix flour and salt in a food processor.
- Add in cubed butter and process until crumbly.
- Add oil, 3 tablespoons very cold water, and lemon juice.
- Pulse until dough ball forms.
- Wrap in plastic, let rest and chill for 20 minutes.

24. Baby Spinach Frittata With Sweet Potato Crust

Serving: Makes 8 slices | Prep: | Cook: |Ready in:

Ingredients

- 8 large eggs
- 3 tablespoons chili garlic sauce
- 1/2 cup lite coconut milk
- sea salt and freshly cracked black pepper
- 2 medium sweet potatoes, peeled and diced (about 4 cups)
- 2 tablespoons extra virgin olive oil
- 2 teaspoons ground cumin
- 1/2 teaspoon cayenne pepper
- 4 green onions, thinly sliced
- 2 cups baby spinach, roughly chopped
- 4 ounces herbed goat cheese, crumbled
- 2 tablespoons chopped cilantro (garnish)

Direction

- Preheat oven 425F.
- In a large bowl, whisk together eggs, chili garlic sauce, coconut milk plus a dash or two of sea salt and pepper.
- Heat olive oil in a large oven-proof skillet (that you have the lid to) over medium heat, add diced sweet potatoes, ground cumin, cayenne pepper, and a dash of sea salt then stir coat. Cook the sweet potatoes for about 15 minutes or until they are tender.
- Top the cooked sweet potatoes with chopped baby spinach and sliced green onions, cover pan and cook for 2-3 minutes or until spinach wilts.
- Remove lid, reduce heat to low then pour egg mixture from step two over contents in the skillet. Sprinkle crumbled goat cheese on top of the eggs.
- Place skillet in the oven and cook for about 14-18 minutes (or until you can shake the pan and the middle eggs are barely set).
- Remove frittata from the oven, let sit for a few minutes before slicing. Top with cilantro then eat!

25. Bacon Baguette Baked Eggs

Serving: Serves 4 | Prep: | Cook: |Ready in:

Ingredients

- 1 tablespoon EVOO, plus brushing pan
- 4 eggs
- 1/2 cup almond milk
- 1/4 cup grated parmesan
- 1 teaspoon salt, divided
- 4 ounces baguette, preferably day-old, cut into 1 inch cubes
- 1 red bell pepper, thinly sliced then cut in half
- 1/2 onion, thinly sliced then cut in half (roughly chopped)
- 1/4 cup goat cheese, crumbled
- 2 slices bacon (I used naturally smoked)
- 1-2 sprigs fresh thyme, for garnish

Direction

- Brush 9×9 pan with olive oil.
- In a bowl, beat eggs, milk, Parmesan, and 1/4 tsp salt and pepper. Add bread, toss until coated; transfer to pan and let sit.
- Heat oven to 400 degrees.
- In large nonstick skillet, cook strips of bacon until crisps. Remove and place on paper towel. In same pan (yes with bacon grease), sauté bell pepper, onion, thyme and remaining 1/2 tsp salt and 1/4 tsp black pepper until onion begins to brown, 10 minutes. Add bell pepper mixture to pan; spread evenly over bread mixture; dot with goat cheese.
- Bake until top is puffed and browned and center is firm, 25 minutes. Let rest for 5 minutes. Garnish with thyme.

26. Baked Butternut Squash And Warm Goats Cheese Salad

Serving: Serves 4 | Prep: | Cook: | Ready in:

Ingredients

- The Salad...
- 1 Medium butternut squash, peeled, cut in half with seeds removed
- 3-4 ounces Chevre goats cheese, sliced in rings or triangles
- 2 cups Mixed blend salad (I use one with watercress, rocket, and baby spinach)
- 1 cup Halved cherry tomatoes
- 1 tablespoon Butter or butter substitute
- 1 tablespoon Agave nectar
- 2-3 Sprigs of fresh Thyme
- The Dressing...
- 3 tablespoons Olive oil
- 1 tablespoon Balsamic vinegar
- 1 teaspoon Lemon juice
- Salt and pepper to taste

Direction

- Preheat your oven to 220C (430F)
- Prepare your butternut squash and place on a baking sheet, spread the butter evenly on each piece and drizzle with the Agave nectar. Place in the oven for approximately 45 minutes.
- Wash your lettuce and wash and chop your tomatoes, place in a bowl.
- Blend your vinaigrette by mixing the olive oil, balsamic vinegar, lemon juice, salt and pepper, then mix well with a fork.
- Slice the goat cheese and stick it in the oven on the baking sheet for the last 5 minutes of the butternut squash cooking. Remove the butternut squash and goats cheese from the oven. If there is any syrup in the butternut squash groove, pour it over the salad. Using a sharp knife and fork, cut the butternut squash into chunks or slices.
- Place the goat cheese on top of the salad, followed by the butternut squash and the

vinaigrette. Sprinkle some fresh thyme on top! And, voila!!!! Enjoy!

27. Baked Eggs

Serving: Serves 2 | Prep: | Cook: | Ready in:

Ingredients

- 1 tablespoon heavy cream
- 2 eggs
- 2 tablespoons chopped tomatoes (or to taste)
- 1 tablespoon chopped onions (green or white)
- crumbled goat cheese, to taste
- sprinkle of bread crumbs
- healthy grate of cheddar or parmesan
- salt and pepper, to taste
- sprinkle of garlic powder and red pepper flakes
- fresh herbs, chopped, if available

Direction

- Coat the bottom of an individual sized shallow baking dish (you can use a larger dish if you're making baked eggs for a crowd) with the heavy cream.
- Crack one or two eggs (for an individual size) into the dish.
- Add the chopped veggies and goat cheese.
- Add herbs and spices.
- Sprinkle the top with bread crumbs and grated cheese.
- Bake at 375 degrees for about 25 minutes or until the cream has just set (less time if you like runnier yolks).

28. Baked Ricotta And Goat Cheese With Candied Tomatoes

Serving: Serves 8-10 | Prep: | Cook: | Ready in:

Ingredients

- For the baked cheese
- 15 ounces whole milk ricotta
- 4 ounces log goat cheese
- 1   egg
- 2 tablespoons fresh marjoram leaves, or leafy herb of your choice
- generous grinding of black pepper
- generous sprinkling of kosher salt
- For the candied tomatoes
- 1 tablespoon olive oil
- 12 ounces cherry tomatoes
- 1/4 cup vermouth
- 1/4 cup light brown sugar
- 3 sprigs marjoram, or leafy herb of your choice
- sea salt

Direction

- For the baked cheese: Place the ricotta in a colander lined with cheese cloth and leave to drain for about 30 minutes, pressing down to help extract liquid.
- Preheat the oven 375 degrees. Brush the inside of a 2 cup baking dish with olive oil.
- In the small bowl of a stand mixer, beat the ricotta, goat cheese and egg until smooth. Beat in the herbs (chopped if the leaves are large), a generous amount of pepper and salt. Taste your goat cheese first, saltier cheeses require less additional salt.
- Spoon the cheese mixture into the prepared baking dish and bake for 40 minutes, or until puffed in the center and browning.
- Let the cheese cool slightly, then invert it out onto a plate.
- For the tomatoes: While the cheese is baking, heat the olive oil in a large skillet over medium heat, then drop in the tomatoes. Cook, stirring frequently, until the skins on the tomatoes start to split. Pull the pan off the flame, add the vermouth and return to the heat. Add the brown sugar and herbs and stir until the sugar is melted. Add a generous pinch of salt. Lower the heat and cook gently

until the liquid is reduced to a syrupy coating for the tomatoes. The tomatoes will collapse and some may disintegrate. That's fine.
- When ready to serve, spoon the candied tomatoes over the warm baked cheese and serve with sliced baguette or crostini.
- The baked cheese can be prepared a few hours in advance and then baked before serving. It is best served warm, but not necessarily right out of the oven. The tomatoes can be prepared ahead too and gently reheated before serving.

29. Balsamic Reduction Burger With Warm Goat Cheese Spread

Serving: Serves 6 | Prep: | Cook: | Ready in:

Ingredients

- Balsamic Reduction
- 1 1/2 cups aged balsamic vinegar
- 3 tablespoons honey
- Warm Goat Cheese Spread
- 1 teaspoon extra-virgin olive oil
- 1 shallot, finely chopped
- 1 clove garlic, minced
- 4 ounces goat cheese
- 2 ounces light cream cheese
- 1 teaspoon chopped fresh thyme leaves
- sea salt and freshly ground black pepper
- 1 1/2 pounds ground beef
- Optional toppings such as: 6 lettuce leaves, 1 thinly sliced red onion, 1 sliced large tomato
- 6 whole wheat hamburger buns, split and toasted

Direction

- For balsamic reduction: Boil the balsamic vinegar and honey in a heavy small saucepan, uncovered, over medium-high heat until reduced to about 1/3 cup, stirring occasionally, about 18 minutes. While mixture reduces make goat cheese spread. Balsamic reduction can be made days in advance and reheated.

- For warm goat cheese spread: In a small saucepan, heat olive oil at medium heat. Add shallots and garlic and cook, stirring from time to time, for 5 minutes or until it has soften. Add goat cheese and cream cheese and stir. Cook, whisking with a whisk, just until cheese has melted and mixture is combined, hot and creamy. Remove from heat. Add thyme, salt and pepper and stir well. Cover with a lid to keep warm.
- Preheat the grill. Divide beef into six portions and shape into patties. Sprinkle patties on both sides with salt and pepper. Cook burgers over medium high heat until meat reaches desired degree of doneness. Baste the burgers with balsamic reduction the last 2 minutes of cooking. To assemble the burger, generously slather each toasted bun with warm goat cheese spread. Layer with the patty and drizzle remaining balsamic reduction on meat. Layer lettuce, tomato, and red onions slices. Top with goat cheese coated toasted bun.

30. Balsamic Roasted Pumpkin With Goat Cheese, Lentils And Crispy Fried Shallots

Serving: Serves 4-6 | Prep: | Cook: | Ready in:

Ingredients

- the salad: the whole shabang
- 1 small to medium pumpkin, chopped and peeled *if it's too difficult to peel prior to roasting, allow pumpkin to cool and remove skin afterwards
- 1 cup dried French lentils
- 4 oz goat cheese (1 small log)
- 1 shallot, peeled and cut into thin rounds or half-moon shapes
- olive oil for "frying" the shallots

- 1-2 Tbsp olive oil for drizzling, extra for roasting
- salt and pepper to taste
- balsamic reduction
- 6 Tbsp balsamic vinegar

Direction

- The salad: the whole shabang
- Preheat oven to 4oo degrees. Soak lentils for 10 minutes.
- In a large mixing bowl, toss pumpkin with 1-2 tablespoons olive oil and season lightly with salt. Spread on a cookie sheet or in a roasting pan and roast until soft, about 30-40 minutes.
- Meanwhile, cook lentils in salted, boiling water until soft, about 30 minutes.
- Pour about 1 inch worth of olive oil into a small-medium heavy pan or skillet (enough oil to cover shallots). Heat oil over medium-high and fry shallots for 3 to 5 minutes until crispy, golden brown. Remove and drain excess oil on a paper towel.
- Toss pumpkin with balsamic reduction and mix with lentils and goat cheese. Drizzle with remaining tablespoon of olive oil and garnish with crispy shallots.
- Balsamic reduction
- Heat balsamic vinegar in a small saucepan on medium-low and reduce to about half, about 10-15 minutes.

31. Barley And Mushroom "risotto"

Serving: Serves 2 generously | Prep: | Cook: | Ready in:

Ingredients

- 3/4 cup uncooked pearled barley
- 2 cups chicken stock
- 1 heaping teaspoons smoked paprika
- 2 cloves garlic, minced
- 1 package mushrooms, sliced or diced
- 1 chorizo sausage, in slices
- 2 tablespoons olive oil

- 1 onion, chopped
- 3 tablespoons soft goat cheese, or another soft cheese
- 1 small onion, diced

Direction

- Cook the pearl barley by bringing it to a boil with about 2.25 cups water, turning it down low and covering until cooked, about 40 minutes. You can also use cooked barley that's been in the fridge.
- While that's happening, heat a pan to medium low heat and add a little olive oil. Add the sausages and let them cook until the fat renders (if you are using raw chorizo, make sure to cook the sausage all the way through)
- When done, remove the chorizo and set aside. Leave as much of the fat in as possible, adding more oil if necessary. Add the sliced mushrooms and some S&P and cook until their water is released and they are nicely cooked. Add in the onion and cook for a few minutes until translucent, then the garlic for another minute. Finally, add the paprika and mix, cooking for another minute. Adjust seasoning if necessary
- Add the two cups of chicken stock, and mix. Bring it to a boil, then turn down to simmer, uncovered, until reduced by about half or even a bit more, until you get a saucy consistency.
- When the sauce is reduced and a little thicker, add back the sausages and then the barley. Mix it all together so that the sauce/mushroom/chorizo mixes with the barley. Keep stirring, the barley will soak up most of the sauce. Towards the end, add in the goat cheese to creamily everything. Serve with a squeeze of lemon.

32. Basil Corn Cream & Goat Cheese Bake

Serving: Serves 4 | Prep: | Cook: | Ready in:

Ingredients

- 1 tablespoon butter
- 1/2 onion, finely chopped
- 1/2 teaspoon paprika
- 1/4 cup white wine
- 2 ears of corn
- 3/4 cup chicken broth
- 1/4 cup instant corn meal
- 1/4 cup whipping cream
- 1/8 teaspoon salt
- Dash freshly ground black pepper
- 1/4 teaspoon red chili flakes
- 1/4 cup black olives, finely chopped
- 1/4 cup fresh basil leaves, finely chopped
- 1/4 cup goat cheese, crumbled

Direction

- in a medium saucepan melt butter over medium heat, add chopped onion and paprika and cook for 3-5 minutes or until onion is soft
- add wine and cook 2 minutes; in the meantime cut kernels off the cobs, then add them to the pan and continue cooking for another 5 minutes
- Add chicken broth and cook on low heat for 15 minutes
- Remove from heat, pour into a food processor bowl and process until fairly creamy; return to pan on low heat
- Add instant corn meal and cook 1 minute, then add cream, salt and pepper and chili flakes and cook 3 minutes longer
- Remove from heat, add olives and basil and mix to blend ingredients
- Preheat oven to 400F; spoon cream into 4 individual small ramekins and top with crumbled goat cheese
- Bake for about 12 minutes or until cheese is golden, serve immediately

33. Basil Goat Cheese Toast With Fresh Peaches

Serving: Serves 1 | Prep: | Cook: |Ready in:

Ingredients

- 3.5 ounces goat cheese
- 5 sprigs basil
- 2 slices hearty bread, thickness is up to your preference
- 1 ripe peach, sliced thick
- honey

Direction

- Remove leaves from basil sprigs, stack them and roll them up, and slice as thinly as you can. Mix this basil with your soft goat cheese. I make up a big batch of this and keep it in the fridge all week.
- Toast your bread, spread the basil goat cheese thickly (I usually use about half of the amount this recipe makes). Drizzle honey across the top, and layer on the peaches.

34. Beans & Rice Go On Spring Break

Serving: Serves 4 to 6 | Prep: 0hours5mins | Cook: 0hours25mins |Ready in:

Ingredients

- 1 1/2 cups vegetable broth (or water)
- 2 cups (100 grams) tightly packed spinach, divided
- 1/2 cup tightly packed cilantro leaves
- 1 tablespoon butter
- 1 small onion (90 to 100 grams; heaping 1/2 cup), minced
- 2 garlic cloves, minced

- 1 cup jasmine or other long-grain rice, rinsed thoroughly until the water runs clear
- 1 teaspoon salt, plus more to taste
- one 15-ounce can white beans, drained and rinsed
- 1/2 cup frozen peas
- 1/4 cup (5 grams) roughly chopped mint
- 1/2 lemon, zested
- 1/3 cup (50 to 60 grams) crumbled goat cheese
- 2 poached eggs, for serving (optional)

Direction

- Heat the oven to 400° F.
- In a blender, combine the broth, 1 cup of tightly-packed spinach, and the cilantro. Blend until mostly smooth.
- In a large, ovenproof pot (like a Dutch oven), melt the butter. Add the minced onion and garlic and cook, stirring, until soft and translucent, 3 to 4 minutes.
- Add the rice and salt and stir to coat the grains in butter. Pour in the green broth and add the beans and peas. Cover the pot and bake for exactly 17 minutes. If the liquid is not fully absorbed, send the pot back into the oven for 10 or 15 additional minutes.
- Remove the pot from the oven and use a fork to fluff it. Add the mint, lemon zest, goat cheese, and remaining 1 cup tightly-packed spinach. Taste for salt.
- Top with a poached egg, if you'd like.

35. Beans And Greens

Serving: Serves 4 | Prep: | Cook: |Ready in:

Ingredients

- 1 cup dried cranberry beans (3 cups cooked beans)
- 2 stalks celery
- 2 carrots
- 1 small white onion

- 2 large cloves garlic
- 1 sprig rosemary
- 4-5 sage leaves
- 1 bunch kale
- 3 ounces soft goat cheese (such as chèvre)
- 1 cup fresh breadcrumbs
- Olive Oil
- Salt and pepper, to taste
- 1 14 oz can crushed tomatoes
- Dash of red pepper flakes

Direction

- Soak your beans overnight in lightly salted water. Change the water to cook them; bring it to a boil then turn it down to a simmer and let them cook, simmered, until tender (this should take about 45 minutes).
- Meanwhile, prepare the kale by stripping the leaves from the thick stems. A quick way to do this is to grip the thick bottom of the stem in one hand while sliding your other hand down the stem, pulling the leaves off. Chop the leaves coarsely. Preheat the oven to 375 degrees.
- Add the kale, the tomatoes (with their juices), and about 1/2 cup of the reserved bean liquid. Season with salt, pepper, and chili flakes, and give a good stir. Cover the dish and let cook, stirring occasionally, until the kale has wilted and cooked down - about 10 minutes.
- Add the beans and stir the mixture to even out the distribution of kale. Add more bean liquid, if needed - you want the liquid to come up close to the top of the beans, but not cover them.
- Use a spoon to scoop out dollops of goat cheese, distributing them across the surface of the dish. Push about half of them down into the beans; let some of the others stay near the top.
- In a bowl, mix your breadcrumbs with about a tablespoon of olive oil to coat them. Sprinkle them over the top of your dish.
- Bake, uncovered, for 30 minutes or until the breadcrumbs are browned and the mixture is bubbling.

36. Beet & Fennel Galette With Walnuts

Serving: Serves 6-8 | Prep: | Cook: | Ready in:

Ingredients

- Make the dough:
- 1 1/4 cups all purpose flour
- 1/4 tablespoon salt
- 8 tablespoons unsalted butter, chilled and cut into small pieces
- 1/4 cup sour cream
- 2 tablespoons lemon juice
- 1/4 cup water
- Make the filling:
- 3/4 pound beets, greens trimmed
- 2 tablespoons olive oil
- 1 yellow onion, sliced thin
- 1 fennel bulb, sliced thin
- 3 garlic cloves, minced
- Kosher salt
- 1/2 cup walnuts, crushed
- 10 mint leaves, chopped
- 10 basil leaves, chopped
- 1/2 cup sour cream
- 6 ounces goat cheese
- 1 egg yolk
- Freshly ground black pepper

Direction

- Make the dough:
- In a food processor, combine flour and salt. Add in butter and pulse until small pebbles form.
- In a small bowl, combine sour cream, lemon juice, and water. Add to food processor and pulse until mixture comes together and forms dough. Wrap dough in plastic wrap and refrigerate for at least one hour, or up to two days.
- Make the filling:

- Bring a medium-sized saucepan of salted water to boil. Add in beets and cook until they soften, about 20-30 minutes, depending on size. Beets don't need to be cooked all the way through, but you should be able to pierce them with a fork relatively easily.
- Preheat oven to 400F.
- Let beets cool. Peel off skins and grate on a box grater or in a food processor. Transfer to bowl.
- In a large skillet, heat olive oil. Add in onion and cook until translucent. Stir in fennel and garlic, season with salt, and cook until fennel softens.
- Add fennel mixture to bowl with beets. Stir in walnuts, herbs, and sour cream.
- Roll out dough into about a 12 inch round. Place vegetables in the center, leaving about a 1½ - 2 inch border around the sides. Use your hands to scatter goat cheese evenly across the top. Fold the edges of the dough in, overlapping where there is extra.
- In a small bowl, whisk together egg yolk and a drop of water. Brush the dough with egg wash and sprinkle with freshly ground black pepper.
- Bake for 30-40 minutes, until dough is nicely browned. Let cool for at least 15 minutes before serving.

37. Beet & Lettuce Salad With Green Onion Vinaigrette

Serving: Serves 3 to 4 | Prep: | Cook: | Ready in:

Ingredients

- 8 ounces lettuce, roughly chopped
- 1 large beet, roasted and sliced as thinly as possible
- 1/2 cup pumpkin seeds
- 2 ounces goat cheese, crumbled
- 1/4 cup chopped green onions
- 1 tablespoon lemon juice
- 1 teaspoon maple syrup

- 1/4 teaspoon cayenne pepper
- 1/4 cup olive oil
- Salt and pepper, to taste

Direction

- Combine chopped lettuce, sliced beet, pumpkin seeds and goat cheese in a large bowl.
- Combine green onion, lemon juice, maple syrup, and cayenne pepper in a food processor or Vitamix; while blending, slowly drizzle in olive oil until the mixture emulsifies and becomes the consistency of a vinaigrette. Salt and pepper to taste.
- Drizzle dressing on lettuce bowl; toss; taste and add more dressing until the salad tastes the way you want it. We used about half the dressing (and are saving the rest in the fridge for later).

38. Beet & Toasted Seed Salad With Pistachios & Goat Cheese

Serving: Serves 6-8 | Prep: | Cook: | Ready in:

Ingredients

- for the salad...
- 4-6 large beets
- 4 tablespoons olive oil
- 1/4 cup shelled, roasted & salted pistachios (not the red ones)
- 2 tablespoons sesame seeds (preferably black & white)
- 2 teaspoons coriander seeds (crushed or whole)
- 1/4 cup shelled sunflower seeds
- 1 drizzle of olive oil
- 1/2 teaspoon salt
- 1/2 teaspoon freshly ground pepper
- 1-2 cups arugula or baby arugula
- 1-2 cups romaine lettuce, sliced
- 6 ounces soft goat cheese
- for the dressing...

- 1/4 cup olive oil (or pistachio oil if you have)
- 2-3 tablespoons fresh lemon juice
- 1/4 cup minced shallots
- 1 tablespoon honey
- 1 teaspoon packed finely grated lemon peel

Direction

- Preheat oven to 375 degrees F.
- Slice beets into thin, bite sized chunks or pieces (peel on or off, your choice), place into roasting pan & drizzle with 4 TB olive oil. Place pan in oven & roast until beets are tender. Set aside.
- In a large pan, place pistachios, sesame seeds, coriander seeds & sunflower seeds. Drizzle with short, light stream of olive oil & sprinkle with salt & pepper. Heat over medium heat until white sesame seeds and sunflower seeds are toasted and golden in colour. Set aside.
- In a small bowl, whisk dressing ingredients & set aside.
- Place arugula, romaine & beets in large salad serving bowl & toss with dressing. Add 3/4 of seed mixture & toss again. Drop bite sized pieces of goat cheese over salad & sprinkle with remaining seed mixture.
- Serve & enjoy.

39. Beet Crostata With A Pepper Parmesan Crust

Serving: Serves 6 | Prep: | Cook: | Ready in:

Ingredients

- Pepper-Parmesan Crust
- 1 cup all-purpose flour
- 1 teaspoon kosher salt
- 1 teaspoon pepper, freshly ground
- 2 tablespoons grated parmesan cheese
- 1/4 pound cold butter (1 stick), diced
- 2 tablespoons ice water
- Beet Filling
- 1 pound beets (any color/type)

- 1 garlic bulb
- extra virgin olive oil
- goat cheese
- walnuts, coarsely chopped
- salt and pepper
- 1/3 cup balsamic vinegar
- 1 egg, beaten

Direction

- Cut greens from beets. Rinse and dry beets. Then wrap in foil. Wrap garlic in foil after drizzling with olive oil. Bake beets and garlic at 350°F for 1 hour. Unwrap and let cool completely.
- For crust, put flour, salt, pepper, and parmesan in a food processor bowl fitted with a steel blade. Add the butter and pulse until the butter is the size of peas. With the motor running, add the ice water while pulsing until just before the dough becomes a solid mass. Turn dough onto a floured surface and form into a disk. You can wrap with plastic and refrigerate while you prepare the filling.
- Preheat the oven to 400 degrees F.
- Reduce balsamic vinegar until it becomes syrupy (reduced to about 1/3). This happens pretty quick. Remove to small bowl.
- Remove peel from beets (they should easily slide off. You can peel directly into the foil and discard). Slice beets into rounds and set aside.
- Divide dough into 3 equal portions. Roll out one portion to ¼ in thick round about 6-8 inches in diameter. Transfer to a baking sheet.
- Cut roasted garlic bulbs cross-wise so each clove is halved. Squeeze out roasted garlic onto dough and spread around leaving a 1 in border. Sprinkle with salt and pepper.
- Arrange 1/3 of beets slices in a round on top of garlic. Generously tuck goat cheese and walnuts between slices. Sprinkle with salt.
- Drizzle with 1/3 of reduced balsamic vinegar. Finely grate a little orange rind evenly on top. Turn and pleat edges over toppings. Drizzle with olive oil.

- Brush dough with beaten egg. Bake at 400°F for 20-25 minutes until tops are golden brown. Let cool slightly.
- Drizzle with olive oil and serve. A squeeze of orange and/or a sprinkling of parmesan is nice too.

40. Beet Greens Frittata With Tarragon And Goat Cheese

Serving: Serves 2 or 3 | Prep: | Cook: | Ready in:

Ingredients

- 4 large eggs
- about 1 cup beet stems, washed and cut into 1" pieces
- about 4 cups beet leaves, washed
- 1 tablespoon olive oil
- 1 garlic clove, minced
- 1 tablespoon chopped fresh tarragon, plus extra for garnish
- salt and pepper
- 1 tablespoon heavy cream
- 2 ounces goat cheese
- **If cooking for a crowd, double the ingredients and make two frittatas

Direction

- In a large pot of lightly salted boiling water, blanch beet stems until tender. With a slotted spoon or spider strainer, remove from water and place in a colander. Gently press out water with the back of a large spoon, the spider strainer, or if cool enough, squeeze in your hands. Place stems in a dish.
- Add beet leaves to boiling water and blanch until tender. Remove from water, cool slightly in colander, and squeeze out excess water again. Roughly chop the beet leaves. Place them in the dish with the stems and salt these very well.
- In a pan, heat olive oil. Add garlic and cook until just barely golden. Add beet greens and sauté for 5 minutes. Taste for salt, and add more if desired.
- Whisk together the eggs, ¼ teaspoon salt, a grating of pepper, the cream, and the tarragon.
- Heat a small 8" cast-iron frying pan or non-stick pan over medium heat. Add a slick of olive oil to pan to coat bottom. Pour in egg mixture and sprinkle beet greens over top. With a rubber spatula, gently lift edges of the frittata and let the uncooked egg run underneath.
- Sprinkle on the goat cheese. Continue lifting the edges, until almost done, and bottom of frittata is golden.
- Carefully invert a dinner plate over the pan, hold tight, grab the hot handle with a dry dish towel and flip upside down. Your frittata should now be upside-down on the plate. If pan is dry, add just a touch of olive oil to the pan. Next, slide the frittata back in the pan and continue cooking until done and bottom is golden. Alternatively, to avoid the fliperoo, place the frittata under the broiler for a few minutes until done.
- Turn out onto a serving dish. Cool slightly. Garnish with additional fresh tarragon, and scoops of goat cheese drizzled with olive oil sprinkled with sea salt. Cut into wedges, or 1" hors d'oeuvre-sized squares, and serve. Frittatas are great warm, room temperature, or cold.

41. Beet Ravioli With Goat Cheese, Ricotta And Mint Filling

Serving: Serves 4 | Prep: 3hours0mins | Cook: 0hours20mins | Ready in:

Ingredients

- For the beet ravioli and filling
- 2 large beets
- 2 1/2 teaspoons olive oil
- 2 eggs

- 3 1/4 cups flour (plus more for dusting)
- 1 teaspoon salt
- 1 cup ricotta cheese
- 3/4 cup goat cheese
- 1 tablespoon chopped parsley
- 1 tablespoon chopped mint
- 1/4 teaspoon salt
- 1/2 teaspoon black pepper
- 1/4 cup grated parmesan cheese, plus more for serving
- For the brown butter sauce
- 8 tablespoons butter
- 3 1/2 tablespoons lemon juice

Direction

- For the beet ravioli and filling
- Preheat oven to 400° F.
- Wrap the beets in tinfoil and place on a baking sheet. Roast about 1 hour or until the beets are tender.
- Remove beets from oven and allow them to cool a bit before handling. Remove the skins, place in a food processor and puree the beets until smooth.
- Add eggs to the food processor and pulse until combined. Add flour and salt and process until dough comes together.
- Transfer the dough to a well-floured surface and knead until smooth about 7 to 10 minutes (add in more flour if the dough is sticky)
- Cover and let rest for 2 hours.
- Before dough is done resting make the filling by combining chopped parsley, mint, ricotta, goat cheese, and salt and pepper in a mixing bowl. Set aside.
- When dough is done resting, cut into 4 pieces. Roll out each piece to form a thin layer (about 1/8") of dough.
- Place 1/2 Tablespoon of filling onto one sheet of the dough about 1/2" from the edge. Continue to place spoonfuls of filling along the dough about 1" from each other.
- Place one of the other pieces of rolled out dough on top of the piece with the filling on it. Pinch the dough around the filling to form the ravioli.

- Use a sharp knife to cut out the ravioli into individual squares.
- Pinch the edges of each ravioli with the edge of a fork. Set aside each ravioli in a single layer on a baking sheet dusted with flour until ready to cook.
- Add ravioli to a pot of boiling water. Stir until the water returns to a boil. When the ravioli float on their own, about 5-7 minutes, they are finished.
- Serve on individual plates drizzled with brown butter sauce (below) and shaved Parmesan cheese.
- For the brown butter sauce
- Melt butter in a pan. Cook over medium heat until the butter is completely melted and brown bits start to form.
- Add lemon juice, remove from heat.

42. Beet Salad With Apple, Quinoa, Kale And Walnuts

Serving: Serves 4-6 | Prep: | Cook: | Ready in:

Ingredients

- Roasted Beet and Apple Salad
- 3 large red beets, peeled and diced
- 2 large Granny Smith Apples, peeled and diced
- 2 cups sliced kale (stems removed and discarded)
- 1 tablespoon freshly squeezed lemon juice
- 1 tablespoon extra-virgin olive oil
- 3/4 cup cooked quinoa
- 1/2 cup raw or toasted walnuts
- 1/2 cup goat cheese, crumbled
- Walnut Vinaigrette
- 1/4 cup sherry vinegar
- 1 teaspoon Dijon Mustard
- 1/2 cup extra-virgin olive oil
- 1/4 cup walnut oil
- 1/2 teaspoon clover honey

- Pinch kosher salt and freshly ground black pepper to taste

Direction

- Roasted Beet and Apple Salad
- Preheat the oven to 350. Place the diced beets on a sheet of aluminum foil and drizzle with the olive oil. Fold the foil so the beets are sealed and place on a large cookie sheet. Roast in the oven for 15-20 minutes or until a fork pierces easily into the beets. You want them soft but still a little firm. Remove the beets from the oven and set aside to cool. Add the kale, lemon juice and a drizzle of olive oil. Massage until the kale starts to soften and wilt, 2 to 3 minutes. Add the apple, beets. Drizzle some walnut vinaigrette over ingredients and toss. Add the quinoa and walnuts and gently toss again. Garnish with goat cheese.
- Walnut Vinaigrette
- Combine the vinegar, honey and mustard in a bowl. While whisking, slowly pour a steady stream of the olive oil and walnut oil. Season with salt and pepper.

43. Beet Salad With Goat Cheese, Apricots, And Pistachios

Serving: Serves 4 | Prep: 0hours5mins | Cook: 0hours5mins | Ready in:

Ingredients

- 3 tablespoons balsamic vinegar

Direction

- Serve immediately.

44. Beet Terrine With Goat Cheese

Serving: Serves 8-12 | Prep: | Cook: | Ready in:

Ingredients

- 1 1/2 - 1 3/4 pounds red beets, about 3 large ones
- 1 1/2 - 1 3/4 pounds yellow beets, about 3 large one
- olive oil
- Kosher salt
- 8 ounces goat cheese
- 1 tablespoon lemon juice
- 1/4 cup whole milk (can substitute 2%)
- 3 tablespoons crème fraîche
- 2 tablespoons basil, chopped, plus more for garnish
- freshly ground black pepper
- sea salt as garnish

Direction

- Preheat oven to 425F.
- Individually wrap each beet in tinfoil, drizzling with olive oil and a pinch of salt. Place covered beets on a baking sheet and bake for 45-50 minutes, until beets are completely cooked through and can be easily pierced with a fork. Let cool completely. (You can store foil wrapped beets in fridge overnight).
- In a large bowl, mix together goat cheese, lemon juice, milk, crème fraîche, basil, and some black pepper. Mixture should be thin but not runny. If it's too thick and hard to spread, add a little bit more milk.
- When you're ready to assemble, use your hands to gently rub the beets and discard the skin (alternatively you can peel them before you roast them, but I find this method easier).
- Using a mandolin or a sharp knife, slice beets into ⅛ inch thick rounds. Start with the yellow beets and transfer to another cutting board/plate before slicing the red beets to avoid juices staining the yellow beets.
- Line a 9 x 4 inch loaf tin with plastic wrap, leaving some hanging over the sides. Drizzle olive oil and rub to coat bottom and sides of tin. Start by placing a layer of red beets into the bottom of the tin, overlapping them

slightly. Top with another layer of red beets. Using a small spatula or a knife, spread about ⅓ of the goat cheese mixture over the top of the beets. Next, add two more layers of red beets, followed by ⅓ of the goat cheese, 2 layers of yellow beets, the last of the goat cheese, and finally 2 more layers of yellow beets.

- Fold the loose plastic wrap over the top to wrap completely (add additional plastic wrap if needed) and refrigerate for at least 8 hours.
- When you're ready to serve, gently unwrap the terrine and flip it onto a serving platter. If you want the edges to look super clean, you can trim each side so you get nice, straight lines, however this is completely optional.
- Slice terrine in ½ inch pieces, and sprinkle sea salt and basil on top right before serving.

45. Beetroot Gratin With Apples And Goatcheese

Serving: Serves 4-6 | Prep: | Cook: | Ready in:

Ingredients

- 3-4 medium beets
- 200 milliliters cream (15%)
- salt and pepper
- 2 apple
- 1 clove of garlic
- 100g fresh goat cheese, crumbled
- 5-6 Basil leaves, finely cut

Direction

- Preheat oven on 400F. If you are using fresh beet, bake them in the oven for about 60-90 minutes. Let cool then rinse under cold water and remove the peel.
- In a bowl, combine cream, 3 tbsp. Basil, crushes garlic and season to taste. Place in a saucepan and cook on low heat for about 15 minutes.
- Cut the apples into slices

- Turn on your oven on 420F and butter an oven dish (gratin dish). Cut the beets into slices. Arrange beets and apples into several layers. Season with salt and pepper. Pour the cream on top then add crumbled goat cheese.
- Bake for about 20-25 minutes. The cream should makes small bubble and cheese should brown slightly. Once it is ready, top with more Basil leaves and also season with some Black pepper.

46. Beetroot Risotto With Goat Cheese

Serving: Serves 4 to 6 | Prep: 0hours10mins | Cook: 0hours50mins | Ready in:

Ingredients

- 2 pounds beets, peeled, cleaned, and roughly chopped (frozen is a great option, too)
- 1/4 cup olive oil
- 1 pinch kosher salt
- 1 pinch freshly ground black pepper
- 2 quarts vegetable or chicken stock
- 4 tablespoons unsalted butter
- 4 shallots, finely minced
- 2 cups Arborio rice
- 1 cup La Crema Rosé
- 1/2 cup sour cream
- 8 ounces goat cheese, chunked into large pieces
- 1 pinch chopped chives, for garnish

Direction

- Preheat oven to 400°F. Toss the beets with olive oil, salt, and pepper roast on a quarter sheet pan until tender, about 25 to 30 minutes. Set aside to cool slightly.
- In a small saucepan, bring stock to a simmer and keep warm over a low flame.
- In a medium braiser or any wide-bottomed, high-sided pan, melt butter and sauté shallots for a couple minutes, or until translucent. Stir

in the rice, coating each grain until butter-slicked. Splash in the wine and reduce, stirring constantly.

- Once the alcohol has evaporated, lower the heat and slowly ladle in the hot stock (one or two ladlefuls at a time), stirring until fully absorbed by the rice between each addition. Keep stirring until the rice is perfectly al dente (to the tooth), about 18 to 20 minutes.
- Meanwhile, puree the roasted beets with sour cream until very smooth.
- When cooked to your liking (I like my rice with a slight bite in the middle), stir in the beet and sour cream puree. Season to taste with salt and pepper.
- Garnish risotto with goat cheese chunks and chives.

47. Beetroot Goat Cheese Moelleux

Serving: Serves 6 | Prep: | Cook: | Ready in:

Ingredients

- 200g   cooked beets
- 2   eggs
- 4 tablespoons Heavy cream or ricotta
- 3 teaspoons walnut oil
- 1 tablespoon chives
- 1/3 cup flour
- Fresh goat cheese
- Walnuts

Direction

- Preheat the oven on 375-400F
- Dice the beetroot and mix it in a blender. Add the eggs, the cream, oil, herbs and flour. Season to taste.
- Fill six individual muffin molds. Place 1 tbsp. of goat cheese at the center then top with one walnut half.
- Bake for 20 minutes. Let the moelleux cool down and serve cold with a salad, such as apple, walnut and spinach salad.

48. Besotes Caliente "Hot Kisses"

Serving: Makes 2 dozen | Prep: | Cook: | Ready in:

Ingredients

- 24   medium to large fresh jalapenos
- 24   medium (21-25) peeled & deveined shrimp
- 24   slices apple smoked (or other slightly sweet) bacon
- 8 ounces goat cheese

Direction

- Plan to pre-heat the grill or the broiler about 15 minutes before finishing the preparation. Medium heat for grill and not too close broiler element.
- Cut the goat cheese into 24 small oblong pieces, ~1" long. Place in freezer while preparing shrimp & jalapenos.
- While wearing latex kitchen gloves, just barely cut the stem top off & core the fresh jalapenos. To do this, you will need to cut a single slice almost the length of the pepper on only one side, but stopping just short of the pointy bottom. An easy way to core the jalapenos without special tools, is to hold it in one hand and rotate a butter knife down the center of the pepper.
- Stuff & wrap each pepper: Tuck a piece of goat cheese and one shrimp in each pepper; then wrap a slice of bacon around covering the whole pepper. Anchor bacon in place with two toothpicks as skewers.
- Cook ~10 minutes, turning several times. The time is very imprecise, because of the variance in grill or broiler temp. You want it hot enough to cook quickly, but slow enough to cook, not blacken the bacon. They are done when the bacon is nice and caramelized.
- These are hard to let cool enough to eat, but are good at room temp. Hot, creamy, smoky and a little sweet, no-one can eat just one.

49. Blackberry Galette With Flaky Goat Cheese Pastry

Serving: Serves 6 to 8 | Prep: | Cook: |Ready in:

Ingredients

- Pastry
- 1 1/4 cups (160 grams) all-purpose unbleached flour
- 1 tablespoon (12 grams) sugar
- 1/8 teaspoon salt (I use fine sea salt)
- 8 tablespoons (4 ounces/113 grams) could unsalted butter
- 4 ounces (113 grams) cold fresh (creamy) goat cheese, with or without herbs or lavender
- Filling
- 3 1/2 cups (14 ounces/400 grams) blackberries
- 3 tablespoons (36 grams) sugar
- 1 1/2-2 ounces (42-56 grams) additional goat cheese, optional
- 1 1/2 tablespoons (22 grams) cold unsalted butter

Direction

- First make the dough: Combine the flour, sugar, and salt in the bowl of a food processor fitted with the steel blade. Pulse a few times to mix.
- Cut the butter in 3/4-inch cubes and scatter them over the flour. Pulse until butter pieces range in size from very coarse breadcrumbs to hazelnuts.
- Crumble or break the 4 ounces of goat cheese into teaspoon size chunks and add them to the processor. Pulse until the mixture looks like crumbs — it should not come together into a dough or look cohesive at all, but it should stick together when you pinch it.
- Pour the mixture into a plastic bag and press it very firmly into a compact ball, don't worry if you notice unblended bits of butter or cheese;

this is correct. Twist the top of the plastic bag and refrigerate the dough for at least two hours and up to three days before using.
- Not, fill and the bake galettes. Position a rack in the lower third of the oven and preheat the oven to 400°F.
- Remove the dough from the refrigerator. Unwrap and cut it in half, and let it rest at room temperature for 10 to 15 minutes until just still firm, but pliable enough to roll; it should not be soft or squishy.
- Set one piece of dough on a flour-dusted surface and press it into a thick patty. Sprinkle it with flour and roll it into an 11-inch circle 1/8-inch thick, sprinkling dough and rolling pin as necessary to prevent sticking. As you work, slide the dough around and/or slip a metal spatula under it frequently, and sprinkle with more flour, as necessary to avoid sticking. Don't bother to trim the circle; uneven edges are part of the charm here. You don't have to patch the edges if they tear a little, but do patch any breaks or tears in the center of the dough, using bits from the edge, to prevent juices from leaking.
- Roll the pastry up around the rolling pin and unroll it on a sheet of parchment — or slip a flexible cutting mat or baking sheet under it to transfer. Brush off excess flour if necessary — and set aside.
- Repeat with the second piece of dough, transferring it to another piece of parchment.
- Distribute half of the berries over the center of each circle, leaving a 3-inch border. There will space between berries. Sprinkle the berries on each pastry with 1 tablespoon of the sugar. If you like, break the optional goat cheese into small pieces and divide and distribute them over and between the berries on each galette. Cut the butter into slivers and distribute them over the berries. Trying not to tear or break the pastry (or juices will leak out), fold the edges up and over some of the berries, letting the pastry pleat it as you go.
- Use a pastry brush dipped in water to moisten all of the exposed pastry around each galette and sprinkle each with half (1 1/2 teaspoons)

of the remaining sugar. Trim parchments so that both galettes will fit — with their parchment — onto one baking sheet.

- Bake galettes until pastry is golden to deep golden brown and very deeply colored around the bottom and underneath (you can lift the parchment slightly and peer through it underneath), 30 to 35 minutes, rotating the pan from front to back halfway through the baking time. Juices will be bubbling and may seem thin; they will thicken as the galettes cool. Set the pan on a rack to cool. Serve once cooled.

50. Blood Orange, Fennel, Goat Cheese And Hazelnut Salad

Serving: Serves 2 | Prep: | Cook: | Ready in:

Ingredients

- Blood Orange, Fennel, Goat Cheese and Hazelnut Salad
- 1/4 cup Chopped Hazelnuts
- 4 cups Mixed field greens and butter lettuces
- 1/2 Bulb Fennel, Julienned (about 1 Cup)
- 1/3 cup Blood Orange Vinaigrette (recipe follows)
- 3 Small (or 2 Medium) Blood Oranges, Supremed
- 2 ounces Goat Cheese
- Blood Orange Vinaigrette
- 1 Medium Shallot, Minced
- 1 teaspoon Zest from Blood Orange (one small)
- 3 tablespoons Blood Orange Juice (from 2-3 small)
- 1 tablespoon White Wine Vinegar
- 1/2 teaspoon Salt
- 1 pinch Sugar
- 1/2 cup Olive Oil
- Ground Pepper

Direction

- Blood Orange, Fennel, Goat Cheese and Hazelnut Salad
- Preheat oven to 350. Spread hazelnuts on baking sheet and place in oven for 5 minutes until toasted and fragrant. Place hazelnuts in a clean dish towel and rub the nuts vigorously to remove the skins (you don't have to get them all), set aside.
- Wash and dry salad greens. Combine salad greens and fennel in salad bowl. Pour 1/3 cup of vinaigrette around the inside edges of the bowl and gently combine with greens. Add more as needed.
- Divide dressed greens onto two serving plates, top each with half of hazelnuts, oranges and goat cheese and serve.
- Blood Orange Vinaigrette
- Combine shallots, zest, juice, vinegar, salt and sugar in a small bowl and whisk to combine.
- Slowly pour in olive oil in a thin stream while whisking into the shallot juice mixture until combined and almost creamy.
- Season with additional salt if necessary and pepper.

51. Braised Calamari With Spinach And Tomatoes

Serving: Serves 2-4 | Prep: | Cook: | Ready in:

Ingredients

- 4 tablespoons Olive Oil
- 2 Large Shallots, thinly sliced
- 2 Cloves of Garlic, Minced
- 1-2 teaspoons Red Pepper Flakes (This puts a little kick in the dish)
- 1/2 cup Dry White Wine
- 2 Cans of Fire Roasted Tomatoes, Juice Reserved (Can also roast your own tomatoes, I love the smokey flavor it adds)
- 1 tablespoon Oregano
- 1 1/2 pounds Calamari, (Tubes and Tentacles) Tubes Cleaned and sliced into 1/2" rings

- 2 cups Chopped Fresh Spinach
- 1 1/2 ounces Chèvre Goat Cheese
- Salt and Pepper to taste
- Serve with Toasted Bread for dipping.

Direction

- Heat oil in a sauté pan over medium heat. Add Shallots and sauté until soft, about 3 minutes.
- Add Garlic and red pepper flakes and continue to cook until fragrant.
- Deglaze with pan with white wine and add tomatoes. Season with oregano. Bring to a soft boil.
- Add calamari and turn heat down to low. Cover and cook for approximately 20-25 minutes. The calamari should not be chewy but tender. Cook longer if needed.
- Stir in the spinach and goat cheese. Allow to cook with the lid off for about 5 more minutes or until the greens are tender and the cheese has melted. Add reserved tomato juice if you desire a thinner sauce.
- Season with Salt and Pepper and serve with toasted bread or on top of cooked pasta.

52. Bread Salad With Sweet Onion Vinaigrette

Serving: Serves 4 | Prep: | Cook: |Ready in:

Ingredients

- Sweet Onion Vinaigrette
- 1 cup sweet onion, diced
- 1 tablespoon minced garlic or green garlic
- 1 cup olive oil
- 6 tablespoons white balsamic vinegar
- 1/2 teaspoon pepper
- 1/2 teaspoon kosher salt
- 1 teaspoon sugar
- Bread Salad
- 10 ounces sourdough or French bread, thick sliced
- 2 1/2 ounces arugula

- 1/4 cup red onion, thinly sliced
- 4 ounces goat cheese, crumbled
- 8 ounces cherry tomatoes, halved
- 1/2 English cucumber, diced
- sweet onion vinaigrette

Direction

- Sweet Onion Vinaigrette
- 1. Chop onion and garlic in a small food processor until minced.
- 2. In a medium bowl place minced onion and garlic, vinegar, sugar, salt and pepper.
- 3. Slowly add in oil with an immersion blender or whisk by hand.
- 4. Reserve for salad.
- Bread Salad
- 1. Grill off the slices of bread. Cool and cut into bite sized cubes.
- 2. In a large bowl mix: bread, arugula, onion, tomatoes and cucumber.
- 3. Pour desired amount of dressing on the salad (I used about 1/3 of the dressing).
- 4. Let sit for 30 minutes or more. Garnish with goat cheese and serve.

53. Breakfast Of Savory Spears

Serving: Serves 1 | Prep: | Cook: |Ready in:

Ingredients

- 3 tablespoons Butter
- 1 piece Bread
- 6 asparagus spears
- 1/4 cup uncooked breakfast sausage
- 2 tablespoons goat cheese
- 2 eggs

Direction

- Prep asparagus by chopping into 1.5 inch pieces (snapping off the bottom bits)
- Melt 2 Tbsp. of butter into the pan

- Add prepped asparagus into pan with pepper (no salt is needed, as it will come from the goat cheese and sausage)
- Once asparagus has been cooked through, remove from pan (no more than 5 minutes - the asparagus will be bright green and soft to bite into) leaving the butter
- Dip both sides of bread into the butter and toast the bread into the pan
- Once toasted, remove from pan and add sausage
- While sausage is cooking, spread goat cheese onto bread and top with cooked asparagus
- When sausage has been cooked through, remove from pan and place on top of asparagus atop the toast
- Melt remaining butter in pan and cook eggs to desired preference (fried or sunny-side up are my preference) careful not to add much salt
- Once eggs are cooked, place atop the sausage and enjoy

54. Bright Salad With Crispy Leeks

Serving: Serves 4 | Prep: 0hours20mins | Cook: 0hours5mins | Ready in:

Ingredients

- For the Salad
- 1 leek, washed and dried, halved lengthwise and then sliced crosswise in 1/4 inch strips
- 1/2 cup canola oil
- Himalayan or sea salt
- 8 handfuls salad greens
- 1 red pear, skin on, sliced very thinly
- 1 juicy orange, segmented in supremes over a small bowl to catch the juice, and then squeeze the remains to release more juice
- 1/2 avocado, sliced very thinly
- 4 tablespoons goat cheese - 1 tablespoon per serving
- For the Citrus Vinaigrette
- 4 tablespoons olive oil, plus more if needed
- juice of segmented orange
- enough lemon juice to make 4 tablespoons of citrus juice when combined with the orange juice
- 1/2 teaspoon honey or agave syrup
- salt and pepper to taste

Direction

- Assemble the salad servings: place 2 handfuls each of the salad greens on 4 salad plates. Arrange 4 thin slices of pear, 3 orange supremes, and 2 slices of avocado atop each plate of salad. Break each tablespoon of goat cheese into bits and scatter around salad serving. Set salads aside.
- Make the vinaigrette by combining all ingredients listed. You may want to add a little more olive oil to create a nice emulsion. Check for seasoning as well as amount or honey or agave syrup. Set aside.
- Slice the leeks as noted. First, chop off most of the green part of the leek, leaving a little of the lighter green part of the leek. Then, slice the leek lengthwise down the middle. Wash very well, and dry the leek even better. Place the leek halves cut side down, and slice each half crosswise into 1/4" half circles. Pat the leeks with a kitchen towel to remove all traces of moisture.
- Heat a medium sized sauté pan over a medium flame. Add the canola oil. After a few moments, test the oil temperature by adding a piece of leek to the sauté pan. If the leek sizzles, the pan is ready.
- Fry the leek bits by half-handfuls. It will take about 10 seconds for the leeks to turn a light golden color, so be hovering over the pan. Have a wire mesh skimmer close by so you can immediately scoop out the golden crisped leeks, and transfer them onto paper towels. Keep frying by half handfuls until all the leeks are fried.
- NB - there is nothing that tastes as bitter as a black, fried leek, so fish out any bits that are overly crisped.

- Lightly salt the leeks, and blot away as much oil as possible.
- Spoon a tablespoon of vinaigrette on each salad serving. Serve extra vinaigrette on the side.
- Place a hearty handful of leeks on the top of each salad serving, and enjoy the crunch and the contrast to the greens and the sliced fruits.

55. Broccoli And Goat Cheese Quiche

Serving: Serves about 4-6 | Prep: | Cook: |Ready in:

Ingredients

- Filling
- 2.5-3 cups of broccoli florets cut to small-medium chunks
- 4 oz of soft goat cheese
- 1/2 cup heavy cream
- 1/2 teaspoon of thyme leaves
- 1/4 cup of grated parmesan + a bit more for the top
- 2 eggs
- 1 teaspoon of salt
- Black pepper
- 1-2 tablespoons of sliced almonds
- Pie Crust
- 1 stick of unsalted butter
- 1.25 cups of flour
- 1 egg
- 0.5 teaspoon of salt

Direction

- Cut the cold butter to small pieces. Put the butter and the flour in the food processor and process for 1-2 minutes until it looks like soft sand. Add salt and egg and mix until just starting to form a ball. If the dough a bit too dry add a tablespoon of cold water. Take out the dough and form a disk, wrap with plastic wrap and let it chill in the fridge for about 1/2 hour.

- Heat the oven to 360 F. Boil a pot with some water. Add salt and the broccoli florets. Cook them for 5 minutes and transfer the broccoli to a bowl of ice water to stop the cooking.
- In a bowl crumble the goat cheese. Add the eggs, heavy cream, thyme, parmesan, salt, pepper and mix well. Add the broccoli.
- Spread the chilled dough in a 9.5" quiche\tart pan. Pour in the filling mixture. Grate a little more parmesan on top and sprinkle the almonds. Bake for 45 minutes until light golden brown on top.

56. Brown Buttered Squash

Serving: Serves 4-6 | Prep: | Cook: |Ready in:

Ingredients

- 1 medium-large butternut squash, seeded, and cut into 1/2 inch cubes
- 2 tablespoons olive oil
- Kosher salt
- 8 tablespoons butter
- 1/2 cup Panko bread crumbs
- 1 1/2 tablespoons fresh sage, chopped
- 2-4 ounces prosciutto, thinly sliced
- 4-6 ounces goat cheese

Direction

- Preheat oven to 425F.
- Toss butternut squash in olive oil and salt. Arrange flat on a baking sheet and bake until squash is tender, about 20-30 minutes.
- Meanwhile, in a medium pan, melt butter over low heat. Cook, stirring occasionally, until butter starts to brown. Add in bread crumbs and sage, stir well, and remove from heat.
- When squash is done cooking, transfer to browned butter and toss to coat.
- Transfer squash to a serving dish and tear pieces of prosciutto, tucking them between the squash pieces. Crumble goat cheese on top, give it a quick stir, and serve.

- Serve in pasta bowls and top with crumbled goat cheese.

57. Brown Rice Pasta With Asparagus And Goat Cheese

Serving: Serves 2 | Prep: | Cook: |Ready in:

Ingredients

- 1 bunch asparagus
- 1 cup cremini mushrooms
- 3/4 cup Pancetta, cubed
- 2 Roma Tomatoes, seeds removed, diced
- 1 tablespoon fresh basil, chopped
- 1 tablespoon fresh oregano, chopped
- 2 cups Brown Rice Penne
- Crumbled Goat Cheese
- 1 clove garlic, minced
- 1 tablespoon olive oil

Direction

- Set pot of water to boil on stove. Once boiling add pasta. Brown rice pasta takes about 10 minutes to cook. With rice pasta, it is important to rinse in cold water after cooked.
- Cook pancetta in frying pan over medium heat. Once browned and fat has rendered, remove and set aside. Drain fat, leaving about a tsp in the pan along with any leftover pancetta bits.
- In same pan, cook garlic for 1 minute. Add asparagus and mushrooms. Season with salt and pepper. Sauté for about 4-5 minutes, until tender. Remove from pan and set aside.
- Add olive oil to same pan. Once heated, add tomatoes and herbs. Cook for about 5 minutes, until tomatoes are softened. Add asparagus, mushrooms and pancetta back to the pan. Add the sauce. (I used a sauce that I picked up at a local farmers market. It had a good kick of spice to it which worked well.)Simmer on low until pasta is finished cooking.
- Add cooked pasta to the other ingredients and blend to ensure tomato mix is well distributed with the pasta.

58. Browned Butter And Sage Pasta With Heirloom Tomatoes

Serving: Serves 2 | Prep: | Cook: |Ready in:

Ingredients

- 5 tablespoons unsalted butter
- 2 shallots, diced
- 1/4-1/3 cups fresh sage, chopped
- 1/2 teaspoon red pepper flakes
- 1 1/2 cups cherry tomatoes, diced
- spaghetti, linguini or cappellini, for two
- salt and pepper, to taste
- 2 tablespoons crumbled goat cheese

Direction

- Bring a salted pot of water to a boil. Add pasta when boiling and cook according to pasta type and instructions.
- Melt 3 tbsps. of the butter in a large saucepan and add sage, shallots and red pepper flakes, cooking over low heat until sage is slightly browned and turning crispy - 5 to 10 minutes.
- When the pasta is halfway done, add the remaining 2 tbsps. of butter and the chopped tomatoes to the sauce. You don't want them to overcook, but they should soften a bit. Note: Add a little more butter or some of the pasta water if you need more liquid.
- Season with salt and pepper. Turn off the heat and mix in the goat cheese.
- Drain the pasta and add it to the sauce, tossing until coated.
- Serve and enjoy!

59. Buckwheat Crêpe Cake With Walnuts, Honey, And Goat Cheese

Serving: Serves 10-12 | Prep: | Cook: |Ready in:

Ingredients

- For at least 25 (or more) crêpes
- 2 cups (260 grams) buckwheat flour
- 2 tablespoons sugar
- 3/8 teaspoon salt
- 1/2 cup (55 grams) unsalted butter, melted, plus more for the pan and top of the cake
- 6   large eggs
- 2 1/2 cups whole milk, plus more as needed
- 1/2 cup water
- For filling
- 3 cups (300 grams) walnuts, finely chopped (or pulsed in a food processor to make a very coarse meal)
- 1/2 teaspoon ground cinnamon
- 1   large orange (for zest)
- 12 ounces (340g) fresh creamy goat cheese, softened
- 3/4-1 cups (320-420g) honey (orange blossom or clover or a mixed flower honey has a bright floral taste)
- EQUIPMENT
- 8-inch crepe pan

Direction

- In a large bowl, combine the flour, sugar, salt, butter, and eggs with about a quarter of the milk and whisk until smooth. Whisk in the remaining milk and the water. Set the batter aside for at an hour (to let the flour hydrate) or cover and refrigerate for longer (up to 2 days). Stir the batter well before and frequently as you use it, as the heavier ingredients tend to settle to the bottom of the bowl. (Buckwheat flour makes a crêpe batter with the slightly unusual "stretchy" texture — the best method for coating the crêpe pan is to pour a little more batter into the hot pan than you really need, swirl the pan to coat and pour excess batter immediately back into the remaining batter. It sounds wrong, but it works perfectly.)
- Set two plates near the stove for the finished crepes. Heat the pan over medium to medium-high heat and brush lightly with butter (a silicon brush is terrific for this). When a drop of water sizzles on the pan, lift the pan off the burner and pour a scant 1/4 cup of batter into the pan, off center at about 2 o'clock. Immediately tilt and rotate the pan counter clockwise, shaking as necessary, to coat the pan entirely (in one pass if possible), and immediately pour excess batter back into the bowl. Set the pan back on the burner and cook the crepe until the surface no longer looks wet and the edges and parts of the underside are browned, 45-60 seconds. Loosen the edges of the crepe with a spatula and flip it over with the spatula or (carefully) with your fingers. Cook 30 to 60 seconds longer. Slide or flip the crepe onto one of the plates. You can trim the edge of the crepe to remove the lip caused by pouring off excess batter at any time — while you are cooking or when the crepe is cooked. As you get the hang of the batter, and how to tilt the pan, you can decrease the amount of batter you pour in the pan and thus the amount of excess.
- Repeat, setting the second crepe on the second plate. Crêpe can be stacked hot — but they are easier to separate if you let each one cool just long enough to cook the next one. Stack the first two crepes in time to put the next hot one on the empty plate, and so forth. If the crepes seem too thick, adjust the batter with a little extra water. You want thin crepes with lacy edges. Repeat to make the remaining crêpes, buttering the pan only as necessary. Make about 25 crepes. Set aside,
- Toss the walnuts and cinnamon in a bowl and grate the zest of the orange over them. Toss to mix.
- Place one crepe on a plate. Leave a 1/2 inch margin bare around the edges of each crepe as you fill. The filling will melt towards the edges to some extent anyway, and naked edges will

be lacy and slightly crisped. Smear a scant tablespoon of goat cheese somewhat evenly over the crêpe — a small offset spatula is your best friend here. (If the cheese is not soft enough to spread easily, microwave it on low for a few seconds.) Drizzle the crêpe with about 1 1/2 teaspoons of honey. Sprinkle with a heaping tablespoon of the nut mixture. Spread the second crêpe with cheese and then set it on top of the first. Drizzle with honey and sprinkle with nuts. Repeat — always spreading cheese on the next crêpe before stacking it. In the end, top with a bare crêpe. Press down gently on the stack to level the cake. (If you are a superb crêpe maker you will have gotten more than 25 crepes from the batter, you can continue to stack and fill them, or wrap and refrigerate or freeze left over crepes for another use).

- The cake can be wrapped airtight and refrigerated for a day or two. To serve, set the cake on a baking sheet, brush the top with a little melted butter. Bake in a preheated 350 F oven for 25-30 minutes (assuming the cake was refrigerated — a little less if not) until heated thoroughly. Transfer to a serving platter. Sieve a little powdered sugar over the top. Serve hot. Cut with serrated knife.

60. Burger With Spicy Slaw

Serving: Serves 2 | Prep: | Cook: |Ready in:

Ingredients

- Burger
- 3/4 cup bbq sauce
- 1/3 cup tomato sauce or chopped canned tomatoes
- 3 chipotle pepper in adobo sauce
- 1/3 cup honey
- 2 beef paties
- 1 log of goat cheese, sliced
- 2 sesame buns
- Spicy Slaw

- 4 cups thinly sliced cabbage
- 2/3 cup blood orange vinegar
- 3/4 cup mayo
- 2 chipotle peppers in adobo sauce

Direction

- Start with the slaw, which can be made several hours ahead of time. Blend the vinegar, mayo, and chipotles, mix with cabbage and refrigerate until ready for use.
- For the burger glaze, blend bbq sauce, tomatoes, chipotles, and honey. Season burger patties with salt and pepper and place over med-high heat on grill. As the burgers cook, paint with about 4 coats of the glaze.
- Once they begin to approach desired doneness, move to indirect heat, add goat cheese and cover grill until cheese begins to melt.
- Toast buns lightly and assemble burgers with spicy slaw.

61. Butternut Squash Mac N Cheese

Serving: Makes enough for an army | Prep: | Cook: | Ready in:

Ingredients

- 1 large box cavatappi
- 3/4 cup mozzarella (crumbled)
- 3/4 cup parmesan cheese (grated)
- 1 1/2 cups raw cows milk white cheddar (grated)
- 1/2 cup soft goat cheese
- 1 cup milk (I used 2%)
- 2 cups half and half + 3 tbsp
- 1 large onion (diced)
- 4 cloves garlic (minced)
- 1/4 pound pancetta - ask for thick slices at your deli (diced)
- 2 tablespoons Dijon mustard (mine was shallot Dijon and it was fab)

- 2 tablespoons fresh thyme leaves
- 1 teaspoon crushed red pepper flakes
- 3 tablespoons flour
- 1/2 teaspoon nutmeg
- 1 medium butternut squash (halved longways and seeds removed)
- 1 1/2 cups Panko breadcrumbs
- 2 tablespoons unsalted butter + 2 tbsp
- 2 tablespoons olive oil
- salt and black pepper
- 1 cup reserved pasta water

Direction

- Preheat oven to 375 degrees. Cover a baking sheet with foil (makes life so much easier). Place the halved butternut squash on the baking sheet and coat in olive oil. Roast in oven for 40 minutes. Remove and let cool. Scoop out the orange squash and puree in a food processor until smooth (about 1-2 minutes). Remove to a small bowl and whisk in 3 tbsps. half and half and some salt and pepper. Set aside.
- In a large (your largest) saute pan with high sides, heat 2 tbsps. butter and 2 tbsps. olive oil over medium heat. Add onion and pancetta and cook for 5 minutes. Add garlic and cook for another 3 minutes until fragrant and soft. Add thyme, crushed red pepper flakes and salt and pepper. Cook for 3 more minutes.
- Add flour to the mixture and stir to form a thick onion, garlic paste. Let cook for about 2 minutes. Whisk in 1 cup milk and 2 cups half and half. Whisk to incorporate the flour into the milk, you don't want chunks. Add the Dijon mustard and nutmeg to the mixture at this point and some more salt and pepper, and simmer until the mixture is thick. Will take about 5 minutes (maybe longer, maybe shorter).
- When thick enough, add the parmesan and cheddar cheeses. Stir until they are melted and the mixture looks cheesy. Stir in the goat cheese and butternut squash puree and mix to combine. Add another layer of salt and pepper. While cooking the cheese mixture,

cook the pasta according to the box, but cook for 2 minutes less.
- Before draining the pasta, add a cup of the pasta water to the cheese mixture. Drain the pasta and add to the cheese mixture. Transfer noodles to a large baking dish. Add more salt and pepper. Spread the mozzarella over the top of the pan for one last coating of cheese that will be ooey and gooey after you put it in the over.
- In a saute pan, melt 2 tbsps. of butter until browed (about 2-3 minutes). Add the panko bread crumbs to the butter and mix around until all bread crumbs are covered in butter. Sprinkle the breadcrumbs over the top of the mac and cheese and pop in the oven for 10 minutes. The bread crumbs will brown up and the mozz. cheese will melt into the crust. YUM!

---

62. Butternut Squash Pasta With Sage And Goat's Cheese

Serving: Serves 2 | Prep: | Cook: | Ready in:

Ingredients

- 400 grams butternut squash
- 3 garlic cloves
- 1 tablespoon olive oil
- 250 grams spelt flour spaghetti
- 10 fresh sage leaves
- 40 grams butter
- 80 grams fresh goat's cheese
- salt and pepper

Direction

- Preheat the oven to 200°C.
- Peel the butternut squash and cut into 1cm cubes. Distribute the cubes in a baking tray, add two unpeeled garlic cloves, the olive oil and a pinch of salt. Mix everything and bake for 20 minutes or until the butternut squash is soft.

- Once the squash has finished baking, cook the spelt spaghetti according to package instructions.
- Peel and crush the remaining garlic clove. Finely chop the sage leaves.
- Melt the butter in a frying pan and fry the crushed garlic and the sage for 2 minutes.
- Add the drained spaghetti and the butternut squash (discarding the baked garlic cloves) mix and season with salt and pepper.
- Distribute the spaghetti between two plates and scatter some crumbled goats' cheese onto each portion.

63. Butternut Squash And Bourbon Bisque

Serving: Serves 10 | Prep: | Cook: | Ready in:

Ingredients

- 3 shallots, chopped
- 3 cloves garlic, chopped
- 4 slices bacon, diced
- 1 teaspoon cumin
- 1/4 teaspoon paprika
- 2 teaspoons fresh grated ginger
- 1/2 teaspoon fresh sage
- 1/2 teaspoon fresh thyme
- 1/2 cup soy sauce
- 1/2 cup sherry
- 1/4 cup bourbon
- 5 cups chicken broth
- 6 cups butternut squash, in 1 inch cubes
- goat cheese, for serving

Direction

- In large pot, cook bacon on medium/high heat till all the fat is melted off and bacon is cooked. The remaining bacon will make an absolutely wonderful garnish. If you prefer no pork, you may use butter or olive oil.

- Remove bacon, leaving fat. Add garlic, shallots, and seasonings and cook for 1 minute.
- Add soy sauce to deglaze pan, scraping bottom of pan to get off all the cooked bits. At this point, add the butternut squash and cook for about 5 minutes to get the seasonings to meld a bit with the squash before adding more liquid.
- Add chicken broth and bring to a boil. As soon as it hits the boil, add the sherry. You MAY use more sherry, but please don't leave it out. It makes all the difference!
- Boil for 15 minutes before reducing it to a simmer. Add the bourbon as soon as you lower the temperature to a simmer. Oh, and you can add more bourbon as well. Bourbon doesn't tend to be sold in ¼ cup increments, so be friendly. Simmer for 45 minutes with the lid on.
- Turn off the stove and add the soup in two batches to a food processor. When you add the soup to the processor, be sure to cover the top with a towel because it might leak from the top. Blend both batches and return to pot. You may serve now or let it simmer a bit longer.
- Serve with a creamy lump of goat cheese and some bacon crumbles. Enjoy!

64. Byrek (spanakopita) With Leaks

Serving: Makes as many you need | Prep: | Cook: | Ready in:

Ingredients

- 1 packet Phyllo dough
- 3-4 pieces Leaks
- 8 tablespoons Butter
- 1 teaspoon Sea salt
- 1 packet goat cheese
- 1/4 teaspoon Nutmeg
- pinch White black pepper

Direction

- Take the leaks and split each leaks in 2. Then run them under the old water washing and opening each layer (leaks tend to be dirty and you don't want the additional crunch :) After you wash them cut them in small little pieces and place them in a bowel full of cold water. After you leave them there for a few minutes drain them and place them in a hot pan that has 3 table spoons of butter melted.
- Lower the heat and place the leaks in the butter, put in the salt, nutmeg and cover the pan. Stir often and wait until the leaks have sweated for about 15 minutes.
- Through in the goat cheese and stir it often until everything is mixed together. Add the pepper and Give it a quick taste to see if it needs more pepper or salt and add what you need.
- Heat the oven at 350
- Tale a large round pan or a large square pan. Melt 4 table spoons of butter and get a pastry brush ready. Open the phyllo dough package (don't leave it open too long or they will dry quickly) Take the pan and brush the bottom with butter and add a phyllo dough and them brush with butter and then continue the layering and buttering process for about 10 phyllo dough. After that take the leak filling and layered across the top of the phyllo dough and make sure is even. Then place on top of the filling a phyllo dough butter the top and continue with each layer of butter and phyllo dough.
- After you have used them all, use an egg wash for the top layer and place it in the oven for about 30 minutes more or less depends on the heat of your oven. Keep an eye on it, if the top is golden brown then it's done.

65. CHA! Vocado Goat Cheese Spread

Serving: Serves 1 tbsp- yeild 1 1/2 cups | Prep: | Cook: | Ready in:

Ingredients

- 1 cup 1 Avocado (ripe, mashed)
- 1/2 cup Goat cheese, whipped
- 1 tablespoon CHA! by Texas Pete
- 1 dash TO TASTE- salt and pepper

Direction

- Place the ripe avocado into a small mixing bowl and mash it well with a potato masher or if you have a food processor, blend the avocado until it is smooth.
- Place the mashed avocado into a mixing bowl and add the goat cheese, CHA! by Texas Pete® and a pinch of salt and pepper. Mix together well.
- Place in an airtight storage container and keep refrigerated until ready to use.

66. Cara Cara Orange, Beet, And Goat Cheese Salad

Serving: Makes 1 salad | Prep: | Cook: | Ready in:

Ingredients

- Dressing
- 1 gallon medium garlic clove, peeled and minced
- 1 tablespoon olive oil
- 1/2 tablespoon balsamic vinegar
- tiny pinch of sea salt
- generous pinch of raw sugar
- Salad
- fresh salad greens- enough to cover your plate (I used baby winter lettuces from my garden)
- 1 Cara Cara orange, peel and all pith removed with a sharp knife, and sliced cross-wise
- 1/2 medium Chiogga beet, peeled and sliced paper thin on a mandoline
- small handful of minced cilantro (or substitute parsley)
- crumbled goat cheese (or substitute feta)

- generous pinch of crushed red pepper-optional

Direction

- Mix dressing in a small bowl and set aside while you make the salad.
- Make the salad by layering the greens, then the orange slices, then the beet slices, then the minced cilantro, then the goat cheese. Sprinkle on the red pepper flakes, if using.
- Spoon the dressing evenly over the top of the salad and dig in immediately.

67. Caramelised Red Onion & Anchovy Tart

Serving: Serves 4/6 | Prep: | Cook: | Ready in:

Ingredients

- 1 packet Ready made puff pastry such as Pepperridge Farm (use one sheet)
- 1 Egg, for glazing
- 1-2 Red onions (one large or 2 small), sliced into rings
- 1/4 cup Brown sugar
- Splash Balsamic vinegar
- 1 packet Whole anchovies, from a jar or a tin
- 1 sprig Fresh Chives
- 1 sprig Fresh Thyme
- 1 packet Soft goat's cheese (Optional)
- 1 handful Flour for dusting and rolling
- 1/4 cup water, for sauteeing the onions
- Pinch Salt & Pepper

Direction

- Take your pastry out of the freezer and allow to defrost. You can make your own puff pastry if you choose to.
- Preheat your oven to 400F
- On a clean work surface, sprinkle some flour and roll out the pastry using a rolling pin. You should ensure that is about 1cm thick. The pastry will be in a rectangular shape.
- Separate your egg and retain the yolk. Beat well with a little water to create an egg wash.
- Using a pastry brush, spread the egg wash along the outer corners of the pastry and fold in the edges to create a crust. Continue to coat the pastry with the egg wash.
- Line a baking sheet with parchment paper, and transfer the pastry to the sheet.
- Put into the oven for approximately 10 minutes. This will help the puff pastry become crispy.
- Whilst the pastry is cooking, slice a red onion into rings, and saute in water over a medium heat until soft. Once the water has evaporated, add 1/4 cup of brown sugar. Stir the sugar into the onions to ensure they are coated.
- The onions usually take around 10 minutes to caramelize in my experience. At this point, add a couple of splashes of the balsamic vinegar and stir.
- Take the pastry out of the oven (it should be starting to crisp), and spread the caramelized onions on to the pastry, ensuring they are evenly distributed.
- Open your anchovies and give them a rinse under cold water if they came packed in salt. Arrange the anchovies as desired over the tart.
- Sprinkle on the chives and thyme, if using.
- Finally, if using, cut the goat's cheese into rounds and place on to the tart.
- Pop the tart back into the oven for a further 15/20 minutes or until golden.
- Remove from the oven, season to taste, cut into slices, and serve hot or cold.

68. Caramelized Fennel, Goat Cheese & Mustard Green Tart

Serving: Serves 6 | Prep: | Cook: | Ready in:

Ingredients

- 1 pie crust
- 1 fennel bulb
- 2 tablespoons butter
- 10 ounces goat cheese (chevre)
- 1 cup heavy cream (or .5 c cream & .5 c half & half)
- 3 eggs
- .5 bunches mustard greens, washed, despined & roughly chopped
- 1/8 teaspoon freshly cracked pepper
- 3/4 teaspoon sea salt or kosher salt

Direction

- Prepare the pie-crust to be filled according to recipe instructions, or bake pre-made crust in pie plate with beans for weights for 10-15 minutes.
- Preheat the oven to 350 F.
- Caramelize the fennel: Cut off the stems, hard core, and any woody parts of the bulb, rinse. Quarter the bulb and chop roughly. Melt butter in skillet (I prefer cast iron) over medium-low heat. Add the fennel and salt liberally (about .5 tsp). Leave in the pan without stirring until the fennel is translucent. Remove from heat. (This step can be done the day before constructing tart).
- Process the goat cheese with a food processor until crumbly. Add cream, eggs, 1/4 tsp salt, 1/8 tsp freshly cracked pepper.
- Spread the fennel in the bottom of the tart. Add the chopped mustard. Pour the goat-cheese/custard mixture over the mustard to fill the tart.
- Bake for 30-45 minutes, until the tart is firm when shaken & the top is lightly browned. Allow to cool for 10 minutes. Can be served warm or room temperature.

69. Caramelized Pecan And Goat Cheese Poppers

Serving: Makes 48 | Prep: | Cook: |Ready in:

Ingredients

- 1 1/2 cups pecan halves
- 2 1/2 tablespoons unsalted butter, melted
- 2 1/2 tablespoons brown sugar
- 1/2 teaspoon sea salt
- 1 teaspoon minced, fresh rosemary
- 1 pound Goat cheese
- 1/2 teaspoon finely ground fresh black pepper

Direction

- Preheat to 400. Toss pecans with butter, sugar, salt and rosemary; toast until browned 8-10 minutes in 400 oven. Cool.
- Finely chop pecans in food processor till finely chopped. Make sure pecans are really cool or cold before rolling cheese.
- Form herbed cheese into 1/2 inch sized balls and roll in seasoned pecans; drop into small paper doily cups and chill in refrigerator or freezer for 1/2 hour before setting out on your party table. Freeze or chill your serving plate as well. I like to chill the plain cheese balls on waxed paper in the refrigerator and roll in the nut mixture as close to serving as possible to retain the crisp crunch of the buttery pecans.
- Note: My original recipe called for Boursin herbed cheese and that is good, but lately I have been using plain Goat cheese mixed with a little pepper; I like the cleaner flavor.

70. Caramelized Shallot, Cabbage And Tasso Tart

Serving: Makes one 9" round tart | Prep: | Cook: | Ready in:

Ingredients

- For Molly's tart crust
- 4 tablespoons ice water (you might need up to 2 additional teaspoons)
- 3/4 teaspoon apple cider vinegar

- 1½ cups all-purpose flour
- 3/4 teaspoon sea salt
- 9 tablespoons unsalted butter, chilled but not frozen, cut into chunks
- For the tart filling
- 3 tablespoons 1 teaspoon extra-virgin olive oil, divided
- 1⅓ cups thinly sliced (lengthwise) shallots
- 1/4 cup 2 tablespoons balsamic vinegar
- 1 cup shredded Savoy cabbage
- 1/2 cup cubed tasso (a cured pork, traditionally from Louisiana); you can also use top-quality smoked turkey
- 1/2 cup crumbled goat cheese
- 1/2 cup whipping cream
- 1/2 cup 2% milk
- 2 large eggs
- 1 large egg white
- 1/2 teaspoon salt
- 1/4 teaspoon freshly ground black pepper

Direction

- For Molly's tart crust
- In a small bowl, stir together the 4 tablespoons ice water and the vinegar, and set aside. In the bowl of a food processor, pulse together the flour and ¾ teaspoons of sea salt. Add the butter and pulse until well-incorporated. With the motor running, pour in the water-vinegar mixture and let the dough come together. If it seems dry, add a teaspoon of additional ice water at a time (I usually add 1-2 teaspoons). Turn the dough into a bowl and shape into a ball. Place the ball on a sheet of plastic wrap, press gently into a disk, cover tightly with the wrap and refrigerate for at least two hours. (You can prepare to this point up to three days ahead).
- For the tart filling
- Make the caramelized shallots: In a large sauté pan (I prefer not to use nonstick), heat 3 tablespoons oil over medium-high heat until almost smoking. Add the shallots and cook, stirring only as necessary, until brown around the edges and soft, about 5 minutes.

- Add the vinegar and stir until the bottom of the pan is dry, about 6 minutes. Remove them from the skillet (don't wipe out the skillet). You might have more than the cup you need. Save these and serve on warm toast with cheese. Aah!
- For the rest of the veggie filling: In the skillet, place the remaining teaspoon of oil. Set pan over medium-high heat and when the oil is warm, add the shredded cabbage. When it's nice and melty, reduce the heat to medium-low and add back one cup of caramelized shallots and the cubed tasso. Stir gently to combine everything well and remove the skillet from heat.
- Preheat the oven to 375° Fahrenheit. Using a lightly floured Silpat or waxed paper or the like, roll out the crust using the plastic wrap or more waxed paper as the top sheet on which you roll. Invert the crust over your tart pan, carefully pressing it to the bottom and up the sides. Fold all overhang back in, leaving at least a 1/3" rim above the top of the tart pan. Prick the bottom of the crust all over with a fork, and then place a sheet of foil or parchment on it. Place pie weights or dried beans on top. Blind bake for twenty minutes. Remove foil/parchment and weights/beans and bake five minutes more.
- Remove from oven and let cool slightly while you ready your goat cheese and remaining ingredients. In a 2 cup measuring cup (or the like), whisk together your cream, milk, eggs, egg white, salt and pepper. Set aside.
- When your crust has cooled a bit, place it on a rimmed baking sheet. Then, evenly pour the crumbled goat cheese over the crust. Top that with the shallot-cabbage-tasso mixture. Over that pour the egg-milk mixture. Carefully slide the pan into the oven and bake 25 minutes or until top is golden and set.

71. Celery And Buttermilk Smashed Potatoes

Serving: Serves 4 people | Prep: | Cook: | Ready in:

Ingredients

- 5-6 medium red potatoes (quartered)
- 3 tablespoons sour cream
- 1/2 cup buttermilk
- 2 tablespoons goat cheese
- 4 stalks celery with lots of leaves (rough chop)
- 1/2 tablespoon celery seeds
- salt and pepper

Direction

- Add potatoes to a large pot of salted water. Bring to a boil, and let it cook until a fork slides in the potatoes easily. Drain and transfer to a large mixing bowl or pot.
- Add the buttermilk, sour cream, goat cheese, celery seeds and salt and pepper to the potatoes. Smash until they are creamy, but still have lumps. Stir in the celery at the end, just to incorporate. Serve piping hot with some delicious food!

72. Cheese Pumpkin Salad With Chipotle Honey Viniagrette

Serving: Serves 4 | Prep: | Cook: | Ready in:

Ingredients

- For the salad
- 1 large wedge cheese pumpkin (about 1.5 lb)
- 2 carrots, peeled and cut into bitesized chunks
- 2 parsnips, peeled and cut into bitesized chunks
- 2 large red or yellow peppers, chopped
- 1 small onion, diced
- 1 jalapeno, minced
- 1 garlic clove, minced
- 1/2 teaspoon cumin
- 1 15 oz can black beans
- 1/2 cup goat cheese crumbles
- 5 ounces baby spinach
- For the vinaigrette
- 2 chipotles in adobo sauce
- juice of 1 lime
- 2 tablespoons red wine vinegar
- 1.5 tablespoons honey
- 1/2 teaspoon oregano
- 1-2 tablespoons EVOO

Direction

- Preheat oven to 400 degrees. Line a large baking sheet with tin foil and EVOO spray (or 1 Tbsp. EVOO). Add pumpkin, carrots, parsnips, and peppers, sprinkle with salt, and roast for ~30 min, flipping once, until veggies are browned around the edges.
- While the vegetables are roasting, heat 1 tbsp. EVOO in a small skillet. Add the onion and garlic, cook for 1-2 minutes. Add the jalapeno, cumin, and a dash of salt, stirring frequently until onions are translucent and have lost their bite, 5 to 7 minutes. Set aside.
- Make the dressing. Combine all vinaigrette ingredients plus a generous sprinkle of salt and pepper in a blender. Adjust seasonings to taste.
- To assemble the salad, chop the cheese pumpkin wedge into large chunks. Mix the veggies from the oven with the veggies from the skillet, plus the black beans. Serve over a bed of spinach, and top with 1 to 2 Tbsp. of goat cheese (per serving) and a few spoonfuls of vinaigrette.

73. Cheesy Fritters & Simple Salad

Serving: Serves 2 to 4 | Prep: 0hours15mins | Cook: 0hours22mins | Ready in:

Ingredients

- For the quinoa patties
- 1/2 cup quinoa, well rinsed
- 1 cup water
- 1/4 teaspoon kosher salt, plus more to taste
- 6 tablespoons fresh goat cheese (90 grams)
- 3 tablespoons extra-virgin olive oil, plus more as needed
- For the salad
- 6 cups baby arugula
- 2 tablespoons extra-virgin olive oil
- 2 tablespoons just-squeezed lemon juice
- 1 pinch kosher salt

Direction

- Cook the quinoa. Combine the quinoa, water, and 1/4 teaspoon salt in a small pot. Bring to a boil. Reduce to a simmer, cover the pot, and cook for about 15 minutes, until the quinoa is tender and the water has absorbed.
- Remove the lid, fluff with a fork, and let sit for a few minutes to absorb any remaining water. Add the goat cheese and stir until completely melted. Season with salt to taste. Let sit for at least 10 minutes to cool and set a bit. Now form into 8 patties, each about 2 inches in diameter. (At this point, you can wrap and refrigerate the patties, then fry them within a couple days.)
- Set a preferably nonstick skillet over medium heat. Add the olive oil, adding more as needed to create a circa 1/8-inch thick depth. When the oil is shimmery and hot, add the quinoa patties. (If they can all fit in one pan, great. If not, no big deal—just do batches.) Pan-fry for about 4 minutes until the crust is deeply golden brown. Gingerly flip and fry for another 3 minutes or so. Transfer to a paper towel-lined plate to drain.
- Meanwhile, add the arugula to a big bowl. Dress with the olive oil, lemon juice, and salt. Toss and adjust each ingredient to taste. Serve the salad with the hot quinoa patties on top.

74. Cherry Orchard Baguette

Serving: Serves 4 | Prep: | Cook: | Ready in:

Ingredients

- 1 baguette
- 2 tablespoons whole grain dijon mustard
- 4 ounces semi soft goat cheese
- 2 ounces sliced prosciutto
- 3/4 cup pitted and chopped Bing cherries
- 1 cup spicy microgreen mix

Direction

- Cut your baguette lengthwise and set both pieces on a cutting board with the inside of the baguette open so that you can begin assembling your sandwich.
- Spread 1 Tbsp. each of whole grain Dijon mustard onto what will become the top and bottom of the sandwich.
- Spread 4 oz. of goat cheese onto the bottom half of the baguette.
- Layer prosciutto on top of the goat cheese.
- Sprinkle the chopped Bing cherries over the prosciutto.
- Sprinkle mirogreens over the cherries.
- Place the top of the baguette on the sandwich, cut into quarters, and serve.

75. Cherry Tomato Clafoutis

Serving: Serves 4 for lunch | Prep: | Cook: | Ready in:

Ingredients

- Cherry Tomato Clafoutis
- 3 eggs
- 1/3 cup whole milk
- 1/3 cup cream
- 1/2 cup flour
- 1/2 teaspoon salt
- 1/4 teaspoon freshly ground black pepper
- 12-14 cherry tomatoes

- 2 ounces goat cheese
- Herb "Salad"
- 2 handfuls fresh basil, chiffonade
- 2 handfuls fresh parsley, rough chop
- 3 tablespoons fresh tarragon, rough chop
- 3 tablespoons fresh chives, chopped
- 2 (drizzles around bowl) extra virgin olive oil
- 1 pinch salt
- 3 turns fresh cracked black pepper

Direction

- Preheat oven to 350, liberally butter a ceramic or glass baking dish (preferably round or oval)
- In a large bowl, whisk together eggs, milk and cream. Add salt, pepper, and flour, whisk until just combined.
- Place tomatoes into buttered baking dish, spread evenly. Pour custard mixture over top.
- Dot with goat cheese. Bake in oven until puffed and lightly browned, about 30-35 minutes.
- Once clafoutis is out of oven, toss together herb salad (make sure to do this at the last minute so the herbs are not wilted). Serve each slice of clafoutis topped with herb salad.

76. Cherry Tomato And Chorizo Tart

Serving: Serves 3 | Prep: | Cook: | Ready in:

Ingredients

- 1 puff pastry
- 20 cherry tomatoes
- 200 grams chorizo slices
- 100 grams goat cheese
- tomato sauce
- salt and pepper
- rocket salad

Direction

- I decided to cut my pastry into 4 to make small tarts, but you can keep it whole. Spread the tomato sauce over the pastry and roll up the edges slightly.
- Add the chorizo slices, crumbled goat cheese on it and finally add cherry tomatoes cut in half. Add salt and pepper and bake 20 minutes at 180 ° C.

77. Chèvre, Chorizo & Chocolate Panini

Serving: Serves 2 | Prep: 0hours5mins | Cook: 0hours10mins | Ready in:

Ingredients

- 2 tablespoons olive oil, divided
- 2 fresh chorizo sausages (about 1 pound)
- 3 ounces chèvre, at room temperature
- 1 teaspoon finely grated lemon zest
- 1 ounce dark chocolate, finely chopped
- 2 demi baguettes or 5-inch pieces of baguette, split lengthwise

Direction

- In a medium pan, heat 1 tablespoon of oil over medium heat until it's fragrant. Add the chorizos and cook, turning every couple of minutes, until they're browned and cooked through, 7 minutes. Set aside.
- Schmear the chèvre on each piece of baguette, sprinkle the lemon zest over the chèvre, and sprinkle the chocolate on top of both. Split the chorizos lengthwise and place one inside each baguette.
- Reheat the pan from the chorizo over medium heat. Warm the remaining tablespoon of oil until it's shimmering and fragrant. Place the panini in the pan and weight them down with a sandwich press (if you don't have one, a tea kettle filled with water works just as well). Wait. The unspoken ingredient in this panini is time. Let the panini get hot and toasted

slowly, about 4 minutes on each side, and then it's ready to serve. The chèvre won't melt, but it should be warm and creamy. The chocolate won't liquefy, but it should be soft and melted. When you take a bite, the sausage juices will bring everything together.

78. Chilled Beet Soup With Chevre Cream And Garnishes

Serving: Serves 3-4, depending on serving size | Prep: | Cook: | Ready in:

Ingredients

- For the Beet Soup:
- 1 pound (500 g) Raw beets
- 1 tablespoon Olive oil
- 6   Green onions (white parts only) -OR- 1 medium Shallot, thinly sliced
- 3 cups (750 mL) light chicken stock/ vegetable stock -OR- 1 15 oz can low sodium chicken broth with water added to create 3 cups total
- Salt and Pepper to taste
- For the Chevre Cream and Garnishes:
- 3-4 ounces Chevre goat cheese
- approximately 3 tablespoons Plain yogurt (not Greek style)
- 1 handful Fresh chives, chopped
- 1   Middle Eastern cucumber, diced
- 1-2 splashes White wine vinegar -OR- Fresh lemon juice
- Salt and Pepper to taste
- 1 handful Fresh Dill

Direction

- Rinse and cut off the tops of the beets. Put them together in a foil packet and place this on a cookie sheet. Roast the beets, wrapped tightly in the foil, at 400 degrees Fahrenheit for anywhere from 45 minutes to an hour, or until they are tender when pierced with a small knife. The timing will really depend on the size of your beets.   If your beets are giant, you

may want to cut them in half before wrapping them in the foil to speed the process along. Allow the beets to cool to room temperature and then rub off their skins. Save any juices that have collected in the foil.
- In a small pan, heat the olive oil until shimmering over medium heat and then add the sliced onions or shallot. Cook until translucent, but not yet browning, then remove from the heat.
- If the beets are not already at a size that your blender can handle easily, chop them up into smaller pieces. Add all of your beets to the blender with your chicken/vegetable stock and the cooked onion/shallot. Puree until silky smooth and uniform. The amount of time this will take and the setting to use will depend on your blender model.
- Taste the soup and season with salt and pepper to taste. Chill the pureed soup until cold.
- Just before serving, prepare your garnishes. For the chevre cream, blend together the goat cheese and yogurt with a fork until a thick cream results. Put this into a separate container, cover and refrigerate. For the diced cucumbers, them into a bowl and toss with a splash or two of either white wine vinegar or fresh lemon juice, then sprinkle with salt and pepper to taste. Set aside for at least ten minutes to let the flavors meld.
- To serve, put a large dollop of the chevre cream in the center of each bowl of chilled beet soup, then sprinkle with fresh chopped chives. At the table, offer the cucumbers, additional vinegar or lemon juice, any leftover chevre cream and the fresh chopped dill as garnishes to add independently.
- Enjoy!

79. Chipotle Pork And Goat Cheese Grilled Cheese Sandwich

Serving: Makes lots of sandwiches! | Prep: | Cook: | Ready in:

Ingredients

- For the Pork Tenderloin
- 3 Adobo Marinaded Chipotles (cans can be found in Mexican section of grocery store)
- 1 shallot (rough chop)
- 3 cloves garlic (halved)
- 2 tablespoons cider vinegar
- 2 tablespoons honey
- 1/2 lime (juice and zest)
- Lots of Olive Oil
- Sea salt and black pepper
- 1/2 tablespoon Paprika
- 1 tablespoon Cumin
- 1/2 tablespoon crushed red pepper flakes
- For the Grilled Cheese Sandwich
- Chipotle marinaded pork (shaved into slices)
- Goat cheese
- Baby spinach leaves
- Chipotle Sauce (from above)
- Fresh crusty bread sliced into 1/2 in slices (like an Italian or Portuguese loaf)

Direction

- For the Pork Tenderloin
- Toss all ingredients except the olive oil into a food processor. Blend the ingredients, streaming in the olive oil as it mixes. Add enough oil until the mixture looks nice and smooth.
- You will use some of the sauce to marinade the pork, and some to use as a sauce for serving. To prepare the meat, first run the meat under water to wash off any excess liquids. Then pat dry with a towel.
- Rub salt, pepper, paprika and cumin all over the meat to coat. Add a few spoonfuls of the marinade to a large freezer bag. I also add a couple of bay leaves to the mixture to give it a little more flavor. Add the pork to the bag

with the marinade and move the meat around to coat all sides. Let the meat marinade in the refrigerator for up to 4 hours.
- After 4 hours, take the meat out about 20 minutes before you are ready to cook it. Preheat oven to 300 degrees. You want the meat to come down to room temperature before cooking. While the meat is resting, heat a grill pan on the stove top over high heat (If you don't have a grill pan you could just use a large sauté pan). Add a little olive oil to the grill pan and toss the pork on! Cook the pork on each side for 5 minutes.
- Once both sides have cooked, transfer meat to a baking pan and put it into the oven at 300 degrees for about 20 minutes. Now, I don't have any clue what the internal temperature should be. I just know what it should feel like when I poke it with my finger. It should be nice and soft, but not so soft that it feels like jello. Let the pork rest on your cutting board for about 10 minutes. Slice up and serve with some of the remaining (microwaved) chipotle sauce.
- For the Grilled Cheese Sandwich
- Butter both pieces of bread. Pile some goat cheese on one side of the bread and stack some pork on top. Crumble some more cheese on top of the pork and add a stack of spinach. On the other piece of bread, add spread some chipotle sauce on the non-buttered side. Make a sandwich and throw it on the skillet!
- Cook both sides of the bread until it's golden and the cheese is melt! Cut it in half and serve! Yummm.

80. Chive, Herb Goat Cheese, And Tomato Frittata

Serving: Serves 6 | Prep: | Cook: | Ready in:

Ingredients

- 1 tablespoon Olive Oil

- 1/2 cup Onion, chopped
- 2 cups Cherry Tomatoes, halved
- 3/4 teaspoon salt
- 1/4 teaspoon pepper
- 8   eggs, lightly beaten
- 2 ounces herb goat cheese

Direction

- Preheat oven to 425 degrees.
- In a 10-inch ovenproof nonstick skillet, heat oil over medium-high. Add onions and tomatoes, season with salt and pepper, and cook about 5 minutes.
- Add eggs and season with salt and pepper, and stir to combine. Sprinkle goat cheese throughout, crumbling with your fingers.
- Cook, undisturbed, until edges are set, about 2 minutes. Transfer skillet to oven and bake until top of frittata is just set, 10 to 13 minutes. Invert or slide frittata onto a plate and cut into 6 wedges. Serve warm or at room temperature.

81. Citrus Salad With Goat Cheese Stuffed Dates

Serving: Serves 1, generously | Prep: | Cook: |Ready in:

Ingredients

- 1   shallot, diced
- 1/2   clove garlic, finely chopped
- 2 teaspoons lemon juice
- 2 teaspoons sherry vinegar
- 2 tablespoons extra-virgin olive oil, plus more for dates
- 8   pitted dates
- 1/4 cup goat cheese (fresh and creamy, not aged)
- A splash good balsamic vinegar
- 2   navel oranges (or Cara Cara or juice oranges)
- 1   seedless tangerine
- Coarse salt

- 1 tablespoon slivered blanched almonds, lightly toasted
- Lemon zest (preferably made with a zester, but a Microplane is fine)
- 8   parsley leaves

Direction

- Combine shallot, garlic, lemon juice, and vinegar. Set aside for a few minutes. Slowly whisk in olive oil. Taste. If it's too acidic, add more oil. If it's too oily, add more vinegar or lemon juice. Set aside.
- Preheat your boiler. Fill each date with goat cheese (no need to be careful -- the cheese can be spilling out). Place dates in a cast iron pan or baking dish. Splash with olive oil and thick balsamic. Broil until dates are just warmed through and the cheese is starting to brown. Watch carefully. Don't let them burn. This should take about 4 minutes. Cool for a few minutes while you slice the citrus.
- With a serrated knife, carefully cut off the skin and the pith off of the oranges and the tangerine. Slice them both longitudinally. Spread slices out on plate, overlapping a bit. With a spoon, splash the citrus with your reserved dressing (make sure to scoop up some of the vinegary shallots). Sprinkle with salt. Nestle in the warm dates. Garnish with almonds, lemon zest, and parsley leaves. Eat with a baguette. You will have some dressing left over for the next day's salad.

82. Citrus Scented, Cheese Cupcake With Lemon Curd And Chocolate Curls

Serving: Makes 16 cupcakes, but depends on the size | Prep: | Cook: |Ready in:

Ingredients

- Crust Base
- 5 ounces Graham crackers with real honey

- 2 ounces Pecans
- 2 tablespoons Sweet (unsalted) butter
- 2 tablespoons Granulated sugar
- 0.5 teaspoons Table salt
- The Filling
- 24 ounces Farmer Cheese (3 packages)
- 4 ounces Goat cheese
- 1 piece Lemon zest
- 0.5 cups Fresh lemon juice (2-3 lemons)
- 4 pieces Large eggs, room temperature
- 1 piece Large egg yolk
- 0.5 cups Heavy cream
- 1.5 cups Baker's sugar
- 0.5 pieces Vanilla bean (content scraped into the heavy cream)
- 2 tablespoons Sour cream
- 0.5 teaspoons Table salt

Direction

- METHODI. Crust. Adjust the oven rack to lower-middle position and heat the oven to 325F degrees. Prepare a muffin/cupcake bake ware with silicon cups (that is what I do for a foolproof method and the look is attractive too); but you can use cupcake liners of your preference. Toast the pecans for 10 minutes; mixing and turning them during half-time. Cool the pecans on a rack then process them in a Food Processor to fine, even crumbs (you should use about 3 ounces for the base)Process the crackers in the Food Processor, to fine, even crumbs (you should use about 5 ounces for the base)Pour both crumbs into a clean bowl and mix them well. Add the sugar and mix well to incorporate. Melt the butter. Pour the warm, melted butter into the crumb mix and mix the mixture until it is evenly moistened and resembles wet sand. Place two tablespoon of the mixture into each of the prepared silicone cups and press it firmly to the bottom and as much as you can to the sides (you can use a small measuring cup to assist you in the pressing of the crumbs). Bake until golden brown (about 10 minutes). Cool on a wire rack to room temperature (about 30 minutes). When cooled, set the pan as is (with the baked crumbs in the silicon cups) into a roasting pan and fill the roasting pan with warm water so that it is about half the height of the muffin/cupcake pan.
- THE FILLING: Zest the lemon. Squeeze the lemons (measure out 1/2 cup juice for use). Cut the vanilla bean into half and scrape the content with the blunt side of the knife into the heavy cream. Warm the cream in a non-reactive pan to the point of boil, then move the pan off the heat source and let it rest until use. Process a quarter cup sugar and lemon zest with a wooden spoon until the zest is absorbed completely into the sugar and makes the sugar moist, and pale yellow in color. Stir into the sugar mixture the rest of the sugar (1 cup)Process the farmer- and goat cheese in the Food Processor until the cheese will resemble cream cheese (It may take up to 5 minutes)Place the cheese mixture into the Kitchen Aid Mixer bowl, add the sugar/lemon zest mixture in a slow, steady stream while using the paddle; increase the speed to medium and continue to beat the mixture until it is creamy and smooth, scraping down the bowl sides with a rubber spatula, as needed. Reduce the speed to medium-low, and add the eggs, 2 at a time; beat the mixture until the eggs are incorporated. Scrape the side and bottom of the bowl well, after each addition. Add the lemon juice and salt and mix until just incorporated. Add the heavy cream with the vanilla, and mix until just incorporated. Give the batter a final scrap, stir with a rubber spatula to make sure that there are no lumps in the batter. Pour the cheese mixture into each of the silicon cups (leave about 1/8 inch at the top). Increase the temperature in the oven to 350F. The first 15 minutes place a wooden spoon in the door of the oven (the oven door will remain open); then take away the spoon, close the oven door and bake the cupcakes for another 20 minutes (but you may need to check earlier, because the timing depends on your oven). The cupcake is done when the center jiggles slightly, the sides just start to puff, the surface is not shiny and the instant-

read thermometer inserted into the center of the cake registers 150F degree. Turn off the oven and prop open the oven door with the handle of the wooden spoon; allow the cupcake to cool in the water bath in the oven for 1 hour. Take out the pan after 1 hour, and place it on a wire rack and continue to let it cool for 2 more hours

- The Lemon Curd: Heat the lemon juice in small non-reactive saucepan over a medium heat, until hot, but not boiling. Whisk the eggs and the egg yolk in a medium non-reactive bowl and gradually whisk in the sugar. Whisking constantly then slowly pour the warm lemon juice into the egg mixture and then return the mixture to the saucepan and cook over medium heat, while stirring constantly with a rubber spoon, until the mixture register 170F degrees on an instant-read thermometer and thick enough to cling to the spoon. Immediately remove pan from the heat source and stir the butter into the mixture until incorporated. Stir in the vanilla extract and salt. Pour the curd through a fine mesh strainer to assure that there are no lumps in the curve, into a small non-reactive bowl. Cover the surface of the curd directly with plastic wrap and refrigerate until needed

- ASSEMBLE THE CUPCAKE: When the cheese cupcake is cool, take about a heaping tablespoon of the curd and spread it on top of each of the cheese-cupcake. Refrigerate at least for 4 hours or overnight. To serve, remove the silicon cup and place the cupcakes on a serving plate (you could also remove the silicon cup prior to placing the lemon curd on the top of the cupcake, but I believe it is easier to work with the cupcake while it is with the silicon cup. Take a vegetable peeler and drop a few chocolate curls on top of the lemon curd

83. Colby Garrelts' Grilled Pork Loin With Green Bean Salad

Serving: Serves 4 | Prep: 0hours0mins | Cook: 0hours0mins | Ready in:

Ingredients

- For the pork loin:
- 1 boneless center cut pork loin
- 1/2 cup olive oil
- 1/2 cup apple cider vinegar
- 1/3 cup Dijon mustard
- 1/4 cup honey
- 3 tablespoons prepared horseradish
- 2 tablespoons minced garlic
- For the salad:
- 1/2 cup rice wine vinegar
- 1/3 cup olive oil
- 1/4 cup honey
- 1 tablespoon fresh lemon juice
- 12 ounces green beans
- 1/2 to 1 cups baby arugula, loosely packed
- 4 ounces goat cheese
- 2 ounces thinly sliced prosciutto, torn into bite-sized pieces

Direction

- Marinate: Place fresh pork loin in resealable plastic food storage bag. Mix together remaining ingredients; pour over pork loin. Marinate in refrigerator for 2 hours.
- Heat grill to medium. Remove pork loin from the marinade and lightly pat dry. Grill the pork loin for 18 to 20 minutes per pound, or until the internal temperature reaches 145°F to 160°F, turning occasionally. Let stand 10 minutes before slicing to serve.
- Make the salad: Whisk together vinegar, olive oil, honey, and lemon juice; set aside. Boil green beans in salted water for 2 to 3 minutes, until green beans are bright green. Remove from water and place in ice water to stop cooking; drain and toss with arugula and vinaigrette in large bowl. Season with salt and pepper.

- Divide beans between 4 plates; top with goat cheese and prosciutto. Slice pork loin and arrange on plates for serving.

84. Corn And Tomato Crustless Quiche With Fresh Tomato Salad

Serving: Serves 8 | Prep: | Cook: |Ready in:

Ingredients

- For the Quiche:
- 2 cups frozen organic sweet yellow corn (thawed)
- 2 cups frozen organic sweet white corn (thawed)
- 16 oz soft Goat cheese (room temperature)
- 6 extra large eggs (room temperature)
- 1 cup cherry tomatoes, halved
- 4 tablespoons crème fraîche
- 2 teaspoons salt
- 1 teaspoon freshly ground black pepper
- 2 tablespoons finely chopped fresh thyme
- For the salad
- • 4 fresh ripe tomatoes
- • 2 medium Persian cucumbers (partially peeled, seeded and cut in thin slices
- • 1 teaspoon coarse salt
- • 1 small red onion, sliced thinly length-wise (about 1/2 cup)
- • 1/4 cup chopped fresh flat-leaf parsley
- • 2 tablespoons fresh dill chopped
- • 2 cloves garlic, minced
- • 3 tablespoons extra-virgin olive oil
- • 1 tablespoon fresh lemon juice
- • 8 Bocconcini balls cut in half

Direction

- Preheat oven to 325 degrees. In a blender puree white corn with the crème fraîche. Strain thru a fine sifts to a large bowl, pressing with a wooden spoon to extract as much of the corn milk as possible, discard the solids.
- In another bowl whisk Goat cheese until smooth, add the eggs one at a time, salt, pepper and thyme; then add this mixture to the bowl with the white corn and crème fraîche mixture.
- Whisk together until well blended; then fold in the yellow corn kernels and tomatoes.
- Butter and flour an 8 by 8-inches baking glass or casserole dish, pour the Quiche mixture and bake for about 80 minutes or until slightly firm and light golden brown.
- Transfer quiche to a wire rack to cool until set, about 20 minutes. Serve warm or at room temperature. To reheat, cover quiche with aluminum foil and bake in an oven heated to 325 degrees for about 15 minutes.
- To make the salad: Bring a small pot of water to a boil. Submerge each tomato for 10 seconds each and immediately run under cold water. The skin should easily peel off. Cut out the core, slice into thin wedges and place in a medium-size bowl. Add the salt and mix.
- Add the onion, cucumber, garlic, herbs, olive oil and lemon juice. Stir until well combined. Chill until ready to serve, preferably at least 30 minutes. Serve in salad bowls alongside with the quiche.

85. Country Style Potato Salad With Pancetta, Goat Cheese & Dried Cranberries

Serving: Serves 4 | Prep: | Cook: |Ready in:

Ingredients

- 2 pounds red bliss potatoes
- 1 tablespoon olive oil
- 6 ounces pancetta, diced
- 1/2 cup finely chopped yellow onion
- 1 tablespoon Dijon mustard
- 2 1/2 tablespoons cider vinegar

- 3/4 cup chicken stock
- 1/2 cup dried cranberries
- 2 tablespoons chopped parsley plus extra for garnish
- Kosher salt
- Freshly ground black pepper
- 2 ounces goat cheese

Direction

- Wash the potatoes and cut them in half. Place them in a large saucepan and fill the saucepan with enough cold water to cover them. Salt the water and bring to a boil over high heat. Cook until potatoes are fork tender. Drain the potatoes and slice them into 1/4-inch slices.
- Heat the olive oil in a large sauté pan over medium heat. Add the pancetta and cook until crisp. Add the onion to the pan and cook until softened. Add the mustard, vinegar, chicken stock, and dried cranberries and stir to combine. Cook 3-4 minutes until liquid is reduced by half. Add the sliced potatoes along with the parsley and salt and pepper to taste. Toss to combine all ingredients well.
- To serve, transfer the potatoes to a serving platter and crumble the goat cheese on top. Garnish with the remaining parsley. Serve warm.

86. Cous Cous And Fresh Veggie Salad

Serving: Serves 2-4 | Prep: | Cook: | Ready in:

Ingredients

- 1 cup couscous
- 1 cup chicken or vegetable broth
- 1 cup grape tomatoes, sliced
- 1/4 cup chopped cilantro
- 1/4 cup scallions
- 1/2 cup carrots, diced
- 1/4 cup radishes, diced

- 1 cup wilted greens, such as spinach or kale (optional)
- 3 tablespoons extra virgin olive oil
- 2 tablespoons red wine vinegar
- 1 tablespoon lemon juice, plus zest of one lemon
- salt and freshly ground pepper to taste
- 1-2 ounces chevre or goat cheese

Direction

- Bring broth to a boil. Stir in couscous and cover. Remove from heat. Let stand 5-10 minutes and then fluff with a fork.
- While couscous is cooking and cooking, chop your vegetables. Feel free to substitute based on what you have on hand.
- Gently combine veggies with couscous. Add olive oil, vinegar, lemon juice, salt, and pepper. Mix to combine. Stir in a few dollops of goat cheese. Chill or serve at room temperature.

87. Crackers With Sweet Cheese And Fried Sage

Serving: Serves 4-6 | Prep: | Cook: | Ready in:

Ingredients

- 2 ounces goat cheese
- 1.5 teaspoons honey
- 4.5 teaspoons olive oil, divided
- handful of fresh sage leaves
- water crackers or some other vehicle with which to get yummies mouth-ward
- flake finishing salt

Direction

- In a small bowl combine the goat cheese, honey and 1.5 teaspoon of olive oil. Set aside.
- Heat the remaining olive oil (or enough to generously coat the bottom) in a small sauté pan over medium-high heat. When hot, fry the

sage leaves until crisp and the sizzling noise stops - about 1-2 minutes. Chopsticks help with the turning. Drain on a paper towel lined plate.

- This is the tricky part. Smear some goat cheese on a cracker, top with a fried sage leave and a sprinkle of salt. Eat. Mop the sweat from your brow and crack open a cold one to reward yourself.

Serving: Serves 4-6 as a starter, easily doubled | Prep: | Cook: | Ready in:

Ingredients

- 3/4 cup fresh cranberries, washed and picked over
- 2 tablespoons unsalted butter
- 3 tablespoons light brown sugar
- 3 tablespoons Frangelico
- 1   round bucheron (goat cheese)

Direction

- Position oven rack in top third of oven. Preheat broiler.
- In a small saucepan, heat butter until it begins to brown.
- Carefully add cranberries (if your butter is sputtering, you may want to remove saucepan from heat momentarily to avoid burning yourself when you add cranberries).
- Add brown sugar and Frangelico. Allow mixture to bubble and cook for about 4 minutes. Cranberries should split open. Remove mixture from heat.
- Meanwhile, place bucheron round in a broiler proof container.
- Spoon all of the cranberries and some of the liquid on to the goat cheese round. Reserve remaining liquid.
- Broil for 3 minutes.

- Transfer cranberry studded bucheron round to serving plate. Spoon additional liquid over cheese and cranberries. Serve with crackers or crostini.

89. Cranberry And Persimmon Filled Endive With Tangy Goat Cheese Dressing

Serving: Makes about 24 stuffed endive spears | Prep: | Cook: | Ready in:

Ingredients

- For the cranberry and persimmon:
- 1   crisp Fuyu persimmon
- 1 1/2 cups fresh whole cranberries, washed
- 2 tablespoons granulated sugar, plus more if necessary
- Pinch of sea salt, if necessary
- ++++++++++++++++++++++
- For the tangy goat cheese dressing:
- 2 ounces Chevre made with vegetable rennet
- 1   small garlic clove, minced
- 1 teaspoon sherry vinegar
- 1/2 teaspoon Dijon mustard
- 2 tablespoons Greek yogurt plus 2 tablespoons water thoroughly blended in a small bowl
- 1 teaspoon finely chopped Italian parsley
- Sea salt to taste
- Black pepper to taste
- ++++++++++++++++++++++
- For walnuts:
- 1/4 cup walnut halves
- ++++++++++++++++++++++
- For serving (scooping and drizzling):
- 3 Belgian Endive heads

Direction

- Carefully remove the stem and peel the persimmon. Slice in half, and then cut each half into six wedges. Cut each wedge into thirds.

- Combine cranberries and persimmon pieces in the bowl of a food processor. Pulse until mixture is uniform and finely chopped, occasionally using a spatula to scrape down the sides of the bowl. If you find yourself with any stubborn chunks of persimmon, simply pick these out and eat them. Add granulated sugar and pulse three more times to combine. At this point, you will want to taste the mixture. Depending on the tartness of the fruit, you may want to add a little more sugar to taste. You do not want it to be really sweet, but you also do not want it to be lip-puckering tart. Transfer fruit to a glass container (you should have 1 1/2 cups), cover with plastic wrap, and refrigerate for at least two hours.
- MAKE THE DRESSING: Using a fork, mash goat cheese and garlic in a medium bowl; add sherry vinegar and mix to combine. Add Dijon mustard and mix to combine. Using a spatula, add yogurt-water mixture and combine until dressing is smooth. Fold in Italian parsley, and season to taste with sea salt and black pepper. At this point, if your dressing is too thick, you can add another Tablespoon of water and mix to combine thoroughly. Transfer dressing to a glass jar with a lid and refrigerate for at least two hours to let flavors meld.
- Preheat oven to 350 degrees. Spread walnut pieces in a single layer on a large rimmed baking sheet. Toast nuts for 5-7 minutes, shaking the pan once, until fragrant and golden.
- Allow nuts to cool. Finely chop. Transfer to an airtight container until needed for garnish.
- Trim ends off Belgian endive heads. Carefully remove spears, discarding any outer layers that look less than perky. Rinse spears and thoroughly dry, using a spin dryer if you have one, or paper towels. You should have at least 24 good-sized spears, plus a few more for tasting. Reserve the tender, innermost spears for another use.

- Arrange spears on a large serving platter if you are going the shared starter route, or individual plates, if you prefer the salad route. Before scooping out the fruit mixture, give it a good stir and taste it. I found that after sitting for two hours the fruits had mingled, mellowed, and needed a pinch of sea salt to perk them up. When satisfied, scoop a generous teaspoon of fruit and fill the stem end, gently pressing down on the fruit with the bottom of the spoon in an aesthetically pleasing way. Drizzle the dressing over the spears and garnish with toasted walnuts. Enjoy!

90. Cream Of Green Tomato Soup

Serving: Serves 4 | Prep: | Cook: | Ready in:

Ingredients

- 2 pounds green tomatoes, cut into quarters
- 1-2 jalapeno peppers (depending on how much heat you like)
- 3   cloves of garlic
- 2-3 tablespoons olive oil
- 1 cup green pumpkin seeds
- 2 cups chicken or vegetable stock
- 1.5 cups milk, or cream if you want a richer soup
- 1 teaspoon cumin
- 1/2 teaspoon dried oregano
- 1/2 teaspoon chili powder
- 1/4 teaspoon cayenne
- 1 tablespoon honey
- 1.5 tablespoons fresh minced cilantro
- 1 teaspoon lime juice
- 1/2 cup spreadable goat cheese/chevre
- sea salt, to taste

Direction

- Start by roasting the first four ingredients. Preheat the oven to 350 degrees. Coat a baking pan with some of the olive oil, assemble the tomatoes, jalapenos and garlic on pan, and drizzle with enough olive oil to coat. Place in oven to roast until softened, 30-40 minutes. Remove from oven, scrape seeds and remove stems from jalapenos and place all in blender along with pumpkin seeds and stock. Puree until smooth.

- Place a large saucepan over low-medium heat. Add puree mixture, as well as the remaining ingredients. Gradually bring the soup to medium heat and simmer until the goat cheese is fully melted into the soup. Season with sea salt to taste.

- Optional: toast the following in 350 degree oven for about 15 minutes, •1 cup pumpkin seeds/pepitas •1 tbsp. maple syrup •1 tbsp. olive oil •1/2 tsp chipotle powder• sea salt. These are also great to top salads. Serve with the soup, as well as crumbled goat cheese and your favorite hot sauce.

91. Creamy Goat Cheese Grits

Serving: Serves dinner for one, or – if you must share – enough for two as a side dish | Prep: | Cook: |Ready in:

Ingredients

- 1/2 cup grits (not instant)
- 1/2 teaspoon salt, plus more to taste
- 1/2 cup milk, plus a few more tablespoons if necessary
- 1/4 cup fresh goat cheese
- 1/4 cup grated parmesan
- coarsely ground black pepper

Direction

- Combine the grits, salt, milk and 2 cups cold water in a medium saucepan. Set the saucepan over medium-high heat and bring the mixture to a boil, whisking frequently. When it reaches a boil, turn the heat all the way down and cover the saucepan. Simmer the grits,

whisking occasionally, until they are creamy and tender to the bite, 8 to 10 minutes.

- Whisk in the goat cheese and the parmesan, adding a bit more milk if the mixture seems too thick. Taste the grits and add more salt if necessary. Whisk in a few generous grinds of black pepper, spoon into a large bowl and eat right now!

92. Creamy Lemon Asparagus Soup With Goat Cheese & Pistou

Serving: Serves 5-6 | Prep: | Cook: |Ready in:

Ingredients

- Lemon Asparagus Goat Cheese Soup
- 2 bunches Asparagus, chopped
- 1 Leek, chopped
- 1 Garlic Clove, minced
- 3 tablespoons Butter
- 5-6 cups Chicken Broth
- 1/2 cup Milk, we used 2% but you can use whole or cream
- 3 ounces Soft Goat Cheese
- 1 Lemon, juiced
- Salt & Fresh Ground Pepper to Taste
- Easy Pistou
- 1 Garlic Clove, peeled
- 2 cups Fresh Basil Leaves
- 1/4 cup Olive Oil
- 1 Small Tomato, peeled, seeded & diced
- 1 1/2 ounces Parmesan Cheese, grated
- 1 pinch Salt

Direction

- In a heavy cast iron pot over medium/high heat melt the butter and cook garlic and leek until the leeks begin to wilt. Once they have wilted and become slightly transparent add the asparagus and cook for a few minutes, stirring. Add the chicken broth and bring to a boil. Cook until asparagus is fork tender, about 10 minutes. Once asparagus is tender, puree your soup with an immersion blender or an upright blender in batches. Once pureed, add the goat cheese, lemon juice and salt & pepper to taste and stir until all ingredients have melded into the soup.

- Pistou is traditionally made with mortar and pestle but since we don't currently have one in the FWE kitchen, we decided to use our small food processor for the job. Combine the basil and garlic in the food processor and pulse while adding the olive oil slowly. Once these are well broken down, add the remaining ingredients and pulse until you have what resembles a fine pesto.
- Serve your soup hot with a dollop of pistou and some rustic bread. Enjoy!

93. Creamy Goat Cheese With Pine Nuts & Cranberries

Serving: Serves 2-3 as a starter | Prep: | Cook: | Ready in:

Ingredients

- 100 grams soft goat cheese
- 30 grams hard cheese, e.g. Gruyère, Comté, finely grated
- 1 teaspoon mustard
- 1 teaspoon honey
- 15 grams pine nuts, roasted and chopped
- 10 grams dried cranberries, chopped (+ 2 for decoration)
- 8-10 sprigs of thyme
- 1 dash of freshly ground black pepper

Direction

- Roast pine nuts in a pan at low to medium heat until slightly golden (no addition of oil/fat needed; takes about 10 min)
- Coarsely chop pine nuts and cranberries.
- Pick leaflets from 4-5 thyme sprigs.
- Grate the hard cheese finely.

- Combine hard and goat cheese in a bowl, then blend in other ingredients using a fork or spoon.
- Form a ball or place mixture into a small baking mold or other dish layered with foil. Cool in refrigerator for at least half an hour.
- Turn baking mold/dish upside-down and decorate cheese with remaining thyme sprigs and cranberries. Serve with Grissini breadsticks, baguette or homemade walnut bread.

94. Crispy Brussels Sprouts With Kale + An Addictive Pomegrante Molasses Vinaigrette

Serving: Serves 4 (scales up easily) | Prep: | Cook: | Ready in:

Ingredients

- 1 pound Brussels sprouts trimmed and quartered
- 1/2 Bunch of curly kale roughly chopped (2 cups)
- 1 tablespoon Olive oil
- 1 Clove garlic - pressed or minced
- 2 tablespoons Golden raisins
- 1 tablespoon Pine nuts - toasted
- 2 tablespoons Pomegrante molasses
- 1 teaspoon Red wine vinegar
- 2 tablespoons Olive oil
- 1/2 teaspoon Dijon mustard
- Vegetable oil for frying
- 3 tablespoons Goat cheese, crumbled.

Direction

- You will need two pots - one deep saucepan for frying and one skillet for sautéing. In the large skillet heat the olive oil and garlic over medium heat. When the garlic is fragrant add the kale and season with salt. Cover and cook for about 5-10 mins until the kale is tender but take care not to burn the garlic.

- Meanwhile heat the oil for the Brussels to 330 degrees. In batches cook the sprouts for about 3 mins until cooked and slightly browned and crispy. Drain on paper towels and season well with kosher salt.
- Meanwhile - or even before you cook the veg - make the vinaigrette. Mix the pomegranate molasses, red wine vinegar, olive oil, and Dijon. Whisk well and season with salt and pepper.
- To assemble - toss the crispy Brussels with the vinaigrette. In a bowl mix in the cooked kale and golden raisins. Top with crumbled goat cheese and pine nuts.

95. Crispy Prosciutto Rosemary Khachapuri (Georgian Cheese Bread)

Serving: Makes 2 large or 4 small breads | Prep: | Cook: | Ready in:

Ingredients

- For the dough
- 4 1/3 cups (522 g) bread flour
- 1 tablespoon (9 g) instant active dry yeast
- 2 tablespoons (25 g) granulated sugar
- 1 teaspoon (4 g) fine sea salt
- 10 tablespoons (142 g) unsalted butter, at room temperature
- 1 cup (242 g) whole milk, warmed to about 100°F
- 1/3 cup (81 g) warm water
- For the filling and finishing
- 1 1/2 cups goat cheese
- 2 1/1 cups diced fresh mozzarella cheese
- Egg wash, as needed for finishing
- 8   slices prosciutto
- 1 tablespoon roughly chopped rosemary

Direction

- Make the dough: In the bowl of an electric mixer fitted with the dough hook attachment, mix the flour, yeast, sugar, and salt to combine. Add the butter and mix on low speed until the mixture looks crumbly, about 1 minute.
- Add the milk and water and mix the dough on low speed for 4 minutes. Raise the speed to medium and mix until the dough is very smooth, 2-3 minutes more.
- Transfer the dough to a large, oiled bowl and cover with plastic wrap. Let the dough rise for 1 1/2 to 2 hours, until the dough is puffed (it may not fully double in size).
- Divide the dough as desired: Cut into two even pieces for larger, more shareable khachapuri, or into four even pieces for smaller, individual khachapuri.
- Pat the dough into an oval shape with your hands. On a lightly floured surface, roll out the dough, maintaining the oval shape, into an oblong oval about 1/3-inch thick.
- Pick the dough up from the ends and transfer it to a parchment lined baking sheet. Gently stretch the dough when you transfer it to help elongate the oval a bit.
- Crumble the goat cheese evenly over the dough, leaving about 1-inch around the edge on all sides. Sprinkle the mozzarella evenly over the goat cheese.
- Working your way around the bread, fold the excess dough up and over the filling to create a little wall and encase it. Gently pinch the ends of the oval to help seal. Cover the breads with a piece of plastic wrap sprayed with nonstick spray, and let the bread rise for 30 minutes – 1 hour.
- Preheat the oven to 375ºF. Brush the edges of the dough with egg wash.
- Arrange the prosciutto over the surface of the cheese—4 slices each for large kachapuri, 2 each for small. Sprinkle a bit of rosemary over each bread.
- Transfer to the oven and bake until the crust is golden brown, the cheese is melted and lightly golden, and the prosciutto is crisp, 30-35 minutes for small, 45-50 minutes for large.

- Let the khachapuri cool for 5-10 minutes before serving warm.

96. Crostini With Whipped Goat Cheese And Hot Pepper Jelly

Serving: Serves a crowd | Prep: | Cook: | Ready in:

Ingredients

- Hot Pepper Jelly
- 3/4 pound red jalapenos
- 2 cups cider vinegar, divided
- 6 cups sugar
- large pinch salt
- 1 packet Certo liquid pectin
- Crostini
- 1 baguette, thinly sliced
- 2 cloves smashed garlic
- olive oil, as needed
- salt and pepper, to taste
- 1 cup goat cheese, or more as needed
- 2 tablespoons heavy cream

Direction

- Hot Pepper Jelly
- Halve the jalapenos. Seed the jalapenos based on how spicy you want the jelly. (Since red jalapenos are sweeter than green jalapenos, I seeded half of the jalapenos, but left the seeds with the other half. It made for an only slightly spicy jelly. Final spice can also be adjusted with red pepper flakes at the end of cooking.)
- Transfer the peppers to a food processor or blender, with half of the vinegar. Transfer the mixture to a large pot. Add the remaining vinegar and sugar. Bring to a boil over medium heat. Boil for 10 minutes.
- Stir in liquid pectin. Boil for 1 minute, until jelly begins to thicken. Remove from heat, and ladle into sterilized jars. If keeping in the fridge, close the jars and refrigerate. If planning to keep on the shelves, process,

covered, in boiling water for 5-7 minutes, or until sealed.
- Crostini
- Rub each baguette slice with garlic. Drizzle with olive oil and season with salt and pepper. Bake in a preheated 350 degree oven until golden brown, about 4-5 minutes. Let cool completely.
- Using a handheld mixer (or in your Kitchenaid), whip the goat cheese with the heavy cream until light and fluffy. Season with salt and pepper.
- Spread a layer of whipped goat cheese on each piece of crostini, and top with a dollop of hot pepper jelly.

97. Crusted Heirloom Tomato With Goat Cheese Mousse

Serving: Serves 6 | Prep: 0hours15mins | Cook: 0hours25mins | Ready in:

Ingredients

- Goat Cheese Mousse
- 1 1/8 cups Heavy whipping cream
- 10.5 ounces Goat Cheese
- Pinch Salt and pepper (to taste)
- Pinch Optional herbs (parsley, chives, etc.)
- Fried Tomatoes
- 2 Large heirloom tomatoes (yellow or green hold best)
- 2 Eggs
- 1 cup Flour
- 1 cup Panko bread crumbs
- Vegetable oil

Direction

- Start with the mousse by adding 1 cup of heavy whipping cream to a mixer
- Mix on medium speed until stiff peaks are reached (like you are making a whipped cream)

- Move the whipped cream to a separate bowl and place in the fridge
- Add the goat cheese and last 1/8 cup of heavy whipping cream to the mixer
- Mix on medium speed until the goat cheese is softened and creamy (may need to scrape sides of the bowl every couple minutes)
- Once the goat cheese is properly mixed, fold the whipped cream in
- Prepare your tomatoes by slicing into 1cm thick slices (you should get about 3-4 per tomato depending on size)
- Begin to prepare your oil by pouring into a pan and over medium-high heat (use enough oil to fry the tomatoes on each side)
- Beat the eggs and lay out the flour and Panko. Prepare your tomatoes for frying by dipping in flour, then the egg mixture, and then in to the bread crumbs
- Place into the oil and fry for about 60-90 seconds, and then flip to the other side. Fry until the tomatoes reach a golden color
- Plate the goat cheese mousse with the tomato, and garnish as you please! I added nectarines which paired nicely.

98. Crème Fraîche Eggs En Cocotte

Serving: Serves 2 | Prep: | Cook: | Ready in:

Ingredients

- Olive oil, for greasing the ramekins
- 2 tablespoons goat cheese crumbles
- 2 to 3 tablespoons diced tomatoes
- 2 large eggs
- salt and pepper, to taste
- 2 tablespoons crème fraîche
- 2 tablespoons grated Parmesan
- 2 tablespoons Gruyere or mozzarella (optional)
- 1/4 cup shredded parsley, for garnish (optional)

Direction

- Preheat oven to 325° F.
- Lightly grease two 4-ounce porcelain ramekins with olive oil. Divide the goat cheese and tomatoes between the two ramekins. Gently crack an egg over the mixture in each ramekin, taking care not to break the yolks. Sprinkle salt and pepper over the eggs. Finally, dollop a tablespoon of crème fraîche over each, and finish with a generous layer of Parmesan, plus mozzarella, or gruyere, if you really want to go all out.
- If you like, prepare a Bain Marie to bake the cocottes in a gentle and even heat. Place them in a baking dish or cake pan, then fill the pan with about 1 inch of hot water. Otherwise, simply place them on a baking sheet. Either way, bake for about 10 to 20 minutes until your desired level of doneness. At 10 minutes, the egg whites will be just set. At 15 minutes, the yolks will still be soft. At 20, the whole egg should be set. If you're one who loves a runny egg, keep a close eye on your eggs before the 10 minutes are up.
- Let cool briefly, then serve with a side of toast or salad.

99. Drunk Cherry Hot Mess Ice Cream

Serving: Makes 6 1/2 cup servings | Prep: | Cook: | Ready in:

Ingredients

- Drunk Cherry Ice Cream
- 1 cup Cherries (fresh, pitted)
- 1 milliliter Amaretto liqueur (or about 2 oz)
- 1 1/2 cups Milk (2%)
- 1 1/4 cups Half & Half
- 1/3 cup Sugar
- 1/4 cup Brown Sugar
- 2 tablespoons Corn Starch
- 1 teaspoon Vanilla

- 2 ounces Goat Cheese (room temp)
- 2 pinches salt
- Hot Mess Mix-Ins
- 1/2 cup Walnuts, chopped
- 1 teaspoon Brown Sugar
- 1/2 teaspoon Sugar
- 1/2 teaspoon Cayenne Pepper
- 1/4 tablespoon Butter
- 1 pinch salt
- 10   Caramels (wrapped candies)
- 4   Serrano Peppers
- 1/2 cup Chocolate Chips

Direction

- Pit the cherries, and place in small bowl. Pour Amaretto and let soak for several hours to overnight.
- In a medium saucepan, heat up the Milk, Half & Half (reserve about 1/4 cup and mix in the 2 TBLS cornstarch until dissolved, then add to the pan), Sugar, and Brown Sugar. Over Low-medium heat, bring to just below boiling (about 180 degrees) or until the mixture around the sides of the pan starts looking foamy, about 10 minutes.
- Remove from heat and let cool for about 5 minutes. Add in the 1 tsp. Vanilla and 2 pinches of salt. Whisk in the goat cheese until blended completely. Place in a covered container and refrigerate for several hours to overnight.
- Nuts: Melt the butter in the microwave for about 30 seconds. In a small bowl, stir in nuts, butter, sugars, Cayenne and pinch salt. Spread the nuts out in a small baking pan, and toast at 350 for about 8 minutes. Let cool completely.
- Caramel Chunks: Cut the Serrano peppers in half and with a spoon remove the seeds and veins. Chop into small pieces. In a saucepan, add the caramels and serrano peppers, and heat over medium heat until caramels are melted. Stir often to prevent burning. Spread the caramel mixture onto parchment paper and place in freezer for a few minutes to cool.
- Meanwhile, melt the chocolate in the microwave, 30 seconds at a time. Stir after

each 30 seconds for about 1 1/2 to 2 minutes. Drizzle the chocolate over the caramel mixture, and return to freezer to harden. Peel the hardened caramel mixture off the paper, flip over and cover the other side with drizzled chocolate. Return to freezer. Remove just before the ice cream goes into the freezer and chop into pieces.
- Once the milk mixture has thoroughly chilled, pour into the ice cream maker, following the manufacturer's instructions. Once the mixture begins to thicken, slowly add in the cherries, including the Amaretto, the nuts, and the chocolate/caramel chunks. Freeze to a soft-serve consistency, then remove to a container and place in the freezer for about 2 hours. Before serving, let it sit out for a few minutes to soften.

100.   Easy Broccoli Salad With Cheese Recipe

Serving: Serves 3 as a lunch | Prep: 0hours10mins | Cook: 0hours0mins | Ready in:

Ingredients

- 1   medium to large head of broccoli
- 8-10   pitted dates
- 3/4 cup walnut pieces, toasted or raw
- 1/4 cup dried sour cherries
- 5 ounces Cypress Grove Humboldt Fog, divided into 2 ounces and 3 ounces, at room temperature
- 1/4 cup extra virgin olive oil, plus 2 tablespoons
- 1 lemon, for 1 tablespoon freshly squeezed lemon juice and 1/4 teaspoon lemon zest
- 1/2 teaspoon kosher salt, plus more as needed

Direction

- On a cutting board, take the head of broccoli and cut off the florets with about 2 inches of stem attached to each. Slice these thinly (aim for between 1/8 inch and 1/4 inch), but roughly—no need to spend too much time getting everything the same size or thinness. Different textures are ideal. You want about 4 cups total of sliced broccoli pieces—add to a large bowl, where we'll build the salad. (Save the remaining stalks for another use!)

- Roughly chop the dates into pea-sized pieces—you should end up with about 1/3 cup. If the walnut pieces are large, give them a quick chop, too, so no piece is so chunky that it'd be unpleasant to get in a bite. Add the dates, walnuts, and dried sour cherries to the bowl of sliced broccoli. Crumble in the 2 ounces of goat cheese.
- In a food processor, blend the remaining 3 ounces of goat cheese with 1/4 cup extra virgin olive oil, 1 tablespoon freshly squeezed lemon juice, 1/4 teaspoon lemon rind, and 1/2 teaspoon salt, until the mixture is creamy. Pause the blending once or twice to scrape down the sides with a spatula, to ensure no cheese clumps are hanging around the perimeter. As it gets fully smooth and homogenous (this takes less than a minute), drizzle in the remaining 2 tablespoons of olive oil, until you have a dressing with the consistency of loose, thick yogurt. Taste and add additional salt and lemon juice if needed.
- Drizzle the dressing over your broccoli salad and toss to thoroughly coat. This salad is excellent right away, but can also sit in the fridge, fully dressed and covered, up to three days. (And it even lasts a few extra days if you prep everything, but wait to dress it until you serve.)

101. Egg Scramble With Zucchini And Goat Cheese

Serving: Serves 2 | Prep: | Cook: |Ready in:

Ingredients

- 4   eggs, beaten

- 1   zucchini, diced
- 2 ounces goat cheese
- 3   cloves garlic, minced
- 2   tomatoes, seeds removed and diced
- Olive oil
- Salt
- Pepper

Direction

- Heat oil in a sauté pan. Add zucchini and cook until tender and slightly browned. Add garlic and cook for just a few minutes (do not let the garlic brown). Add the tomato, then pour the eggs into the pan. Season with salt and pepper, and cook stirring occasionally until eggs are cooked but still soft. Fold in the goat cheese. Serve with toast.

102. Egg And Goat Cheese Breakfast Bake

Serving: Serves 12-14 | Prep: | Cook: |Ready in:

Ingredients

- 4 cups Seasoned Salad Croutons
- 1.5 cups Crumbled Goat Cheese
- 8   Eggs
- 4 cups Milk
- 1 tablespoon Chopped Rosemary
- 1/4 teaspoon Cracked Pepper
- 1 cup Shredded Cooked Chicken
- 1 cup Sauteed Mushrooms
- 1/2 cup Cooked Spinach

Direction

- Preheat Oven to 325 degrees.
- In a large bowl combine croutons and goat cheese.
- Transfer mixture to a greased 13 x 9 inch baking dish.
- In a large bowl whisk the eggs, milk, rosemary, and cracked pepper.

- Slowly pour over the crouton mixture.
- Sprinkle the shredded chicken, mushrooms, and spinach over the top.
- Bake uncovered at 325 degrees for 60-65 minutes or until knife inserted near the center comes out clean.
- Sprinkle with additional goat cheese on the top if desired.
- Let stand for 10 minutes before cutting.

103. Egg Topped Spicy Cornbread Pudding

Serving: Makes 1 large casserole of goodness | Prep: | Cook: | Ready in:

Ingredients

- Cornbread
- 1 1/3 cups butter
- 1 cup sugar
- 6 large eggs
- 2 3/4 cups buttermilk
- 1 tablespoon baking soda
- 2 1/2 cups masa
- 1 1/2 cups cornmeal
- 1 1/2 cups AP flour
- 1 tablespoon salt
- Custard & assembly
- 15 large eggs, divided
- 3 cups heavy cream
- 1 cup buttermilk
- 1 teaspoon olive oil
- 3 poblano peppers, sliced into 2" strips
- 1 yellow onion, halved and sliced
- 1 cup sliced mushrooms
- 1/2 to 1 tablespoons hot sauce, depending on your taste
- salt and pepper, to taste
- 1/2 teaspoon chipotle chile powder
- 1/2 cup crumbled goat cheese
- 1 tablespoon fresh cilantro or parsley, for garnish

Direction

- For the cornbread: Preheat oven to 375, butter a large sheet pan and line with parchment. Melt butter in large skillet, then remove from heat and stir in sugar. Quickly add eggs and beat until well blended, being sure not to let them sit in the hot liquid and curdle...keep that whisk moving! Combine buttermilk with baking soda and stir into mixture in pan. Stir in cornmeal, masa, flour, and salt until very few lumps remain. Pour batter into prepared pan. Bake 30 to 40 minutes, until a toothpick inserted in the center comes out clean.
- For the veggies: Heat the olive oil in a pan. Once hot, add the onions and allow them to brown nicely, beginning to caramelize. Add the poblanos and let the two cook until the poblanos are near doneness, then add the mushrooms, hot sauce, chipotle, and S&P. Cook until the onions are nice and caramelized and all veggies are tender.
- Make the custard: Blend the cream, buttermilk and 9 of the eggs together. Season with S&P.
- Bringing it all together: Oil or butter a large casserole dish. Break up the cooled cornbread into large pieces. Add the veggies and goat cheese; fold together, trying not to break up the cornbread too much. Add the custard and fold gain, then put it into your casserole dish. Rap on the counter a little so everything settles in nicely. Let the bread pudding sit for 3 hours to allow the custard to set in. When ready to bake, preheat the oven to 300 degrees and cover the casserole with foil. Bake for 1 hour and 15 minutes or until the custard looks nice and soaked in and set. Sprinkle the cilantro or parsley overtop and let cool completely (might I recommend overnight?).In the morning, when ready to serve, you have two options: If you like your bread pudding warm, reheat in the oven with the 6 eggs cracked over top until they are set, 10-15 minutes at 375 degrees. If you like it room temp, cook your eggs as you would normally, sunny side up, and place atop a nice slice of your delicious cornbread pudding.

104.   Eggplant Cilantro Pumpkin Seed Pesto Sandwich

Serving: Serves 2 | Prep: | Cook: |Ready in:

Ingredients

- 4   Sourdough bread slices
- 2 tablespoons Mayonnaise
- 4 tablespoons Goat cheese
- Breaded eggplant cutlets (I used Trader Joe's frozen breaded eggplant cutlets)
- Green leaf lettuce
- 4   Garlic cloves
- 1 bunch Cilantro
- 1/2 cup Olive oil
- 1/2 cup De-shelled, unsalted Pumpkin seeds
- 1/4 cup Parmesan cheese
- Salt&pepper to taste
- 1 tablespoon Lemon juice
- Dash Balsamic vinegar
- Dash Olive oil (for lettuce)

Direction

- Bake eggplant cutlets (follow box instructions)
- For the pesto: blend together garlic cloves, cilantro, olive oil, pumpkin seeds, Parmesan cheese, lemon juice, salt, and pepper to taste.
- Dress four leaves of lettuce with a dash of balsamic vinegar and a dash of olive oil.
- Lightly toast sourdough bread slices.
- Combine mayonnaise with 2 tablespoons of pesto.
- To assemble: spread goat cheese on one slice of bread, per sandwich, then spread mayo-pesto blend onto the other slice of bread. Place five cutlets on each sandwich, over the goat cheese, then add the dressed lettuce leaves and tomato slices. Top with other slice of bread and enjoy!

105.   Eggs In A Wintry Tomato And Kale Sauce

Serving: Serves 4 to 8 | Prep: 0hours10mins | Cook: 0hours28mins |Ready in:

Ingredients

- 3 tablespoons extra virgin olive oil
- 1   yellow onion, peeled and minced
- 1   small carrot, scrubbed and minced
- 1   small celery stalk, minced
- 3 tablespoons Italian (flat-leaf) parsley, minced
- 1   large clove of garlic, minced
- 1 sprig fresh rosemary, about 1-inch
- 1 sprig fresh thyme, more to taste
- 1   bunch lacinto kale, washed and finely chopped
- 1 tablespoon tomato paste
- 28 ounces can of whole tomatoes
- 1 pinch Salt and pepper
- 4   large eggs (up to 8, depending on how many each person wants to eat)
- 2 ounces crumbled goat cheese, for serving (optional)

Direction

- In a large deep frying pan, heat your olive oil over medium heat until shimmering, then add the onion, carrot, celery, and parsley. Cook, stirring frequently, until deeply browned, 8-10 minutes.
- Add the garlic, rosemary and thyme and cook for one minute, then add the kale. Cook, stirring, until the kale has softened somewhat, about 5 minutes.
- Add the tomato paste and canned tomatoes plus their juice. Smash up the tomatoes with a wooden spoon (if you smash enthusiastically, your stovetop may wind up looking like a crime scene. It's a good excuse to ask your spouse to clean the stove!). Add a few pinches of salt and pepper, cover the sauce and simmer for 8 minutes. Taste and add more salt and pepper to taste.

- Use your wooden spoon to make little wells in the sauce for your eggs. Crack each of the eggs into its well and sprinkle them with a little more salt and pepper. Cover the pan and cook over low heat until the egg whites have set but the yolks are still runny, about 5 minutes. Crumble the goat cheese over the eggs, if using, and serve warm. Crusty bread for mopping up the sauce is not out of order here.

106. End Of Summer Tagliatelle

Serving: Serves 2 | Prep: | Cook: |Ready in:

Ingredients

- 2 punnets mixed cherry tomatoes
- 2-3 tablespoons olive oil
- kosher salt, freshly cracked black pepper
- 1 ear of corn
- 1/4 cup toasted hazelnuts
- 1 tablespoon unsalted butter
- 1/4 pound tagliatelle, preferably fresh
- 2-3 ounces fresh goat cheese
- 1/8 teaspoon red pepper flakes
- 1/4 cup pesto
- grated Parmesan

Direction

- Heat the oven to 250F.
- Wash and pluck the stems from the cherry tomatoes; pat them dry. In a mixing bowl, toss the tomatoes with the olive oil, as well as a generous pinch of kosher salt and a few cracks of the black pepper. Move the tomatoes to a baking sheet and the baking sheet into the oven. Bake the tomatoes for 2 hours at 250F, and then lower the heat to 200F; continue baking for 1 more hour. (If you are making the tomatoes a day ahead, allow them to cool, move them to an airtight container, and into the refrigerator.)

- Set a medium pot of water on the range, and turn the heat to high. Allow the water to come to a rolling boil. Shuck the corn. When the water is boiling add the corn; cook for about 4 minutes. Remove the cob from the water and, when it's cool enough to handle, cut away the kernels; set the corn aside. Add new water to the pot, along with quite a lot of kosher salt, until it tastes like the sea. Set the heat to high, and wait for the water to once again reach a boil.
- Meanwhile, crush the hazelnuts—I moved them to a plastic bag, and whacked them with a mallet. Set the hazelnuts aside. Melt the butter in a pan over medium-low heat. Add the tomatoes and corn kernels to the pan.
- When the water reaches a boil, add the tagliatelle. Cook it for about 2-3 minutes, or until the pasta rises to the top of the water. Using tongs, transfer the pasta directly to the saucepan, along with about 1/4 cup of the pasta cooking water.
- Increase the heat under the pan to medium. Stir in the goat cheese, the red pepper flakes, the pesto, and grated Parmesan (however much you like). Use the tongs to toss the pasta and the sauce together. Add a little more pasta water, if it looks too dry. Cook the tagliatelle in the pan for another 1-2 minutes. Divide the pasta between two bowls. Enjoy hot.

107. Endive Autumn Salad

Serving: Serves 4 | Prep: | Cook: |Ready in:

Ingredients

- 16 endive leaves
- 3 tablespoons soft goat cheese
- 1 tablespoon Greek yogurt
- juice and zest of half a small lemon
- 1 handful dried cranberries
- 1 handful diced apple (skin on if you like – I do) – I had mini apples in my veg box, so I used 4

- 1 handful candied walnuts (I buy them that way, but they can be made by tossing the nuts with a tbsp of balsamic, a tbsp of brown sugar and some salt and roasting in a medium oven for a few minutes – watch them or they burn)
- salt and pepper

Direction

- Mix the goat cheese with the yogurt, lemon and lemon zest
- Add the apple and the cranberries and season well
- Spoon the mixture into the solid end of the endive (or spoon into a bowl and use the endive leaves and other raw veg as scoops)
- Put the walnuts into a zip lock bag, seal and bash with a mug or rolling pin so that they're crushed buy still lumpy, then sprinkle on top
- If you can make that you can make this:
- Add diced celery for a more classic Waldorf note
- Add diced roasted chicken and serve on chopped salad leaves
- Or serve on top of couscous
- Add a tsp of chopped fresh tarragon to the goat cheese mixture
- Toast slices of French bread then sub with a cut clove of garlic and drizzle over some olive oil. Spread the mixture (minus the endive) on top to make crostini.

108. Fall Squash Salad With Maple White Wine Vinaigrette

Serving: Serves 1 person | Prep: | Cook: | Ready in:

Ingredients

- 1 bunch mixed baby greens
- 1/3 cup diced roasted butternut squash, warmed
- 2 tablespoons goat cheese (plain, pumpkin spice, or cranberry cinnamon)
- 1 tablespoon raw shelled pumpkin seeds

- 1 tablespoon extra virgin olive oil
- 2 teaspoons white wine vinegar
- 2 teaspoons dark maple syrup
- 1/4 teaspoon garlic powder
- salt and pepper to taste

Direction

- Place the mixed baby greens in a small bowl. Sprinkle the warmed squash, goat cheese, and pumpkin seeds on top. (If roasting the butternut squash, cut into 1/2 inch pieces roast in a 350 degree oven for about 30 minutes, tossing halfway through).
- To make the vinaigrette, combine olive oil, white wine vinegar, maple syrup, garlic powder, and salt and pepper in a small dish and whisk to combine. Pour over the top of the salad. Enjoy!

109. Fiddlehead And Goat Cheese Quiche

Serving: Serves 8 | Prep: | Cook: | Ready in:

Ingredients

- 1 store-bought or homemade pie crust
- 2 cups fiddleheads (read note above)
- 2 garlic cloves, minced
- 1 cup whole milk
- 1/2 cup heavy cream
- 3 large eggs
- 2 egg yolks
- 1 teaspoon kosher salt
- Pinch red pepper flakes
- 8 ounces goat cheese, crumbled

Direction

- To prepare the fiddleheads, trim the bottom stalks from the shoot. Once well-trimmed, rinse well, doing the best you can to rid them of the brown papery skins. Bring 6 cups of water and a healthy pinch of salt to a rolling boil in a large pot. Add fiddleheads and boil for about 10 minutes. Drain fiddleheads in a colander and run under cold water to halt cooking. Note: it's okay if the water you drain is a little brown.

- Preheat the oven to 350 degrees. Fit the pie crust in a 10 inch pie plate. Trim any overhanging dough and crimp the edge if you're feeling fancy. Note: if using a homemade pie crust, consider adding pie weights and baking for 20-30 minutes, or until the crust is firm and lightly browned. This will make for a crispier quiche crust. If using store-bought, this step isn't necessary.
- In a medium bowl, whisk together the eggs and egg yolks. Add the milk, cream, and salt. Whisk until everything is well-combined.
- Spread fiddleheads along the bottom of the pie crust. Crumble goat cheese over the fiddleheads. Sprinkle red pepper flakes over the goat cheese.
- Pour the egg and milk mixtures over the fiddleheads and goat cheese.
- Bake until the center of the quiche has set and the top is golden brown, about 40 minutes.
- Remove from the oven and cool slightly. Cut into 8 wedges and serve.

---

110.   Fig, Prosciutto & Goat Cheese Panini

Serving: Makes 1 sandwich | Prep: | Cook: | Ready in:

Ingredients

- 2 fresh figs, stems removed and sliced
- 4 slices prosciutto
- 1-2 ounces goat cheese
- 3-4 fresh basil leaves
- 2 slices good quality white bread
- olive oil
- salt
- pepper

Direction

- Preheat a Panini press or grill pan.
- Brush both sides of the two pieces of bread generously with olive oil. Season both sides with salt and pepper.
- Layer the goat cheese, figs, basil and prosciutto onto the bread.
- Cook in the Panini press (or grill both sides on a grill pan) until the cheese is melted. Serve immediately.

---

111.   Fig Goat Cheese Hors D'Oeuvre

Serving: Serves 6-8 | Prep: | Cook: | Ready in:

Ingredients

- 8-10   fresh, ripe figs
- fresh goat cheese (I use Monterey goat cheese)
- thyme sprigs
- honey
- 16-20   roasted walnut halves

Direction

- Pre-heat oven to 375 degrees.
- Cut figs in half and top each half with a dollop of fresh goat cheese and a small sprig of fresh thyme.
- Drizzle with honey.
- Place figs on a baking sheet and place in pre-heated oven for about 5-10 minutes until goat cheese oozes a bit.
- Remove from oven and top each fig half with a roasted walnut half and serve.

112. Flammkuchen With Apples, Hazzlenuts Und Goat Cheese

Serving: Makes 1 | Prep: | Cook: | Ready in:

Ingredients

- Dough
- 200g flour
- 10g yeast
- Salt and pepper
- 1/2 teaspoon Sugar
- 1 tablespoon Olive oil
- Topping
- 1 Boskop or Braeburn Apple
- 1 red onion
- 2 teaspoons Hazelnuts
- 40 milliliters Crème fraîche
- 2 ounces fresh goat cheese (50g)
- 3-4 sprigs Thyme
- 4 Sage leaves
- 2 teaspoons Honey
- some sugar

Direction

- Dough: Mix the yeast with 125ml water and let stand. Add ½ tsp sugar. In a bowl, stir together flour and salt. Forma well in the middle and pour in water-yeast mixture. Let stand for a little then add the oil. Knead the dough with your hands. Work for about 10 minutes until the dough is soft and smooth. To make it rise, place the dough in a bowl, cover it with a clean cloth and in place it warm room for about hour. The dough must double in volume.
- In the meantime, cut into thin slices. Sprinkle with some sugar. Cut the onion into thin slices. Coarse the hazelnuts.
- Preheat the oven the highest temperature possible. Line a baking tray with parchment paper.
- Once the dough has lifted, roll out very thinly. Put the dough on the baking sheet. Spread crème fraîche on top, then lay the apple slices,

onions and hazelnuts (in that order). Sprinkle with pepper and salt. Top with crumbles of fresh goat cheese.
- Bake the Flammekueche for 20 minutes, placing the baking tray in the middle of the oven.
- Wash the thyme and pluck off the leaves. Simply wipe the sage leaves with a clean kitchen towel. Once the Flammekueche is backed, sprinkle with thyme leaves, sage and honey. Serve immediately.

113. Flowers And Beetroot Salad With Soft Goat Cheese

Serving: Serves 1 | Prep: | Cook: | Ready in:

Ingredients

- Salad
- 150 grams goat cheese
- 5 edible flowers
- 250 grams arugula
- Handful cress
- Balsamic Vinaigrette
- 3 tablespoons olive oil
- salt
- 2 teaspoons balsamic vinegar

Direction

- Simply compote the salad with all ingredients, sliced beetroot and diced goat cheese.
- Mix olive oil, salt and balsamic vinegar and season the salad. Garnish with the delicate flowers.

114. Friday With San Marzanos

Serving: Serves 2 to 4 | Prep: | Cook: | Ready in:

Ingredients

- For the Barley Flour Dough:
- For the sponge-
- 1/2 cup warm water
- 1 tablespoon dry active yeast
- 1/2 cup barley flour
- For the dough-
- 1 cup warm water
- 2 tablespoons buttermilk
- 4 tablespoons olive oil
- 1 teaspoon kosher salt
- 2 1/2 cups unbleached all purpose flour
- 3/4 cup unbleached bread flour
- For the topping:
- 1 small onion, finely diced
- 2 garlic cloves, minced
- 1 1/2 cups San Marzano tomato sauce, or strained tomatoes by Pomi
- 6 prosciutto slices, torn into thin strips
- 12 ripe San Marzano tomatoes, sliced into 1/4 inch rounds
- 24 slow roasted San Marzano tomato halves, minced (see head note)
- 1 1/2 cups fontina cheese, grated
- 3/4 cup goat cheese, crumbled
- 2 tablespoons fresh rosemary, finely minced
- Kosher salt and fresh ground black pepper
- olive oil
- cornmeal for dusting

Direction

- Make the sponge by placing the water into a mixing bowl with a dough hook attachment. Sprinkle the yeast over the top and let it bloom. Once it has dissolved add the barley flour and mix to combine. Cover and set aside for 30 minutes.
- If the sponge is good and frothy add the rest of the dough ingredients and mix with the dough hook until the dough comes together. If it is too wet add a little flour. It is a soft dough and might be a little sticky but it is manageable.
- Remove the dough from the bowl and kneed it briefly to build the gluten.

- Wipe a little olive oil over the interior of the dough bowl and place the dough back into it rolling the dough around to cover it with a little oil. Cover the dough with a wet towel or plastic wrap and let it rise for 1 to 1 1/2 hours. Place a medium sauce pan over medium heat and add some olive oil and sweat the onions until they soften and then add the garlic. Stir and then add the tomato sauce. Bring to a boil and then reduce the heat and simmer until the sauce is reduced to a cup. It should be somewhere between tomato sauce and tomato paste.
- Preheat the oven to 500 degrees. Sprinkle a little cornmeal over the bottom of an 18 x 12 sheet tray.
- Remove the dough from the bowl and punch it down. Kneed it a few times to bring it together. Cover it and let it rest for 10 minutes.
- After the dough has rested, dust the dough with some flour on both sides and then flatten it into an 8 inch disk. Then roll it with a rolling pin into a square that fits the 18 x 12 sheet tray. Place the dough into the sheet tray. Cover it and let the sough rise for 20 minutes.
- It is important to put the ingredients on the right order so everything cooks right. Start with the sauce, just a light coating is all that is needed, by placing a large spoonful in the middle and use the spoon to spread it outwards. Then spread the fontina out across the sauce. Now the fresh tomato slices followed by the minced slow roasted tomatoes and finally top with the goat cheese, prosciutto and rosemary. Drizzle a small amount of olive oil across the top and then season the pizza with pepper and a touch of salt.
- Side the pizza into the oven and set a time for 8 minutes. At the end of the 8 minutes rotate the pizza 180 degrees. Turn the oven down to 450 degrees. Set the timer for another 8 minutes and bake it until the crust and cheese start to brown.
- Remove it from the oven and let it rest 5 minutes before slicing. Serve immediately.

115. Fried Stuffed Olives With Black Garlic Aioli

Serving: Makes 2 dozen | Prep: | Cook: | Ready in:

Ingredients

- For the Aioli:
- 6 cloves of black garlic
- 2 egg yolks at room temperature
- 1/2 cup canola oil or other mild flavor oil
- 1/2 cup olive oil
- 1 tablespoon fresh lemon juice
- sea salt to taste
- For the fried olives:
- 24 pitted castelvetrano olives
- 1/2 cup of soft goat cheese (room temp is best)
- 1 cup flour
- 1/2 cup panko crumbs
- 1/2 cup grated parmesan
- 1 egg beaten
- canola oil for frying

Direction

- To make the aioli, mash the cloves of black garlic in a mortar or bowl, into a paste. (Super easy, black garlic is already so soft). I used my mortar and pestle for this step.
- Scrape the garlic paste into a deep bowl and add the beaten egg yolks to the garlic and salt and whisk it all together.
- Blend the olive oil and canola oil together in a vessel and start adding the oil to the garlic and egg mix very slowly, that is to say, the *drop at a time, kind of slowly* and whisk like crazy. As the aioli begins to thicken and emulsify, the remaining oil and lemon juice can be added in a slow stream but be sure to whisk continually. I'm a lover of shortcuts, but for aioli, I prefer to whisk it myself. The call is up to you if you prefer a food processor.
- For the olives: Get breading stations ready. Place the flour in one bowl, beaten egg in another and in the last bowl, mix the panko and grated parmesan together.
- Pat the olives dry with a paper towel and set aside while you place the soft goat cheese in the pastry bag.
- Pipe the goat cheese into the olives and then roll them one at a time in the flour, then the egg and finally in the panko/parmesan mix. Repeat.
- Place canola oil in a deep pan (about 3 inches) and heat until hot. Working in batches, carefully place the olives into the oil and fry them until the crust becomes golden brown, turning them as necessary to brown all sides. About 45 seconds to 1 minute.
- Place olives on paper towels to drain. Serve immediately with the aioli and enjoy!

116. Frittata With Prosciutto, Potatoes, Goat Cheese & Thyme

Serving: Serves 6-8 | Prep: | Cook: | Ready in:

Ingredients

- 12 eggs
- 1/2 cup milk
- 1 tablespoon fresh thyme
- 2 ounces arugula
- 1 russet potato (about 8 oz)
- 2 ounces thinly sliced prosciutto
- 1/2 yellow onion thinly sliced
- 1 teaspoon olive oil
- 2 ounces goat cheese, crumbled
- 1 ounce butter

Direction

- Preheat oven to 350 degrees.
- Peel the potato and thinly slice. I used a mandoline to slice the potato as thin as for chips/crisps. Put the sliced potatoes in bowl and cover them with cold water to keep them from turning brown.

- Slice the onion and sauté in olive oil until soft and translucent.
- Butter a 9x12 baking dish and lay down an overlapping layer of potato slices on the bottom of the dish (you will use about half the potatoes). Spread out the layer of cooked onions and then the prosciutto. Put down a layer of arugula and top with crumbled goat cheese and half of the thyme.
- Whisk together the egg and milk and gently pour over the layers in the pan. Top with the remaining slices of potato and sprinkle fresh thyme on top.
- Cover with foil and put in 350 degree oven. Bake for about 30 min before removing the foil. The frittata is done when the eggs are set. I wanted it to be a little more brown on top, so for the last 5 minutes, I brushed the top with melted butter and put it under the broiler.

117.   Garlicky Goat Cheese Toast

Serving: Serves 2 | Prep: | Cook: | Ready in:

Ingredients

- 1   roasted garlic head
- 2 ounces goat cheese
- 2   slices sourdough or olive bread
- Pinch Maldon Sea Salt
- 1 tablespoon extra virgin olive oil
- Smoked paprika - optional

Direction

- Preheat oven to 350 degrees. Slice top off whole head of garlic, drizzle with olive oil and kosher salt. Wrap tightly in foil and roast for 1 hour. Remove from oven and let cool in its wrapper. Use in recipe now or store in refrigerator for future use.
- Toast bread slices. Squeeze goodness out of roasted garlic head, divide and spread between the two slices of toast. Crumble 1 oz.

of goat cheese on each slice and crunch a few grains of flaky sea salt on top. A shake of smoked paprika will make it look prettier. Serve open-faced.

118.   Goat Cheese & Fig Pizza

Serving: Makes 2 | Prep: | Cook: | Ready in:

Ingredients

- 2   naans
- 1/2 cup goat cheese
- 1/4 cup chopped dried figs (soaked in water for 15-20 minutes then chop them)
- Extra Virgin Olive Oil

Direction

- Pre-heat oven at 350° F.
- Generously drizzle EVOO on each naan.
- Place the naans in the oven for 5 minutes.
- Remove the naans from the oven.
- Spread goat cheese and evenly spread chopped dried figs.
- Drizzle a bit more EVOO on top.
- Bake for another 10 minutes or until crust gets crispy.
- You can garnish with chopped pistachios.

119.   Goat Cheese Biscuits

Serving: Makes 6 medium biscuits | Prep: | Cook: | Ready in:

Ingredients

- 2 cups (8 1/2 ounces) all-purpose flour
- 2 teaspoons baking powder
- 1/2 teaspoon baking soda
- 1/2 teaspoon salt
- 6 tablespoons cold unsalted butter
- 4 ounces fresh goat cheese

- 1/2 cup cold milk

Direction

- Preheat the oven to 450° F. Line a baking sheet with parchment paper.
- In a large bowl, whisk together the flour, baking powder, baking soda, salt, paprika, and cayenne (if using).
- Cut the butter into the dry ingredients using a fork or pastry cutter until it's in mostly pea-sized chunks—some chunks can be slightly larger and some smaller, but don't overwork it.
- Crumble the goat cheese into the bowl and stir to combine.
- Add the milk, stir the dough with a fork until it is somewhat evenly moistened, then knead it a few times in the bowl so it mostly comes together in a ball but don't overwork it at all. It should not be cohesive and there should be chunks of drier areas and some wetter areas.
- Turn the dough out onto the parchment-lined sheet, and fold it over onto itself until there aren't any dry spots remaining. Don't think of this as kneading: You want to handle it gently and as you fold, the wet/dry areas will disappear. Fold about 10 times, then gently press the dough down to a rectangle about 2" high.
- Using a sharp knife, cut the dough into 2" squares and separate them slightly on the baking sheet.
- Bake for about 12-15 minutes, or until golden brown. Let cool slightly, then eat!

---

120.   Goat Cheese Caesar Salad With Roasted Tomatoes And Parmesan Crisp

Serving: Serves 2 or more | Prep: 0hours30mins | Cook: 0hours25mins | Ready in:

Ingredients

- For the Caesar dressing
- 1/3 cup buttermilk
- 2 tablespoons mayonnaise
- 1   garlic clove, grated
- 1 1/2 tablespoons lemon juice
- 1/2 teaspoon anchovy paste
- 2 teaspoons dijon mustard
- 1 pinch salt and pepper, plus more to taste
- For the salad
- 3/4 cup freshly grated parmesan cheese
- 10   cherry tomatoes
- 1/2 tablespoon olive oil
- 1 teaspoon balsamic vinegar
- 2   heads of romaine lettuce (or how ever many you are serving)
- 4 ounces good goat cheese
- 1   garlic clove, grated
- 1 teaspoon dried oregano
- 1 tablespoon heavy cream

Direction

- Mix all of dressing ingredients together. Add salt and pepper to taste. Place in refrigerator until ready to use.
- Take goat cheese out of refrigerator to soften. Grate garlic and mix with oregano and cream. Mix softened goat cheese with herb cream mixture and set aside.
- Preheat oven to 375° F. Toss cherry tomatoes with olive oil, balsamic vinegar, salt, and pepper. Roast in oven for about 20 minutes or until tomatoes burst and brown in a few spots. Take out of oven and set aside.
- Raise oven temperature to 400° F.
- Pour a heaping tablespoon of parmesan on a silicone or parchment lined baking sheet. Repeat with 1/2 cup parmesan cheese spacing cheese at least 1/2 inch apart. Reserve 1/4 cup parmesan for serving. Bake for about 5 minutes until crisp and golden brown. Cool.
- Clean romaine lettuce and trim. Place between damp paper towels and place in refrigerator until ready to use.
- Pipe a portion of goat cheese mousse on bottom of one salad plate (depending on how much goat cheese you like). I use a ziploc bag

with the corner cut off to make a pretty design or you can always spoon on the bottom. Repeat with remaining salad plates.

- Toss romaine very lightly with dressing (be very sparse as I always put a little dressing on top of finished salad). Divide lettuce between salad plates.
- Divide roasted tomatoes on top of salad. Drizzle about a tablespoon of dressing on lettuce and sprinkle with parmesan. Add parmesan crisp and serve.

---

121. Goat Cheese Caramel Swirl Ice Cream

Serving: Serves 4 | Prep: | Cook: |Ready in:

Ingredients

- Goat Cheese Ice Cream
- 3/4 cup milk (use whole, low-fat, or skim, they're all good!)
- 3/4 cup cream
- 4 egg yolks
- 2/3 cup sugar
- 6 ounces goat cheese, crumbled
- Caramel Swirl (adapted from David Lebovitz's The Perfect Scoop)
- 3 tablespoons salted butter
- 1/2 cup sugar
- 1/2 cup cream
- 1/2 teaspoon vanilla extract
- More salt, to taste

Direction

- Goat Cheese Ice Cream
- Crumble goat cheese in a medium bowl with strainer set on top.
- Heat milk and cream in a medium saucepan until simmering. Meanwhile, whisk egg yolks and sugar in medium bowl. Pour milk mixture slowly over yolks, whisking constantly. Return mixture to saucepan. Cook over low heat, stirring constantly with a silicon spatula, until

mixture thickens and coats spatula. Pour custard through strainer into the bowl with the goat cheese and stir till smooth. Cover and chill the custard in the fridge, at least 4 hours or overnight.

- Freeze custard in an ice cream maker according to the manufacturer's instructions. Once it is finished, scoop some ice cream into a container then spoon a layer of caramel over it. (See caramel recipe below.) Continue to layer the ice cream and caramel. Let ice cream harden in the freezer for at least 3 hours before digging in! It keeps in the freezer for about a week.
- Caramel Swirl
- Melt the butter in a medium saucepan. Once melted, stir in the sugar. Let it cook, stirring often, until deep golden brown and just starting to smoke. Remove from heat and whisk in half of the cream. Whisk until smooth, then stir in the rest of the cream, the vanilla, and the salt. If you have lumps, gently rewarm and keep whisking.
- Let caramel cool to room temperature before layering with the ice cream. Leftovers can be stored in the fridge for at least a month, but it is delicious warmed up and poured on top of the ice cream!

---

122. Goat Cheese Croquettes

Serving: Serves 2-4 | Prep: | Cook: |Ready in:

Ingredients

- 1 log of goat cheese (you can use either seasoned or plain)
- 1/4 cup all purpose flour
- 1 egg
- 1/2 cup Panko bread crumbs
- 1 tablespoon salt (I use Maldon flakes)
- 1 tablespoon black pepper
- 1 tablespoon smoked paprika
- 1 tablespoon dried oregano

Direction

- Freeze goat cheese for about 10 minutes (so it's easy to work with), then divide into round balls.
- Roll the balls in a bowl with 1/4 cup flour, then dip them in a bowl with the beaten egg, and roll in another bowl of a mixture of panko, salt, pepper, oregano and paprika - coat evenly.
- Heat 1 inch of vegetable oil in a large skillet over medium-high heat. Gently drop the chilled croquettes into the oil and fry until golden brown on all sides. It should take about 2-4 minutes.
- Transfer to paper towels to drain, serve hot.

---

123.   Goat Cheese Grits With Red Eye Gravy, Country Ham, And A Fried Egg

Serving: Serves 4 | Prep: | Cook: | Ready in:

Ingredients

- For Grits
- 4 cups goat's milk (whole cow's milk will do)
- 1/2 teaspoon kosher salt
- 1/4 teaspoon nutmeg
- 1 cup grits
- 1/2 cup goat cheese
- 1 tablespoon honey (or to taste)
- For Ham, Egg, and Gravy
- 3 tablespoons butter, plus extra as needed for frying
- 4 thin slices country ham
- 1/2 cup brewed coffee
- 4 eggs
- 2 tablespoons chopped chives (optional)

Direction

- For Grits

- Bring milk, salt, and nutmeg just to a boil over medium high heat, stirring frequently to prevent scorching.
- Slowly whisk in grits and reduce to a simmer. Cover and simmer for about 20 minutes, stirring every so often to prevent sticking.
- When thick and cooked through, remove from heat and stir in goat cheese, honey, and salt to taste if desired.
- For Ham, Egg, and Gravy
- While your grits are cooking, melt 1/2 tablespoon of butter in a cast iron skillet and fry your ham until browned over medium heat, about 2 minutes per side. I fry two slices at a time to fit them in the pan.
- Once all your ham is fried up, deglaze the pan with the coffee, scraping at the browned bits with a wooden spoon.
- Simmer until reduced by a third and then swirl in one and a half tablespoons of butter. Pour off into a bowl and reserve.
- Wipe down your pan and fry your eggs in the rest of the butter, and serve the grits topped with ham, gravy, and an egg. And a napkin.

---

124.   Goat Cheese Ice Cream With Honey And Fig Jam

Serving: Makes 1 quart | Prep: | Cook: | Ready in:

Ingredients

- 2 cups heavy cream
- 1 cup milk
- 1/3 cup honey
- 1/4 teaspoon salt
- 4 egg yolks
- 1/2 cup (4 ounces) fresh goat cheese, like Le Cornilly
- 1/2 cup fig jam

Direction

- Heat cream, milk, honey, and salt in a saucepan until just simmering. Meanwhile, in a light bowl, lightly whisk the egg yolks. Once milk mixture is simmering, slowly pour it into the yolks, while whisking constantly.

- Add the egg and cream mixture back into the saucepan and cook on low heat, stirring constantly, until the mixture thickens and coats the back of a wooden spoon, about 5 to 7 minutes. Remove from the heat.
- Crumble the goat cheese into a large bowl. Strain the warm custard through a fine mesh strainer onto the goat cheese and whisk until fully incorporated and smooth.
- Cover and cool in the fridge until thoroughly chilled, at least 2 hours or overnight.
- Freeze the mixture in an ice cream maker. Once it is frozen, transfer dollops of ice cream into a one-quart container, adding tablespoons of fig jam as you go so that ice cream and jam are layered together. Run a butter knife through the mixture in a swirling motion two to three times to gently swirl the ice cream and jam.
- Seal the container and let the ice cream set in the freezer for at least 4 hours before serving. The ice cream will keep for a week in the freezer.

---

125. Goat Cheese Pasta With Caramelized Onions And Roasted Butternut Squash

Serving: Serves 4 to 6 | Prep: | Cook: | Ready in:

Ingredients

- 1 cup butternut squash, peeled and diced
- 2 tablespoons olive oil
- 1 pinch coarse salt
- 1 pound pasta (almost any will work; I use spaghetti)
- 8 ounces goat cheese
- 5 tablespoons butter
- 2 garlic cloves, minced or pressed
- 1/2 cup vermouth (or white wine)
- 1/4 cup fresh basil, chopped
- 1 tablespoon fresh thyme, finely chopped
- 1 cup caramelized onions
- 1 pinch salt and pepper, to taste
- 1 handful toasted pecans, optional

Direction

- Preheat the oven to 400° F. Place the squash on a sheet pan, then drizzle with olive oil and sprinkle with coarse salt (a good pinch or two). Toss to combine, then make sure all the pieces are flat on the pan, not on top of each other. Bake until the squash is tender and browned, stirring occasionally, 20 to 25 minutes.
- Bring a large pot of water to a boil. Add salt (I add 1 tablespoon), then add the pasta and cook until al dente. Drain, reserving 1/2 cup of the pasta water.
- While the pasta is cooking, crumble the goat cheese in the bottom of large bowl and set aside. Melt the butter over medium heat, and then stir in the garlic and sauté until fragrant, about 30 seconds. Stir in the vermouth and cook until slightly reduced, about 2 minutes. Turn off the heat, and add the basil and thyme.
- Add the pasta to the goat cheese, and using tongs or serving spoons, toss until the goat cheese is evenly coating the pasta (pour a little of the reserved water on top if you need to loosen the cheese). Pour the butter-herb mixture on top, and toss until combined. Add the roasted butternut squash and caramelized onions, and toss gently until combined; season with salt and pepper to taste, and top with toasted pecans, if desired.

---

126. Goat Cheese Pumpkin Cheesecake

Serving: Serves 8-12 | Prep: | Cook: | Ready in:

Ingredients

- 6 ounces vanilla wafers (about 46)
- 2 ounces pecans
- 3 tablespoons brown sugar
- 1 pinch ground nutmeg
- 1/4 teaspoon ground ginger
- 1/4 teaspoon ground cinnamon
- 1/4 teaspoon salt
- 5 tablespoons butter, melted
- 6 ounces crumbled goat cheese
- 1 1/2 cups granulated sugar
- 16 ounces cream cheese at room temperature
- 3 eggs
- 1 cup pumpkin puree
- 1 cup sour cream
- 1 teaspoon vanilla extract
- 1 large pear (Bosc or Bartlett)
- 4 tablespoons maple syrup

Direction

- Preheat oven to 350 degrees F. In a food processor, pulse cookies and pecans until finely ground (it makes about 2 cups). Add sugar, cloves, nutmeg, ginger, cinnamon, salt and butter; pulse until combined. Firmly press crumb mixture into bottom and up the sides of a 9-inch springform pan. Bake for 8-10 minutes or until crust is golden and set. Cool completely before filling.
- Meanwhile, with an electric mixer set on low speed, beat together the goat cheese and sugar. Add the cream cheese and beat until combined. Add eggs one at a time mixing on low speed after each is added. Combine the remaining ingredients and continue to beat until the mixture is very smooth.
- Pour the batter into the prepared crust and bake for about 1 hour and 15 minutes, until edges begin to pull away from sides of pan; the center should be still soft. Cool to room temperature then cover with plastic wrap and refrigerate for at least 5 hours or overnight.
- Roasted pears: Preheat oven to 450 degrees F. Slice pear lengthwise 1/8-inch thick (I used a mandoline slicer, but knife works well too).
- Line a large baking sheet with parchment paper. Coat with cooking spray. Arrange pear slices in a single layer on sheet and brush with 2 tablespoons maple syrup. Roast until pears are soft, about 15 minutes. Remove from oven and heat the broiler. Brush pears with remaining syrup and broil until browned in spots, about 3-4 minutes. Let cool.
- Arrange pear slices, overlapping slightly, on cheesecake.

127. Goat Cheese Stuffed Grapes

Serving: Serves 4 | Prep: | Cook: |Ready in:

Ingredients

- 7 ounces creamy goat cheese
- 1 teaspoon honey
- large red seeded grapes
- chopped sugared or plain pecans

Direction

- It is a simple formula which depends on how many you wish to make. In a small bowl combine goat cheese and a bit of honey (for 7 ounces of goat cheese I use 1 tsp of honey). Smooth it together and refrigerate for a few minutes.
- Slice the top off of your grapes, then slice a tiny bit off of the bottom of each grape so your they will stand on their own. Using the small end of a melon baller scoop out a bit of each grape (including the seeds).
- Roll the goat cheese in your clean hands until a small ball is formed, and place one ball in each grape (size depends on the size of your grapes).
- Chop up a few nuts for garnish and drizzle with a bit of honey if you like.

128. Goat Cheese And Asparagus Tart

Serving: Makes one 9-inch tart | Prep: | Cook: | Ready in:

Ingredients

- 1 package frozen puff pastry, or equivalent homemade (https://food52.com/recipes...)
- 3/4 cup grated, aged goat cheese, like Tomme de Chèvre Bethmale
- 8 ounces (1 log) soft-ripened goat cheese, like Sainte Maure de Touraine
- 1 bunch asparagus
- Freshly ground pepper and sea salt, to taste

Direction

- Preheat your oven to 400 °F. Piece together two rectangles of puff pastry by overlapping them. Roll up the edges until they're about 1/2 inch high.
- Sprinkle the aged goat cheese over the puff pastry in a thin layer.
- Halve the soft-rind goat cheese log, and then slice lengthwise into 1 inch strips. Layer on the strips intermittently in three rows.
- Snap the asparagus into shorter pieces when necessary, and arrange them around the pieces of soft cheese—something like making a frame around the slices.
- Bake for 20 to 25 minutes, until puff pastry is golden. Be mindful to stab any bubbles that crop up in the puff pastry so they don't deform the finished product. Serve hot or at room temperature.

129. Goat Cheese And Balsamic Vinaigrette

Serving: Makes 1/2 cup dressing | Prep: | Cook: | Ready in:

Ingredients

- 3 tablespoons softened Goat Cheese (I used the one with herbs)
- 1/4 cup good quality Balsamic Vinegar
- 1 teaspoon honey
- 1 pinch Sea Salt
- 1 pinch Cracked Black Pepper
- 1 dash of garlic salt

Direction

- Using a fork, mix all ingredients together in a bowl until the Goat cheese is smooth. The dressing will be a thick creamy espresso color. Drizzle it over an arugula and tomato salad (or any salad of your choice) and enjoy!!

130. Goat Cheese And Date Flatbreads

Serving: Makes 6 flatbreads | Prep: | Cook: | Ready in:

Ingredients

- 6 pieces Trader Joe's 100% Whole Wheat Middle Eastern Flatbreads
- 1 cup Pitted Medjool Dates
- 8 ounces Goat Cheese
- 1 sprig each of assorted fresh herbs (I used Rosemary and Dill)
- Extra Virgin Olive Oil (to taste)
- Honey (to taste)
- Coarse Sea Salt (to taste)

Direction

- Preheat the oven to 400 degrees Fahrenheit. While the oven is heating, prepare the date spread: pulse 1 cup pitted dates in a food processor while slowly adding warm water, one tablespoon at a time, until the mixture resembles a sticky jam, with some chunks remaining. Add a pinch of salt and pulse once more.
- Arrange the breads on a large cookie sheet and distribute the date paste evenly between the

flatbreads, spreading out evenly to the edges of each piece. Crumble the goat cheese and sprinkle across evenly, topping with half of the fresh herbs, a sprinkle of salt, and a drizzle of olive oil.

- Bake in the preheated oven for 10 minutes. Turn the oven to broil and cook 3–5 minutes more, until the goat cheese is browned and bubbling.
- Upon removing the breads from the oven, drizzle with the honey and top with the remaining herbs and salt to taste. To serve, cut into wedges and arrange as for finger foods.

131. Goat Cheese And Fig Jam Knife And Fork Burger

Serving: Serves 4-5 | Prep: | Cook: | Ready in:

Ingredients

- 2 ground hamburger with a fat ratio of 90/10 or 85/15
- 1 1/2 tablespoons finely minced shallot
- 3 tablespoons fig jam
- 2 ounces crumbled goat cheese
- Salt and black pepper to taste
- Minced herbs, such as sage, thyme, or parsley leaves, and soft, baby greens for serving

Direction

- Prepare ingredients: Peel and mince the shallot. Preheat the grill — or stove-top grill pan — to medium-high.
- In a medium mixing bowl, add salt and pepper to the ground beef and gently hand mix until combined.
- In a small mixing bowl, combine the goat cheese, fig jam, and minced shallots.
- Complete the other three sections and then freeze the patties for about 15-20 minutes until firm.
- Lightly brush each burger with olive oil.

- Grill burgers over high heat for about 7-10 minutes per side until the beef is cooked through with an internal temperature of 160 F.
- Grill burgers over high heat for about 7-10 minutes per side until the beef is cooked through with an internal temperature of 160 F.

132. Goat Cheese And Herb Mashed Potatoes

Serving: Serves 4-5 | Prep: | Cook: | Ready in:

Ingredients

- 1 pound Russet Potatoes
- 2 tablespoons Rosemary
- 2 tablespoons Thyme
- 4 tablespoons Goat Cheese
- 1-2 cups Whole Milk
- 2 tablespoons Butter
- Salt and Pepper

Direction

- Peel and quarter potatoes
- Boil potatoes, rosemary, and thyme
- Drain potatoes and herbs
- Mash potatoes and add goat cheese, warm milk, and butter. You may need more or less milk to get the texture you want
- Salt and pepper to taste

133. Goat Cheese And Tomato Chutney Pie

Serving: Makes one 9" tart | Prep: | Cook: | Ready in:

Ingredients

- 2 pieces puff pastry sheets or malawach dough, 9" circles

- 1/3 cup tomato chutney (prefer Le Bon Magot brand)
- 4 ounces crumbled goat cheese
- 1 tablespoon whole nigella seeds
- 1 medium onion, thinly sliced
- 1/4 cup finely grated grana padano or parmigiano reggiano
- salted butter

Direction

- Preheat the oven to 375°F.
- Grease a pie dish or baking sheet with butter and lay down the first dough circle, spread the chutney evenly over the surface, then the onions, half the nigella seeds, the goat cheese, and half the grated cheese.
- Top with the other pastry disk and pinch the edges closed. Top with the remaining grated cheese and the nigella seeds.
- Bake for approximately 35 minutes or until crisp and browned. Allow to cool on a rack, then serve in slices.
- Also great filled with fresh fruits, ricotta, and powdered sugar with, or lamb, spinach, and my Kibbeh spice!

134.   Goat Cheese With Tangy Clementine Jam And Fresh Thyme

Serving: Serves 4 to 8 | Prep: | Cook: |Ready in:

Ingredients

- 1 mini log goat cheese (110 grams)
- 3 pieces medium clementines (or other mandarin oranges)
- 1 tablespoon fresh thyme
- 2 tablespoons raw cane sugar
- 1/3 medium-sized hot chili pepper
- 1 teaspoon cornstarch
- 1 tablespoon water
- 3 slices farmer's bread

Direction

- Wash and pat dry the clementines.
- Shred the clementine peel with a shredder or peeler.
- Squeeze the clementines and pass the juice through a sieve.
- Chop the thyme and the hot chili pepper.
- In a small skillet, add clementine juice and peel, thyme, chili pepper, and sugar, and stir well.
- Bring to a boil, reduce heat, and let it shimmer for 5 minutes.
- Dissolve cornstarch into the water, add it to the skillet, and stir. It will take 2 to 3 minutes for the clementine juice to thicken.
- Remove from heat and let cool.
- Cut the bread slices into bites and the goat cheese into slices.
- Arrange each goat cheese slice on a bit of bread and add 1 to 2 tablespoons of the clementine jam on top.

135.   Goat Cheese, Pancetta, And Chive Stuffed Mushrooms

Serving: Makes 40 mushrooms | Prep: | Cook: |Ready in:

Ingredients

- 8 ounces cream cheese or neufchatel cheese, left at room temperature for 30 minutes to soften
- 6 ounces goat cheese, left at room temperature for 30 minutes to soften
- 3 ounces thinly sliced pancetta
- 1/3 cup minced shallots
- 3 cloves garlic, peeled and minced
- 1/4 cup plus 1 tablespoon tablespoons minced fresh chives, divided
- 2 pounds crimini mushrooms
- 1 cup panko breadcrumbs
- olive oil or canola oil for spraying the mushroom tops

Direction

- Wash and season the Mushrooms: Pour some salt into your hand. Wet each mushroom, and rub it in the salt to remove the dirt (this also seasons the mushrooms). Rinse and dry the mushrooms, then remove to a large rimmed baking sheet.
- Heat a medium frying pan over medium-high heat. Cook the pancetta until golden (about 1 1/2 to 2 minutes per side--the pancetta will crisp up as it cools). Remove to paper towels. When cool, crumble the pancetta and set aside.
- In the same pan, sauté the shallots in the pancetta drippings until softened (about 3 minutes). Add garlic and cook for another minute. Set aside.
- In a medium bowl, stir together the cream cheese and goat cheese until smooth. Add the crumbled pancetta, shallots and garlic, chives, salt and pepper. Stir to combine.
- In a different bowl, stir together the panko, 1 tablespoon minced chives, 1/4 teaspoon kosher salt, and 1/4 teaspoon freshly ground black pepper.
- Using a spoon, generously fill each mushroom cap with the goat cheese mixture. Dip the top of each mushroom in the panko mixture, and then put back on the baking sheet. Lightly spray or brush the mushroom tops with olive oil or canola oil.
- Bake the mushrooms in a 400 oven for 12-18 minutes, or until the tops are golden brown

---

136. Goat Cheese Pesto Pasta

Serving: Serves 1 | Prep: | Cook: | Ready in:

Ingredients

- 1/2 packet Gluten free or rice pasta
- Handful Small shrimp
- 4 ounces Soft goat cheese
- 6 Mushrooms
- 3 Sun dried tomatoes
- Handful Pine nuts
- 1 pinch Red pepper flakes
- 1 Clove garlic
- Olive oil
- Salt & Pepper
- 4 sprigs Fresh basil

Direction

- Boil salted water for the pasta. Set timer and monitor the pasta during the preparation of the sauce. Strain when finished, and drizzle with olive oil.
- For the sauce: sauté the garlic in olive oil. Add shrimp (or chicken, if you prefer), salting to taste. Add sliced mushrooms.
- Add goat cheese, stirring gently until melted. Add water if needed to create more of a sauce (you can also use cream or milk, but I don't consume non-goat dairy).
- Sprinkle red pepper flakes on top of the sauce, then add sun dried tomatoes and pepper, if desired. Add basil last, mixing well before serving on top of pasta. Enjoy!

---

137. Goat Cheese Biscuits With Herbes De Provence

Serving: Makes 20 | Prep: | Cook: | Ready in:

Ingredients

- 3/4 cup flour
- 2/3 cup oats
- 2 ounces log of soft fresh goat cheese
- 2 tablespoons Butter
- 1/2 teaspoon Herbes de Provence
- 1/2 teaspoon coarse salt
- 1 tablespoon olive oil
- 3 tablespoons single cream

Direction

- Pour the flour, oats, crumbled goat cheese and diced butter in a bowl. Work the mixture with your fingers so that the butter and goat cheese gather up the flour

- Add the oil, herbs, salt and single cream. Mix the wet and dry ingredients with your hands until a smooth consistent ball of dough is formed.
- Form small round cookies and place them on a baking tray. Bake for 15 minutes on 350F

138. Goat Cheese, Pear And Jamon Iberico Salad

Serving: Serves 2-3 | Prep: | Cook: | Ready in:

Ingredients

- The salad
- mixed salad
- 1/2 pear
- jamon iberico, sliced
- soft goat cheese
- 1/4 red onion
- black pepper, freshly grounded
- The vinaigrette
- 2 tablespoons olive oil, like arbequina
- 1 teaspoon honey mustard
- 1/2 teaspoon vinagre de jerez

Direction

- Wash the salad leaves, dry them in a kitchen cloth, tear into smaller pieces and mix together. You can use mixed salad if you like. Place the leaves in a bowl
- Skin the pear and remove the hard nest, cut into slices and place on the salad
- Slice the goat cheese and add it into the bowl, twist the jam on slices and add them into the bowl
- Mix the vinaigrette, add the ingredients together in a cup or small bowl and mix them hard with a fork. You can drizzle it over the dish or salad, or serve separately on the table with a teaspoon

139. Goat Cheese Herbs Quenelles

Serving: Makes 20 small quenelles | Prep: | Cook: | Ready in:

Ingredients

- 100g log of fresh, soft goat cheese, without the skin
- 1 egg white
- 1/3 cup flour
- salt and pepper
- 1 teaspoon dried oregano
- 1 teaspoon dried basil
- 2 tablespoons olive oil
- 2 teaspoons balsamic vinegar

Direction

- Remove the skin of the goat cheese if necessary. Cut cheese into small dices. In a bowl, combine cheese with flour, salt, pepper, basil and oregano. Crush with a fork. Incorporate egg white and mix well to obtain consistent mixture. You can also use your hands.
- Make quenelles with the help of two teaspoon. Pour a little bit of flour in a bowl and flour the quenelles. Place in a sealed box and set in the fridge for the night.
- The next day, heat some water in a large saucepan. Poach the quenelles until they come out on the surface, about 2-3 minutes. Dry well and fry them gently in a pan with some olive oil and a few drops of balsamic vinegar

140. Goat's Cheese And Stone Fruit Tarts, Two Ways

Serving: Serves 4 | Prep: | Cook: | Ready in:

Ingredients

- Shortcrust pastry made from 250g plain flour and 150g butter (or use ready-made).
- 1 sweet plum, halved, stones removed
- 1 nectarine, halved, stone removed
- 100 grams goat's cheese or goat's curd
- 2 eggs
- 125 milliliters single cream
- 1/2 teaspoon dried lavender
- 2 teaspoons chopped fresh tarragon
- 1 tablespoon honey

Direction

- Preheat oven to 180°C. Line 4 lightly greased small tart tins with pastry. Bake blind for 10 minutes (I use cling-film to line the pastry cases, filled with baking beans).
- Remove the baking beans and return to the oven for 5 minutes.
- Divide the goat's cheese and fruit between the cases. If necessary, slice a piece from the base of each fruit half to ensure it fits flush with the pastry edge. Drizzle a little honey onto the fruit.
- Whisk eggs and cream until well combined. Carefully pour the mixture into cases. You may not need all the mixture.
- Sprinkle the lavender onto the plum tarts and the tarragon onto the nectarine tarts and bake for 25 mins.
- Serve warm or at room temperature.

141. Grandma Lilly's Cottage Cheese Dip

Serving: Serves a small group as an hors d'oeuvre | Prep: | Cook: | Ready in:

Ingredients

- 1 cup 2% cottage cheese, small curd
- 1 tablespoon spicy brown deli mustard (in the family tradition, I use Guldens)
- 1 tablespoon shallots, finely minced, more to taste
- 1 tablespoon goat cheese
- sweet Hungarian paprika

Direction

- Place cottage cheese in bowl. Add 2 teaspoons or about 2/3 of the mustard. Mix well and taste. It should be a little sharp but the mustard should not completely overtake the cottage cheese flavor. If it is too creamy and the cottage cheese flavor is still dominant, add more mustard.
- Add the shallots and goat cheese and mix. Taste again and add more mustard if necessary.
- Place into serving bowl and top with a healthy sprinkling of paprika.

142. Grape And Feta Flat Bread

Serving: Makes one 8" x 14" flat bread | Prep: | Cook: | Ready in:

Ingredients

- 1/2 Package of Trader Joe's pizza dough
- 4-5 ounces Goat cheese
- 3 Fist sized bunches of grapes of different colors sliced in half
- 3 cloves garlic peeled and sliced
- 2-3 tablespoons grated parmesan cheese
- olive oil
- sea salt

Direction

- Cut pizza dough in half on floured surface. Wrap and store remainder for another flatbread.
- Place dough on floured surface and stretch until it is a rectangle of approximately 8"x14". The middle will be thin.

- Place teaspoons sized dollops of goat cheese on the dough. Place grape halves on the dough. Sprinkle sliced garlic on dough.
- Drizzle with olive oil. Just a quick zigzag.
- Bake in a preheated 500 degree oven for 12-15 minutes.
- Remove from oven. Sprinkle with sea salt and cut into serving slices.

143. Green Goat Carbonara

Serving: Serves 4 | Prep: | Cook: | Ready in:

Ingredients

- 1 pound pasta, preferably fresh, dried fettucine
- 1/2 pound thick-cut bacon
- 4 eggs
- 4 ounces goat cheese
- 1/2 cup chopped fresh parsley
- salt and pepper to taste

Direction

- Slice the bacon crosswise into lardons, then crisp in a large pot like a Dutch oven. Remove the bacon from the pan, and pour off most of the bacon fat. A little bit left in the pan will add flavor to the pasta.
- Bring a large pot of salted water to a boil. If using Wide Awake Bakery Pasta, cook for 4 minutes. Otherwise cook pasta al dente and reserve 1/2 cup pasta cooking water before draining.
- While the pasta is cooking, lightly beat the eggs with the goat cheese until combined. Place the drained pasta in the pan you crisped the bacon in and toss vigorously with the egg and goat cheese mixture. Add a little pasta water if necessary and toss until the eggs thicken but don't scramble. Mix in the bacon and parsley. Garnish with grated parmesan or crumbled goat cheese if desired.

144. Green Lentil & Trout Salad

Serving: Serves 4 | Prep: | Cook: | Ready in:

Ingredients

- 1 cup green lentils, sorted and rinsed
- 2 1/4 cups chicken broth or water
- 1/4 cup white wine
- salt to taste
- 4 cups arugula (loose packed)
- 4 small persian cucumbers, chopped
- 1 avocado, chopped
- 4 ounces smoked trout, crumbled
- 2 ounces goat cheese, crumbled
- 1/4 cup chives, chopped (dill works nicely here too)
- 1/4 cup olive oil
- 2 tablespoons fresh lemon juice (from about 1 large lemon)
- freshly ground black pepper
- flaky sea salt

Direction

- Add lentils, broth and wine to a sauce pan and bring to a boil. Reduce heat to low, cover with a lid, and simmer until lentils are tender, about 35-40 minutes. Drain and cool, then add salt to taste.
- In a large bowl, combine the cooled lentils, arugula, cucumbers, avocado, smoked trout, goat cheese, chives, olive oil, and lemon juice. Mix well, then divide between 4 plates and season with freshly ground black pepper and flaky sea salt. Alternately, you can make individual salads if you won't be eating all four servings at once. For each salad, you'll use about ⅔ cup lentils, 1 cup arugula, 1 Persian cucumber, ¼ avocado, 1 oz. smoked trout, ½ oz. goat cheese, 1 Tbsp. chives, 1 Tbsp. olive oil, and ½ Tbsp. lemon juice.

145.   Green Quinoa Patties

Serving: Makes approximately 25 patties | Prep: | Cook: | Ready in:

Ingredients

- 2 cups Organic Quinoa
- 1 packet Organic Spinach (large clamshell, about 11 oz), chopped finely
- 2 Large Zucchinis , grated
- 2 Large Leeks, chopped finely
- 2 Organic Eggs
- 1 teaspoon Cayenne Pepper, or more if you like spice!
- 1 dash Chili Flakes
- 1 cup Goat Cheese (or 1 10 oz package)
- 1 teaspoon Olive Oil
- 1 dash Salt
- 1 dash Pepper

Direction

- Rinse quinoa. Bring 4 cups of salter water to a boil and add quinoa. Cook covered for 15 minutes. Let stand for 5 minutes, covered, and transfer to a bowl to cool.
- Heat olive oil in a large sauté pan. Add chopped leeks and sauté with salt and pepper until soft but not brown. Add zucchini and sauté for about 2 minutes. Add spinach and let wilt. Allow vegetable mixture to cool.
- Combine quinoa and vegetable mixture together in a large mixing bowl. Add eggs, goat cheese, cayenne, and chili flakes. Combine thoroughly. Season with salt and pepper to taste.
- Fill a quarter cup measurement with quinoa mixture. Place upside down on a lined baking sheet to form patty shape (the same way you may build a sand castle!). If the quinoa is not sliding out easily, rinse the measuring cup with water between each patty. Continue until all patties are formed.
- Bake for about 40 minutes at 400 degrees, or until brown and crispy.

146.   Green Soup!

Serving: Serves 6 | Prep: | Cook: | Ready in:

Ingredients

- 1 Sweet onion, chopped
- 4 cloves garlic, minced
- 1 box of chicken broth
- 1-2 teaspoons dried thyme
- 1-2 sprigs fresh rosemary leaves
- 1/4 cup quick cook brown rice
- 1/2 bunch kale leaves (torn from stems)
- 1 tablespoon olive oil
- goat cheese
- hot sauce
- 1 teaspoon red or white wine vinegar

Direction

- Sauté the onion and garlic in a large pot until well caramelized.
- Add chicken broth, thyme, and rosemary, and bring to a boil.
- Turn the heat down to a simmer, and add brown rice and kale leaves to the pot. Simmer for approximately 10 minutes (or until the rice is done and the kale is tender).
- Remove from heat. Pour contents of the pot into a blender and puree. You may have to do this in several batches.
- Mix the pureed batches all together back into the pot and stir in vinegar.
- Serve garnished with goat cheese (or whatever cheese you prefer) and hot sauce. You may also substitute Greek yogurt or sour cream for the cheese.

147.   Green And Red Endive Boats

Serving: Makes about 40 endive boats | Prep: | Cook: | Ready in:

Ingredients

- 5 heads of endive
- 1 log creamy goat cheese
- 2-3 Golden Delicious apples, cored and minced
- 1 bunch fresh chives, minced
- 1.5 tablespoons paprika

Direction

- Separate the endive leaves and lay them on a baking sheet or serving platter. Spoon a small portion of goat cheese into each one, and then sprinkle the minced chives next to each morsel of cheese. Drop some apple next to the cheese and chives. Finish with a dusting of paprika.

---

148. Green And Fruits Salad

Serving: Serves 4 | Prep: | Cook: | Ready in:

Ingredients

- 4 cups Lettuce sucre
- 2 cups Spinach (uncooked-fresh)
- 3 tablespoons spearmint (fresh)
- 3 ounces cranberries dried
- 200 grams strawberry (fresh in slices)
- 200 grams pineapple (fresh)
- 250 grams goat cheese
- 3 ounces pecans
- 150 grams Panela cheese or fresh cow milk cheese
- 2 ounces olive oil extra virgen
- 2 ounces lemon juice
- 3 dashes salt and pepper

Direction

- Clean all green leaves, dry and cut in pieces, then mix together.
- Cut all fruits and mix together with green leaves, put over pecans and cranberries.
- Mix lemon juice with salt, and pepper, when you felt the flavor is ok, mix with olive oil for

make a "Limonetta". Mix everything with the dressing.
- Cut the goat cheese and Panela cheese and put in over the salad.

---

149. Greens Goat Cheese Lemon Ravioli

Serving: Serves 2-3 | Prep: | Cook: | Ready in:

Ingredients

- For the ravioli dough
- 1 cup "00" flour
- 1/4 cup whole wheat pastry flour
- 1/2 teaspoon salt
- 2 large egg yolks, reserve 1 egg white for sealing ravioli
- 1½ tablespoons extra-virgin olive oil
- 1/4 cup water
- For the mixed greens and goat cheese filling, and the lemon-butter sauce
- 8 ounces mixed baby greens (I used lacinato and red russian kale, and mustard greens)
- 2 large garlic cloves, peeled and minced
- extra-virgin olive oil
- 2 tablespoons 1 tsp fresh lemon juice, divided
- zest of 1 lemon, divided in half
- 1/2 teaspoon salt
- 2 tablespoons white wine
- 2 ounces young, fresh goat cheese, crumbled
- 3 tablespoons butter (salted or unsalted)
- white pepper
- grated Parmesan

Direction

- For the ravioli dough
- Combine all ingredients in a food processor and combine until a ball starts to form. Turn out onto a lightly floured surface and knead for about 6 minutes, incorporating only enough flour to keep the dough elastic. It should not be sticky. When smooth and pliable, shape into a ball, wrap tightly in

plastic wrap and let sit at room temp for 1 hour. Make the filling.

- For the mixed greens and goat cheese filling, and the lemon-butter sauce
- Wash the greens well, removing any thick center ribs. Chop well. In a 10" or 12" skillet set over medium-high, heat enough olive oil to slick the bottom of the pan. When hot, add the garlic and 1 tsp lemon juice. Stir 30 seconds or so and add the greens, half the lemon zest, salt and white wine. Cook, stirring and tossing, until the greens are cooked but still a pretty green and not overdone.
- Pour into a mixing bowl, stir in the crumbled goat cheese and set aside while you roll out the pasta dough. Set a large pot of well-salted water to boil. Wipe out the skillet you used for the greens, and put the butter and the rest of the lemon juice in it.
- Set up your pasta machine, and roll your dough through repeatedly until you reach number 8. You may have to cut your dough in half at some point because it will get quite long as you roll it out. Place your dough on a lightly floured work surface and if it's not roughly the shape of a long rectangle, trim it conservatively to become such. Find your egg white and set it (in a bowl) next to you.
- Place a scant tablespoon of your greens filling equally spaced down the length of the pasta rectangles near one of the long edges. You're going to cut and fold over to make the ravioli. Using your finger, wipe egg white along the edges and press firmly to seal the ravioli. Place the finished ravioli on a lightly floured cookie sheet as you go and keep them covered.
- Put the skillet with butter and lemon juice over medium heat and when the butter has melted, add the rest of the lemon zest, season with salt and white pepper and turn the heat to low. You'll be draining the ravioli and putting them directly into this sauce. When you've filled and sealed all the ravioli (24 to 30 depending on size), cook them in batches in the boiling salt water 2 minutes or a very slight bit more. It won't take long and you

don't want them overdone as they head into the hot lemon-butter sauce.

- When they're all cooked and sauced, grate Parmesan generously over the top and serve immediately. Do not plan to talk much as these are so good you won't be able to. You'll just be savoring every bite. :)

---

150.   Grilled Bread With Goat Cheese & Green Olives

Serving: Serves 4 | Prep: 0hours5mins | Cook: 0hours10mins | Ready in:

Ingredients

- 1/4 cup extra-virgin olive oil
- 1/4 cup walnut halves
- 12   green olives, preferably Castelvetrano, pitted and roughly chopped
- 1   large handful Italian parsley leaves
- 2 tablespoons freshly squeezed lemon juice
- 1 dash kosher salt
- 1 dash freshly ground black pepper
- 4 ounces plain goat cheese, at room temperature
- 4   large, 1-inch-thick slices country bread, grilled or toasted

Direction

- Place the olive oil and walnuts in a small skillet and set it over medium heat. When the nuts begin to sizzle, immediately transfer them and the oil to a mixing bowl. Add the olives, parsley, and lemon juice, and stir well to combine. Season the mixture to taste with salt and pepper.
- Evenly divide the goat cheese between the pieces of toast and spread to cover. Season the goat cheese with salt and pepper. Divide the walnut mixture between the toasts and serve immediately.

151. Grilled Goat Cheese With Apple On Cranberry Pecan Bread

Serving: Serves 1, but easily multiplied | Prep: | Cook: | Ready in:

Ingredients

- 1 loaf Cranberry-Pecan bread, or any good quality fruit and nut bread
- 1 1/2 to 2 ounces goat cheese
- 1 apple
- 1 tablespoon butter

Direction

- Slice bread into 1/2 inch pieces
- Spread goat cheese on one slice of bread
- Slice apple into 1/16 to 1/8 of an inch slices
- Place several slices on sandwich, and place another piece of bread on top.
- Melt 1/2 tbsp. of butter in a non-stick skillet over medium-low heat
- Cook sandwich until first side is just beginning to get toasty, then add a bit more butter and flip. Continue cooking and flipping relatively frequently until both sides are toasty and cheese is melty. You're done!

152. Grilled Olathe Sweet Corn And Chicken Chowder With Goat Cheese

Serving: Serves 6 | Prep: | Cook: | Ready in:

Ingredients

- 1 tablespoon Olive oil
- 3 pieces Thick bacon, cut into 1/2-inch pieces
- 4 Chicken thighs, skinless/boneless, diced
- kosher salt +fresh ground pepper
- 1 pinch Crushed red pepper
- 1 Onion, medium, diced
- 3 Carrots, medium--trimmed, peeled, and sliced into 1/4-inch coins
- 3 Celery stalks--trimmed and sliced into 1/4-inch pieces
- 1 Garlic clove, minced
- 2 teaspoons Thyme, dried
- 1 Bay leaf
- 4 cups Chicken broth, low-sodium
- 1/2 cup Water
- 4 Red potatoes, small and unpeeled, cut into 1-inch pieces
- 4 Ears Grilled Olathe corn, husked, silks removed, kernels cut off (reserve cobs for broth)
- 4 ounces Colorado goat cheese, crumbled
- 3 Scallions, minced (green and white parts) for garnish
- 6 sprigs Fresh thyme for garnish

Direction

- In a 6-quart heavy pot, heat a tablespoon of oil over medium heat and sauté chopped bacon until crisp. Remove bacon to a paper towel-lined plate and reserve for garnish. Carefully pour out or spoon the bacon grease into a heat-proof container, leaving 2 tablespoons in the bottom of the pot.
- Add diced chicken to hot pot; season with 1/2 teaspoon kosher salt, 1/4 teaspoon freshly ground black pepper, and crushed red pepper. Cook, stirring often, until beginning to brown. Add onion, carrots, and celery; cook, stirring, until vegetables are softening and chicken is browned. Add garlic, thyme, and bay leaf.
- Pour in broth and water. Raise heat; bring to a boil. Lower to simmer; add potatoes and corn cobs to flavor broth. Cook 10 minutes; add corn kernels. Simmer another 10 minutes or until all vegetables are tender. Remove cobs and discard. With a potato masher, mash through soup lightly and briefly–just to thicken a bit, not to purée.
- Add goat cheese and stir until melted. Taste, adjust seasonings. Serve hot garnished with reserved bacon, green onions, and a sprig of

fresh thyme for each bowl. (Diners should pull the thyme leaves off into the bowl before eating soup. This truly makes the soup!) Whoever gets the bay leaf does the dishes.

- COOK'S NOTE: While I've used leftover grilled corn here because I like the taste, you can use boiled corn or frozen corn for any season soup. Fresh corn would also work perfectly well as the cobs help make a tasty broth and the corn cooks very quickly.

153. Grilled Pork Tenderloin With Goat Cheese, Tomato, And Blueberry Salad

Serving: Serves 4 | Prep: | Cook: | Ready in:

Ingredients

- one 1-pound pork tenderloin, at room temperature
- 3 tablespoons olive oil, divided
- Freshly ground black pepper
- 2 pints cherry tomatoes, halved
- 1 cup blueberries
- 1/4 cup fresh goat cheese, finely crumbled
- 1/4 cup fresh basil leaves
- 1 tablespoon balsamic vinegar

Direction

- Preheat grill to medium-high. Rub pork tenderloin with 1 tablespoon olive oil and season generously with salt and pepper. Add seasoned pork to the grill. Grill, turning often, until pork has grill marks on all sides and is barely pink in the center, about 15 to 18 minutes. Remove the pork from grill and set aside to rest, 5 minutes.
- While the pork rests, scatter tomato, blueberries, goat cheese, and basil leaves around a platter. Drizzle vinegar and remaining 2 tablespoons olive oil over salad. Season the salad with salt and pepper and serve with pork.

154. Grilled Sirloin, Goat Cheese, And Arugula Pockets

Serving: Serves 3 | Prep: | Cook: | Ready in:

Ingredients

- 1-1/4 pounds grassfed, boneless sirloin steak
- 1/2 small log of goat cheese
- 1 cup arugula
- 3 pita pocket breads, toasted
- 1/2 cup mayonnaise (any healthy type)
- 1 teaspoon sriracha
- 1/2 cup basil pesto

Direction

- Grill the steak until medium rare. Let rest at least 10 minutes. Slice thinly.
- Combine mayo and sriracha in a small bowl.
- Put steak, goat cheese, arugula, mayo mixture and pesto in pitas. Enjoy!

155. Grilled Stuffed Red Peppers

Serving: Serves 4 | Prep: | Cook: | Ready in:

Ingredients

- 2 large red peppers
- 1 white onion, medium dice
- 1 garlic clove, minced
- 10 ounces Spinach
- 6-8 slices of goat cheese
- 8 kalamata olives, quartered lengthwise
- 1 tablespoon fresh oregano, rough chop
- 3 tablespoons olive oil
- kosher salt
- black pepper

Direction

- Get your grill going. Cut peppers in half lengthwise. Remove the seeds and membranes. Brush 1 tablespoon of olive oil over the inside and outside of the peppers, then sprinkle all over with salt and pepper. Place the peppers on the grill over medium-hot coals skin side down. Cover and let cook for about 10 minutes, until the skins are lightly charred, then turn and cook for about 4 more minutes. The peppers should be soft, but still hold their shape. Remove from grill.
- While the peppers are on the grill, sauté the spinach. Pour 2 tablespoons olive oil in a large sauté pan over medium heat. Once the oil is hot, add the onions. Cook, stirring occasionally for about 3 minutes, or until they are translucent. Season with salt and add the garlic; cook for about 2 more minutes, until pale golden. Add spinach, season with salt and cook, covered, stirring occasionally, until wilted, about 3 minutes.
- Divide the spinach equally and fill the bottom of each pepper. Sprinkle the oregano and olives over the spinach, then add the slices of goat cheese. This can be done several hours ahead.
- Put back on the grill to heat through, or pop them in the oven. Enjoy!

Direction

- Get your grill going. Brush the ears of corn with olive oil and sprinkle with salt and pepper. Once the grill is at medium heat, you can put these directly on the grill, turning frequently until caramelized evenly. Once cooled, cut the kernels off of the cob.
- Cut the squash thinly, into rounds, brush with olive oil and season with salt and pepper. Using either a sheet pan or a grill basket, grill the squash until browned in spots.
- Gather your toppings: corn, squash, crumbled goat cheese, rosemary. Roll out the pizza dough until it's even all around and no thinner than 1/4 inch. It does not have to be round. Brush the grill with olive oil.
- The grill should be medium heat. Place the dough directly on the grill and let stand for 2-3 minutes. You will see bubbles rising in the dough as it cooks.
- Once browned on the bottom, remove dough from the grill onto a floured board with the grilled side up. Brush with olive oil and add toppings evenly.
- Return the pizza to the grill. Cover and cook for an additional 2-3 minutes until the dough is cooked through and the cheese begins to melt.
- Remove from grill, cut into wedges or squares and serve.

---

156.   Grilled Summer Pizza

Serving: Serves 2-4 | Prep: | Cook: | Ready in:

Ingredients

- 1 pound fresh pizza dough
- 8 ounces goat cheese, crumbled
- 2 ears sweet corn, husks and silk removed
- 2-3 small zucchini and/or summer squash
- 1 tablespoon chopped fresh rosemary
- olive oil
- salt + pepper

---

157.   Grilled Vegetable Sandwiches With Herbed Goat Cheese

Serving: Serves 4 | Prep: | Cook: | Ready in:

Ingredients

- 1/2 cup soft goat cheese
- 2 tablespoons chopped fresh chives
- 1-1/2 tablespoons chopped fresh basil
- 8 slices whole grain bread

- 2 portobello mushroom caps
- 2 red bell peppers, stemmed, seeded and quartered
- 2 zucchini, cut lengthwise into 1/4-inch thick slices
- Nonstick cooking spray
- Kosher salt and ground black pepper, to taste
- 1/2 cup baby spinach leaves

Direction

- Preheat grill for direct grilling over medium-high heat. In a small bowl, stir together goat cheese, chives and basil. Toast bread in a toaster or toaster oven.
- Lay mushrooms, bell peppers and zucchini on baking sheet. Spray both sides with nonstick spray and lightly sprinkle with salt and pepper. Place vegetables on hot grill rack and grill until just tender, turning occasionally (time will vary for each vegetable, so just pull them off the grill and transfer back to the baking sheet as they finish cooking). Depending on your grill, the zucchini slices and mushrooms should take about 4 minutes, and the bell peppers will take about 6 minutes. Make sure not to overcook the vegetables, because you don't want them to be mushy, just tender. At this point, you can either leave the vegetables whole, or slice them into strips.
- Spread toasted bread with goat cheese mixture. Build sandwiches using grilled vegetables and spinach.

158.   HATCH CHILI RELLENOS

Serving: Serves 4-6 | Prep: | Cook: |Ready in:

Ingredients

- 8-10 large Hatch or Poblano chili peppers, roasted, stemmed, seeded, and sliced lengthwise down one side
- 9 ounces goat cheese

- 3 ounces raisins, chopped
- 2 ounces pine nuts, lightly toasted
- kosher or sea salt, to taste
- 1 cup Crema Mexicana
- 1/4 cup fresh cilantro, chopped

Direction

- MAKE STUFFING: Preheat the oven to 350. In a bowl, combine the goat cheese, raisins, and pine nuts. Season with salt.
- STUFF AND BAKE: Lay the chile peppers in a large baking pan. Stuff them with the cheese mixture then securely close them with toothpicks. Place in the oven and bake 15 minutes.
- HEAT CREMA AND SERVE: In a small saucepan, heat the cream Mexicana over LOW heat until it is warm. When chiles are ready, place 1 or 2 on a plate and drizzle with warm cream. Garnish with cilantro and serve.

159.   Hazelnut Chocolate Rugelach With Goat Cheese Pastry

Serving: Makes 24 cookies | Prep: | Cook: |Ready in:

Ingredients

- Pastry/dough
- 1 1/4 cups (160 grams) all-purpose unbleached flour
- 1 tablespoon (12 grams) sugar
- 1/8 teaspoon salt (I use fine sea salt)
- 4 ounces (8 tablespoons/113 grams) cold unsalted butter
- 4 ounces (113 grams/1/2 cup) cold fresh goat cheese
- Filling
- 1/3 cup (66 grams) sugar
- 1/2 teaspoon (generous) ground cinnamon
- 1 medium orange, organic or unsprayed

- 1/2 cup (50 grams) finely chopped toasted and skinned hazelnuts
- 1/2 cup (85 grams) dark chocolate chips
- a couple pinches salt (I use fine sea salt)

Direction

- Make the pastry: Combine the flour, sugar, and salt in the bowl of a food processer fitted with the steel blade. Pulse a few times to mix.
- Cut the butter in 3/4-inch cubes and scatter them over the flour. Pulse until butter pieces range in size from very coarse breadcrumbs to hazelnuts.
- Crumble or break the 4 ounces of goat cheese into teaspoon size chunks and add them to the processor. Pulse until the mixture looks like crumbs—it should not come together into a dough or look cohesive at all, but it should stick together when you pinch it.
- Pour the mixture into a plastic bag and press it very firmly into a compact ball, don't worry if you notice unblended bits of butter or cheese; this is correct. Twist the top of the plastic bag and refrigerate the dough for at least two hours and up to three days before using.
- Fill, shape and bake the cookies: Position a rack in the upper and lower thirds of the oven and preheat the oven to 350° F. Line two baking sheets with parchment paper.
- Remove the pastry from the refrigerator. Unwrap and cut it in half and let it rest at room temperature for 10 to 15 minutes until just still firm but pliable enough to roll; it should not be soft or squishy.
- Meanwhile, mix the cinnamon with the sugar in a small bowl. Set a heaping tablespoon of it aside for sprinkling on the cookies later. Use a microplane (or other fine grater) to grate the zest of the orange over the remaining cinnamon sugar and mix thoroughly. Set aside.
- Roll one piece of dough between sheets of wax paper into a 12-inch circle a scant 1/8-inch thick. Peel off the top sheet of paper and set it on the counter next to you. Flip the dough over onto the loose sheet of paper and peel off the second sheet.
- Sprinkle half of the cinnamon orange sugar evenly over the dough. Scatter half of the hazelnuts and half of the chocolate chips over the sugar. Sprinkle with a pinch of salt. Roll over the filling with a rolling pin to press it gently into the pastry.
- Cut the pastry like a pizza, into 12 equal wedges. Roll the wide outside edge of a wedge around the filling towards the points as though shaping a miniature croissant. Place it on a parchment lined baking sheet, with the point of dough on the bottom to prevent it from unrolling. Repeat with the remaining wedges, placing them about 1 1/2-inches apart.
- Roll, fill, cut and shape the second piece of pastry. Moisten the cookies with a wet pastry brush and sprinkle each with the reserved cinnamon sugar.
- Bake 20-25 minutes, until deep golden and brown on the bottom. Rotate the baking sheets from back to front and top to bottom about halfway through the baking time. Set baking sheets racks to cool. Cool cookies completely before storing in an airtight container. Rugelach are always best on the day they are baked, but they remain delicious for several days. Store in an airtight container.

---

160.   Heirloom Tomato Flatbread "Pizza"

Serving: Serves 2 | Prep: | Cook: |Ready in:

Ingredients

- For the flatbread dough
- 2 1/2 cups all purpose flour
- 1/2 teaspoon baking powder
- 1/2 teaspoon baking soda
- 1/2 teaspoon salt
- 1 teaspoon sugar

- 1/2 teaspoon ajwain (carom/caraway seeds)
- 1-2 garlic cloves, finely chopped
- 1 egg
- 1/4 cup yogurt
- 1/4 cup milk
- 1 tablespoon olive oil
- For the flatbread pizza
- 4 large heirloom tomatoes
- 1 teaspoon salt
- 6 ounces (170 gm) fresh goat cheese
- 10-12 fresh basil leaves, slivered
- Freshly ground pepper, to taste
- 3 tablespoons good quality, extra-virgin olive oil

Direction

- Sift together the flour, baking powder, baking soda and salt. Sprinkle over the sugar, ajwain and garlic. Make a well in the center and add the egg and yogurt. Start stirring, incorporating flour as you go till it all clumps together. Add the milk a little at a time and knead to get a smooth dough. Apply the oil and keep dough covered with a damp cloth for an hour.
- Preheat the oven to 450F (230C).
- Divide the dough into two. (Use one half and freeze the rest for later. Or double the ingredients for the pizza and make 2 of them.) Flour your work surface, form the dough into a ball and flatten with your hand. Roll out the dough into a circle, oval or a rectangle, as you would do for your thin-crust pizza. Prick the dough all over with a fork.
- Line a baking sheet with parchment paper. Place the rolled out dough on the sheet and bake in the preheated oven for 8 mins. (You can also use a pizza stone.)
- Prep the tomatoes while the crust bakes - the key is to get excess moisture out so you don't get a soggy crust. Line the counter with a double layer of absorbent paper towels. Slice the tomatoes and spread them in a single layer over the towels. Sprinkle with salt. Place another layer of paper towels over the

tomatoes and press lightly. Leave the tomatoes till ready to use.
- Roughly shred the goat cheese over the baked crust and bake for another 5-6 mins.
- Layer the prepped tomatoes over the cheese. Sprinkle over the basil and season with freshly ground pepper. Drizzle with the olive oil. Bake for another 5-6 mins. Cut into wedges and serve hot.

---

161. **Heirloom Tomato, Goat Cheese & Greek Yogurt Tart With Basil & Almond Pesto**

Serving: Serves 6 | Prep: | Cook: | Ready in:

Ingredients

- For the crust:
- 1 1/3 cups of all-purpose flour
- 3 tablespoons of grated parmesan
- Freshly ground black pepper
- 100gr of cold butter, chopped
- Pinch of salt
- ¼ cup cold water
- For the Filling:
- For the tomatoes:
- 3 big heirloom tomatoes, sliced about 1.5 to 2 cm thick
- 5 cherry tomatoes, sliced in half
- 1 teaspoon of sugar
- Salt
- Drizzle of olive oil
- For the goat cheese filling:
- 1 cup of Greek yogurt
- 200gr soft goat cheese, at room temperature
- 2 eggs
- Pinch of salt
- Pinch of pepper
- For the pesto:
- 45gr peeled roasted almonds
- 1 bunch of basil, reserve a few small leaves to decorate the tart later
- 30gr of grated parmesan

- 1/3 cup of olive oil
- Pinch of garlic powder
- Pepper
- Pinch of salt

Direction

- To oven dry the tomatoes: Place the tomato slices on a baking tray lined with parchment paper. Sprinkle with salt, sugar and drizzle some olive oil. Dry them for 2 hours at 130C/270F. Once the 2 hours are up, remove them from the oven and set aside to cool.
- To make the pesto: Place all of the ingredients in the food processor and pulse until everything is mixed. Cover with plastic wrap and keep it in the fridge until ready to use. You will only need 5 tablespoons of this pesto; you can use the leftover for something else.
- To make the crust: Place the butter, flour, Parmesan, salt & pepper in the bowl of the stand mixer fitted with the paddle attachment. Mix on low speed for a few minutes until the pieces of butter get smaller. Then add the cold water and mix on low for a few extra minutes, until you get an even dough. Form a ball with the dough, flatten it a bit with your hands, wrap it in plastic and let it sit in the fridge for 30 minutes.
- Once the dough has rested in the fridge, preheat the oven to 180C/350F. Grease and flour a 9 inch – 23cm pie mold. It is better if it has a detachable bottom, just makes it easier to slice the tart later. Lightly flour your working area and roll out the dough in a circular shape, enough to cover the pie mold. Line the pie mold with the dough, pressing firmly on the edges. Place it in the fridge for 15 minutes.
- Take the pie out of the fridge and pinch the bottom with a fork. Line it with parchment paper and fill it with uncooked rice or pastry weights. Bake for 10 minutes. Then remove the rice and parchment paper, and bake for 5 more minutes. Remove it from the oven but the keep the oven on.

- To make the goat cheese & Greek yogurt filling: Just blend all of the ingredients until evenly combined.
- To assemble the tart: Pour the goat cheese filling over the partly baked crust. Just don't pour it up to the edges, because it still needs the pesto and you don't want it to overflow. Separate 5 tablespoons of the pesto and spoon it over the filling. Then grab a knife and swirl it around, be careful not to touch the crust. Bake for 20 minutes.
- After the 20 minutes are up, remove the tart from the oven. Spread the oven dried tomatoes over the top and bake for 10 extra minutes. Allow the tart to cool down for 1 hour before slicing it. You can decorate it with some fresh basil leaves. I like to serve it with a simple salad.

---

162.   Herbed Goat Cheese And Root Vegetable Galette

Serving: Serves 4 to 6 | Prep: 0hours40mins | Cook: 1hours0mins | Ready in:

Ingredients

- For the dough:
- 2 cups whole-wheat flour
- 1 teaspoon salt
- 12 tablespoons unsalted butter, cold and cut into little pieces
- 2 eggs, beaten
- For the assembly:
- 1 tablespoon unsalted butter
- 4   small or 2 large shallots, peeled and thinly sliced
- Kosher salt and freshly ground black pepper
- 6 ounces goat cheese, at room temperature
- 1/2 teaspoon (heaping) finely chopped fresh rosemary
- 1/2 teaspoon (heaping) finely chopped fresh thyme

- 1 carrot, peeled and sliced into 1/8- to 1/4-inch thick rounds
- 1 sweet potato, sliced into 1/8- to 1/4-inch thick rounds
- 1 turnip, peeled and sliced into 1/8- to 1/4-inch thick rounds
- 1 egg, beaten
- olive oil

Direction

- To make the dough, mix flour and salt together in a large bowl. Add the butter pieces and mix and mush using your fingers until the flour resembles wet sand, with some small butter chunks bits remaining. Add the beaten eggs into the bowl and mix in with a fork. Use your hands again to bring the dough together, then dump it onto a lightly floured surface to knead a few times. Form dough into a disc and wrap in plastic wrap. Refrigerate for at least 30 minutes.
- To assemble the galette, melt the remaining butter in small pan over medium-high heat. Add the sliced shallots and season with salt and pepper. Sauté until soft and slightly golden, about 8 to 10 minutes. Set aside.
- In a small bowl, use a fork to mash together the goat cheese, rosemary, and thyme.
- Preheat oven to 375° F.
- Unwrap the dough disc and set on a lightly floured surface. Roll out to 1/4-inch thickness, about an 11- by 14-inch rectangle. Transfer to a parchment paper-lined sheet pan.
- Spread the herbed goat cheese onto the dough rectangle, leaving about a 1/2-inch edge around the edges. Sprinkle the shallots evenly across the cheese layer. Finally, shingle the vegetable rounds over the cheese and shallots. You may not use all of the rounds that you cut (depending on the size of the original vegetables), but don't be afraid to really load it up!
- Fold the edges of dough over the vegetables, overlapping as you go. Neatness is not required or even requested! This will be delicious even if it's amorphous.

- Brush the crust lightly with the beaten egg. Brush the visible vegetables with olive oil. Sprinkle salt and pepper over the whole thing, and then stick it in the oven. Bake for 40 minutes, rotating halfway through. Allow to cool slightly on the baking sheet before transferring to a cutting board to slice. Brownie-style or pizza-style, the slicing is dealer's choice. This is great warm and at room temperature.

---

163.   Honey & Goat Cheese Stuffed Grapes

Serving: Serves 6 | Prep: | Cook: |Ready in:

Ingredients

- 7 ounces plain goat cheese, room temperature
- 1 teaspoon honey
- 18 large seeded red globe grapes
- 2 tablespoons sugared or spiced nutes, chopped
- 1 tablespoon additional honey for drizzle

Direction

- Combine your goat cheese and your honey in a small bowl, mix until combined. Place in the refrigerator until ready to use.
- Slice a small piece from the bottom of each grape to allow it to later stand on its own. Slice off a bit of the top of each grape, then using the small side of a melon baller scoop out 2/3 of the inside of each grape - making sure you get all the seeds. Discard innards.
- Get your chilled goat cheese and honey mixture and begin rolling into small balls - the size varies depending on the size grapes you have on hand as well as the size scoop you created. Place one ball into each grape allowing a bit of the ball to stick out on top.
- Plate your stuffed grapes, place a few bits of sugared nuts (or plain nuts) on each stuffed

grape and scatter a few over the plate, drizzle with a bit of additional honey and serve.

- To serve: Scoop ice cream in to bowls. Top with macerated nectarines, using reserved liquid as a sauce. Garnish with additional thyme. Enjoy!

164. Honey Goat Cheese Ice Cream With Lemon And Thyme Macerated Nectarines

Serving: Serves 4-6 | Prep: | Cook: | Ready in:

Ingredients

- For the lemon and thyme macerated nectarines:
- 1 pound nectarines
- 1 lemon, zested and juiced
- 1 teaspoon olive oil
- 1 teaspoon sugar
- 1 teaspoon fresh thyme
- For the honey goat cheese ice cream:
- 2 cups heavy cream
- 1 cup milk
- 1/3 cup honey
- 3 ounces creamy goat cheese

Direction

- For the honey goat cheese ice cream: In a medium saucepan, add cream, milk, and honey. Bring to a low simmer, stirring every so often.
- Once combined, remove from heat and whisk in goat cheese. Transfer to a covered glass dish, allowing to cool. Chill in refrigerator for at least 4 hours (or overnight).
- Once mixture is completely chilled, transfer to an ice cream maker, processing according to manufacturer's instruction. Freeze additionally to reach desired consistency (I froze mine for an additional 24 hours prior to enjoying).
- For the lemon and thyme macerated nectarines: In a medium bowl, combine sliced nectarines, lemon zest and juice, olive oil, sugar, and thyme.
- Allow to macerate at least 1 hour.

165. Hot As You Want Them Lamb Burgers With Basil Lemon Goat Cheese

Serving: Serves 4 | Prep: | Cook: | Ready in:

Ingredients

- Herbed lamb burgers
- 1 pound ground lamb
- 3 cloves garlic, minced
- 1 scallion or spring onion, thinly sliced
- 2 tablespoons fresh thyme (leaves stripped from stems)
- 2 sprigs fresh rosemary (leaves snipped off the stem in small pieces)
- 1 teaspoon salt or to taste
- 1/2 teaspoon freshly ground pepper or to taste
- 2 tablespoons minced fire-roasted green chilies (or about half of a small can, the Hatch brand is sold at Whole Foods)
- 2 tablespoons pitted green or mixed olives
- 1 tablespoon Balsamic vinegar
- 4 pita pockets
- For the filling and glaze
- 2 tablespoons fresh goat cheese
- 1 tablespoon fresh basil leaves snipped into small pieces
- grated zest of one Meyer lemon or regular lemon
- juice of 1/2 Meyer lemon or regular lemon
- 1/2 tablespoon honey
- 1-2 tablespoons minced fire-roasted green chilies (or finish up the can)

Direction

- In a large bowl, mix the thyme, rosemary, minced garlic, sliced scallion, salt and pepper with the ground lamb.
- Puree 2 tablespoons of the green chilies (hot or mild, as you prefer) in a food processor with the pitted olives and Balsamic vinegar. Add the green chili mixture to the seasoned lamb and stir gently but thoroughly until well mixed. Refrigerate for several hours.
- Blend the goat cheese, lemon zest and basil and refrigerate. Mix the glaze ingredients-- honey, lemon juice, and 1 tablespoon or more of the green chilies--and refrigerate.
- About half an hour before grilling time, divide the lamb mixture in half, and form 4 thin patties, making a thumbprint indentation in the center. Put a teaspoon of the goat cheese mixture in the indentation and spread it out a little, but not all the way to the edges. (Don't use up all of the goat cheese mixture.) Make four more thin patties, using up the remaining lamb, to top each bottom patty. Press the layers firmly to seal the edges against goat cheese leaking on the grill. Mix one to two teaspoons of the green chili-honey-lemon mixture into the remaining goat cheese, which will become the final topping.
- Grill for about 2 minutes until bottom sides are nicely browned. Flip and spoon some of the honey-lemon-chili glaze on top of each burger. Remove finished burgers and top with a dollop of the goat cheese-glaze mixture. Serve in a warm pita pocket.

166.   Hurricane Irene Special Tarragon White Wine Chicken With Goat Cheese Pasta

Serving: Serves 2 | Prep: | Cook: | Ready in:

Ingredients

- Tarragon White Wine Chicken
- 2 skinless, boneless breasts of chicken, washed and dried.
- 2 tablespoons extra virgin olive oil
- 1 small yellow onion, chopped (I used a "Candy Onion" from Union Square Farmer's Market. Delicious.)
- 3 tablespoons chopped fresh tarragon
- 2 cloves garlic, minced
- 2 tablespoons white wine of your fancy
- 1/4 teaspoon sea salt
- pepper to taste
- Goat Cheese Rice Pasta
- 3 cups cooked rice pasta shells (I used Organ Garlic and Parsley Rice Pasta, available online or at health food stores.)
- 1/2 cup Boucheron Goat's Cheese (or any soft goat's cheese, but this one is extra creamy.)
- 1/4 cup grated aged goat's cheese (preferably 4 months or more)
- pepper to taste

Direction

- Pre-heat oven to 375 degrees Fahrenheit.
- Prepare the pasta: in a medium saucepan, heat the 1/2 cup soft goat's milk cheese over medium low heat. Add in aged goat's cheese. Stir until melted and completely blended. Remove from heat. Add cooked pasta (prepared according to package's directions) directly to melted cheese mixture. Pepper to taste. Stir until combined. Pour cheesy pasta into a bread baking dish (this is the perfect size for two people) and set aside.
- Prepare chicken: Oil a casserole dish/baking pan with 2 tbs. olive oil. Place chicken breasts on oiled surface, and flip a few times to coat completely. Set aside for a moment.
- In small bowl, combine onion, tarragon, garlic, white wine, sea salt, and pepper. Pour herb mixture over oiled chicken breasts.
- Place both pasta and chicken in oven at the same time. Cook for 25 minutes, or until chicken and cheese on pasta are both browned, and chicken is not pink on the inside.

- Remove, let cool for about 3 minutes, and serve with some leafy greens.

167. Impromptu Winter Salad

Serving: Serves 2, generously | Prep: | Cook: | Ready in:

Ingredients

- 1/2 cup Marcona almonds
- 1 tablespoon Meyer lemon juice
- 3 tablespoons walnut oil
- 1 teaspoon organic wildflower honey
- 1 teaspoon grated ginger root
- 1 large, organic Pink Lady apple
- 1/2 cup freshly squeezed orange juice
- 4 ounces organic arugula
- 3 ounces goat cheese
- 1/2 cup pomegranate seeds
- ground black pepper

Direction

- Heat a small, dry skillet and gently toast the almonds until they become light brown, about 5 minutes. Set aside.
- In a small, deep bowl, whisk together the walnut oil and lemon juice. Whisk in the honey and grated ginger. Set aside.
- Cut and core the apple into quarters. Thinly slice the apple (but do not peel it) and place slices in a shallow bowl. Cover the fruit with the orange juice.
- Add the arugula to a salad bowl. Crumble the goat cheese into the greens. Add the sliced apple, toasted almonds and pomegranate seeds.
- Add the vinaigrette to the salad. Grind black pepper to taste. Toss and serve immediately.

168. Jack's Pear, Bacon, & Goat Cheese Quesadillas

Serving: Makes two 10-inch quesadillas | Prep: 0hours0mins | Cook: 0hours15mins | Ready in:

Ingredients

- 3 slices thick bacon, diced
- four (10-inch) flour tortillas
- 2 cups cups shredded Monterey Jack cheese
- 1/2 cup cup crumbled goat cheese
- 1 firm ripe Bartlett, Bosc, Comice or Anjou pear, peeled and thinly sliced

Direction

- Cook the bacon in a large skillet until browned and crispy. Remove with a slotted spoon and drain on a paper towel. Discard extra fat and wipe out the skillet well.
- Cook two of the tortillas over medium heat until one side on each one is pale golden brown and they are no longer soft and doughy.
- Remove one tortilla from skillet and reduce the heat to low. Flip the other tortilla uncooked side down and sprinkle the browned side with 1/2 cup Monterey Jack cheese and 1/4 cup goat cheese.
- Distribute half of the bacon over the cheese and layer with half of the pear slices. Cover pears with 1/2 cup more shredded cheese and top with the second tortilla, uncooked side up. Press firmly with a spatula.
- Cook until bottom tortilla is golden brown and bottom layer of cheese is melted. Carefully flip quesadilla over and cook second side until cheese is melted and tortilla is golden brown.
- Transfer to a cutting board. Cut into wedges and repeat with remaining ingredients.

169. Jerusalem Artichoke Soup With Figs And Goat Cheese

Serving: Serves 4 | Prep: | Cook: | Ready in:

Ingredients

- 700g Jerusalem artichoke
- 2 parsnip
- 1 garlic clove
- 500 milliliters water
- 500 milliliters milk
- 2-3 sprigs thyme
- 2 fresh figs
- 1 tablespoon maple syrup
- Salt and pepper
- crumbled goat cheese
- 4 tablespoons greek yoghurt

Direction

- Peel and dice the Jerusalem artichoke and parsnip. Chop the garlic clove and remove the thyme leaves from the sprigs. Place vegetables, thyme leaves and garlic in a cooker cover with water and milk. Cook for 20 minutes
- In the meantime, cut the figs in slices. Melt some butter in pan and add the figs and maple syrup. Season with some pepper and cook for about 2 minutes on low heat.
- Once the vegetables are cook, mix well and season to taste.
- Once you're ready to serve, pour the soup into individual bowls and decorate with figs and crumbled goat cheese

170. Jewels Of The Winter Salad

Serving: Serves 6 | Prep: | Cook: | Ready in:

Ingredients

- Salad

- 1 large bunches Lacinato Kale- cut into 1/2" slivers
- 1 cup Pomegranate airils, plus more for garnish
- 1 cup Roasted beets- cut into 1/2 inch pieces
- 1/2 cup Walnuts- toasted
- 1/2 cup goat cheese- crumbled
- Salad Dressing
- 1 teaspoon mustard- I like Stonewall Kitchen Maple Mustard
- 1 shallot-minced
- 1 tablespoon Red currant Jam
- 1/4 cup Pomegranate Vinegar(can substitute white balsamic)
- 1/2 cup Olive oil
- salt & pepper to taste

Direction

- Make the dressing: In a small bowl whisk together the mustard, shallots, jam & vinegar. Slowly add the olive oil while whisking until well blended. Add salt & pepper to taste.
- Place the slivered kale a large salad bowl. Add 1/2 the dressing & massage into the kale. Let it sit for 10-15 minutes so that the kale softens & absorbs the dressing.
- Arrange the beets, pomegranate seeds, walnuts & goat cheese on top of kale.
- Pour the remainder of the dressing over the salad & toss. Sprinkle salad with extra pomegranate seeds & serve.

171. Kale & Barley Cake

Serving: Makes 1 8-inch cake | Prep: | Cook: | Ready in:

Ingredients

- 2 tablespoons olive oil, divided
- 1 large shallot, thinly sliced
- 2 garlic cloves, smashed and sliced
- 2 teaspoons chopped fresh rosemary
- 6 cups shredded lacinato kale
- Salt, to taste

- 1.5 cups Cooked barley
- 4 eggs
- 1 cup goat cheese, crumbled

Direction

- Heat 1 tablespoon of the olive oil over medium-high heat in an 8-inch oven proof pan or skillet. Add the shallots and garlic and cook until beginning to turn golden, about 5 to 8 minutes.
- Add the rosemary and shredded kale and a generous pinch of salt. Cook, sitting until the kale has just began to wilt, about 4 minutes. Stir in the cook barley and heat through, then turn off the heat.
- In a large bowl, lightly whisk the 4 eggs then add in the kale and barley mixture.
- Wipe the sauté pan clean, then heat the remaining 1 tablespoon of olive oil over medium heat. Pour in half of the kale and egg mixture, then dot with half the goat cheese. Pour in the remaining kale and egg mixture, then top with the remaining goat cheese.
- Preheat the broiler.
- Cook covered over medium-low heat, for about 8 minutes or until the egg begins to set and the bottom is beginning to brown. Move to finish in the broiler for 5 minutes. Let cool slightly and serve warm or at room temperature in wedges.

172.   Kale Salad With Roasted Beet Dressing

Serving: Serves 4 | Prep: | Cook: | Ready in:

Ingredients

- Roasted Beet Dressing
- 3 Small Sliced & Roasted Beets
- 5 tablespoons Olive Oil
- 4 tablespoons Lemon Juice
- 2 tablespoons Apple Cider Vinegar
- 1 tablespoon Honey

- 1 pinch Salt & Pepper
- Salad
- 2 bunches Kale
- 1/2 cup Slivered Almonds
- 1/2 cup Cranberries
- 4 Beets
- 4 ounces Goat Cheese (omit if you want to keep this vegan)
- 1/4 cup Panko Bread Crumbs

Direction

- Slice the washed beets and toss with salt and pepper and a little bit of your favorite high heat oil. Roast at 375 until tender, about 20 minutes.
- Thoroughly clean the kale and finely chop. I pulsed it in the food processor to minimize the effort. Adding the hot beets will gently wilt the kale, warming it all up but keeping it fresh.
- Combine the ingredients for the dressing and blend in a blender, food processor or immersion blender.
- Lightly brown panko bread crumbs. Cover goat cheese slices with the crumbs.
- Season with salt and pepper and toss. Add the dressing when you serve the plate.

173.   Kale, Avocado, Pomegranate Salad Dressed With Balsamic Reduction

Serving: Serves 4 | Prep: | Cook: | Ready in:

Ingredients

- Preparing the salad
- 10-14 full size leaves of DIno Kale or Luciano Kale
- 1 Avocado
- 1 small vine ripe tomato diced
- 1 pomegranate
- 1/3-1/2 cups chopped pecans
- 1 handful goat cheese

- 4 ounces Baby Bella mushrooms
- 1.5 teaspoons brown sugar
- 1 tablespoon canola oil
- Basalmic reduction
- 1/4-1/3 cups Balsamic vinegar

Direction

- Preparing the salad
- Take the chopped pecans and put it over medium to high heat in a pan.
- Heat until the oil starts to come off the pecans, stirring frequently.
- Lightly sprinkle brown sugar coating both sides of the pecan.
- Continue on medium to high heat for 2-3 minutes until sugar melts and lightly coats pecans.
- Take off heat, spread pecans on parchment paper to dry, and keep aside
- Continue on medium to high heat for 2-3 minutes until sugar melts and lightly coats pecans.
- Cut pomegranate in half and put it in a bowl of water to separate the pomegranate seeds from the pith. Keep separated pomegranate seeds aside.
- Cut kale leaves vertically in half and separate stem from the leaf
- Take bunches of kale leaves in your hand and rip into 1-2 pieces
- Slice mushrooms
- Coat pat with canola oil and put kale leaves in the pan over medium high heat
- Place mushrooms on top of kale and cover the pan till kale leaves starts to turn a brighter green and mushrooms are fully cooked
- Slice avocado
- Place kale and mushrooms onto serving plates with diced tomatoes.
- Sprinkle with pomegranate seeds, goat cheese, sliced avocado, and chopped pecans
- Balsamic reduction
- Place balsamic vinegar in a pan just under high heat stirring frequently until balsamic starts to take a syrupy form
- Drizzle over the salad to taste

174.   Kale, Leek & Goat Cheese Galette

Serving: Serves 4 | Prep: | Cook: | Ready in:

Ingredients

- 1 bunch Kale
- 1 bunch Leeks
- 1 Onion
- 3 ounces Goat cheese
- 1 Pie Crust
- 1 cup Walnuts
- 3 Egg
- 1 tablespoon Garlic

Direction

- Sautee kale, leeks, onions (garlic optional) in a covered sauce pan on low for 15-20 minutes.
- Assemble sauteed vegetables into large mixing bowl. Fold in eggs and walnuts.
- Place pie crust flat onto a cookie sheet and pour the vegetable mixture in the middle of the crust so that there is 1-2 inches of dough that remains surrounding the vegetables.
- Arrange goat cheese in small bits around the edge of the mixture. Fold up extra 1-2 inches of pie crust to form the shape of the galette.
- Bake at 400 degrees for 35-40 minutes- until the crust is golden brown and starting to flake. Enjoy!

175.   Khachapuri (Georgian Cheese And Egg Bread)

Serving: Makes 2 large or 4 small breads | Prep: 3hours0mins | Cook: 1hours0mins | Ready in:

Ingredients

- For the dough
- 4 1/3 cups (522 g) bread flour
- 1 tablespoon (9 g) instant active dry yeast
- 2 tablespoons (25 g) granulated sugar
- 1 teaspoon (4 g) fine sea salt
- 10 tablespoons (142 g) unsalted butter, at room temperature
- 1 cup (242 g) whole milk, warmed to about 100°F
- 1/3 cup (81 g) warm water
- For the filling and finishing
- 1 1/2 cups goat cheese
- 2 1/2 cups diced fresh mozzarella cheese
- 1 egg, beaten with a splash of water
- 6 large eggs

Direction

- Make the dough: In the bowl of an electric mixer fitted with the dough hook attachment, mix the flour, yeast, sugar, and salt to combine. Add the butter and mix on low speed until the mixture looks crumbly, about 1 minute.
- Add the milk and water and mix the dough on low speed for 4 minutes. Raise the speed to medium and mix until the dough is very smooth, 2-3 minutes more.
- Transfer the dough to a large, oiled bowl and cover with plastic wrap. Let the dough rise for 1 1/2 to 2 hours, until the dough is puffed (it may not fully double in size).
- Divide the dough as desired: Cut into two even pieces for larger, more share-able khachapuri, or into four even pieces for smaller, individual khachapuri.
- Pat the dough into an oval shape with your hands. On a lightly floured surface, roll out the dough, maintaining the oval shape, into an oblong oval about 1/3-inch thick.
- Pick the dough up from the ends and transfer it to a parchment lined baking sheet. Gently stretch the dough when you transfer it to help elongate the oval a bit.
- Crumble the goat cheese evenly over the dough, leaving about 1 inch around the edge

on all sides. Sprinkle the mozzarella evenly over the goat cheese.
- Working your way around the bread, fold the excess dough up and over the filling to create a little wall and encase it. Gently pinch the ends of the oval to help seal. Cover the breads with a piece of plastic wrap sprayed with nonstick spray, and let the bread rise for 30 minutes to 1 hour.
- Preheat the oven to 375° F. Brush the edges of the dough with egg wash.
- For small khachapuri, crack an egg on each piece, in the center of the bread. Transfer to the oven and bake until the crust is golden brown, the cheese is melted and lightly golden, and the egg white is set, but the yolk is still runny, 30 to 35 minutes.
- For large khachapuri, transfer the breads to the oven and bake for 15 to 20 minutes. Remove the breads from the oven and crack three eggs evenly over the center of each bread. Return to the oven and continue to bake for 25 to 30 minutes more, until the bread is golden, the cheese is melted, and the egg white is set but the yolks are still runny.
- Let the khachapuri cool for 5 to 10 minutes before serving warm.

176.   Leek And Cherry Tomato Clafouti

Serving: Serves 4-6 | Prep: | Cook: |Ready in:

Ingredients

- for the clafouti batter
- 3/4 cup milk
- 3/4 cup cream
- 3 eggs
- 1/2 cup flour
- 2 tablespoons melted butter
- Pinch salt
- for the leek filling
- 6 slender leeks

- 1 pint cherry tomatoes
- 4 sprigs marjoram
- drizzle of olive oil
- 2 tablespoons butter, divided use
- 1/4 cup dry white vermouth
- 2 to 3 ounces mild goat cheese
- salt and pepper to taste
- 1 tablespoon chopped fresh chives

Direction

- Preheat the oven to 350 degrees. In an oven dish toss together the cherry tomatoes and marjoram leaves from 4 sprigs with a generous drizzle of olive oil and a pinch of salt. Place in the oven and roast, jiggling the pan occasionally to turn the tomatoes, for about 30 minutes until the tomatoes have collapsed and are very fragrant.
- Meanwhile, prepare the clafouti batter. In a blender, mix the milk, eggs, and flour and a pinch of salt. Drizzle in the melted butter. Let the batter rest for at least 15 minutes before using.
- Remove the roots and most of the green parts of the leeks. Cut a slit down the length of each leek so that you can fan apart the layers, and wash them thoroughly to remove accumulated dirt. Cut them into 1/4 inch rings. Heat a large ovenproof skillet or paella pan and add 1 tablespoon of butter. When the butter froths, add the leeks, salt, and pepper, and cook over medium heat until they are soft, about 8 minutes. Add the white vermouth and cook this down. Remove the leeks to a dish and return the skillet to the stovetop.
- Add the remaining tablespoon of butter to the skillet and swirl to cover the bottom and sides of the pan. Pour a thin film of batter into the bottom of the pan and swirl to spread, as if you were making a crepe. Let the batter cook until it turns from pale white to a more yellowish color. Turn off the heat and assemble the clafouti. Spread on the leeks, and then crumble over the goat cheese. Distribute the roasted tomatoes and pour over any accumulated pan juices. Finally pour over the

rest of the clafouti batter and transfer the pan to the oven.
- Bake the clafouti for 50-60 minutes until it is nicely browned on top and a fork poked into the center comes out clean. Garnish with chopped chives and serve.

---

177.   Leek And Goat Cheese Tart

Serving: Serves 4-6 | Prep: | Cook: | Ready in:

Ingredients

- 1 1/4 cups flour
- 1/4 pound chilled butter (1 stick), cut into cubes
- 1/4 teaspoon salt
- 2 tablespoons ice water
- 6 leeks, halved, cleaned, white and really light green part only
- 2-4 tablespoons butter
- 2 teaspoons herbes de Provence
- 1 cup whipping cream
- 3 eggs
- 1 egg yolk
- 8 ounces soft goat cheese, such as Montrachet or Chevre

Direction

- Put the flour and salt into the bowl of a food processor and pulse a couple of times.
- Open up the top and drop the cubes of chilled butter onto the flour; close and pulse a few times till it begins to combine.
- Pour 1 T of the water in through the feed tube and pulse, adding more water as necessary until the dough nearly comes together. Dump it out onto a piece of plastic wrap, knead it into a disc and refrigerate for about a half-hour.
- Put 2 T of butter into a saute pan, heat till bubbly then add the leeks; lower the heat and cook them slowly, never allowing them to

brown, adding more butter if you feel it's necessary. You can add an additional 2 T of butter. When the leeks are soft and cooked through, sprinkle them with the herbes de Provence and let them cool down in the pan, covered.

- Meanwhile, preheat the oven to 350°. Remove the dough from the refrigerator and roll out to less than 1/4" thickness. I use a 4.5 x 13.5 rectangular tart pan but you can also use a 9" springform pan or a tart pan with a removable bottom. Carefully put the pastry in the pan, smoothing it into the corners, prick the bottom and blind-bake it for 20 minutes, poking any bubbles with a fork should they erupt during the baking. Remove the crust from the oven and cool on a rack while you're fixing the filling.
- Beat the yolk with the eggs, then add the cream. Season with a bit of salt and pepper if you wish; I like to use finely ground white pepper.
- Lay the leeks across the bottom of the tart pan, fitting them snugly against one another. Crumble the goat cheese over the leeks, then pour the egg-cream mixture over all. If you use the rectangular pan I mentioned, you'll have extra crust and extra cream, don't think you can use it all in this one tart!
- Place in center of the oven and bake for 30-35 minutes or until the filling is set. Depending on the shape of your pan it may cook faster or it may require more time. With the rectangular pan it usually takes 25-30 minutes to be nicely done.
- Let cool before slicing. This is a nice appetizer or, paired with a green salad, makes an elegant light lunch. Enjoy!

---

178. Leek, Bacon And Goat Cheese Pizza

Serving: Serves 3 | Prep: | Cook: | Ready in:

Ingredients

- Pizza Crust
- 5 1/3 cups AP flour
- 1 tablespoon kosher salt
- 1 teaspoon instant yeast
- 2 tablespoons sugar
- 2 cups room temperature water
- 2 tablespoons olive oil, plus more to work with
- For the toppings
- 4 leeks, white and light green parts only
- 1 tablespoon butter
- 1/4 cup white wine
- 1/4 cup cream
- salt to taste
- 4 pieces bacon
- olive oil
- 4 ounces fresh goat cheese

Direction

- Pizza Crust
- Combine all ingredients in the bowl of your stand mixer. Mix with the paddle attachment at low speed for about a minute. Let the dough rest for 5 minutes.
- Switch to the dough hook on your stand mixer. Mix at medium speed for about 5 minutes. The dough should be wet but not too tacky.
- Transfer the dough to an oiled board, and knead by hand for a few minutes. Divide into 5 equal portions, form each portion into a ball, and store each portion in a lightly oiled ziplock bag. (At this point, you should be able to freeze the bags you don't plan to use immediately).
- Let the dough sit in the refrigerator at least overnight, or up to 4 days.
- About 90 minutes before you plan to bake the pizzas, take the dough out of the refrigerator, form into a neat ball, and let rest at room temperature on a floured or parchment lined baking sheet.

- Preheat oven to 500 degrees (or higher). Form the pizza dough into a flat dish on a floured sheet. It is now ready for toppings.
- For the toppings
- Clean the leeks by slicing them lengthwise and running them under water until all the layers are clean. Roughly chop into 1 inch pieces.
- In a large skillet, melt the butter. Add the leeks, and cook over medium heat until they start to soften.
- Add the wine, and cook until absorbed. Add the cream, and cook until absorbed. Salt to taste and remove from heat.
- Meanwhile, chop the bacon into bite sized pieces and fry until cooked but not too crisp (it cooks further in the oven).
- Brush each pizza crust with olive oil. Arrange the leeks, the cooked bacon, and crumbled goat cheese over the top of each pizza.
- Bake at 500 degrees 15 minutes.

---

179. Leek, Shallot And Goat Cheese Tart

Serving: Serves 6 | Prep: | Cook: | Ready in:

Ingredients

- Tart pastry shell
- 2 cups all purpose flour
- 8 tablespoons cold unsalted butter, cut in pea-size cubes
- 1/2 teaspoon salt
- 1 large egg
- 2 tablespoons ice cold water
- Filling and baking
- 3 leeks,white parts only, thinly sliced
- 4 medium shallots, thinly sliced
- 4 tablespoons olive oil
- 1 cup heavy cream
- 3 large eggs
- 1/4 teaspoon ground nutmeg
- 1 tablespoon Dijon mustard
- 1 cup crumbled goat cheese

Direction

- Tart pastry shell
- Sift the flour in the bowl of a stand mixer. Add the salt and the butter. Using the paddle attachment, mix at speed 2 until the butter is incorporated.
- Add the egg and keep mixing, about 1 more minute.
- Add the water and mix until you get a crumbled dough, about another minute.
- Scrape the dough onto a clean work surface. Make a ball with it using your hands. Flatten it to make a thin disc. Cover with plastic wrap and refrigerate for a minimum of 1 hour.
- Preheat the oven to 375 F.
- On a floured surface, roll the dough until you have a 12 inch diameter circle. Place the dough in a 9-inch tart pan and crimp the edges
- Place a round of parchment paper inside the shell and cover with pie weights. Bake for 15 minutes, until lightly golden.
- Filling and baking
- Preheat the oven to 375 F.
- Heat the olive oil in a medium skillet and add the leeks and the shallots. Cook over medium heat for 10 minutes, until very soft.
- In a medium bowl, beat the eggs. Add the cream, mustard, nutmeg, salt and pepper. Whisk until blended, about 30 seconds.
- Spread the leeks and shallots over the tart shell using a spatula to level. Pour the cream and egg mixture over. Sprinkle with the goat cheese.
- Bake for 35 minutes, until golden.

---

180. Leftover Pie

Serving: Serves 8 | Prep: | Cook: | Ready in:

Ingredients

- 1 cup fingerling potatoes
- 1 bunch of radishes
- 3 carrots

- olive oil
- sea salt, black pepper
- 1 celeriac bulb (aka celery root)
- 2 apples
- 1/2 cup chicken or vegetable stock
- 2 sprigs of thyme
- 2 tablespoons unsalted butter
- 1 tablespoon apple vinegar (optional)
- 3-4 sausages (I used Italian-herbed pork sausages)
- 2 small white onions
- 4-6 ounces goat cheese
- grated Parmesan (optional)

Direction

- Heat the oven to 425F.
- Scrub the fingerlings clean. Move them to a pot of cold water, and set the pot over high heat. Cook the potatoes until you can stick a fork about halfway into each potato, about 10 minutes.
- Scrub the radishes clean. Cut off any stems, whiskers, or any bits you can't get clean. If you have any black radishes in the bunch, you should peel the skin off those. Cut each radish into slightly larger than bite-sized pieces (they will shrivel a little in the roasting). When you're done, move the radish pieces to a large bowl.
- Pour a generous measure of olive oil over the radishes, carrots, and fingerlings. Thoroughly salt and pepper the vegetables, and toss them with your hands to coat evenly.
- Move the vegetables to a baking sheet. Use a fork to smash down the fingerlings a bit, and then move the baking sheet into the oven. Roast the vegetables until all are wrinkled and caramelized, about 35 minutes.
- While you are waiting for the vegetables to roast, tackle the celery root. Cut off all the whiskery bits. Cut the celery root into small-ish pieces. Peel, core, and dice the apples.
- Add the celery root and the apple to a Dutch oven, or to a wide sauté pan with a lid. Add the chicken stock and the thyme, and set the heat to medium. Put the lid on and let

everything cook uninterrupted for 10 minutes. (Seriously, check after 10 minutes. Do not do as I did and resist checking under the lid until the smell of burnt apple becomes palpable.) When you can pierce the celery root with a fork, remove the pot from the heat. Discard the thyme sprigs. Use a potato masher (a large fork works too) to roughly puree the apple and celery root. Stir in the butter, and salt to taste. Set the pot aside.

- At this point, or near about, the vegetables should be coming out of the oven. Give them a little splash of apple vinegar, if you like.
- Now, tackle the sausage: Pour about 1 tablespoon of olive oil into a wide sauté pan, and let it start heating up over medium/medium-low heat. Meanwhile, use a paring knife to gently peel the casings off each sausage. When the oil is heated, add the sausage meat to the pan. Cook, stirring occasionally to break the sausage into pieces, until no longer pink. You should have time to slice up the onion while the sausage is cooking.
- When the sausage is finished cooking, remove it to a small bowl. Add the onion to the sausage pan, stirring as you go to dissolve the brown bits. Cook the onion until at least translucent. If you want to caramelize them, go for it. Whatever you have time for.
- Now that everything is prepared, you want to layer all the ingredients into a casserole. I followed this order: radishes/carrots/fingerlings; onions; sausage; goat cheese; celery root mash. Try to seal in the other ingredients with the celery root mash. I sprinkled the top with freshly grated Parmesan and black pepper.
- Pop that puppy into your 425F heated oven and cook for about 25 minutes. The crust should have hardened slightly, and the color should be more deeply golden than when it went into the oven. Serve warm.

181. Lemon Goat Cheese Cheesecake

Serving: Serves 10 | Prep: | Cook: |Ready in:

Ingredients

- 1/4 cup unsalted butter, plus 1 teaspoon (for greasing the pan)
- 8 ounces cookies (lemon, shortbread, vanilla wafers, or your favorite cookie)
- 1/2 teaspoon kosher salt, divided
- 10 ounces cream cheese, room temperature
- 6 ounces creamy fresh goat cheese, room temperature
- 1/2 cup sugar
- 3 eggs, room temperature
- 1/2 cup crème fraîche or sour cream
- 2 tablespoons lemon juice
- 2 teaspoons firmly packed lemon zest (not strips, make sure it's very finely zested)
- 8 ounces cookies, enough to circle the cake (preferably the same kind you used for the crust)
- 2 tablespoons of your favorite jam or honey (for gluing on cookies)

Direction

- Heat oven to 350° F. Butter the interior of your springform pan. Cut a piece of parchment to fit the bottom of the pan and press it into the pan. Butter the parchment. Set aside. Place butter for the crust in a medium-sized pan over medium heat. The butter will melt, sizzle, and foam up. Once it smells nutty and the noise stops, watch closely. Turn off the heat once the brown bits drop down to the bottom of the pan. Set aside. Pulverize your cookies in the food processor. Pulse in the brown butter and a 1/4 teaspoon of the salt. Press into the bottom and up about 1 inch of the greased spring form pan. Bake until just starting to brown (about 10 minutes). Remove from the oven to cool. Turn oven down to 300° F.
- Place cream cheese and goat cheese in the bowl of a standing mixer, and beat until light and smooth (about 3 minutes). Scrape down the sides. Add the sugar and beat for another minute. Scrape down the sides. Add the eggs one at a time, scraping down between each addition. Add the remaining salt, crème fraîche, and lemon juice and zest. Beat for another 30 seconds. If you see any lumps, beat for another 30 seconds or so.
- Pour into the crust in the prepared springform pan. Bake for 40 minutes. Don't peek. Not even once. After 40 minutes, turn off the oven and open the door. Leave the cake to cool for an hour in the oven. After an hour, remove from the oven to cool completely. (Otherwise, the cake will sweat in the fridge.) Cover and place in the fridge for 8 hours or overnight.
- To serve, place the bottom of the pan over a medium flame on the stove. Move it around for about 5 seconds over the flame. Use a warm paring knife (warmed under hot water or over the flame) to separate the cake from the side of the pan. Remove outer ring from the spring form pan. Don't stress if it looks like a mess because you will be covering the sides up with cookies. Try to slide the cake off of the bottom of the pan. If it won't budge, put it over the flame for a few more seconds and/or use a spatula to loosen things up. I've found that once the cake is off the base and on the plate, you can easily slide out the circle of parchment paper. Sometimes, the parchment will even stay behind on the pan.
- Encircle the side with the same cookies you used for the crust. They will need a little help sticking; you can use any kind of jam or honey.
- Eat immediately, or store in the fridge until serving -- though be warned, the cookies might get a big stale the longer it sits.

182.   Lemon Verbena Goat Cheese Ice Cream With Blackberry Sauce

Serving: Makes 1 quart | Prep: | Cook: | Ready in:

Ingredients

- 2 cups whole milk
- 1 tablespoon cornstarch, plus 1 teaspoon
- 4 ounces goat cheese, mild
- 3 tablespoons cream cheese
- 1/4 teaspoon kosher salt
- 1 1/4 cups heavy cream
- 2/3 cup sugar (I used coconut palm sugar)
- 1 tablespoon lemon verbena leaves, torn

Direction

- In a small bowl, whisk 2 tablespoons of the milk with the cornstarch. Whisk together the goat cheese, cream cheese and salt in a medium bowl; set aside. Fill a large bowl with ice and water.
- In a large saucepan, combine the remaining milk, cream and sugar. Bring to a boil, boil for 4 minutes, stirring frequently. Remove from heat and add lemon verbena leaves; let steep 10 minutes.
- Bring mixture back to a boil, then remove from heat and gradually whisk in the cornstarch slurry. Bring to a boil, and stir until slightly thickened, about 1 minute. Remove from heat.
- Gradually whisk the ice cream base into the goat cheese mixture until smooth. Pour into a 1-gallon freezer bag and submerge in the ice bath for 30 minutes.
- To make the blackberry sauce: Combine 2 cups of fresh blackberries with 3/4 cup sugar (again, I used coconut palm sugar) and bring to a boil in a medium saucepan. Reduce heat and simmer for 10 minutes. Let cool completely (can make ahead).
- Pour the ice cream base into your ice cream machine and run until thick, about 25-30 minutes.
- When ice cream has frozen, pack into a storage container, alternating layers of ice cream with pools of blackberry sauce (make sure to scoop some sauce into the base of the container.) Freeze at least 4 hours; enjoy!

183.   Lentil Salad With Roasted Radicchio & Cauliflower

Serving: Serves 4 | Prep: | Cook: | Ready in:

Ingredients

- For the Salad:
- 1 small head cauliflower, cut into small florets (450 g), see notes above
- 3 teaspoons olive oil, plus more as needed
- 1/2 teaspoon Aleppo pepper or freshly ground black pepper
- kosher salt
- 1/2 cup French green lentils, rinsed
- 1 bay leaf, if you have it
- 1/3 cup walnuts or more to taste
- 1 head radicchio, cored and chopped
- 1/4 to 1/2 cups coarsely chopped fresh tarragon
- 3 ounces goat cheese
- For the Dressing:
- 3 anchovy fillets
- 5 tablespoons extra-virgin olive oil
- 2 tablespoons minced shallots
- 2 tablespoons balsamic vinegar
- 1 teaspoon Dijon mustard
- 1 tablespoon fresh lemon juice, plus more as needed
- 1/2 teaspoon honey
- 3 tablespoons currants or more to taste

Direction

- Heat the oven to 400°F. Line a large rimmed baking sheet with parchment paper. Spread the cauliflower into a single layer on the baking sheet. Toss with 2 tablespoons of the oil, the Aleppo pepper, if using, and kosher salt all over. Add more oil if necessary. Spread into a single layer again and roast until the cauliflower is light brown, 20 to 25 minutes.

- Meanwhile, place the lentils, bay leaf, if using, and a few pinches of salt in a saucepan and add enough cold water to cover by at least an inch. Bring to a boil, then turn down the heat and simmer until tender, 20 to 25 minutes (or longer—sometimes mine take as long as 30). Add additional water if needed.
- Place the nuts in a medium sauté pan and toast over low heat until golden brown — keep a close watch! Transfer nuts to a board and coarsely chop.
- Meanwhile, in a large bowl, toss half of the radicchio with the remaining 1 tablespoon of olive oil. When the cauliflower is light brown, scatter the remaining undressed radicchio on the sheet and roast until the radicchio is wilted and the cauliflower is tender, 3 to 5 minutes more. Let cool.
- To make the vinaigrette, finely chop the anchovies and smash them into a paste with the side of a chef's knife. Combine with the remaining ingredients and whisk until emulsified. Add more lemon to taste.
- Drain the lentils well, discard the bay leaf, and transfer to the large bowl with the dressed radicchio. Toss the lentils, while they are still warm, with enough vinaigrette to lightly coat. Add a few pinches of salt.
- Toss in the roasted cauliflower and radicchio, 1/4 cup of the tarragon, and walnuts to the bowl. Toss with more vinaigrette until evenly dressed. Taste and adjust the seasoning, adding more lemon juice if needed. Add the remaining 1/4 cup tarragon if you wish. Just before serving, crumble the goat cheese over the salad and gently toss. Serve warm or at room temperature.

---

184. Maple Pecan Cran Apple Salad With Lemon Maple Vinaigrette

Serving: Serves 4 | Prep: | Cook: |Ready in:

Ingredients

- 4 cups chopped romaine lettuce
- 4 cups fresh spinach
- 1/2 sweet vidalia onion, thinly sliced
- 1/2 honeycrisp apple, thinly sliced
- 1/2 cup dried cranberries
- 1/2 cup Salted Maple Pecans (http://www.tiffanythyme.com/salted-maple-pecans/)
- 4 ounces goat cheese, roughly chopped
- 1 teaspoon brown sugar
- 1 teaspoon dried minced onion
- 1 teaspoon dried minced garlic
- 1 teaspoon lemon pepper
- 1/2 teaspoon paprika
- 1/4 teaspoon crushed red pepper flakes
- 1/4 teaspoon salt
- 1 pound thinly sliced chicken breast filets
- 1 teaspoon coconut oil or extra virgin olive oil
- Lemon-Maple Vinaigrette
- 1/4 cup fresh lemon juice
- 3/4 cup extra virgin olive oil
- 2 tablespoons dijon mustard
- 4 tablespoons 100% pure maple syrup
- 1/2 teaspoon salt
- 1/2 teaspoon black pepper

Direction

- Toss chopped romaine with spinach. Add thinly sliced Vidalia onions and apples. Top with craisins, Salted Maple Pecans, and goat cheese.
- Combine brown sugar, minced onion, minced garlic, lemon pepper, paprika, crushed red pepper flakes, and salt to create spice rub.
- Massage spice rub into chicken breast filets on both sides.
- Preheat your skillet on medium heat and add your oil.

- When hot, add your chicken and sear on each side for roughly 4-5 minutes or until cooked through. Remove chicken from skillet and place on a plate to rest.
- For the vinaigrette, add lemon juice, olive oil, maple syrup, Dijon mustard, salt, and pepper to a small bowl. Whisk until well combined.
- Finish salad with Sweet & Tangy Seared Chicken Breast and Lemon-Maple Vinaigrette, if desired.

185. Mashed Potatoes With Caramelized Onions & Goat Cheese

Serving: Serves 4 | Prep: 0hours10mins | Cook: 0hours15mins | Ready in:

Ingredients

- 4 tablespoons unsalted butter, divided use
- 1 tablespoon olive oil
- 1 1/2 pounds yellow onions (approximately 2 large onions), thinly sliced
- 1 pinch kosher salt
- 1/4 teaspoon sugar
- 3 pounds Russet potatoes, peeled and cut into 1-inch pieces
- 1 1/2 cups half and half
- 1 clove garlic, smashed
- 1 bay leaf
- 3 ounces goat cheese
- 1 pinch Black pepper

Direction

- To make the caramelized onions, heat 2 tablespoons of butter and the olive oil in a large sauté pan over medium heat. Add the sliced onions and stir them to coat with the fat. Add 1/4 teaspoon salt and the sugar and cook, stirring frequently, until onions are golden brown and caramelized, about 30-40 minutes. If the onions get too dry, add a small amount of water to deglaze the pan. Set aside.

- Place the potatoes in a large pot of cold, salted water. Bring to a boil and cook until fork tender.
- While the potatoes are cooking, heat the half and half, garlic, bay leaf, and remaining 2 tablespoons of butter in a small saucepan over medium heat.
- Drain the potatoes and return them to the hot, dry pot. Stir them over low heat for 2 minutes until they are dry. Pass the potatoes through a ricer into a large bowl. Gently stir in the hot cream mixture a little at a time until the potatoes are smooth and creamy (discard the garlic and bay leaf). You may not need to use all of the liquid. Set aside a small amount of the caramelized onions for garnish and stir the remaining onions into the mashed potatoes. Crumble the goat cheese into the potatoes and stir to combine well. Season with salt and black pepper to taste.
- Spoon the mashed potatoes into a serving bowl and garnish with the remaining caramelized onions. Serve hot.

186. Mediterranean Pressed Picnic Sandwich

Serving: Serves 6-8 | Prep: | Cook: | Ready in:

Ingredients

- 1 loaf of good, round rosemary bread, or olive bread - about 12 inches across
- 1/4 cup sun dried tomatoes in olive oil, drained and julienned - reserve oil.
- 8 oz. jar of marinated artichoke hearts, drained, reserving marinade, chopped
- 2 tablespoons balsamic vinegar
- 2 teaspoons fresh lemon juice
- 1 tsp Dijon Mustard
- salt and pepper to taste
- 1/2 cup of purchased black olive tapenade
- 10 oz. of good, high quality, prosciutto slices

- 1 cup (large handful) of baby spinach and / or arugula leaves
- 8 ounces jar of roasted red peppers, drained and cut into strips for layering.
- 6 oz. of crumbled goat cheese
- 10-12 whole, large basil leaves

Direction

- Slice the loaf of bread in half horizontally, like a sandwich or hamburger bun, and remove the inside crumb from the top and bottom, leaving a 1/4 inch border all around. Save the crumbs for bread crumbs.
- Drain the artichokes and sun dried tomatoes, save their oils / marinades, and combine them together. To the marinade, add the balsamic vinegar, lemon juice, Dijon, and salt and pepper. Whisk well to incorporate and taste for seasoning - set aside. If the dressing is too strong, add a few teaspoons of olive oil as needed. You can also add some dried basil, oregano or rosemary if you like.
- Spread the inside of the TOP of the loaf with the olive tapenade, and lay the prosciutto slices in the BOTTOM, covering thoroughly.
- Layer the spinach, artichoke hearts, red pepper, goat cheese, basil leaves, and sun dried tomatoes on the prosciutto in that order. Make sure to cover the sandwich all the way to the edges as evenly as possible with every layer.
- Whisk the dressing well and carefully spoon in about 4 Tablespoons over the layers in the bread boule. Save the rest of the dressing for another use.
- Place the top with the tapenade back on top of the loaf and press down well to secure the top.
- Wrap the loaf securely in wax paper and butcher's twine, and then wrap again securely in aluminum foil. Place in the refrigerator overnight with a heavy cast iron pan or brick on the sandwich to weigh it down.
- When ready to serve, simply unwrap the sandwich and cut into wedges with a serrated knife. It will go quickly. Can be unrefrigerated for up to 4 hours as long as it isn't blazing hot,

but I normally keep it in the cooler until about 1/2 hour before it's needed.

187.   Mediterranean Sandwich

Serving: Serves 4 | Prep: | Cook: |Ready in:

Ingredients

- 2 tomatoes, diced
- 1/2 pound andouille sausage
- 1/2 pound hot italian sausage
- 7 ounces jar of roasted red peppers
- 4 ounces goat cheese crumbles
- salt and pepper to taste
- 4 tablespoons olive oil
- 2 small zucchini, cut thinly lengthwise
- 1 tablespoon basil paste
- 2 garlic cloves, minced
- 4 small baguettes/buns
- sriracha sauce (optional)

Direction

- Preheat oven to 375 F.
- If your sausage is in casing, cut them out of the casing and dump contents into food processor. I bought mine just ground up so I didn't have to fool with any casing. Then add red peppers and goat cheese. Season with salt and pepper. Pulse a few times until everything is well combined.
- In a large skillet, brown the sausage mixture under medium high heat for about 8-10 minutes, but not cooked all the way. Then bake in oven for 10 minutes.
- While the sausage is in the oven, in a separate skillet, heat 1 tablespoon of oil over medium high heat. Add zucchini and season with salt and pepper. Sauté until tender, about 5-7 minutes.
- In a small bowl, combine the tomatoes, garlic, basil paste, and remaining 1 tablespoon of olive oil. This is like a quick bruschetta that

sets the sandwich off, in my opinion. Season with salt and pepper to taste.

- Cut your baguettes in half and brush cut side with olive oil and sprinkle with salt. Toast in oven for about 5 minutes. Remove from the oven and start building your sandwich. Bottom baguette, sausage mixture, zucchini, tomato mixture, and top with top of baguette. Return to oven for about 5 minutes to crisp bread more.
- Serve hot and with sriracha sauce!

188.   Mediterranean Style Steak Fajitas

Serving: Serves 2 | Prep: | Cook: | Ready in:

Ingredients

- Steak Fajitas
- 1   package of corn tortillas
- 1 1/2 pounds cap steak
- 3 cups red cabbage
- 1 1/2   red peppers
- 4   large onions
- 4   cloves of garlic
- 3 tablespoons butter
- 4 tablespoons olive oil
- one bunch cilantro
- 1/4 cup goat cheese
- 1   lime
- Almond, Basil Pesto
- 2 cups fresh basil
- 1/3 cup freshly grated parmesan
- 1/4 cup almonds
- 1/4 cup olive oil
- 3   cloves of garlic
- 1   juice of one fresh lemon

Direction

- Roughly chop the onions; it may seem like a lot but they are going to reduce a ton while you caramelize them. Heat a pan on medium and add in 2 tbsp. of olive oil. Add the onions and then bring the heat down to a low/med and let the onions sweat out until they are a gorgeous golden hue. This takes about 20 minutes.
- While the onions are caramelizing make the basil almond pesto, throw all of the ingredients into a blender or food processor and whiz until smooth. This will make a big batch but it will keep in the fridge for about 2 weeks. Set aside. Tip: add a little olive oil on the top each time you use some pesto from the jar and this will keep it from going brown.
- Thinly slice the red pepper and the cabbage and in a large pan on medium heat add 2 tbsp. of olive oil. Throw in the veggies and 3 tbsp. of the pesto you made earlier and braise on low for about 15 minutes. You still want them to be colorful and have a little crunch.
- Preheat the oven to 200 degrees, once the onions and veggies are done you can put them on a tray to keep warm while you make the steak.
- Mince 4 cloves of garlic and season your steak generously with salt and pepper and rub on the minced garlic. In a large pan on medium – to high heat add in 3 tbsp. of butter. Add in your steak and sear on both sides so you get a nice crisp then cook to your liking. Some people like their steak more rare, some medium so I will leave this up to you!
- Warm your tortillas, I rubbed them on the pan I was cooking the steak in and then threw them in the oven with the veggies for a couple of minutes. Garnish with fresh cilantro, goat cheese and a slice of lime.

189.   Merguez And Goat Cheese Stuffed French Toast

Serving: Serves 2 | Prep: | Cook: | Ready in:

Ingredients

- French Toast

- 1 Merguez sausage
- 3 ounces Goat cheese
- 2 Eggs
- 1/4 cup Almond or regular milk
- 1 handful Sliced toasted almonds
- 1 teaspoon Chopped fresh mint
- 2 Very thick slices raisin challah
- 1 teaspoon Powdered sugar
- Citrus syrup
- 1/2 cup Orange or tangerine juice
- 1/2 cup Sugar
- 1 teaspoon Lemon zest
- 1 teaspoon Fresh mint, chopped
- 1/4 teaspoon Orange blossom water

Direction

- French Toast
- Remove sausage from casing and crumble or dice and sauté until cooked through.
- Beat eggs into milk in a bowl.
- Make a slit in the center of each challah slice and fill with merguez and goat cheese.
- Dip each side of bread in egg mixture.
- Heat olive oil on a pan and fry in each side until golden brown.
- Serve sprinkled with powdered sugar, fresh mint, a sliced almonds and drizzles with citrus syrup.
- Citrus syrup
- Combine ingredients and bring to a boil, stirring.
- Cook until reduced to syrup.

190.　　　Mini Beet Wellingtons

Serving: Makes 4 servings | Prep: | Cook: | Ready in:

Ingredients

- Beets
- 4 large beets, peeled
- 2 tablespoons unsaltdd butter, melted
- kosher salt and freshly ground black pepper
- Coating + Wellington

- 12 ounces goat cheese
- 6 ounces gorgonzola dulce
- 1 bunch chives, minced
- 8 ounces smoked almonds, very finely chopped
- 14 ounces prepared puff pastry, (thawed if previously frozen)
- egg wash, as needed

Direction

- Preheat the oven to 400° F. In a large bowl, toss the peeled beets with the melted butter. Season each beet with salt and pepper, then wrap in foil. Transfer to a baking sheet and then to the oven. Roast the beets until just barely fork tender, 40-45 minutes.
- Unwrap the beets and let cool completely. Raise the oven temperature to 425° F, and line a baking sheet with parchment paper.
- In a medium bowl, stir the goat cheese, gorgonzola, and chives to combine. Divide the cheese mixture into 4 even portions, and use your hands to press the mixture in an even layer around each beet.
- Roll each cheese-coated beet in the finely chopped nuts. Refrigerate the beets while you prepare the pastry.
- On a lightly floured surface, roll out each piece the puff pastry to 1/4-inch thick. Once the dough is rolled out, cut it into 4 large circles, large enough to fully wrap the beets in pastry.
- Working with one beet at a time, wrap the beet in pastry, using a small amount of egg wash to seal the pastry together at the base. Use scissors to trim away and discard any excess dough.
- Transfer the wrapped beet to the prepared baking sheet, and repeat with the remaining beets and pastry.
- If desired, you can score the top of the pastry with a paring knife to create a decorative pattern. For a sharper look, egg wash the pastry before you score it – the score marks will be paler than the surface of the pastry and the pattern will be very clear! For a more even look, score the pastry after scoring it – the

pattern will be subtler and the pastry will be evenly golden brown. Use the tip of a sharp paring knife to barely score the surface of the dough without cutting fully through it – create any design you like!

- Transfer to the oven and bake until the pastry is golden brown and fully baked through, and the beets are very tender when pierced, 25-30 minutes. Let rest for 5-10 minutes before slicing and serving.

191.   Minted Summer Succotash

Serving: Serves 4 to 6 | Prep: | Cook: |Ready in:

Ingredients

- 1/2 pound green beans (both haricot verts or Romano work well), trimmed and snapped in halves or thirds
- 2 tablespoons sherry or red wine vinegar, or more to taste
- 4 tablespoons extra virgin olive oil, or more to taste
- 8 ounces dried Christmas lima beans, cooked according to package instructions (regular lima beans can be substituted)
- 1 1/2 cups cherry tomatoes, halved
- 2 cups fresh corn kernels (from about 3 ears)
- 1 tablespoon fresh chives, coarsely chopped
- 3 tablespoons fresh mint, coarsely chopped
- 1 cup goat cheese, crumbled
- Kosher salt and freshly ground black pepper
- Lime wedges, for serving

Direction

- Bring a large pot of water to a boil and prepare an ice bath in a large bowl. Add a generous amount of kosher salt, then the beans. Cook until tender but still slightly crisp in the middle (about 2 to 3 minutes for haricot verts and slightly longer for Romano beans).

Transfer to the ice bath to stop the cooking and lock in the color. Drain and set aside.

- Place vinegar in a small bowl, then gradually whisk in oil.
- In a large bowl, combine green beans, Christmas limas, cherry tomatoes, corn, chives, mint, and 3/4 cup goat cheese. Pour dressing over salad, a little at a time, tasting as you go. Toss to coat. Season with kosher salt and pepper. Garnish with remaining 1/4 cup goat cheese. Serve at room temperature, with lime wedges on the side.

192.   Minted Zucchini Soup

Serving: Serves 4 | Prep: | Cook: |Ready in:

Ingredients

- 4 zucchini
- 2 shallots, chopped
- 1/2 yellow onion, chopped
- 4 cups low sodium chicken or vegetable broth
- 1/3 cup fresh mint leaves
- 5 ounces fresh baby spinach
- 1 lemon, juiced
- 1/2-1 teaspoons salt
- 1/4 teaspoon ground black pepper, plus more to serve
- goat cheese or yogurt, to serve
- mint, torn into pieces, to serve

Direction

- Throw zucchini, shallots, onion and broth into a pot and bring to a boil. Once boiled, turn heat to medium-low and simmer until vegetables are soft.
- Stir in mint leaves, spinach, lemon, salt and pepper. Purée in blender or with an immersion blender. Adjust lemon, salt and pepper.
- Serve immediately and top with goat cheese or yogurt, pepper and a sprinkling of torn mint. (Great cold too!)

193. Mission Fig Rolls

Serving: Serves 6 | Prep: | Cook: | Ready in:

Ingredients

- 1/2 pound prossuto de parma
- 1 packet fresh arugula
- 1/2 pound mission figs
- 4 ounces goat cheese
- 1 pinch salt
- 1 pinch fresh ground pepper
- 1/4 cup light olive oil

Direction

- Cut the stems of the figs and cut them into quarters lengthwise
- Using a cutting board, carefully spread a slice of prosciutto at a time
- Add few leaves of arugula in one end of the slice allowing it to come out a bit from the prosciutto
- Using 2 teaspoons for scooping and scraping goat cheese which can be a bit sticky, scoop approximately 1 teaspoon of goat cheese on top of the arugula; you may also use plane dental floss
- Add about 4 quarters of figs spreading it evenly on top of the cheese
- Sprinkle fresh ground pepper and drizzle olive oil
- Using both hands, start rolling the prosciutto tightly without squeezing ingredients out
- Repeat process until you run out of prosciutto
- Place them in a platter and sprinkle more pepper and olive and enjoy!

194. Mixed Greens Salad With Warm Goat Cheese Rounds And Balsamic Vinaigrette

Serving: Serves 2 | Prep: | Cook: | Ready in:

Ingredients

- For the Salad
- 5 ounces mixed leaf lettuce
- 1 small cucumber, sliced lengthwise, then cut into 1/4" pieces
- 2 small tomatoes, diced
- 2/3 cup Balsamic Vinaigrette, preferably homemade
- 2 ounces pecan or walnut halves (optional)
- 1 ounce butter (optional)
- 1 ounce brown sugar (optional)
- For the Goat Cheese Rounds
- 6 1/2" slices of goat cheese (log type)
- 1 egg, beaten
- 1/2 cup breadcrumbs, preferably homemade
- 2 pinches of Herbes de Provence
- 2 pinches of dried parsley
- 2 pinches of dried thyme
- 1/8 teaspoon salt
- black pepper, as desired
- 1 tablespoon light olive oil

Direction

- Place the lettuce, cucumber and tomatoes in two large bowls or plates in which you will serve the salads.
- (This step is optional if you prefer no nuts in the salad) In a non-stick sauté pan, cook the pecans or walnuts, butter and brown sugar over medium low heat until caramelized. Remove from heat and place the nuts on aluminum foil to cool.
- Next, mix the breadcrumbs, Herbes de Provence, parsley, thyme, salt and pepper and place in a bowl. Dip the goat cheese slices in the beaten egg, then the breadcrumb mixture and set aside. Heat the olive oil in a nonstick pan over medium heat, then add the breaded goat cheese rounds. Cook until browned, and

gently turn to brown the other side. If the heat is too low, the goat cheese will melt before becoming brown. Remove from pan.

- Place 1 to 3 warm goat cheese rounds on top of each salad, sprinkle with the caramelized nuts, if using, and serve immediately, drizzled with balsamic vinaigrette.
- TIP: The nuts can be made ahead of time and kept in a tin. The goat cheese can also be prepped ahead of time and kept refrigerated until the salad is ready to be assembled and served. This salad goes well with warm crusty Italian bread or rolls.

195.   Morel Crostini

Serving: Serves 4 to 6 | Prep: | Cook: | Ready in:

Ingredients

- 1 fresh baguette, sliced thin
- 1 splash extra-virgin olive oil
- 3 tablespoons butter
- 6 ounces fresh morels, cleaned and sliced lengthwise
- 2 teaspoons fresh thyme leaves
- Salt and freshly ground black pepper, to taste
- 3/4 cup thinly sliced leeks, white and pale green parts only
- 1 teaspoon fresh lemon juice
- 2 tablespoons Italian flat-leaf parsley
- 1 package of goat cheese, to taste

Direction

- MAKE THE TOAST: Preheat oven to 350° F. Place sliced bread on a baking sheet. Brush each piece with olive oil. Bake until bread is lightly toasted, 10 to 15 minutes. Arrange toast on a serving tray.
- SAUTÉ THE MORELS: In a large skillet, melt butter over medium-high heat. Add morels and sauté 2 to 3 minutes. Add thyme and season with salt and pepper. Sauté until morels are tender, about 3 minutes.

- SEASON: Add leeks to mushrooms and sauté until soft, 3 to 4 minutes more. Stir in the lemon juice and parsley. Season to taste with salt and pepper.
- ASSEMBLE AND SERVE: Pour mixture into a serving bowl and then place the bowl on top of the serving tray with the toast. Place goat cheese on the tray. Let everyone assemble their own crostini: Smear a bit of goat cheese on toast, then top with a spoonful of morels.

196.   Mucho Salad

Serving: Serves 4-6 | Prep: | Cook: | Ready in:

Ingredients

- Maple-Orange Vinaigrette
- 1/2 cup orange juice
- 2 tablespoons pure maple syrup
- 1/4 cup lemon juice
- 2 teaspoons dijon mustard
- 6 tablespoons peanut or canola oil
- salt and pepper, to taste
- Salad
- 8 cups Romaine or Mixed Greens
- 2 tomatoes, cut into large pieces
- 1/2 cup red cabbage, finely sliced
- 1 cup frozen roasted corn kernels, thawed
- 2 avocadoes, cut in large chunks
- 6 medjool dates, cut each into 3-4 pieces
- 1/2 cup almonds, toasted & coarsely chopped
- 4 ounces goat cheese, crumbled
- 2-3 cups roaster chicken, cut into large chunks

Direction

- Maple-Orange Vinaigrette
- Place the orange juice & maple syrup in a small saucepan and bring to a boil. Reduce the heat & simmer until reduced to about 1/3 cup. 15-20 minutes
- Salad

- Preheat oven to 350 degrees. Place almonds on a baking sheet & toast for about 10-12 minutes. Cool & coarsely chop
- Put the lettuce in a large Salad bowl. Top with chicken, tomato, cabbage, corn, avocado, dates, toasted almonds & goat cheese. Do not toss.
- Drizzle generously with Maple-Orange Vinaigrette. You may not use all of the dressing.

197. Mushroom & Goat's Cheese Tart Diabetes.co.uk

Serving: Serves 6 | Prep: | Cook: | Ready in:

Ingredients

- 250 grams Cream Cheese
- 100 grams Soft Goats Cheese
- 2 teaspoons Rosemary
- 250 grams Filo Pastry
- 50 grams extra-virgin olive oil
- Salt and Freshly Ground Pepper

Direction

- Preheat the oven to 200°c of Gas Mark 6.
- Then mix the cream cheese, goat's cheese, fresh rosemary and pepper in a bowl and set aside.
- Heat the butter in a big pan on medium-high heat and add the onions, mushrooms and salt. Cook for around 3 minutes until the onion softens and the juices from the mushrooms are released; this ought to take approximately 4 minutes. Then place aside.
- Next line a large baking sheet (approximately 12 by 17 inches) with greaseproof paper. Place a large sheet of filo pastry on the tray. Lightly oil the sheet with a pastry brush. Repeat this process and layer the rest of the filo pastry sheets on top.
- Spread the cheese mixture evenly over the filo pastry and spoon the mushroom mixture on

top. Carefully roll around 3/4 inch of each side of the tart towards the center to create the outer rim of the tart.
- Bake the tart until the crust is brown and crispy, 25 to 30 minutes. Allow the tart to cool down on the tray on a wire rack for several minutes.
- To serve, lift up the parchment paper and slide the tart onto a sizeable platter. Ideally serve this tart warm as filo pastry can lose its texture when cold.

198. Mushroom Toast With Goat Cheese, Parmesan, Shallot, Garlic & Herbs

Serving: Serves 2 | Prep: 0hours10mins | Cook: 0hours20mins | Ready in:

Ingredients

- 1 10oz bag sliced crimini mushrooms
- 2 small shallots, or 1 large, thinly sliced
- 1 clove garlic, minced
- 1 splash grapeseed oil
- salt & pepper for seasoning
- 1 splash white wine
- 2 sourdough slices
- 1/3 cup goat cheese, +/- to personal taste
- 1/2 cup freshly grated parmesan
- 1 bunch fresh herbs to garnish (parsley), chopped
- 1-2 tablespoons butter

Direction

- Pour a splash of grape seed oil into a non-stick sauté pan that's been warmed to medium-medium high. Add mushrooms, season with salt and pepper, stir occasionally, cook for 4 minutes. Add the garlic, stir, and cook for 1 minute. Add splash of wine, stir, and when it's beginning to cook out add a pat or two of butter. Once that tightens and is no longer watery then remove pan from heat

- While mushrooms cook, toast 2 slices of sourdough bread in a toaster, then smear with desired amount of goat cheese. Pile toasts with mushroom mixture and top with freshly grated parmesan. Place on middle rack in a pre-heated oven with broiler set to high. Watch closely, broil about a minute, remove when cheese is melted (or if desired let parmesan crisp and start to brown then remove). Top with chopped parsley and serve

199. Mushroom, Goat Cheese And Brown Rice Risotto

Serving: Serves 2 as a main dish, 4-6 as a starter or side | Prep: | Cook: | Ready in:

Ingredients

- 5-6 cups mushroom and/or chicken broth (I used 4 c mushroom and 1 c chicken)
- 3 tablespoons butter, divided
- 5 ounces mushrooms (preferably a blend of type), washed and coarsely chopped
- 2 tablespoons 1 tsp extra-virgin olive oil, divided
- 1/3 cup shallots, finely chopped
- 1 tablespoon fresh marjoram, chopped (plus more for garnish if you like)
- 2 teaspoons fresh mint, chopped
- 1½ cups long grain brown jasmine rice
- 1/4 teaspoon salt
- 1/2 cup good quality dry white wine
- 1¼ ounces young goat cheese

Direction

- Pour the broth in a saucepan, cover and set over medium-high heat. Bring to a solid simmer and keep it that way. In a 10" skillet, put 2 T of butter. Melt and then brown it. When brown, put a third or so of your mushrooms. Don't crowd them; in fact, don't let them touch. When they're golden and just cooked through, about 2-3 minutes (flip

during that time), remove them with tongs or a slotted spoon to a plate. Repeat with the remaining mushrooms (you shouldn't need to add more butter). When the mushrooms are done, set them aside.

- In the same skillet (don't wipe it out), pour 2 T of olive oil. Because the skillet is already warm, it should heat up quickly. Add the shallots, marjoram and mint, stir to combine, and remove the skillet from heat. Set aside.
- In a 4 quart saucepan, add the remaining 1 T of butter and 1 tsp of olive oil. Heat over medium-high until the butter is melted. Add the rice and stir to combine. Cook 2-3 minutes, until the rice is nice and toasty. Add the salt and white wine and stir.
- When the wine looks to be almost totally gone, add the broth, ½ c at a time, stirring fairly continuously and adding the next ½ c only when there looks to be just a tiny bit of liquid remaining in the rice. After you've added 2 c of broth, stir in the shallot-herb mixture. Continue adding the broth. When you have added 4½ cups of broth, stir in 2/3 of your browned mushrooms, reserving the remaining third for garnishing the finished risotto. After you've added 5 cups of broth total, check the doneness of the rice. If it's still too al dente for you, add another ½ c of broth and then check again.
- When it's done to your liking, stir in the goat cheese until it's well-incorporated. Spoon risotto into bowls, and top with remaining mushrooms and a sprig of marjoram if you want. Serve immediately.

200. Nettle Tortellini In Brodo

Serving: Serves 4 | Prep: | Cook: | Ready in:

Ingredients

- 3 cups fresh nettle leaves (packed fairly tightly, some stems are OK)
- 2 teaspoons salt

- 1/4 cup pine nuts
- 2   garlic cloves
- black pepper and salt
- 2 tablespoons olive oil
- 6 ounces crumbled goat cheese
- 30-40   round wonton wrappers
- 6 cups chicken broth (or veggie broth or water)
- fresh lemon juice
- fresh mint leaves, shredded
- good quality olive oil

Direction

- Wearing gloves, rinse your nettles well in a colander. Look for any stowaways or stray weeds.
- Bring about 3-4 quarts of water and salt to a boil. Using tongs, grab bunches of nettles and submerge them in the water. Blanch for about 20-30 seconds. Remove nettles and drain in a colander and reserve about 2 cups of the nettle cooking water (optional).
- Once they're cool enough to handle, squeeze out as much water as you can with your bare hands (you don't need gloves anymore!). Add the nettles, pine nuts, garlic, salt and pepper and olive oil to a food processor and process until fairly smooth. Remove to a bowl and stir in goat cheese until it's fully incorporated and you don't see any white streaks.
- Set up a work space with your wonton wrappers, nettle filling and a little dish of water. Also have a baking sheet and a tea towel nearby so you can set your completed tortellini on the sheet and keep them covered with a towel while you work.
- Take one wonton wrapper and drop a scant teaspoon of the filling onto the center. Dab the edge of the circle with water. Fold the wrapper in half and you now have a semi-circle. Press your finger into the middle of the bottom of the semi-circle and bring the two corners together. Press firmly and look at that: tortellini! Continue with the rest of the tortellini.

- In a large pot (4+ quarts) bring to boil the reserved nettle water and chicken broth (or water). Drop about half the tortellini in the water and cook at a low boil for about 5 minutes. You don't want them to get too crowded so you may have to work in smaller batches depending on how large your pot is. Remove tortellini and repeat with the remaining ones.
- Equally divide tortellini and broth among 4 bowls, top with a squeeze of fresh lemon, a sprinkling of shredded fresh mint leaves and a drizzle of very good olive oil. Buon appetito!

---

201.   No Bake Goat's Cheese And Roasted Peppers Cheesecake

Serving: Makes 4 individual cheesecakes | Prep: | Cook: | Ready in:

Ingredients

- For the Parmesan shortbreads (makes 25-30 5cm/2in. shortbreads)
- 100 grams / 3½ oz / ⅔ cup flour
- 75 grams / 1 cup grated Parmesan
- 100 grams / 3½ oz / ½ cup (minus 1 tbsp) cold unsalted butter
- 1 teaspoon mustard powder
- a pinches Cayenne pepper or smoked paprika
- 1   egg, beaten
- For the cheesecake
- 400 grams / 14 oz fresh goat's cheese
- 2-3 tablespoons fresh basil leaves, chopped
- 2   red pepper bells
- 2   yellow pepper bells
- 2 tablespoons olive oil
- 1 tablespoon balsamic vinegar
- 4 tablespoons sun-dried tomato tapenade or pesto rosso (optional)

Direction

- For the shortbreads: Place all the ingredients in a food processor. Process together for about a minute, until the mixture resemble coarse breadcrumbs, then pulse in short spurts. The dough will eventually bind. Wrap in food wrap and leave to chill in the fridge for at least 30 minutes. Preheat your oven to 180°C/350°F and grease or line 1 or 2 baking sheets with baking parchment. Lightly flour your work surface and gently roll out the pastry to about 5mm/0.2 in thickness. Cut out the biscuits to the size and shape you wish - anything between 3cm/1¼in and 5cm/2in. Lay them out on the baking sheets about 2cm/¾in apart. Carefully brush the surface of each biscuit with the egg. Bake for 10 minutes, or until golden brown. Carefully lift the biscuits off the tray using a palette knife and place on a rack to cool. Store in an air-tight container for a few days … if that's possible!
- For the cheesecake: Preheat your oven to 220°C/425°F and line a baking sheet with aluminum foil. Place your peppers under the grill, turning them regularly until roasted all over, about 45 minutes. As soon as the peppers are out of the oven, place them in a Zip-top back, zip the bag and leave to cool for about 15 minutes. Remove the peppers from the bag and, using your fingers, peel them carefully and remove the stem and seeds, then slice them thinly. Place the peppers in a bowl with the olive oil and vinegar, toss lightly and leave to marinate for about 15 minutes. In a bowl, combine the goat's cheese and chopped basil. If the mixture is too dense, add a little olive oil. Season to taste.
- To assemble: In a bowl, or using a pestle and mortar, crush the shortbreads – you will need 4 or 5 per person. Place a 9cm/3.5 in pastry circle on a plate and press the shortbread crumbs in. If using tomato tapenade, add 1 tbsp. and spread it evenly across the shortbread base. Top with ¼ of the cheese mixture, then ¼ of the marinated peppers. Carefully remove the pastry circle and repeat to make the other cheesecakes. Decorate with basil leaves and olives (optional).

---

202. No Churn Strawberry Cheesecake Ice Cream

Serving: Makes one 9x13-inch baking pan | Prep: 6hours30mins | Cook: 0hours0mins |Ready in:

Ingredients

- 1 pound ripe strawberries, hulled and quartered
- 1 tablespoon granulated sugar
- 1 (14-ounce) can sweetened condensed milk
- 1/2 teaspoon kosher salt, plus 1/4 teaspoon
- 2 1/4 cups very cold heavy cream, plus 6 tablespoons
- 2 (4-ounce) packages of Cypress Grove Purple Haze goat cheese (note: Ms. Natural works really well here, too)
- 1/2 cup confectioners' sugar
- 1/2 cup roughly smashed Nilla Wafer crumbs, or cookie crumbs of your choice

Direction

- Mash the strawberries well in a large bowl — aim for as smooth as possible to avoid icy chunks in the ice cream — and mix in the sugar. Let sit 5 minutes, then add the sweetened condensed milk and 1/2 teaspoon salt. Combine with a spatula.
- In another bowl or in a stand mixer, whip 2 1/4 cups heavy cream until stiff peaks form.
- Use a spatula to transfer about 1/4 cup of whipped cream to the strawberry–sweetened condensed milk mixture, and gently fold to loosen it up. Add another blob of whipped cream, and gently fold to incorporate. Keep doing this with a heaping half-cup of whipped cream at a time, until you've folded in all the whipped cream. (It's better to under-mix than over-mix, for fluffier ice cream.)
- Pour into a 9- x 13-inch baking pan, cover with plastic wrap, and put in the freezer. Set a timer for 1 hour.

- In a food processor or blender, combine goat cheese, remaining 6 tablespoons heavy cream, confectioners' sugar, and 1/4 teaspoon kosher salt. Blend until smooth and creamy, stopping to scrape down the sides as needed — it should be between loose yogurt and frosting in consistency.
- After the ice cream has been in the freezer for an hour, take it out and pull back the plastic wrap. Spoon the cheese mixture in lines over the top, so it's evenly distributed. Do the same with the cookie crumbs. Use a spoon to gently swirl the cheese and crumbs into the ice cream. Cover with plastic wrap and put back in the freezer for at least 5 hours.
- Before scooping, let it soften at room temperature for about 10 minutes.

203.   Not Your Same Ole' Bruschetta

Serving: Makes 10 bruschetta rounds | Prep: | Cook: | Ready in:

Ingredients

- 1/4 cup goat cheese
- 2 cups cherry tomatoes, quartered
- 1/2 french baguette
- 2 garlic cloves, minced
- 2 tablespoons olive oil
- 1/4 teaspoon salt
- 1.4 teaspoons pepper
- 4 fresh basil leaves, minced

Direction

- Turn oven broiler on (500 degrees F)
- Quarter tomatoes and add to mixing bowl
- Mix olive oil, salt, pepper, garlic and basil in another small bowl and pour olive oil mixture over tomatoes
- Stir in goat cheese with wooden spoon and place in fridge to chill

- Slice baguette into 1/4 inch rounds (roughly 10 slices) and place on baking sheet and broil in oven until browned
- Top crostini with chilled bruschetta mixture

204.   Oatmeal And Lavender Shortbread With Whipped Goat Cheese And Lemon Coulis

Serving: Serves 4-6 | Prep: | Cook: | Ready in:

Ingredients

- For the cookies
- 1 ¼ cups rolled oats, gently toasted
- 8 tablespoons (1 stick) butter, softened
- 1/2 cup all purpose flour
- 1/4 cup sugar
- 1 teaspoon salt (I like my shortbreads on the salty side, if you do not start with 1/2 tsp)
- 3/4 tablespoon dry lavender flowers
- For the whipped goat cheese and couils
- 4 ounces goat cheese, at room temperature
- 3 tablespoons creme fraiche
- Juice and zest of one lemon
- 1/2 cup good quality extra virgin olive oil
- 1/4 cup brown sugar
- A pinch of salt

Direction

- Preheat the oven to 325°F convection (or 350°F regular bake). Toast the oats for about 10 minutes. Let the oats cool completely and then process in a food processor, until powdery.
- Beat the butter with sugar until creamy. Stir in the oats, flour, salt and lavender. Mix on low speed until the dough comes together. Scrape the dough out onto a work surface and pat it into a log 1 1/4 inches in diameter. Wrap up the log in plastic wrap and refrigerate until very firm, about 2 hours.
- Preheat the oven to 325°F convection (or 350°F regular bake). Slice the dough into 1/4-inch-

thick slices and arrange on baking sheet lined with parchment paper. Prick the top of the shortbreads with a fork. Bake for about 20 minutes, or until golden (somehow, for a lot of cookies in my oven I found 22 minutes to be the magic number). Slide the parchment onto a wire rack and let the shortbreads cool. (The shortbreads can be kept in an airtight container for about a week.)

- To make the whipped goat cheese, beat the goat cheese and crème fraiche until light and fluffy (if needed add a bit more crème fraiche).
- To make the coulis, in a small bowl (or mini-blender) combine the lemon juice, lemon zest, brown sugar, olive oil and salt. Blend until emulsified. Refrigerate for about an hour or two.
- Remove the coulis from the refrigerator and mix well. Place 4-5 cookies on a plate next to a scoop of whipped goat cheese. Top generously with the coulis and serve.

205.   Olive CHA! Penade Goat Cheese Spread

Serving: Serves 1 tbsp-- yeild 1 cup | Prep: | Cook: | Ready in:

Ingredients

- 3/4 cup Goat cheese, whipped
- 1/4 cup Olive tapenade
- 1 tablespoon CHA! by Texas Pete
- 1   Salt and Pepper -- TO TASTE

Direction

- Place the goat cheese into a small mixing bowl and lightly whip the cheese.
- Add the olive tapenade, CHA! by Texas Pete® and a pinch of salt and pepper and mix well.
- Place in an airtight storage container and keep refrigerated until ready to use.

206.   Olive Pizza

Serving: Serves two or more | Prep: | Cook: | Ready in:

Ingredients

- Pizza Dough
- 2 1/2 cups all-purpose flour (about 11.25 oz., or 319 grams; I use King Arthur All-Purpose Unbleached)
- 1 1/2 teaspoons kosher salt
- 3/4 teaspoon active dry yeast (not rapid rise), or 3 grams fresh yeast (about a dime-size ball)
- 8 ounces or 227 grams lukewarm water
- 1/4 cup olive oil
- Olive Pizza
- Pizza dough, about 10 ounces
- 1/2 cup whole milk ricotta cheese (you may need a little more or a little less, depending on the size of your pizza)
- grated zest of half a lemon
- 1/2 cup pitted and chopped oil-cured olives
- about 2 ounces goat cheese
- 1/4 cup red onion, sliced thin
- 2   sprigs fresh thyme
- olive oil
- salt and pepper
- crushed red pepper flakes

Direction

- Pizza Dough
- These instructions are for a stand mixer, but you can do it all by hand, if you so choose. In the bowl of a stand mixer fitted with the paddle attachment, mix flour and salt together.
- Dissolve yeast into warm water. Stir in the oil. With mixer on low speed, pour the liquid into the flour until dough comes together.
- Scrape off the paddle and switch to the dough hook. Knead for 5 or so minutes.
- Scrape mixer bowl and hook, and gather dough into a ball. Place in a well-oiled bowl. Cover bowl tightly with plastic wrap, lay a dish towel over it and place in a warm spot,

like in the microwave. Sometimes, before putting the dough in, I heat a mug-full of water, to get the microwave nice and warm.

- Let rise for 1 hour. Punch dough down, and let rise for another hour.
- This step is totally optional, but worth it if you have all day. Punch dough down again and let rise for 2 - 3 more hours. Alternatively, you can stash the dough in the fridge overnight after the first rise. Bring refrigerated dough to room temperature about an hour before forming pizzas.
- Olive Pizza
- Place a pizza stone on bottom-most rack in oven. Preheat oven to BROIL HIGH at least a half hour before you will bake the pizza.
- Cut dough from above pizza dough recipe into two equal pieces, about 10 ounces each, weighing it with a kitchen scale if you have one. Place the second piece of dough in a freezer bag and freeze, or make a second pizza of your choosing.
- Flatten dough very slightly, and fold in top, bottom, left side, right side, towards center. Turn over, and gently form into a round. Place on lightly floured parchment-lined sheet pan, sprinkle with flour and cover with a kitchen towel. Let rest 10 minutes.
- Lightly oil (just a dab to keep the paper in place) a 12" pizza pan. Line with a piece of parchment paper, and lightly dust paper with flour. Place dough on paper. Dust dough lightly with flour and press down with your fingertips as you turn the pie and spread the dough evenly in all directions until you have a nice thin layer, about 1/4" thick. It probably won't cover the entire pan; that's okay. If dough is not cooperating, it helps to let the dough rest for a few minutes.
- Alternatively, flour your fists very well, and the ball of dough. Stretch dough over your fists and move your fists along the outside edge of the dough, stretching it out. Lay the dough on parchment-lined pizza pan. Tug edges slightly to form a rough circle.
- Spread ricotta onto pizza dough with a small offset spatula if you have one, leaving about a

½ inch border. Sprinkle the lemon zest over. Scatter the olives over the ricotta. Next, shower your red onion slices over the top. Then, spoon little nuggets of goat cheese over. Strip the thyme leaves off of the sprig and sprinkle over the pizza. Lastly, just a touch of salt and pepper, a drizzle of olive oil, and your pizza is ready to bake!

- Place pan directly on pizza stone. Or, if you've got a pizza peel, pull the parchment and pizza onto the peel, then slide parchment and pizza directly onto pizza stone. TURN HEAT TO 550 DEGREES F. Bake for 5 minutes, or until crust is nicely browned and crisp, and bottom of pizza has some nicely browned spots as well. Use a long-handled metal spatula or metal tongs, or the pizza peel, to lift up the pizza and take a peek underneath. The parchment will turn black, but it won't catch fire, so don't worry.
- Remove from oven. Add a touch more salt, a drizzle of oil, and a sprinkle of red pepper flakes if desired. Cut into pieces with kitchen shears and enjoy!

---

207.   Oma's Bavarian Cheesecake Bites

Serving: Makes 20 bite size pieces | Prep: | Cook: | Ready in:

Ingredients

- Base
- 1 1/2 sticks unsalted butter, cubed
- 2 large eggs
- 1/3 cup granulated sugar
- 2/3 cup all-purpose flour
- 1 teaspoon baking powder
- 1 vanilla bean cut length wise and scraped
- Cheesecake
- 3 large eggs, separated. set egg yolks aside and beat egg whites until stiff, chill
- 1 pound cream cheese, cubed

- 1 vanilla bean cut length wise and scraped
- 1/2 teaspoon fresh lemon juice
- 1 small handful lemon zest
- 1/2 cup granulated sugar
- 1 package vanilla sauce mix
- 1 12 oz log goat cheese, cubed

Direction

- Preheat oven to 325 degrees Fahrenheit. In a bowl, cream butter, 2 eggs and 1/3 cup sugar until fluffy. Add half of flour, mix well. Add remaining flour, baking powder and 1 vanilla bean. Mix until smooth. Pour mixture into a greased spring form pan.
- In a separate bowl, cream 3 egg yolks, cream cheese, 1 vanilla bean, lemon juice, lemon zest, 1/2 cup sugar, vanilla sauce mix and goat cheese. Mix until smooth. Gently fold in 3 chilled egg whites. Pour on top of base and bake 50 minutes. Let cool and refrigerate overnight. Before serving, cut into bite size pieces.

---

208. One Pot Kale & Quinoa Pilaf

Serving: Serves 2 to 4 | Prep: 0hours15mins | Cook: 0hours30mins | Ready in:

Ingredients

- 2 cups salted water
- 1 cup quinoa
- 1 bunch lacinato kale, washed and chopped into 1" lengths
- 1 meyer lemon, zested and juiced
- 2 scallions, minced
- 1 tablespoon toasted walnut oil
- 3 tablespoons toasted pine nuts
- 1/4 cup crumbled goat cheese
- Salt and pepper

Direction

- Bring the water to a boil in a covered pot. Add the quinoa, cover, and lower the heat until it is just enough to maintain a simmer. Let simmer for 10 minutes, then top with the kale and re-cover. Simmer another 5 minutes, then turn off the heat and allow to steam for 5 more minutes.
- While the quinoa is cooking, take a large serving bowl and combine half of the lemon juice (reserving the other half), all of the lemon zest, scallions, walnut oil (you can substitute olive oil if you desire), pine nuts, and goat cheese.
- Check the quinoa and kale when the cooking time has completed — the water should have absorbed, and the quinoa will be tender but firm, and the kale tender and bright green. If the quinoa still has a hard white center, you can steam a bit longer (adding more water if needed). When the quinoa and kale are done, fluff the pilaf, and tip it into the waiting bowl with the remaining ingredients. As the hot quinoa hits the scallions and lemon it should smell lovely. Toss to combine, seasoning with salt and pepper, and the remaining lemon juice if needed.

---

209. Orecchiette With Roasted Butternut Squash, Kale, And Caramelized Red Onion

Serving: Serves 4 | Prep: 0hours15mins | Cook: 1hours0mins | Ready in:

Ingredients

- 1 large butternut squash, cut into small cubes, divided
- 4 tablespoons olive oil, divided
- Salt and pepper, for seasoning
- 1 pinch cayenne pepper
- 1/4 teaspoon nutmeg
- 1 red onion, sliced thinly
- 1/2 pound orecchiette

- 1 or 2 large cloves garlic, minced
- 2 cups chicken broth, divided
- 1 bunch kale
- 1/2 cup white wine
- 1/2 cup heavy cream
- 1 ounce goat cheese, optional
- 1 tablespoon chopped sage
- parmesan cheese, to serve

Direction

- Preheat oven to 425° F. Toss all but 1 cup of the butternut squash with 1 tablespoon olive oil, salt, pepper, a pinch of cayenne pepper, and the nutmeg. Roast until butternut squash pieces are tender and caramelized, about 30 minutes. Set aside.
- Heat 1 tablespoon olive oil in a medium saucepan over low heat. Cook sliced red onions until caramelized, about 30 minutes. Set aside.
- Heat a pot of water over high heat until boiling. Salt water generously. Cook orecchiette according to package instructions until al dente.
- Meanwhile, heat another tablespoon of olive oil in a heavy pan over medium-high heat. Cook the remaining cup of butternut squash for approximately 3 minutes. Add garlic and cook for another minute. Add 1/2 cup of the chicken broth and cook until broth is almost completely absorbed.
- Remove the middle stems from the kale and roughly chop the leaves. Add kale to butternut squash and stir until kale has softened. Add caramelized red onions.
- Add white wine and cook for 2 minutes. Add remaining chicken broth and reduce, about 10 minutes.
- Turn heat to low and add the heavy cream. When the pasta is al dente, add it to the pan with the sauce. Add the roasted butternut squash.
- Loosen sauce with pasta water if needed. Sprinkle with goat cheese (optional), sage, and Parmesan cheese.

210. Orzo Salad With Scallions, Hazelnuts, And Golden Raisins

Serving: Makes 1 quart | Prep: | Cook: | Ready in:

Ingredients

- 1/2 cup hazelnuts
- 1/2 cup red wine vinegar
- 1/2 cup golden raisins
- 1 cup orzo
- 1 lime, juiced
- 2 tablespoons rice wine vinegar
- 2 tablespoons champagne vinegar
- Kosher salt
- 1/4 cup sesame oil
- 2 tablespoons good olive oil, plus more for coating the orzo
- 6 scallions
- Small handful of chives
- 1/4 teaspoon red pepper flakes
- 2 ounces fresh goat cheese
- 1/4 teaspoon flaky sea salt

Direction

- Heat the oven to 350° F. Scatter the hazelnuts across a baking sheet, then put in the oven for 10 minutes. Take them out and allow them to cool, then remove the skins. Leave the nuts whole, or roughly chop them -- however you prefer. Set aside.
- Bring the red wine vinegar and 1/2 cup of water to a healthy simmer. Add the raisins and turn down the heat to low. Cover, then cook for 10 minutes. Turn off the heat and allow the raisins to sit in the vinegar solution for an additional 20 minutes. Drain the raisins and set them aside.
- Bring a pot of water to a rolling boil, then add enough kosher salt to make the water taste like the sea. Add the orzo to the pot and cook until al dente (for me, this was consistently 2 minutes less than the bag recommended).

Drain the orzo, transfer to a bowl, and stir in a bit of olive oil -- just enough so that the pasta doesn't stick. Allow the orzo to cool for 20 to 30 minutes.

- Make the dressing: Add the lime juice, rice wine vinegar, and champagne vinegar to a small bowl. Whisk in a little pinch of kosher salt. Add the sesame oil and 2 tablespoons of olive oil. Whisk the dressing to emulsify the oil, then set aside.
- Clean and thinly slice the whites and light greens of the scallions. Mince the chives.
- Stir the red pepper flakes into the orzo. Add the hazelnuts, raisins, scallions, and chives. Fold in the dressing. Stir in the sea salt. Using a fork, break up the goat cheese, then crumble it into the bowl and lightly fold to combine. Serve chilled or at room temperature. Author's Note: If you are eating the salad fresh, I think 1/2 cup of dressing is sufficient. I usually save the remaining 1/4 cup for just before serving, especially if I make the salad ahead of time. But add the dressing bit by bit, then stop when it tastes right to you.

211. Orzotto With Spring Ramps & Goat Cheese

Serving: Serves 2 | Prep: | Cook: |Ready in:

Ingredients

- 24 Ramps
- 1 quart water
- 1 tablespoon salt
- 1/2 pound orzo
- 3 tablespoons unsalted butter
- zest of 1/2 lemon
- black pepper
- 3 ounces goat cheese - crumbled

Direction

- Bring 1 quart of salted water to a boil.

- Meanwhile separate the bulb end of the ramps from the leafy green part. Save the bulbs ends for another use. Roll the leaves and cut them into a chiffonade.
- When the water is boiling add the orzo, reduce the heat to medium-low to gently boil for 10 minutes, stirring occasionally until the water is almost all absorbed. Add the ramps and stir until wilted. Stir in the ramp butter. Using a micro plane, add the zest of 1/2 a lemon and several grinds of black pepper.
- Transfer to serving plates and top with crumbled goat cheese.

212. Panzanella Salad

Serving: Serves 4 | Prep: | Cook: |Ready in:

Ingredients

- Bread
- 2 1/2 cups of a nice french baguette, cut into 2 inch cubes
- Olive oil
- Kosher salt
- Salad
- 1 large or 2 medium cobs of corn, shucked
- 8 ounces cherry tomatoes, quartered
- 8 ounces figs, cut in half lengthwise, then each half cut sliced into 3-4 pieces
- 2 tablespoons olive oil
- 1 tablespoon balsamic vinegar
- Kosher salt
- 3 ounces goat cheese
- 8 mint leaves, chopped
- Freshly ground black pepper

Direction

- Preheat oven to 425F.
- Place bread cubes on a baking sheet. Drizzle with olive oil and sprinkle generously with kosher salt. Bake for 7-12 minutes, until nicely browned. Let cool completely.

- Meanwhile, bring a large pot of salted water to boil. Add cobs and cook until corn is done, about 10 minutes. Set aside to let cool, then cut corn off the cob and measure out about 1 cup.
- In a large bowl, combine cooled corn, cherry tomatoes, figs, and bread.
- In a small bowl, whisk together olive oil, balsamic vinegar, and a pinch of salt. Pour over vegetables and bread and toss to coat. Let sit for 30 minutes to soak in, then toss in goat cheese, mint, and top with freshly ground black pepper.

213. Party Sandwich Loaf Redux...

Serving: Makes one mini party loaf | Prep: | Cook: | Ready in:

Ingredients

- 4 slices of soft, but really good sandwich bread
- softened sweet cream butter
- 2 or 3 different kinds of your prize sandwich fillings (you can repeat one filling if you prefer)
- 3 ounces softened goat cheese mixed with 1 oz full fat Greek yogurt and 1 tbl. of aioli
- 2-3 ounces homemade aioli
- herbs, pickled vegetables, vegetables for garnish
- greens for garnish (red cress featured)

Direction

- Stack all the slices of bread together on a cutting board; then cut the largest rectangle you can from the stack by trimming away all the crusts and then some. You want these 4 slices to stack up perfectly. Lightly butter all sides of the slices except the bottom face.
- Spread each of selected sandwich fillings, layer by layer: What you select should all go well together. Crab meat salad, roasted pepper

hummus, egg salad, spinach pesto aioli, whipped goat cheese with roasted tomatoes and rosemary, chopped cucumber and cress (good to include a salad course in your trio), salmon salad in mustard dill, ham salad in horseradish mustard, or chicken tarragon are some ideas to consider...but design a compatible combination you will love. Make sure you will be able to slice through each layer effortlessly, and that the layers will remain intact, so select wisely. One interior layer can use aioli in the mix, but I would not use it on more. Reserve the rest of the aioli for the top. Keep the mini loaf straight. Press down gently as you build the layers.
- Next frost the loaf. I suggest you use a goat cheese mixed with yogurt and aioli as a spread for all the sides. Maybe use straight aioli for the top. Garnish with suitable herbs and pickled vegetables. Chill for a few hours for the flavors to permeate and for the layers to meld a bit together: this makes slicing easy later. Garnish the plate with greens. Slice and serve. Don't hate me if you don't like this! But if you do like this, then you could make a whole full size loaf of unsliced bread, which you then slice horizontally into 3 or 4 layers.

214. Pasta With Tomato And Basil

Serving: Serves about 3 to 4 | Prep: | Cook: | Ready in:

Ingredients

- 8 ounces pasta (anything goes)
- 6 tablespoons Olive oil
- 1 or 2 cloove(s) garlic crushed
- 1 small onion chopped finly
- 1 to 2 large tomatoes (skinned and de-seeded) cubed
- 1 handful of fresh basil leaves
- 1 or2 mint levaes
- 4 tablespoons Parmesan grated

- 8 to 10 ounces Goat cheese crumbled

Direction

- Cook pasta according to the instructions on the box. Please don't overcook!
- While the pasta is cooking: Combine Tomatoes, onion, garlic, olive oil, and herbs in a bowl and let it sit for the aromas to melt
- When Pasta is done toss it with the goat cheese, the cheese with get creamy and eventually melt. (Feta will not melt) Mix in the tomatoes and top with Parmesan.

215.   Pea Greens And Sugar Snaps With Preserved Lemon Cream

Serving: Serves 6 | Prep: | Cook: | Ready in:

Ingredients

- 6 ounces soft goat cheese
- 1/2 cup crème fraîche
- 2 tablespoons finely chopped preserved lemon, seeds removed
- 3 tablespoons Meyer lemon juice (or substitute regular lemon juice and add 1/2 teaspoon of honey)
- 6 tablespoons extra virgin olive oil
- salt and freshly ground black pepper
- 1 pound sugar snap peas, rinsed
- 4 cups densely packed pea greens
- 2 cups densely packed pea shoots
- 1/3 cup loosely packed basil leaves
- 1 tablespoon snipped chives

Direction

- Using an electric mixer, whip the goat cheese for 2 minutes at medium speed. Fold in the crème fraîche and preserved lemon and set aside (you can cover and refrigerate this for up to a week). Whisk together the Meyer lemon

juice and olive oil and season with salt and pepper to taste.
- In a large saucepan of boiling, salted water, blanch the sugar snaps for 30 seconds, remove with a slotted spoon and immerse in ice water. Drain well and set aside.
- Gently rinse and dry all of the greens, including the basil.
- When you are ready to assemble the salad, gently toss the pea greens, pea shoots, and sugar snaps with the dressing and season with salt and pepper to taste. Cut the basil leaves into thin ribbons and add to the salad with the chives, tossing gently. Run a thick smear of the goat cheese mixture along the center of each plate and arrange some of the salad on top. Serve immediately.

216.   Peach Basil Goat Cheese Galette

Serving: Serves 6 | Prep: | Cook: | Ready in:

Ingredients

- Lemon Pate Brisee (adapted from the Bouchon cookbook)
- 2 1/4 cups flour
- 1 teaspoon kosher salt
- 8 ounces cold unsalted butter, cubed
- 1/4 cup ice water
- 1/2 teaspoon lemon zest
- flour
- Cheese Filling and Peaches
- 4 ounces goat cheese
- 6 tablespoons whole milk ricotta
- 1 extra large egg
- 2 tablespoons basil, chopped
- 2 large peaches, skins removed
- 1 1/2 teaspoons sugar
- juice of 1/2 a lemon
- 1 tablespoon basil, chopped
- 1 egg white. beaten

Direction

- Make the dough a day ahead. Place 1 cup flour in salt in standing mixer with dough hook attachment, turn on low and add the butter in a handful at a time, in about 4 batches, increase to medium speed and when butter is incorporated, stop machine, scrape down sides or dislodge dough from mixing arm, turn on to low again and slowly add in remaining flour, followed by the water, mix until just incorporated.
- Remove and divide in to two, wrap one disk in plastic wrap and freeze for later use.
- Return the other half to the mixer and add in the lemon zest, turn on low until incorporated. Shape in to a disk, wrap in plastic wrap and refrigerate overnight.
- Boil a small pot of water. Score an 'X' in the bottom of each peach place them in boiling water turn off the heat, put the lid on and let them sit in the hot water for 2 minutes.
- Remove the skins from the peaches. Slice the peaches in quarters, slice in to 1/8" slices and place in a bowl, toss with sugar, lemon juice and basil.
- Using a mixer combine the goat cheese, ricotta and egg. Fold in the basil.
- Roll out the dough on a floured surface to 10'-12" in diameter, place on parchment on a baking sheet, spread the cheese mixture in the center of the dough staying clear of the outer 1.5". Arrange peaches on top. Roughly fold over the edges and brush with the egg wash. Bake at 375 for 35 minutes. Remove from oven let cool on the baking sheet on wire rack. Take care when transferring it to a plate or cutting board, the pastry is very flaky.

217.   Peach And Goat Cheese Tart With Rosemary Cornmeal Crust

Serving: Serves 10 | Prep: | Cook: | Ready in:

Ingredients

- 1 cup unbleached, all purpose flour
- 1/4 cup finely ground white cornmeal
- 2 tablespoons sugar
- 1 1/2 teaspoons finely chopped rosemary
- 1/2 teaspoon salt
- 1 stick butter, which has sat in the freezer for 10 minutes or so
- 1/4 cup ice water
- 3/4 cup soft goat cheese
- 2 ounces cream cheese
- 1/4 cup greek yogurt
- 1 tablespoon sugar
- 5 medium peaches, cut into thin wedges
- 1 10 inch spring of rosemary
- 1/2 cup water
- 1/4 cup sugar

Direction

- Whiz the flour, cornmeal, sugar, rosemary and salt in a food processor until combined. Cut butter into ½ inch cubes and add to food processor. Pulse until large crumbs form. Add ice water, pulsing until incorporated, but the mixture still looks like crumbs – the dough shouldn't come together until you pinch it with your fingers. Pour crumbs out onto a sheet of plastic wrap, press together into a disk, wrap, and refrigerate for at least a half hour.
- Preheat the oven to 400. Spray a 9 inch fluted tart pan with nonstick cooking spray. Unwrap the dough and cut ¼ inch slices off of it, laying slices in the bottom and sides of pan to cover and cutting more as you go. Press the slices together to smooth and cover the pan evenly. Stab the dough with the tines of a fork a few times, cover with parchment paper and fill with beans or pie weights. Bake for 10 minutes, remove the parchment and beans, and continue baking 10 to 15 minutes, until golden. Cool completely.
- While the crust is baking, combine the water, sugar, and rosemary spring in a small saucepan over high heat. Swirl until the sugar

dissolves, then swirl occasionally while mixture boils, turning the heat off when the mixture just starts to look thick - about 3 minutes. Let the syrup cool for 10 minutes, reserve the rosemary for garnish, and pour the syrup into a wide, shallow pan (like a lasagna pan). Place the peach slices in one layer on top of the syrup and let them sit for at least a half hour - there will be more peach slices than necessary to account for any unattractive slicing casualties (those can be your snack). After a half hour, flip the slices and let the other side sit for at least a half hour.

- Just before serving, mix the goat cheese, cream cheese, Greek yogurt and sugar. Spread the goat cheese mixture into the tart shell and arrange the peach slices in circles on top. Use the reserved rosemary to garnish.

218. Peach At Its Best

Serving: Serves one | Prep: | Cook: | Ready in:

Ingredients

- 1 homemade baguette or other bread
- 1 perfectly ripe peach
- dash fruity olive oil
- generous smear goat cheese (I use cheese that's been marinated in olive oil and herbs)
- handful optional: fresh cut herbs (basil or thyme or mint)
- small clove optional: garlic

Direction

- Toast a generous slice of bread. Spread with goat cheese. Meanwhile, slice and peel peach. Arrange slices on top of bread. Add dash of olive oil and herbs, if using. (As a variation, depending on time of day, rub bread first with a halved clove of garlic.)

219. Pear Ricotta Goat Cheese Tart

Serving: Makes 1 pie | Prep: | Cook: | Ready in:

Ingredients

- 2 sheets of puff pastry, defrost
- 3 sprigs thyme
- 1 tablespoon honey
- 1 tablespoon lemon juice
- 1/2 tablespoon grainy mustard
- 1/2 tablespoon hot mustard
- 1-2 handfuls walnuts
- 1 pear
- 50g fresh goat cheese
- 50g fresh ricotta cheese
- Salt and pepper
- Splash Honey

Direction

- Preheat oven on 425F
- Peel the pear and cut into thin slices. Then coarsely break the nuts into pieces.
- Crumble the goat cheese and ricotta. In a bowl, gently mix both cheese with a wooden spoon.
- Whisk together maple syrup, lemon juice, and mustard. Wash the thyme and pluck off the leaves. Add to the mustard dressing. Season to taste.
- Spread two sheets of puff pastry on a floured surface. With a rolling pin, thin out the dough. Press the dough into a pie plate, cover bottom and sides.
- Spread out the pear slices. Add the walnuts, then spread out the crumbled goat cheese and ricotta evenly on the dough. Drizzle with the mustard dressing.
- Bake the pie for 20 minutes then grill for three minutes until golden. Take the pie out of the oven and let cool a little. Before serving, add drizzle some honey on top.

220. Pearl Couscous With Roasty Roots, Chickpeas, And Pepitas

Serving: Serves 8 | Prep: | Cook: | Ready in:

Ingredients

- 1 bunch of carrots
- 1 sweet potato
- 4 tablespoons olive oil, divided
- Sea salt, black pepper
- 2 garlic cloves
- 2 cups Israeli (pearl) couscous
- 4 cups chicken or vegetable stock
- 2 tablespoons fresh lemon juice
- 2 teaspoons Dijon mustard
- 4 tablespoons pumpkin seed oil (or olive oil)
- 1 small red onion, minced
- 1 1/3 cup chickpeas
- 4 ounces crumbly goat cheese
- 2 teaspoons za'atar
- 1/4 cup pumpkin seeds

Direction

- Heat the oven to 425F.
- Peel the carrots and the sweet potatoes. Chop them up however you like, but I would cut them into small-ish pieces. (You want them bite-sized, so you can eat this traveling, without a knife.)
- Line a baking sheet with foil or parchment paper. Toss the sweet potato and carrot pieces with 3 tablespoons of the olive oil, and generously with sea salt and black pepper. Move the vegetables to the baking sheet, arranging them so they aren't too crowded. (You want them to roast and caramelize, not steam.) Move the baking sheet to the oven: roast for about 30 minutes, moving the vegetables around every 10 minutes or so. They are done when blackened in spots, and cooked through.
- In a small pot, bring the chicken or vegetable stock to a simmer.
- Meanwhile, mince the garlic. Heat the remaining tablespoon of olive oil in a medium pot over medium heat; when the oil is warm, add the garlic. Cook for about 30 seconds, until fragment, and then add the couscous. Toast the couscous for about 1 minute, and then add the hot stock. (Make sure the heat is on medium; if the heat is high enough to boil the stock, the couscous will overcook. You can also boil for 8 minutes, and then drain any excess stock.) Put the lid on the pot, and set the timer for 15 minutes. After 15 minutes, remove the lid: there should only be a little liquid left in the pot. (If not, put the lid back on, and continue cooking for up to 5 minutes.) Then, cook for another 1-2 minutes with the lid off, until the liquid is largely dissolved. Take the pot off the heat. You can add a tiny bit of olive oil now if you like: it will help prevent the couscous from sticking together.
- Make the dressing: add the lemon juice and the Dijon mustard to a small bowl, along with a pinch of salt and pepper. Use a fork, or the back of a spoon, to mix. Pour in the oil, and whisk to emulsify.
- Mince the red onion. Wash the can-goop off the chickpeas. Crumble the goat cheese.
- Now you can mix everything together, right in the couscous pot. Add the: sweet potatoes, carrots, dressing, red onion, chickpeas, goat cheese, za'atar, and pumpkin seeds to the couscous; stir. You can eat the salad warm, or at room temperature.

221. Peppery Goat Cheese Ravioli With Pineapple Tomato Sauce

Serving: Serves 4 | Prep: | Cook: | Ready in:

Ingredients

- For Ravioli
- 10 ounces Soft Goat Cheese

- 3 tablespoons Extra Virgin Olive Oil
- 2 tablespoons Freshly-Cracked Black Pepper, toasted
- 1/2 teaspoon Salt
- 1 pound Fresh Pasta Dough, rolled out in 1/8-inch thick sheets
- For Sauce
- 1 Large Yellow Heirloom Tomato, peeled (optional) and diced
- 1 Large Red Heirloom Tomato, peeled (optional) and diced
- 2 tablespoons Extra Virgin Olive Oil
- 2 Garlic Cloves
- 2-3 sprigs Fresh Thyme
- 1/2 cup Pineapple, diced
- 1 pinch Dried Lavender Blossoms
- 1 handful Fresh Basil Leaves
- 1 cup Baby Arugula, coarsely chopped
- 1 teaspoon Salt
- 1 pinch Black Pepper

Direction

- In a small bowl, mix the goat cheese, black pepper and salt with a teaspoon of the olive oil until smooth.
- For half-moon ravioli, cut pasta sheets into circles. Place a heaping teaspoon of the goat cheese filling in the middle. Dab edge with water, fold over and press down to seal. Set your ravioli aside to rest while you prepare the sauce.
- Heat the olive oil in a pan. Add the thyme sprigs and garlic, sauté until garlic cloves have slightly browned. Add the diced tomatoes, pineapple, salt, pepper, and lavender. Simmer for 7-10 minutes (until tomatoes have softened and released their juices). Remove from heat, add the basil and arugula.
- Fill a large pot with water and bring to a boil. Add salt and add the ravioli and cook for 2-4 min, until the pasta is tender yet al-dente. Strain the ravioli and immediately toss with the sauce.

222.   Persimmon Bruschetta

Serving: Serves 4 | Prep: | Cook: |Ready in:

Ingredients

- 4 Ripe but not too ripe Fuyu persimmons
- 1/2 cup fresh tangy goat cheese (at room temperature)
- 1/2 cup fresh ricotta
- 1/4 cup light colored honey (not buckwheat)
- 8 Slices crusty country bread
- 1 tablespoon olive oil
- 1/4 cup toasted hazelnuts (or pistachios), coarsely chopped
- Coarse ground black pepper
- Flaky sea salt
- 1 tablespoon chopped fresh rosemary (or mint if using pistachios)
- 1 tablespoon lemon zest (Meyer, if you have it)
- 1 tablespoon lemon juice (Meyer if you have it)

Direction

- Brush bread with olive oil on both sides. Sprinkle with salt & pepper, and bake at 375°F until crisp and lightly browned.
- Cut the persimmons into 8 lovely juicy orange petals. Remove seeds and peel (I use a paring knife), and sprinkle with a bit of lemon juice.
- Whisk together ricotta, goat cheese, lemon juice, lemon zest and rosemary.
- Dollop cheese mixture on warm toasts. Lay 4-6 slices of persimmon on each toast, and sprinkle with coarse pepper and sea salt flakes.
- Heat honey gently.
- Drizzle with warm honey and sprinkle with toasted Hazelnuts. Garnish with rosemary sprigs.

223.   Persimmon And Goat Cheese Salad

Serving: Serves 4 | Prep: | Cook: | Ready in:

Ingredients

- 6 cups mixed greens, any style
- 1   Fuyu persimmon, diced
- 1   small apple, diced
- 1/2 cup soft goat cheese, crumbled
- 3 tablespoons sliced almonds, toasted
- 4 tablespoons tangerine juice
- 2 tablespoons olive oil
- 1/2 teaspoon dijon mustard
- 1 pinch salt
- 2 dashes pepper

Direction

- Place the greens in a salad bowl and top with the fruits and goat cheese.
- In a small bowl, whisk tangerine juice, mustard, salt and pepper. Whisk in olive oil in a small stream. Adjust to taste. Combine with greens and toss. Sprinkle almonds over all. Serve.

224.   Pesto Grilled Vegetable Wellington With Goat Cheese

Serving: Serves 6 | Prep: | Cook: | Ready in:

Ingredients

- Pesto and Puff Pastry
- 1 1/2 cups Fresh Basil
- 1/4 cup Extra Virgin Olive Oil
- 2   Cloves Garlic, chopped
- 3 tablespoons Toasted Pine Nuts (optional)
- 4 1/2 Sticks Unsalted Butter
- 1 teaspoon Table Salt
- 3 1/2 cups Flour (unbleached regular)
- 1 cup Cold Tap Water
- Vegetable Filling

- 2   Red Bell Peppers (Holland)
- 2   Zuchinni
- 2   Yellow Squash
- 2   Japanese Eggplant
- 1 bunch Asparagus (small)
- 2   Portabella Mushrooms
- 11 ounces Goat Cheese (low moisture variety)
- 1   Large Egg
- 1/8 cup Water
- 1/2 cup Olive Oil
- 1   Clove Garlic
- 1 pinch Salt
- 2 pinches Fresh Black Pepper

Direction

- Pesto and Puff Pastry
- First, begin making your puff pastry dough, as this is the most time consuming part of the recipe. If you would like to skip this step, store bought works well also.
- Soften butter by leaving it out of the refrigerator. Let it get soft enough that when you press on it, there is an indentation, but not so soft that it is melting.
- Take 1/2 stick of butter, cut into smaller pieces and place in stand mixer (with dough hook attachment).
- Add 3 cups of the flour, salt, and half of the water to the bowl and mix on low adding the rest of the water until a dough is just formed. You may not need all of the water, depending on the altitude and humidity where you live.
- Take the dough out of the mixer bowl and place on a clean silpat on a tray (you can also use wax paper or parchment dusted with flour) and refrigerate for 30 minutes.
- While the dough is in the fridge, make your pesto.
- In a food processor, add basil, cheese, and pine nuts (optional). Pulse until basil is chopped. Slowly add oil until the pesto is a consistency that you like. Some people like it smooth, other like a chunkier pesto.
- Place pesto in a container and refrigerate until needed later.

- Now, make the butter layer for the puff pastry dough. Take one pound butter and 3 TB flour and mix until smooth. There shouldn't be any lumps.
- After the 30 minutes is up, take the puff pastry dough out of the refrigerator and place on a flour dusted surface.
- Roll the dough into a large rectangle about 1/8 of an inch thick.
- Spread the butter mixture over 2/3 of the dough, leaving 1/3 without any butter. Leave a 1/2 inch boarder around the outside of the dough.
- Fold the dough without any butter over the first third that does have butter. Then fold over the last third over the middle. Press around the outsides to "seal" the butter in. Place the dough back in the refrigerator until the butter has hardened slightly. Don't let it get too hard.
- During this time, you can begin the vegetables (below)
- Take the dough out of the refrigerator and roll it out (being careful not to squeeze the butter out) to about 12x18 inch rectangle.
- Then fold the dough in thirds again, rolling it to about 1/2 inch thick. Place back the refrigerator. These last two steps should be repeated about 6 times. These are called "turns". You can mark your dough with a knife to keep track of how many times you have done the process. After this, your puff pastry is complete.
- Vegetable Filling
- First, wash all vegetables and dry them well.
- Use a garlic press to mash garlic and add it to the olive oil in a small bowl, along with a pinch of salt and a couple turns of fresh black pepper.
- Slice all vegetables into 1/4 inch slices using a mandolin if you have one. For "long" vegetables, it is better to cut lengthwise. For asparagus, remove the bottom end as usual and keep whole.
- As you are slicing, heat up your grill. If you are using an indoor electric grill, turn it up to "Sear" or 450 degrees. If you are using a cast iron grill pan, heat to the point that if you throw some water on it, it sizzles and evaporates right away.
- Brush vegetables with a pastry brush (or grilling brush, if you have one) lightly with olive oil and garlic mixture on one side, placing that side on the grill. If you have an electric grill, brush the other side of the vegetables and close it.
- Cook all vegetables until tender, but not mushy, and set aside to cool.
- When the vegetables are reasonably cool, begin to roll out your puff pastry dough on a lightly flour dusted surface. Remember to work quickly as pastry dough gets sticky and messy very quickly. You will only need about half of the prepared dough. The rest can be wrapped and placed in the freezer for another project (such as pastries, croissants, palmers, etc.)
- Preheat your oven to 450 degrees.
- Roll out the dough into a long rectangle, about 18x8 inches on a large sheet pan with parchment paper. Spray the parchment very lightly with cooking spray.
- Spread the goat cheese thinly across the entire length of the dough, leaving a 1/2 inch boarder around the outside.
- Then, spread a thin layer of pesto on top of the goat cheese.
- Begin layering your vegetables on top of the goat cheese, layering different vegetables next to each other so that when sliced, the Wellington has all different vegetables in each piece (you never get a mouthful of just peppers, for example).
- Depending on the size of the vegetables cooked, you may have extra, simply set them aside for leftovers (unless of course these vegetables were leftovers to begin with). Keep adding vegetables until the layer is about 3 inches thick. Be careful not to add too much liquid with the vegetables as they will make the pastry soggy.
- Crack your egg and add the water, mixing to make an egg wash.

- Fold up the dough to the middle of the top, creating a seam down the middle of the "log". Use some egg wash to seal. Then roll the log over, making the seam on the bottom of the roll touching the pan. Fold under the ends of the roll, again pushing the seams under to the bottom.
- At this point, if you wish, the entire log can be wrapped in wax paper and plastic wrap and frozen for a meal in the future. If you do this, remember to defrost the Wellington slightly before putting it in the oven and do so at 375 for 10 minutes, and then raise the temperature to 450 and cook the rest of the way.
- Cook at 425 degrees for 30-40 minutes, or until the top of the pastry is browned evenly. If your oven cooks unevenly, remember to rotate the pan about half way through.
- Brush the entire log lightly with egg wash, and place in the middle rack of the oven.
- When the Wellington is cooked, remove from the oven and let cool for about 10 minutes. Then slice 2 inch pieces, and serve. This can be served with some of the leftover pesto as a sauce.

---

225. Petit Pea Whip On Rye Pancakes

Serving: Serves /covers about 8 pancakes | Prep: | Cook: | Ready in:

Ingredients

- Spring Pea Whip
- 10 ounces frozen spring peas, thawed
- 1 handful spinach
- 1 bunch Italian flat leaf parsley
- 2 ounces goat cheese, crumbled
- zest of 1 lemon
- 1 good squeeze of fresh lemon juice
- 1/2 teaspoon salt, more to your taste
- freshly ground black pepper
- thinly sliced red onion

- 1 handful capers, rinsed and drained
- best quality smoked salmon
- Rye Pancakes
- 3/4 cup rye flour
- 3/4 cup white whole wheat flour/all purpose flour
- 1 teaspoon salt
- 1 teaspoon baking powder
- 1 1/2 cups milk
- 1 cup water
- 1 egg
- 1 tablespoon butter, melted

Direction

- Spring Pea Whip
- Blitz the peas, spinach, parsley, goat cheese, lemon zest, juice, salt and pepper in your food processor till smooth. Add more salt and pepper to your taste. Chill.
- Put the red onion, capers, and salmon aside until ready to serve.
- Rye Pancakes
- Sift the dry ingredients in a bowl. Combine the wet ingredients together in another bowl and add to the dry. Stir until combined and set aside for at least 15 minutes before cooking.
- Grease a large non-stick pan/griddle with a bit of butter and be prepared for your first pancake to be a dud. Bring your griddle to medium high heat and drop about three tablespoons of batter per pancake on the griddle.
- Cook pancake until bubbles appear on the surface of the pancake and the pancake lifts easily from pan/griddle. Flip the pancake over and cook for a few more minutes (1-2).
- Spread pea mixture on pancake. Top with red onions, capers, and salmon. Roll up and serve. Alternatively, just roll up and serve. It's delicious both ways.

226.   Picnic In A Pie: Tomato, Corn, Basil And Bacon Pie

Serving: Serves 4-6 | Prep: | Cook: |Ready in:

Ingredients

- Pie crust
- 2 cups all-purpose flour, sifted
- 1.5 teaspoons salt
- 1/8 - 1/4 teaspoons freshly ground black pepper
- 1/4 cup milk
- 1/2 cup canola oil
- Pie filling
- 2-3 large tomatoes, sliced 1/2" thick
- kosher salt
- 1 large ear of corn, kernels removed
- 1/3 cup thinly sliced shallot
- 1/2 cup purple and green basil, chopped
- 3-4 slices speck (or regular bacon), chopped
- 2 cloves garlic, peeled and thinly sliced
- Bucheron or other tangy goat cheese, sliced
- freshly ground black pepper
- extra-virgin olive oil, for drizzling

Direction

- Preheat oven to 375. In a medium mixing bowl, combine sifted flour, salt and pepper, and whisk well. Add milk and oil, and using a fork, stir and mash together until mostly combined. Place dough onto a sheet of waxed paper, cover with another sheet of waxed paper, and roll to 1/8 " - 1/4" thick. Put into a deep pie plate and trim excess.
- Bake crust in oven for 20 minutes or until starting to turn golden (use pie weights or beans on foil so the crust doesn't buckle).
- While the crust bakes, put the tomato slices and a nice pinch of kosher salt in a bowl. Let sit 10 minutes, then drain. Add chopped basil and slivered garlic to the tomatoes and set aside.
- In a small skillet, cook the speck (or bacon). Once crispy, remove bacon and turn off heat. Pour the corn kernels in that same skillet, stir

them around in any drippings, and set aside on another burner. You don't want to cook them much; rather you're just tossing them around in the warm drippings to incorporate that flavor.
- When you pull the crust from the oven (leave the oven on), place it on your workstation and begin to layer in the filling: goat cheese, tomato/garlic/basil mixture, shallots, corn, and bacon. Finish with tomatoes and drizzle the whole pie with some olive oil and a grind of pepper. Don't worry if the filling is higher than the pie plate; it will settle as it cooks.
- Place the pie back into the oven and bake for 20-25 minutes. Cool and serve at room temp.

227.   Pink Moscato Soaked Watermelon, Baby Lettuce & Goat Cheese Crunchy Toast Salad

Serving: Serves 5 | Prep: | Cook: |Ready in:

Ingredients

- For the Salad:
- 5 cups baby lettuce mix
- 5 cups arugula leaves
- 1/4 red onion cut into half , thin sliced
- 2 cups watermelon cut into 1/2" cubes, soaked in pink moscato (I used "Barefoot") for at least 3 hours, refrigerated
- 1/3 cup toasted pumpkin seeds
- 10 pieces whole grain bread
- butter
- clove garlic
- 1 packet soft goat cheese
- 1/4 cup Parmesan cheese flakes
- 30 cilantro leaves
- For the Pomegranate Citrus Champagne vinaigrette dressing:
- 1.5 tablespoons pomegranate syrup
- 1/8 cup orange muscat champagne vinegar (I used "traders Joe")

- 1/8 cup extra virgin olive oil (good quality)
- 1/3 teaspoon salt
- Pinch ground black pepper

Direction

- Add all the ingredients into a jar with a lead. Shake well till combined.
- Toast the bread just for a 1-1.5min, take the garlic clove and rub it into the toasted bread. Spread butter and goat cheese between each couple of bread slices, and with a 1" round cookie cutter cut small round bites from each sandwich. Preheat a pan, add few drops of olive oil or butter, and toast the goat cheese bites until it gets crispy.
- Combine the dish: just before serving the salad, pour the dressing over the salad and gently mix. Put in a serving plate, add 4-5 crunchy goat cheese toast to each serving plate, sprinkle toasted pumpkin seeds on top, sprinkle Parmesan cheese flakes and cilantro leaves. Bon apetit!
- If you want to prepare in advance, keep the salad green mix separately from the watermelon cubes, refrigerated. Mix the dressing ingredients in a jar, combine just before serving otherwise the vegetables will get soggy and will lose their freshness.

228.   Pink Potato Pizza

Serving: Serves 2-3 | Prep: | Cook: |Ready in:

Ingredients

- 1 pizza dough
- 2 cups tightly packed basil
- 1/2 teaspoon sea salt
- 2-3 tablespoons olive oil
- 1 small garlic clove
- 2-3 small waxy potatoes
- 2 ounces goat cheese, crumbled
- 2 ounces micro, or baby, greens

Direction

- Preheat oven to 500 for at least 20 minutes. Place a baking stone or baking sheet in the oven to preheat.
- Combine basil, salt and garlic in a food processor. Turn on to puree. With the machine running, drizzle in the olive oil. You may need to stop and scrape the sides of the work bowl a few times. Set aside.
- Lay out a sheet of parchment paper on your work space. Using floured hands, pull and press the pizza dough into your desired shape on the parchment.
- Spread the basil mixture over the dough. Top with potato slices, mostly in a single layer, but some can overlap. Layer dollops of goat cheese on top.
- Take the baking stone out of the oven. Transfer the pizza, parchment and all, to the stone, and place back in the oven. Cook for 10-15 minutes. The dough should be starting to brown, and potatoes should be cooked through.
- To serve, lay the greens atop the pizza and cut into wedges.

229.   Pinot Pea Puree

Serving: Makes enough for a party! | Prep: | Cook: |Ready in:

Ingredients

- Pinot Pea Puree
- 2 pounds bag frozen peas
- 1 shallot, diced
- 2 teaspoons dried tarragon
- 1/4 cup Pinot Gris
- 2 tablespoons butter
- 2 tablespoons grated Parmesan
- 1/4 teaspoon salt
- 1 tablespoon goat cheese
- 1 bunch basil or mint
- freshly cracked black pepper (optional)

- Optional serving suggestion: Crostini
- 30-40 pieces crostini
- Ricotta cheese
- grated Parmesan
- flake salt (Maldon or similar)

Direction

- In unsalted boiling water, cook shallot and peas for 9 minutes (until peas are tender but not mushy). Drain.
- Place peas, tarragon, wine, and butter in food processor. Pulse until peas become broken down but not completely smooth, about 5-10 pulses.
- Add Parmesan, salt, and goat cheese. Blend until puree is the desired texture.
- Chiffonade basil or mint and sprinkle over the top of the finished puree with cracked pepper, or reserve for garnishing before serving.
- Optional serving suggestion: Top crostini with a spoon of pea puree. Add a dollop of ricotta if desired. Sprinkle Parmesan, flake salt, pepper and basil over top before serving.

---

230.   Pita Bread With Oven Baked Goat Cheese Croquettes

Serving: Serves 4 | Prep: | Cook: |Ready in:

Ingredients

- 6   slice of wholegrain crisp bread
- 8   slices of fresh goat cheese
- 4 tablespoons flour
- 2   beaten eggs
- 4 pinches baking soda
- 2   Pita breads (medium size)
- 1 handful Arugula leaves
- 1   pear, cut into slices
- 2 handfuls cooked chickpeas
- 4 tablespoons hummus
- Salt and pepper

Direction

- Combine flour and baking soda. In a mixer, crumble the crisp bread. Season with salt and pepper.
- Form eight croquettes with the slices of goat cheese. Dip each croquette into flour, egg then crisp bread. Set in the refrigerator for an hour.
- Fry in a pan with olive oil until golden or bake them in the oven for 10 minutes on 400F. I like to bake them, including to guarantee that the cheese doesn't melt too much.
- Slightly heat up the pita breads and cut in two
- Garnish Pita half with arugula, slices of pear, and some chickpeas. Add two fried goat cheese croquettes then season with salt and pepper and add 1 tbsp. of hummus to finish. Enjoy!

---

231.   Pizza Tiles

Serving: Serves 4 | Prep: | Cook: |Ready in:

Ingredients

- Peach and chorizo topping
- 1   peach
- 1   chorizo sliced
- goat's cheese
- watercress or rocket
- sun dried tomato paste
- Tomato, pepper and courgette topping
- 1   tomato sliced
- 1   courgette
- 1   yellow pepper
- beetroot cooked in malt vinegar
- buffalo mozarella
- balsamic vinegar glaze

Direction

- For the first pizza spread a couple of tbsp. sun dried tomato paste on the stretched dough.
- Place the chorizo neatly on the pizza, slice the peach and place it on top of it. Finish by crumbling the goats cheese.

- For the second pizza slice the tomato and the pepper length wise in order to have a nice round shape. Slice the courgette the same way. Place the peppers first and then inside them the tomato slices so that they work as frames.
- On top of the tomatoes place the courgette and the beetroot in small cubes. Sprinkle with a little bit of mozzarella. It doesn't need much because the flavours are already rich.
- Bake for 10 minutes and take out of the oven. Grind some pepper, add the watercress (or rocket) and the balsamic glaze.

232. Poblanos Stuffed With Goat Cheese And Greens

Serving: Serves 6 | Prep: | Cook: | Ready in:

Ingredients

- The chiles
- 6 poblano chiles. Choose firm, shiny ones about 4" long
- 2 pounds greens, such as spinach, chard, watercress, mustard greens or a mix
- 3 tablespoons olive oil, or mild-flavored oil such as grape seed or avocado, divided
- 1/2 small onion, finely minced
- 1/3 cup (60g) raisins, preferably golden, roughly chopped
- 1/3 cup (60g) pine nuts
- 9 ounces (250g) soft goat cheese log
- The sauce
- 2 pounds (1kg) plum tomatoes, about 12 large or 16 small
- 1 small onion sliced into thick rings about 1/2 inch wide
- 4 good-sized cloves of garlic
- 2 tablespoons of olive oil, or as above
- Salt
- Up to 1 tsp. sugar, if needed
- Optional: sour cream or crème fraiche

Direction

- Roasting the chiles. This is best done on a gas stove, if possible. Place the chiles directly on the burner grills over a med-high flame. (Use two burners with two to three chiles on each.) You will hear the skin blister and pop. Rotate just as it turns black — excessive charring will result in thin-walled chiles. If you have an electric stovetop, you can either use a skillet over high heat or place the chiles directly on the burner. (In this case, choose chiles that have a flatter profile. Some can be rather undulating and are difficult to char thoroughly on an electric burner or skillet.)
- Once the chiles are charred all over, place them in a bowl and cover with a tea towel to cool. The towel absorbs some of the steam so the chiles don't get too wet. When the chiles are cool enough to handle, peel and gently scrape the charred skin off, using the back of a paring knife. If some of the skin did not get charred and wants to remain, don't worry about it. Leave the stems intact. Make a slit about 2 inches long in the side of each chile, starting close to the top, and remove the seeds. (It can be helpful to carefully make a cut just at the top of the seeds and remove them as a unit — it's a little less messy). If necessary, rinse very briefly under cold water to remove bits of skin and seeds.
- The stuffing: Stem and wash the greens. If using chard, reserve some of the more tender stems, chop into 1/4 inch pieces and set aside. If leaves are large, chop coarsely. Heat a large, deep skillet or wide saucepan, coat the bottom with about 1 tbsp. of olive oil and toss in the still-damp greens with a sprinkling of salt. Depending on the size of your pan, it may be necessary to do this in two batches. Toss frequently. When greens are wilted (about 3 minutes), remove from heat and drain off the excess liquid. Spinach, in particular, releases a lot of liquid, so use a mesh strainer and press on the greens to drain. Chop the greens down a little more.
- Add the remaining oil to the pan over medium heat. Add the minced onion. If using chard stems, add these now and sauté until the

onion is translucent and the stems softened. It may help to add a couple of tablespoons of water to help soften the stems. When the water has evaporated, add the raisins, pine nuts and greens, and sauté these until the greens become quite dry (3 to 5 minutes).

- Taste goat cheese for saltiness and salt the greens accordingly.
- Transfer the greens to a bowl to cool. Crumble the goat cheese in with the cooled greens and combine. To portion the filling, pat the mixture down into the bowl so the surface is relatively flat and you can divide it into 6 "pie wedges." Scoop out each portion, form into a log and stuff into each chile.
- The sauce: I use a Comal (heavy steel or cast iron griddle) for the following step. If you don't have one, you can use a large skillet. I recommend covering the skillet surface with a sheet of foil because the sugars from the tomato can really make a mess of your pan. The foil allows for easy clean-up.
- Heat skillet or griddle over high heat. Cut about 1/3 of the tomatoes in half lengthwise. Place the whole tomatoes, halved tomatoes, onion slices, and whole cloves of unpeeled garlic on the skillet. Turn each as it colors — the cut tomatoes will begin to caramelize on the cut side, and the whole ones will blister black in spots. The onions will turn a dark golden brown, and the skin of the garlic will brown. Transfer each to a bowl as it becomes soft.
- If desired, you may remove the core of the tomato, and if the skin is very black, remove some of that, too, but leave some for the flavor. Peel the garlic. Transfer all ingredients to a blender or food processor and blend to a slightly rough puree. Taste the sauce. If it is acidic or bitter, add the sugar.
- In a skillet large enough to accommodate the pureed sauce, heat 1 to 2 tbsp. oil over med-high heat. When the oil begins to glisten, pour in the sauce carefully — it may splatter a bit. Cook the sauce down for 3 to 5 minutes or until the liquid at the edges has evaporated. Salt to taste.

- To finish the dish: Preheat oven to 350° F. Place the stuffed chiles in an appropriate-sized baking dish that has been lightly oiled, and cover loosely with foil, matte side out. Warm in oven 12 to 15 minutes. Warm the tomato sauce separately.
- Puddle about 1/3-1/2 cup of sauce on each plate, and place the stuffed chile on top. If desired, drizzle with sour cream thinned with cream or milk, or, if you can get it, Mexican crema to serve.

233.   Pork Torta

Serving: Serves 8 | Prep: | Cook: |Ready in:

Ingredients

- Pork tortas
- 8   good quality, large sandwich rolls
- slow cooked, lime marinated pork (see below)
- 2   avocados, pits and peels removed, chopped and just barely mashed with a little salt
- 8 ounces goat cheese, crumbled
- 3 cups very coarsely shredded/julienned jicama root
- 1   carrot, coarsely shredded
- 4   scallions, quartered lengthwise and then cut into julienne length strips
- 1   cucumber, peeled, seeded, and cut into thin matchsticks
- 3 tablespoons chopped, fresh cilantro
- 1/4 cup olive oil
- 1/2 cup plain yogurt
- 2 tablespoons honey
- 2   limes, juiced
- 3 tablespoons rice vinegar
- 1 tablespoon chili powder
- 1 teaspoon ground cumin
- 1 teaspoon salt
- 1/2 teaspoon ground black pepper
- slow cooked, lime-marinated pork
- 3 pounds pork shoulder or butt, trimmed of excess fat, cut into 2 inch cubes

- 1 tablespoon salt
- 1 tablespoon ground black pepper
- 2 tablespoons dried oregano
- 1 large onion, chopped
- 6 garlic cloves, minced
- 5 large limes, juiced (plus a bit more lime juice, for basting)

Direction

- Pork tortas
- In a small bowl, whisk together the olive oil, yogurt, honey, lime juice, and spices. Set aside in the refrigerator for at least 10 minutes for flavors to combine.
- In a large bowl, combine jicama, carrot, scallions, and cucumber. Toss with the dressing.
- Split open sandwich rolls, and scoop a little bit of bread out of each side to make extra room for the fillings. Spread the bottom of each roll with some of the avocado. Top with pork, crumbled goat cheese, and jicama slaw. Put the top of each roll on each sandwich, and serve. Have lots of napkins!!
- Slow cooked, lime-marinated pork
- Toss the pork with the rest of the ingredients and allow to marinate in the refrigerator overnight (at least 8-12 hours).
- Put pork and marinade together in a Dutch oven or roasting pan, cover tightly, and bake in a 350F oven for 2 1/2 - 3 hours. (Peek at 1 1/2 hours to check the liquid levels and pour in a half cup, or so, of mixed lime juice and water if the pork looks totally dry - my pork often looks like it has no liquid by the end, but is extremely tender and falling apart nicely)
- Use forks to shred the meat apart. Stir any cooking juices into the meat, and use the pork in assembling the tortas.

234.　　Potato Salad With Pancetta And Lemongrass

Serving: Serves 4 as side dish | Prep: | Cook: | Ready in:

Ingredients

- 1 pound small waxy potatoes
- 1 handful diced celery
- 1 red onion, diced
- 4 ounces pinenuts, toasted
- 4 ounces pancetta, cubed
- 1 tablespoon minced lemongrass
- 1/4 cup goat cheese
- 2 tablespoons light cream
- 1 dash red chilli flakes
- juice of 1 lemon plus zest
- sea salt and pepper to taste

Direction

- Steam potatoes until tender, perhaps 15 minutes.
- Fry pancetta cubes till crisp and brown, then drain on a paper towel.
- Drain and quarter potatoes and place in a large bowl.
- Add all other ingredients up to goat cheese.
- Shake up all the ingredients from goat cheese on into a dressing, in a jar with a tight-fitting lid.
- When ready to serve, mix pancetta with salad ingredients, then toss with dressing and serve immediately.

235.　　Potato, Leek, And Goat Cheese Tart

Serving: Serves 4-6 | Prep: | Cook: | Ready in:

Ingredients

- 1/2 pound packaged frozen puff pastry, (usually one sheet), defrosted
- 1 egg, whisked

- 5 ounces goat cheese
- 1/2 cup heavy cream
- 3 tablespoons olive oil, divided
- 1   small leek, white and light green parts, thinly sliced
- 3   garlic cloves, minced
- Kosher salt
- 1   medium yukon gold potato, sliced thinly on mandolin
- 3-4   thyme
- freshly ground black pepper

Direction

- Preheat oven to 425°F.
- Lightly roll out puff pastry on parchment to smooth out creases. Transfer dough with parchment paper to a baking sheet. Using a knife, lightly score a 1" border around the dough and prick a couple times in the center with form. Brush with egg wash and bake until golden and slightly puffed, about 10 minutes.
- Meanwhile, in a medium sized bowl, mix goat cheese and cream. Set aside.
- Next, heat 2 tablespoons of olive oil in a medium sized sauce skillet over medium-high heat. Add leeks and cook until they soften. Season with salt, and stir in garlic for 30 seconds.
- When puff pastry is done, let cool slightly. If it puffs up too much, prick with a fork to deflate. Spread goat cheese mixture evenly within the 1 inch border. Next, pull leaves off of 2 sprigs of thyme and sprinkle on top. Place potato slices, 1-2 layers deep, on top of goat cheese, drizzling with olive oil and salt in between if doing 2 layers. Top with leeks and black pepper.
- Bake until pastry is golden brown and baked through, about 18-20 minutes. Let cool slightly. Sprinkle remaining thyme on top before serving.

236.   Prosciutto Basil Rolls With Goat Cheese And Orange Gastrique

Serving: Makes 24 | Prep: | Cook: |Ready in:

Ingredients

- 1 cup sugar
- 1/2 cup rice wine vinegar
- 1/2 cup fresh orange juice
- 6 ounces goat cheese
- 12 pieces prosciutto, halved crosswise
- 24 pieces large fresh basil leaves
- Fresh ground black pepper

Direction

- Combine sugar, vinegar and orange juice; bring to boil in small saucepan. Reduce heat and cook until liquid is a syrup, about 15-20 minutes. Cool.
- Spread a thin layer of goat cheese on each piece of prosciutto; drizzle with gastrique and top with basil leaves. Sprinkle with black pepper and roll up. Place seam side down.

237.   Prosciutto Goat Cheese Stuffed Dates

Serving: Serves 2-4 | Prep: | Cook: |Ready in:

Ingredients

- 8   Medjool dates
- 2 ounces goat cheese, preferably Bucheron or Cana de Cabra
- 8   Basil leaves
- 4   strips Serrano ham or Prosciutto, cut in half

Direction

- Cut a split lengthwise in the dates to remove the pit and stuff with goat cheese. Make sure to close them as much as possible.

- Wrap a basil leaf around the stuffed date and wrap a half strip of prosciutto around that.
- Bake at 375 degrees for 5-10 minutes, just until the fat on the prosciutto starts to render and brown and the cheese melts.

---

238. Prosciutto And Goat Cheese Strata

Serving: Serves 10 | Prep: | Cook: | Ready in:

Ingredients

- 18   slices firm white bread, crusts removed
- 6 ounces bacon or prosciutto, thinly sliced, divided
- 8 ounces Boursin or goat cheese, crumbled, divided
- 4 ounces provolone, grated (about 1 1/2 cups), divided
- 1/4 cup chopped green onions or leeks, divided
- 6 tablespoons fresh basil, chopped, divided
- 5   large eggs
- 2 cups whole milk
- 1 tablespoon Dijon mustard
- 1/2 teaspoon salt
- Pepper, to taste
- 3 tablespoons butter, melted

Direction

- Line bottom of 13 x 9 x 2-inch glass baking dish until completely covered with one layer of bread, cutting some slices to fit. Arrange half of the prosciutto evenly over bread. Sprinkle half of the goat cheese and half of the provolone on top of the prosciutto, then add half of the green onions and half of the basil. Cover with second layer of bread. Layer remaining prosciutto, goat cheese, provolone, green onions, and basil atop bread. Cut remaining bread into 1/4-inch cubes. Sprinkle over top.

- Whisk eggs, milk, mustard, and salt in bowl. Season with pepper. Pour egg mixture over layered bread mixture, then press down on the bread with a spatula. Drizzle melted butter over bread and egg mixture. Cover and refrigerate overnight.
- To bake the strata, preheat oven to 350° F. Uncover strata and let stand at room temperature, 30 minutes. Bake until center is set, about 1 hour. Remove from oven, and set aside. Preheat broiler, then place strata under broiler until top is golden, about 30 seconds. Cut into large squares and serve.

---

239. Proscuitto, Goat Cheese, And Fig Pear Balsamic Jam Rolls

Serving: Makes 24 rolls | Prep: | Cook: | Ready in:

Ingredients

- Fig Pear and Balsamic Jam
- 1.5 pounds figs, stems removed and coarsely chopped
- .5 pounds pears, peeled and pit removed and coarsely chopped
- 1 cup brown sugar
- .5 cups balsamic vinegar
- .25 cups fresh lemon juice
- Proscuitto, Goat Cheese, and Fig, Pear, Balsamic Jam Rolls
- 1 cup fresh arugula
- 3 teaspoons fresh lemon juice
- 3 tablespoons extra virgin olive oil
- Pinch of freshly ground black pepper
- 12 pieces proscuitto, cut in half crosswise
- .5 cups goat cheese (chevre)
- .25 cups fig, pear, balsamic jam

Direction

- For the jam, combine the figs, pears, brown sugar, and balsamic in a large saucepan.

- Bring to a simmer over medium to high heat. Then lower the heat to maintain a gentle simmer and cook.
- Break up the large pieces and stir periodically until the jam thickens.
- Remove from the heat and squeeze about a tablespoon of lemon juice, stir. Taste and add more lemon juice if desired.
- Spoon the jam into a container with a lid.
- Using sterilized jars, spoon into jars, seal jarm and process in boiling water for 10 minutes. Let cool and lids should seal.
- For the prosciutto rolls, place arugula in a medium bowl. In a small bowl, whisk the lemon juice, evoo, salt, and pepper. Toss the arugula in the dressing until lightly dressed (you may not need all of the dressing).
- Spread one tablespoon of goat cheese across one of each piece of prosciutto. Top each with 1/2 tsp. fig, pear, and balsamic jam. Divide the dressed arugula evenly across each of the pieces of prosciutto. Starting from the end covered with the filling, carefully roll each piece of prosciutto. Serve

240.   Prune And Goat Cheese Tart With Walnut Spice Crust

Serving: Serves 16 | Prep: | Cook: | Ready in:

Ingredients

- Crust
- 1 cup flour
- 1/2 cup powdered sugar
- 1/2 cup walnuts
- 1/4 teaspoon salt
- 1/4 teaspoon cinnamon
- 1/4 teaspoon nutmeg
- 1/4 teaspoon ground cardamom
- 1 teaspoon dried thyme
- 5 tablespoons cold butter, cut into 1/2 inch cubes
- 1 egg

- Filling
- 6 ounces prunes
- 1/4 cup cognac
- 8 ounces soft goat cheese that has sat at room temperature for while
- 1 cup ricotta
- 3 tablespoons sugar
- 1 tablespoon olive oil
- 1/4 teaspoon nutmeg
- 1/3 cup honey

Direction

- Microwave cognac and prunes for 45 seconds and let sit at room temperature while you prepare the rest of the tart.
- Blend flour, sugar, walnuts, salt, nutmeg, cinnamon, cardamom and thyme in a food processor until nuts are finely ground. Add butter and pulse until the dough looks like coarse cornmeal. Add egg and pulse until dough start to form large clumps. Press the dough into a 9 inch tart pan with removable bottom and chill for at least an hour.
- Line crust with foil and fill with pie weights. Bake in a preheated 350 oven for 15 minutes. Remove foil and weights and bake for another 15 minutes, until golden. Let cool completely.
- Blend prunes and cognac in food processor until smooth. Place in a medium bowl and add goat cheese, ricotta, sugar, olive oil and nutmeg. Spread filling in cooled crust and chill for at least an hour.
- Just before serving, bring the honey to a boil in a small saucepan. Boil for about two minutes, until the honey gets very bubbly. Turn off the heat, stir until the bubbles subside, and pour over the tart.

241.   Pumpkin Ale Caramelized Figs

Serving: Makes 16-24 bites | Prep: | Cook: | Ready in:

Ingredients

- 8-12 fresh, ripe figs
- 1 cup + 2 tablespoons brown sugar
- 3 tablespoons butter
- 1/4 cup pumpkin ale (or other medium bodied beer of your choice)
- 1 ounce goat cheese, crumbled

Direction

- Halve figs lengthwise.
- Pour 1 cup of brown sugar into a shallow bowl or dish. Press cut side of figs into sugar (doing so will start to pack the brown sugar, so you will need to rake or stir the sugar frequently to keep it loose). Repeat process twice with each fig.
- In a large skillet, melt 1 tablespoon of butter over medium heat.
- Once butter is melted, place figs, cut side down, in skillet. Let sit 2-3 minutes. Carefully turn each fig over and cook and additional 2-3 minutes. Remove figs from pan and set aside.
- Add remaining butter and 2 tablespoons brown sugar, stir until sugar is dissolved. Stir in beer and let mixture reduce slightly.
- Pour caramel beer sauce over figs. Crumble goat cheese over top and serve.

242. Quinoa Salad With Spinach, Strawberries And Goat Cheese

Serving: Serves 4 | Prep: | Cook: | Ready in:

Ingredients

- Quinoa Salad
- 1 cup quinoa, rinsed (I used red quinoa)
- kosher salt and black pepper
- 2 cups baby spinach leaves
- 2 tablespoons fresh basil, cut into chiffonade (ribbons)
- 2/3 cup sliced strawberries

- 1 ounce goat cheese, crumbled
- 1 1/2 tablespoons sliced almonds, toasted
- Balsamic Dressing
- 2 tablespoons balsamic vinegar
- 1 teaspoon Dijon mustard
- 1/2 teaspoon honey or agave nectar
- 2 tablespoons extra virgin olive oil
- Kosher salt and black pepper

Direction

- Place the quinoa in a medium saucepan along with 2 cups water and ¼ teaspoon salt. Bring to a boil then cover with a lid and reduce to a simmer. Simmer the quinoa about 15 minutes until cooked. Remove the lid and cook another 2-3 minutes until all of the water has evaporated. Remove from the heat and fluff with a fork. Let the quinoa cool to room temperature.
- Meanwhile, make the balsamic dressing. Whisk the vinegar, mustard and honey together in a small bowl. Slowly pour in the olive oil while you continue to whisk. Season the dressing with salt and pepper.
- Place the quinoa in a salad bowl along with the spinach, basil, strawberries, goat cheese and almonds. Add the dressing and toss to combine all ingredients well. Serve the salad alone or if desired, topped with slices of grilled chicken breast.

243. Radish Goat Cheese Galette

Serving: Serves 4-6 | Prep: | Cook: | Ready in:

Ingredients

- For The Crust
- 4 ounces unsalted butter
- 2 cups unbleached all purpose flour
- 6 ounces sour cream (not low fat or fat free)
- 2-3 tablespoons ice water
- 1 pinch kosher salt

- Radish and Goat Cheese Galette
- 5 ounces chevre goat cheese
- 1 tablespoon sour cream (optional)
- 1   sour cream pie crust, see above
- 1 tablespoon dijon mustard
- 6   medium size, firm radishes, sliced thin with a mandoline or very sharp knife
- 1/2 tablespoon sherry vinegar
- kosher salt and black pepper to taste
- 1 tablespoon fresh rosemary leaves, or to taste

Direction

- For The Crust
- Combine flour and salt
- Cut butter into flour / salt mixture, mix should be dry and crumble easily
- Slowly add sour cream, while cutting flour / butter mix with a fork
- If dough still looks a bit too dry add a tablespoon of ice water at a time until dough is a fully formed ball, wrap and refrigerate 10 minutes.
- Radish and Goat Cheese Galette
- In a small bowl, combine goat cheese and use sour cream to soften to a spreadable texture, season to taste with kosher salt and pepper
- Roll out chilled pie crust to a roughly round shape and an even thickness.
- Spread the raw crust first with a thin layer of Dijon mustard, the with the goat cheese mixture
- Fold the edges of the galette in, pinching or folding as you go.
- Bake the galette on parchment paper on the middle rack of a 350 degree oven for 20-25 minutes, check frequently for varying oven temps. Crust should be lightly brown and flaky, the goat cheese mix will be lightly cracked. Remove from oven to cool.
- Combine thinly sliced radishes with a scant tablespoon of sherry vinegar, as well as salt and pepper to taste, top the warm - but not hot - galette with radish mixture, and rosemary, slice and serve

Serving: Serves 10-12 | Prep: | Cook: | Ready in:

Ingredients

- Rapturous Morel Marmalade
- 8 ounces Fresh or Rehydrated Morels
- 4   Bacon or Pancetta Slices
- 2 sprigs Fresh Thyme
- 1/2 cup Veal Stock
- Salt & Pepper to Taste
- 1 cup Carrots, Diced
- 1 cup Shallots, Diced
- 1 cup Port Wine
- 1/2 cup Red Wine Vinegar
- 3 tablespoons Brown Sugar
- 1 teaspoon Black Pepper
- Salt to Taste
- Goat Cheese Polenta
- 4 cups Unsalted Chicken Stock
- 1 cup Polenta
- 1/2 cup Goat Cheese
- Salt & Pepper to Taste
- 1 tablespoon Freshy Thyme Leaves

Direction

- Rapturous Morel Marmalade
- In a large sauté pan, cook the bacon till lightly crisp. Remove the bacon and add morels, pinch of salt, and 2 tbs of butter. Cook till the mushrooms develop a nice brown crust. Add veal stock and thyme, simmer rapidly till the stock is more or less evaporated, leaving the mushrooms moist with the tiniest amount of liquid. Set aside.
- In a separate large pan heat 3 tbsps. butter. Saute the shallots and carrots with a pinch of salt till softened, about 10 minutes, stirring frequently. Stir in the sugars, vinegar, port wine, kosher salt and pepper. Cook over medium heat until the liquid has reduced.

- Chop the sautéed mushrooms and bacon bits. Add to the warm sauce and combine gently but thoroughly over low heat till warmed. Check for black pepper, it should be fairly peppery. Serve with goat cheese polenta and crème fraîche. Be warned – highly addictive!!
- Goat Cheese Polenta
- Bring the chicken stock, 2 tbsps. butter, pepper, thyme, and salt to a boil in a heavy-bottomed pot. Sprinkle polenta slowly while constantly stirring the liquid. Reduce the heat to a gentle simmer, and constantly stir the polenta till it pulls away from the sides of the pan. The polenta is cooked when it is creamy and no longer grainy. It should take about 20-25 minutes to get the right consistency. (I cook polenta for at least an hour when I want it extra creamy as I serve it with my short ribs).
- Stir in the goat cheese and taste the seasonings. Pour immediately into a butter glass pan. When cool, cover and refrigerate overnight.
- Cut the polenta into any shape you wish. I usually cut them into bite size since I serve this at my cocktail parties. Heat a big skillet with some olive oil. Pan fry the bites till golden brown on each side. Top it with Morel Marmalade and crème fraîche. Serve warm.

- Put the juice of two fresh limes, the flesh of two whole avocados, and 2 to 4 tablespoons of fresh, local honey into a food processor. Blend until smooth. The puree can be as sweet as the palate of the person making it desires. We use about two tablespoons.
- Put the package of goat cheese, along with at least two tablespoons of water into the stand mixer. The water is also approximate. Blend with the whisk attachment until the goat cheese is soft and smooth. The water is just enough to make it thinner, a similar consistency to the avocado-lime puree. Thicker than pancake batter but not as thick as muffin batter.
- Compose the parfaits in a clear glass. Add a hearty scoop of the lime/avocado puree, a layer of raspberries, a healthy scoop of goat cheese, a layer of raspberries and repeat until the parfaits are full. Add many raspberries as they are the star of the dish, and the goat cheese's strong flavor and lime puree just enhance the berries.

245.   Raspberry Lime Parfaits With Whipped Goat Cheese

Serving: Serves 4 | Prep: | Cook: | Ready in:

Ingredients

- 2 avocados
- 2 limes
- 2-4 tablespoons Honey
- 1 package goat cheese, softened
- 2 tablespoons water
- 1 pint fresh raspberries

Direction

246.   Rich And Creamy Tomato Pie Without Mayo

Serving: Serves 6-8 people | Prep: | Cook: | Ready in:

Ingredients

- Tomato Filing
- 4 large, ripe tomatoes
- 2 pinches Margarita Himalayan Pink Salt
- 1/4 cup fresh basil
- 1 tablespoon garlic, minced
- 1/4 cup shallots, minced
- Goat and Cream Cheese Filling
- 4 ounces cream cheese, softened
- 6 ounces goat cheese
- 1 cup white cheddar, shredded
- 1 tablespoon garlic, minced
- 2 tablespoons shallots, minced

- 1/2-1 teaspoons Oregano and Sage French Grey salt
- 1 tablespoon lemon juice, freshly squeezed
- 2 tablespoons red wine vinegar
- 1/2 cup extra virgin olive oil
- 1 buttery pie crust, preferably homemade
- 1 cup white cheddar cheese, shredded for top of pie

Direction

- Make the crust or thaw a frozen one. I highly recommend making a buttery homemade crust. You can make it ahead of time and freeze it or place in your refrigerator for a week well wrapped in plastic. If you do not have time, Wholly Wholesome pie crusts are very good and there are gluten free crusts as well.
- Wash and cut up the tomatoes. Remove the seeds and place tomatoes in a strainer over a bowl to catch the juices. Add some Margarita Himalayan Pink Salt to the tomatoes to help them start breaking down. Let the juices drain into a bowl for at least 10 minutes. If you skip this step, you will have a soggy pie.
- Chop the basil leaves, 1 shallot, and 2 cloves of garlic. Pack the chopped basil into a 1/4 cup measuring cup and add the basil to the tomatoes. Measure 1/4 cup of chopped shallots and 1 tablespoon of minced garlic. Add to the tomatoes. Toss all the ingredients together.
- Make the goat or feta and cream cheese spread. I use goat but you choose what cheese you like best. Place 6 ounces of goat cheese crumbles in a food processor. Add 4 ounces of softened cream cheese and 1 cup of cheddar cheese. Now add 1 tablespoon minced garlic, 2 tablespoons minced shallot, 1/2 teaspoon Oregano and Sage French Grey, 1 tablespoon freshly squeezed lemon juice, 2 tablespoon red wine vinegar, and 1/2 cup of good olive oil. Mix together until smooth. Taste and see if you want another 1/2 teaspoon of Oregano and Sage herb salt.

- Squeeze the tomatoes again to make sure you removed as much liquid as possible. Place the tomatoes in the pie crust. Spread the cream cheese spread over the tomatoes. Sprinkle 1 cup of cheddar cheese over the cream cheese spread.
- Bake at 350 degrees conventional or 335 degrees convection for 25 to 30 minutes until the sides are bubbling and the cheddar cheese has browned. Let sit for 15 minutes to cool and firm up or it will be a little soupy. We usually cannot wait and cut into within 5 minutes. It is so good! Enjoy.

---

247. Ricotta And (Not Fresh) Goat Cheese Stuffed Shells

Serving: Serves 8 | Prep: | Cook: |Ready in:

Ingredients

- 1 12-oz pack shells
- 1 large egg
- 12 ounces fresh ricotta
- 4 ounces funky goat cheese (rind intact, nothing in the grim tube!)
- 12 ounces thawed spinach, wrung dry and chopped fine
- 4 tablespoons fresh basil, chopped
- 4 sprigs fresh bread crumbs
- 1 tablespoon kosher salt
- 1/2 teaspoon black pepper, freshly ground
- 1 28-ounce can fire-roasted chopped organic tomatoes
- 2 ounces grated Parmesan

Direction

- Preheat oven to 375 degrees.
- Cook pasta shells according to package directions; make sure to use plenty of salted water. Drain and set aside.
- Beat egg in large bowl. Add ricotta, goat cheese, spinach, herbs, bread crumbs, nutmeg,

salt and pepper. Mix until thoroughly combined.

- Spread half a cup of the tomato "sauce" in the bottom of each cooking vessel. (I used 2 9 X 13 baking dishes)
- Use medium-sized metal spoon to fill the shells with the stuffing, arrange in cooking dishes.
- Pour the remaining pasta sauce over the shells
- Cover in foil and pop in the oven for 30 minutes. Remove from oven, remove foil, add Parmesan and cook uncovered for 5 minutes, until cheese has melted and serve.

---

248.   Roast Corn, Goat Cheese, And Caramelized Onion Quesadilla

Serving: Serves 2 | Prep: | Cook: | Ready in:

Ingredients

- 1 ear of corn
- 1/2 of a medium white onion
- 1/4 cup grated pepper jack cheese
- 4 ounces chevre or other soft goat cheese
- 2 ten inch flour tortillas
- Vegetable oil, for cooking

Direction

- Remove the corn kernels from the cob. Heat a large skillet over medium high heat, and put the kernels in it. Cook, stirring and shaking frequently, until the kernels are slightly browned and smell fragrant (about 10 minutes). Remove from the skillet and set aside.
- Next, cut the onion into thin slices. Heat some vegetable oil in a pot over medium heat and add the onions with some salt and pepper. Cook, stirring occasionally, while the onions soften and brown. Deglaze the pan as needed with a splash of water, white wine, or stock (splash the liquid in and then use it to scrape

the browned bits off the bottom of the pan). Continue until the onions are a deep golden brown (20 to 30 minutes). Remove and set aside.
- Heat about a teaspoon of vegetable oil in a large skillet over medium heat, and spread the oil out across the bottom. Lay the first tortilla in the pan.
- Sprinkle the tortilla with half the pepper jack cheese (this cheese is just here to hold the quesadilla together, since the goat cheese does not really melt).
- Distribute the corn, onion, and dollops of the goat cheese evenly across the tortilla, then add the rest of the pepper jack.
- Put the second tortilla on top.
- Cook until the bottom tortilla has browned (about five minutes), then carefully flip it over (we find that two spatulas does the job well). Cook until the other side is browned (3-4 minutes), remove, and serve.

---

249.   Roast Pumpkin, Peppers And Goats Cheese Frittata

Serving: Serves 4 | Prep: | Cook: | Ready in:

Ingredients

- For the roasted vegetables
- 2 cups pumpkin, cubed
- 1 1/2 cups red peppers, sliced
- 4 Garlic cloves, unpeeled
- 4-5 tablespoons Olive oil
- For the frittata
- 4 Bacon strips, chopped
- 1 piece Goat's cheese
- 2 handfuls Parmesan
- 5-6 eggs, depending on depth of pan
- 1 cup frozen peas
- 1 handful Fresh Basil

Direction

- For the roasted vegetables

- The amount of pumpkin and peppers added are entirely to your preference, and therefore adjust the amount to your own liking. Preheat oven to 400(°F). Line baking tray with baking paper.
- Place rosemary, pumpkin, peppers, garlic and olive oil in bowl and toss till fully coated. Season well with salt & pepper. Arrange on baking tray in a single layer, bake for 45-50mins or until tender. You want to achieve those gorgeous brown bits on the vegetables when it's out from the oven. Discard the garlic cloves.
- For the frittata
- Preheat Oven to 400(°F). Using an oven-proof pan, on high heat, crisp up bacon bits. Add spring onions to bacon fat and cook on medium heat, 3-4minutes. Throw in peas, pumpkin, peppers and fresh basil, and continue cooking for 1-2minutes. Season well with salt and pepper.
- Crack eggs into large bowl, crack in black pepper, dash of milk and 1 handful of parmesan. This seasons the eggs. Mix well with fork.
- Combine the eggs into the pan with the rest of the ingredients. Use a wooden spoon to ensure the egg mixture flows to the bottom of the pan, covering the entire pan. Crumble goat cheese into pockets of the egg mixture, bring the heat up to high, until a slow boil. At this point, sprinkle the remainder of the parmesan onto the surface of the egg mixture and transfer to the oven. Be generous with the cheese to ensure a golden brown top. Bake for 15minutes or till golden brown. The end result you are seeking would be a golden crust on the top and an extremely moist center of the frittata.
- Using a paring knife, run your knife around the surface of the pan to release the frittata. Cut into wedges and serve straight hot from the pan.

250. Roasted Apple & Fennel Salad With Toasted Hazelnuts & Goat Cheese

Serving: Serves 4 to 6 people | Prep: 0hours20mins | Cook: 0hours30mins | Ready in:

Ingredients

- 3 baking apples (those that retain their structure when baked like Granny Smith, Honeycrisp, Jonagold, Pinklady, etc.)
- 2 fennel bulbs with fronds
- Extra virgin olive oil
- Salt and pepper
- 1 pinch red pepper flakes
- 1 handful mint leaves
- 4 scallions, thinly sliced
- 1/2 cup hazelnuts, toasted, peeled and chopped
- 4 ounces fresh goat cheese, crumbled (crumbled mild blue cheese would be delicious as well)
- 1 lemon, zest and juice

Direction

- Preheat the oven to 425*F. Cut the fennel bulbs into 1-inch wedges, reserving the fennel fronds for finishing the salad. Cut the apples into similarly sized wedges. Spread the fennel on one parchment-lined sheet pan, and spread the apple on another. Drizzle both generously with olive oil, and season with salt, freshly cracked black peppers, and a pinch of red pepper flakes. Roast the apple pan for 15 to 20 minutes, and roast the fennel pan for ~30 minutes, flipping each halfway through, until all are caramelized, golden brown, and tender. Remove from the oven and allow to cool on sheet pans.
- Meanwhile, prep mint leaves and fennel fronds. Slice scallions. Toast, peel and, chop hazelnuts. Crumble goat cheese.
- To finish the dish, carefully layer the roasted apples, roasted fennel, mint leaves, fennel fronds, sliced scallions, toasted hazelnuts and

crumbled goat cheese on several layers on a shallow serving platter. Zest over 1 lemon and shower the whole thing with lemon juice and a drizzle of best quality extra virgin olive oil. Enjoy as a filling salad on its own or serve with roasted pork or chicken.

---

251. Roasted Beet And Arugula Salad

Serving: Serves one | Prep: | Cook: |Ready in:

Ingredients

- For the salad:
- 4 large beets, peeled and chopped
- 1 tablespoon olive oil
- salt
- pepper
- 1 handful of arugula
- 1/2 cup garbanzos
- 1/4 cup pistachios, shelled
- goat cheese
- For the dressing:
- 1 tablespoon extra-virgin olive oil
- 1 splash balsamic vinegar, plus more if you want more tang
- pepper
- 1 dollop coarse ground or Dijon mustard

Direction

- Preheat oven to 425 degrees F.
- Use a vegetable peeler to peel the beets. Chop the beets to about the size of a quarter.
- Toss chopped beets in a mixing bowl with a tablespoon or so of olive oil. Season with salt and pepper. Place the beets on a large baking sheet lined with parchment paper. Bake for 20 to 25 minutes. At this point the beets should be firm but you should be able to cut into them with the side of a fork. Let them cool. For a crispier beet, give them 5 to 10 more minutes in the oven. If you're short on time, chop the beets into smaller pieces. (Four beets will leave

you with enough for the salad and a cup or so of leftover roasted beets to save for salads throughout the week).

- Use the same mixing bowl to toss a handful of arugula with salad dressing. To make the dressing, mix a tablespoon of extra-virgin olive oil, a splash of balsamic, a few grinds of pepper, and a small dollop of mustard. Feeling feisty? Add a squeeze of Sriracha. Mix in the garbanzos with the arugula. Set aside.
- Break the shells off of the pistachios, leaving you with no more than a 1/4 cup. Add pistachios and about a 1/2 cup of beets to the bowl with arugula. Toss the salad together.
- Move salad to a plate, and finish it by crumbling some small pieces of goat cheese on top of the salad.

---

252. Roasted Beet And Goat Cheese Salad With Dijon Vinaigrette

Serving: Serves 4 | Prep: | Cook: |Ready in:

Ingredients

- 4 medium fresh beets, with greens cut off
- 2 tablespoons olive oil
- 1/4 teaspoon sea salt
- 3 cups mesclun or baby greens
- 2 ounces goat cheese, roughly crumbled
- 2 tablespoons broken walnuts
- 1 tablespoon coarse dijon mustard
- 3 tablespoons red wine vinegar
- 2 tablespoons olive oil

Direction

- Cut beets into quarters, toss with 2 tbsp. olive oil and salt, and put beets on a baking sheet in a 350 degree oven.
- Roast beets for 20 minutes or until fork tender, stirring about halfway through cooking time.
- Let beets cool for 5-10 minutes. Toss with greens, walnuts and goat cheese.

- Combine Dijon mustard, vinegar and oil until well combined and pour over salad. Toss lightly and serve.

253.   Roasted Beet And Goat Cheese Skewers

Serving: Makes 24 bites | Prep: | Cook: | Ready in:

Ingredients

- Roasting The Beets
- 3 Golden Beets
- 3 Red Beets
- Rolling the Goat Cheese and Assembling The Skewers
- 8 ounces Herbed Goat Cheese
- 1/4 cup Sliced Toasted Almonds
- 1 tablespoon Wildflower Honey

Direction

- Roasting the Beets
- Clean the beets and chop off both ends. I like working with the golden beets first as the red variety will stain your cutting board (and hands, and countertop, etc.).
- Wrap each beet individually in a square of aluminum foil, tenting the top to allow for some steam release.
- Roast at 375 degrees until a fork can be inserted with only minimal resistance. This takes approximately 45 min-1 hr. depending on the size of your beets. Once cooked, take out of the oven and unwrap the foil, but leave the beets in the "cups" until cool enough to handle.
- Peel the skin off each beet and cut off each of the rounded sides until you have a fairly uniform square of beet. Cut each square in half, and then each half in half again, and each in half once again for 8 small uniform squares per beet. Allow to cool completely- this can be made even a couple days in advance.

- Rolling the Goat Cheese and Assembling the Skewers
- Crush the toasted almonds roughly by hand into a wide dish.
- Divide the goat cheese into 24 portions. Take a portion and roll in between your hands, forming into a small ball.
- Take the goat cheese ball and roll in the dish of almonds until coated. Repeat until you have rolled and coated all 24.
- Assemble your ingredients sliding one of each onto a short skewer, beginning with a square of the golden beet, then the almond coated goat cheese ball, and finally the red beet on the bottom.
- Lay your skewers on their sides next to each other and drizzle lightly with honey. Flip and drizzle the opposite side.

254.   Roasted Beet, Baby Spinach, And Goat Cheese Quiche

Serving: Serves 6 | Prep: | Cook: | Ready in:

Ingredients

- 1 cup 2 tbsp stone ground whole wheat flour
- 1/2 teaspoon salt
- 6 tablespoons cold butter, cut in cubes
- 2 ounces cold water
- 2 tablespoons toasted sesame seeds
- 3 medium beets, sliced
- 1 sweet onion, sliced
- 2 tablespoons olive oil
- 1/4 cup balsamic vinegar
- salt and pepper
- 1 cup baby spinach
- 3 eggs
- 1/2 cup Greek yogurt
- 1/2 cup milk
- 1 tablespoon dry rosemary
- salt and pepper
- 6 ounces goat cheese

- 1/4 cup grated parmesan

Direction

- Gently grease quiche pan and sprinkle with 1 tbsp. toasted sesame seeds.
- In a food processor, add flour, salt, and cold butter. Pulse until crumbly. Add water and pulse until dough forms. Add 1 tbsp. toasted sesame seeds and pulse 2-3 times, until combined.
- Remove pastry and form into a ball. Using a rolling pin, roll out pastry on a lightly floured surface. Line prepared quiche pan with the pastry and set aside.
- Preheat oven to 375°F.
- Add beets and onions to a baking sheet in a single layer. Drizzle with olive oil, balsamic vinegar. Season with salt and pepper.
- Roast 30 minutes. Remove from oven and add baby spinach to baking sheet. Roast an additional 5 minutes.
- Remove from oven and set aside.
- Reduce oven temperature to 350°F.
- In a mixing bowl, whisk eggs, yogurt, milk, rosemary, salt, and pepper.
- Add roasted beets, onions, and spinach to quiche crust. Sprinkle in crumbled goat cheese. Pour egg mixture into the quiche crust.
- Bake 50 minutes.
- Sprinkle grated parmesan over quiche and bake another 5 minutes.
- Remove from oven and let sit 10 minutes before slicing.

255.   Roasted Beetroot Salad W Goat Cheese + Watercress Salad

Serving: Serves 2-4 | Prep: | Cook: | Ready in:

Ingredients

- PROVISIONS
- 1 bunch baby beetroot
- 100g goats cheese

- Olive oil
- Salt & freshly cracked pepper
- WATERCRESS DRESSING
- 1 bunch watercress
- 1 tsp salted capers, rinsed
- ¼ cup pistachios
- 1 tsp Dijon Mustard
- 1 tsp cider vinegar
- ¼ cup extra virgin olive oil

Direction

- Preheat oven to 220 °C.
- Wash and trim the tops of your beetroot. Place beetroot in a backing tray, drizzle with a little olive oil, and season with salt & pepper. Roast for 20 minutes, or until tender. When beetroot is cool enough to handle, peel the skin, cut in half.
- With your watercress, rinse, chop off the top half of the watercress, arrange leaves on your serving dish. Place the remaining watercress stems into a food processor along with your capers, pistachios, Dijon mustard, cider vinegar, olive oil and pepper. Pulse until combined and chunky.
- To assemble, arrange your goat's cheese and beetroot on top of the watercress leaves, then spoon over your dressing. Enjoy. Share

256.   Roasted Butternut Squash With Goat Cheese, Beet Greens And Walnuts

Serving: Serves 4 | Prep: | Cook: | Ready in:

Ingredients

- 1 1/2 pounds Butternut Squash(peeled and cut into 1 inch pieces)
- 1 bunch beet greens, washed
- 3 tablespoons Olive Oil
- 1/3 cup walnuts, toasted
- 1/3 cup Goat Cheese

- 1/4 cup mint, finely chopped
- 1/4 teaspoon cayenne pepper
- 1/4 teaspoon ground cinammon
- 1 teaspoon sea salt

Direction

- Preheat oven at 400
- On a parchment lined baking sheet, drizzle the squash pieces with 2 Tablespoons olive oil and add the cinnamon, cayenne and sea salt, toss to evenly coat and roast for 45-50 minutes.
- Cut the leaves of the beet greens off of the stalks. Chiffonade leaves, rolling three at a time and then making thin slices on a diagonal.
- When the squash is cooked through, remove from oven and mix in the beet greens right on the baking sheet. If needed, add the T olive oil.
- Then add the mint, goat cheese and walnuts. Serve immediately and enjoy!

---

257. Roasted Carrots With Goat Cheese, Peanuts, And A Balsamic Drizzle

Serving: Makes enough to fill your favorite platter | Prep: | Cook: | Ready in:

Ingredients

- Carrots
- Goat cheese
- Roasted peanuts (Spanish if you have them, they look swankier)
- Balsamic vinegar
- Parsley, chopped, for garnish

Direction

- Heat your oven to 400 degrees.
- Wash your carrots. Peel them if you like to make more work for yourself or if they look especially gnarly. Cut them in half, or quarters if they are especially large.

- Spread out your carrots on a baking sheet. Drizzle with olive oil and lightly sprinkle with salt. (No, these items aren't listed in the ingredients. They don't count. They should be in your kitchen at all times.) Roast in the oven until just tender and starting to get some crisp edges -- 20 to 30 minutes or so.
- Meanwhile, reduce your balsamic vinegar (bring it up to a boil, and then reduce the heat to keep it at a low simmer until it reduces to about 1/3 of the original volume). What's that you say? It's a weeknight and you don't want to muck about with reducing balsamic vinegar, and you happen to have a bottle of Trader Joe's Balsamic Glaze on hand? That's cool, it will work, and I won't reveal your secrets.
- Once your carrots are sufficiently roasted, put them on a platter, drizzle them with the balsamic reduction, scatter little blobs of goat cheese, sprinkle with peanuts, and then a bit of chopped parsley.
- If the lack of concrete numbers is horrifying you right now, I started with about 2 pounds of carrots, and that was just enough to completely fill one baking sheet. I probably used 2 to 3 tablespoons of reduced balsamic, about 2 ounces of goat cheese, a small handful of peanuts (between 1 and 2 ounces), and around 1 tablespoon of chopped parsley -- but I would bump up the amounts of all of the toppings if I was plating the dish instead of serving it family style.

---

258. Roasted Cherry Tomato Tart

Serving: Serves 6-8 | Prep: | Cook: | Ready in:

Ingredients

- 1 small tart crust
- 1 1/2 - 2 cups cherry tomatoes (the exact amount may vary, depending upon the size

and shape of your tomatoes - if you roast too many, that's not a bad thing at all)

- olive oil
- 1 tablespoon dijon mustard
- 8 ounces soft goat cheese
- 2 eggs
- 1/2 cup half-and-half or milk
- 2 teaspoons chopped fresh thyme (or other herb of your choice), divided
- salt

Direction

- Preheat the oven to 200 degrees. Halve the cherry tomatoes along their equators, and place them cut-side up in a baking dish. Drizzle with a bit of olive oil, and place them in the oven for 2-3 hours. They should shrink up somewhat, to maybe 2/3 their size, but still be juicy. Set aside.
- Raise the oven temperature to 375 degrees. Spread the mustard along the bottom of the tart shell, leaving a very thin layer. In a mixer (or using a whisk or fork and a lot of patience), blend together the goat cheese, eggs, half-and-half, and half the fresh herbs. Pour this mixture into the tart shell. Gently place the tomatoes on top, cut-side up, in an arrangement that strikes you.
- Transfer the tart to the oven, and bake ~45 minutes, until the filling has puffed and begun to brown, and the tomatoes are caramelized a touch on top. Remove from the oven and let cool slightly. Scatter the remaining fresh herb and a light sprinkling of salt across the top, and serve.

---

259.   Roasted Delicata Squash Salad With Toasted Almonds, Mint And Tahini

Serving: Serves 4 | Prep: 0hours15mins | Cook: 0hours45mins |Ready in:

Ingredients

- 3 Delicata squash, seeded and sliced into large chunks
- 5 ounces Baby arugula
- 4 ounces Fresh goat cheese, crumbled
- 1/2 cup Almonds, well toasted and chopped
- 1 cup Dates, pitted and chopped
- 1/2 cup Mint, torn
- 1 Lemon, zest and juice
- 1/4 cup Tahini
- 2 tablespoons Extra Virgin Olive Oil
- Salt and pepper, to taste

Direction

- Drizzled squash with olive oil and season with salt and pepper. Roast at 425 for 30-45 minutes until well browned, flipping halfway through. Set aside to cool completely.
- Meanwhile, make tahini drizzle by combining tahini with juice of half lemon, warm water to thin (2-4 tablespoons), and salt and black pepper to taste.
- Layer cooled squash with greens, crumbled goat cheese, toasted almonds, dates, mint and lemon zest. Dress the whole salad with a generous drizzle of olive oil and the juice of remaining half lemon. Lightly drizzle the whole thing with tahini dressing. Enjoy!

---

260.   Roasted Garlic And Caramelized Onion Tart

Serving: Makes one 11 inch tart | Prep: | Cook: |Ready in:

Ingredients

- Tart Crust
- 1 1/4 cups all purpose flour
- 1/2 teaspoon salt
- 1/2 teaspoon sugar
- 1/4 pound cold unsalted butter (1 stick)
- 1/4 cup ice cold water

- Roasted Garlic and Carmelized Onion Tart
- 1 Pie Dough Disc (from recipe)
- 1 Head of Garlic
- 1 anchovy fillet
- 1 tablespoon Olive Oil
- 1 Large Onion
- Salt and Pepper to Taste
- 2 ounces Goat Cheese, crumbled
- 1/4 cup grated parmesan cheese
- 1/4 cup toasted walnuts, chopped
- 1 beaten egg white
- 1/2 teaspoon Herbs de Provence

Direction

- Tart Crust
- Mix together the flour, salt and sugar in a food processor.
- Dice the butter into 1/2 inch cubes.
- Add to the processor and pulse 5 times (1 1/2 seconds each pulse) until the mixture has pea-sized globules of butter still visible in the flour.
- Add the cold water while quickly pulsing the flour mixture to evenly distribute the water through the butter-flour mix (do not overmix).
- Dump out the mixture onto plastic wrap. Bring together into a ball inside the plastic wrap and then flatten into a disc.
- Refrigerate for at least 30 minutes and up to 24 hours. Roll out or freeze dough for up to 1 month.
- Roasted Garlic and Caramelized Onion Tart
- Preheat the oven to 425 degrees.
- Cut the top of the head of garlic. Wrap the garlic in foil and roast for about 45 minutes until the garlic cloves are soft. Mash the softened garlic together with anchovy into a paste and set aside.
- Heat olive oil in saute pan. Slice onion and place in the pan. Saute for 20-25 minutes until onion is browned and caramelized. Season with salt and pepper.
- Roll out the pie dough into an 11 inch round. Place on parchment paper on a baking tray.
- Smear the garlic/anchovy paste onto the bottom of the pie dough, leaving a 2 inch

border. Load the onions, goat cheese and parmesan cheese into the middle and sprinkle the top with walnuts.
- Fold the outside 2 inch edge of the pastry over the center in an overlapping fashion (think rustic tart). Brush the folded edge with egg white and sprinkle with Herbs de Provence.
- Bake the tart at 425 F degrees for 10 minutes, then turn down to 375 degrees F and bake for another 20-25 minutes until the crust is golden. Serve warm.

---

261. Roasted Potato Pizza With Goat Cheese, Spring Herbs And Urfa Biber

Serving: Serves 2 to 4 | Prep: | Cook: | Ready in:

Ingredients

- Pizza Dough
- 2 teaspoons yeast
- 1 1/2 cups water
- 1 tablespoon olive oil
- 2 teaspoons kosher salt
- 1 cup rye flour
- 3 cups white flour, plus more as needed
- Assembling the Pizza
- 3 Yukon Gold potatoes, scrubbed and sliced 1/8" thick
- olive oil
- 1 bunch thyme, leaves removed, lightly chopped
- kosher salt
- 1 cup chopped herb mixture: chives, sorrel and parsley
- 1-2 radishes, julienned
- squeeze of lemon juice
- 1/2 recipe pizza dough, above
- 4 ounces crumbled goat cheese
- 0 Urfa Biber, to taste

Direction

- Pizza Dough
- Combine the water with the yeast and let stand until foamy. Add the olive oil and the salt. Stir in the rye flour and white flour, a little at a time, until the dough comes together and looks a bit ragged.
- Turn the dough onto a floured surface and knead for a minute. The dough should feel soft and a little tacky, but not sticky. Well-floured hands can help you knead it without adding too much additional flour. A wet dough makes a crisp crust. Put the dough into an oiled bowl, cover with a towel, and let it rise for about 2 hours.
- Once risen, turn the dough onto the counter and deflate it. Divide the dough into two pieces and let it rest on the counter for about 30 minutes. This recipe makes enough dough for 2 pizzas. You can reserve the rest of the dough in a ziploc bag in the refrigerator for another time, or double the amount of topping ingredients and make two pizzas.
- Assembling the Pizza
- Preheat the oven to 450 degrees. If you are using a pizza stone, have it heating up in the oven on a lower rack. Have another rack ready to roast the potatoes.
- Toss the sliced potatoes with a glug of olive oil, the chopped thyme leaves and a teaspoon of kosher salt. Spread them out on a heavy baking sheet. Roast about 15 minutes, or until the slices turn golden on their undersides. Remove from the oven. Try not to nibble on too many of the potatoes.
- Turn the oven temperature up to 500 degrees. The oven needs to be thoroughly pre-heated.
- Just before you are ready to assemble the pizza, make the herb salad. Combine the herb mixture in a small bowl with the radish, a teaspoon of olive oil, a squeeze of lemon juice and a sprinkle of kosher salt. Fluff with fork and taste for seasoning.
- Flatten one piece of pizza dough, sprinkle it with flour, and press it into an oval on a floured surface. Brush a piece of parchment paper with olive oil, then lift the dough onto it. Press or roll the dough out until the dough is very thin, but not transparent in any places. An average pizza could be 14 inches long and 10 inches wide. At this point, transfer the dough and parchment onto a peel, if you are using one. Alternatively transfer the dough and parchment onto a baking sheet.
- Lay the potato slices evenly over the top of the dough, overlapping a little to get good coverage. Sprinkle the crumbled goat cheese over the potatoes.
- Slide the whole pizza, parchment and all, onto a pizza stone. Alternatively, place the baking sheet into the oven. Bake the pizza for about 15 minutes. The crust should be golden and the cheese melted and bubbly. Use the peel to slide the pizza out, or remove the baking pan.
- Transfer the pizza to a cutting surface. Spoon the herb salad liberally over the top and sprinkle the Urfa Biber in place of the typical red pepper flakes--more pepper means more heat. Slice and enjoy!

---

262.   Roasted Red Peppers With Anchovies, Garlic, And Goat Cheese

Serving: Serves 4 | Prep: | Cook: | Ready in:

Ingredients

- 2 red bell peppers, cored, seeded, and cut lengthwise into eighths
- 16 anchovy fillets, packed in oil
- 1 tablespoon unsalted butter
- 1 tablespoon extra-virgin olive oil
- 3 cloves garlic, peeled and sliced lengthwise as thinly as possible
- 4 ounces creamy fresh goat cheese, chilled
- A handful baby arugula, chopped

Direction

- Heat oven to 350° F.
- Place peppers skin side-down in a baking dish. I like to snuggle them up nice and tight. Place

one anchovy fillet in the belly of each red pepper slice. Evenly distribute the butter, olive oil, and garlic between the slices.

- Cover with tin foil. Roast until peppers are starting to soften (about 25 minutes). Agitate the pan a bit to make sure all the slices are evenly coated with oil and not sticking to the bottom of the pan. Remove tin foil and cook for another 15 minutes or so until everything starts to brown. You want the peppers tender but not falling apart. This can take anywhere from 40 minutes to an hour. Just be vigilant and don't let anything burn. It's fine to turn down the temp or place the tin foil back on.
- Slice chilled goat cheese into about 8 discs. If they fall apart, just pat them back together like clay. Place on top of cooked peppers. Bake until goat cheese is warm all the way through, about 5 minutes. Cool for 5 minutes. Garnish with chopped arugula. Serve on grilled bread.

263. Roasted Seminole Pumpkin, Sage & Goat Cheese Wontons

Serving: Makes 24 wontons | Prep: | Cook: | Ready in:

Ingredients

- 24   wonton wrappers
- 1 seminole pumpkin, roasted and cooled
- 1 small goat cheese log (4oz)
- 1-2 tbsp dried sage
- sea salt (optional)

Direction

- Roast pumpkin, let cool.
- Remove the seeds. Use only the pumpkin flesh in this recipe. No skin.
- For the filling: mash roasted pumpkin and goat cheese together in a bowl, leaving as big of chunks of goat cheese as you'd like. Let the mixture have vibrant orange color from the pumpkin, speckled with white from the

chèvre. It is ok to have excess of this mixture. Make more wontons or just eat it if so :)
- Place a little bit of filling (1-2 tsp) in center of wonton. Too much filling will cause the wonton wrapper to break, believe me I tried to put in a ton of filling.
- Crumble the sage on top, as much as you'd like. Alternatively, you could mix the sage in with the chevre/pumpkin filling if you wish.
- You could also add some salt now if you'd like, I felt it didn't need but others/you may disagree. Add a sprinkle on top of the filling, to taste.
- Follow directions on wonton package for adding water to corners and folding wontons. You can also look this up online, very easy.
- Steam wontons until soft in a steamer or similar device
- Eat, share

264. Roasted Vegetables And CousCous

Serving: Serves 4 | Prep: | Cook: | Ready in:

Ingredients

- 2   med zucchini diced into 1" chunks
- 1   carrot diced into 1" chunks
- 1   onion peeled and cut into 1" squares
- 2   beetroot diced
- 1   parsnip cut into 1" chunks
- 1 pound tomatoes skinned, deseeded & chopped
- 2   fat garlic cloves (crushed)
- 10 ounces medium couscous
- 18 ounces (fluid) vegetable stock
- 3 ounces olive oil
- 4 ounces firm goat cheese
- salt and pepper

Direction

- Cut your vegetables as required above. It's up to you whether you peel the root ones or not. I don't.
- Preheat the oven to 475°F (240°C).
- Arrange everything in a roasting tin, sprinkle with the crushed garlic, and olive oil, toss it all around in the oil to get a good coating and season with salt and pepper.
- Place the tin on the highest shelf of the oven for 30-40 minutes or until the vegetables are soft and toasted brown.
- Place the couscous in a large, heatproof bowl, then pour the boiling stock over it, add some salt and pepper, stir it with a fork, then leave on one side for 5 minutes, by which time it will have absorbed all the stock and softened.
- While the couscous is absorbing the stock cut the cheese into sugar cube-sized pieces.
- To serve, put a layer of couscous at the bottom of a glass bowl, then add a layer of veggies, then some of the cheese. Keep going in layers until you end with some veggies arranged on the top. The goat cheese will melt into the veggies and couscous.

265. Rosemary & Goat Cheese Crostini

Serving: Serves 4 | Prep: | Cook: | Ready in:

Ingredients

- 1/2 baguette (day old is great)
- goat cheese
- fresh rosemary
- red pepper flakes
- dried parsley
- garlic salt
- butter or non-dairy spread (I like Earth Balance)

Direction

- Cut baguette into very thin slices. Place on a tray and toast in the toaster oven on one side about one minute on 250-300 degrees.
- Butter the untoasted side, and then put them back in the oven for another minute. Be careful not to burn them.
- Remove them from the oven and add a dollop of goat cheese. Sprinkle with parsley, red pepper flakes, and garlic salt.
- Top each crostini with a sprig of rosemary. Place back in the oven for another couple minutes, until crispy. Enjoy!

266. Rosemary And Goat Spuds

Serving: Serves 2-3 | Prep: | Cook: | Ready in:

Ingredients

- 2 Sweet Potatoes
- 2 teaspoons Rosemary (or, to your taste)
- 8 ounces Goat cheese
- 2 tablespoons Oil (I used olive but you could use coconut or vegetable)
- Salt and pepper

Direction

- Pre-heat oven to 400.
- Chop the sweet potatoes in 1 inch size pieces.
- Toss the potato pieces with the oil, rosemary, and some salt and pepper.
- Put the potatoes on a parchment or foil lined baking sheet and roast for 45-55 minutes. Toss them once about halfway through the cooking time.
- Crumble the goat cheese and sprinkle it over the potatoes. Return them to the oven until the cheese melts.
- Enjoy!

267. Rustic Beet Tart And Wilted Greens

Serving: Serves 4 | Prep: | Cook: |Ready in:

Ingredients

- 3 small (2 to 3 inch diameter) beets, any color, with the greens
- 1/2 package of frozen puff pastry, or equivalent of homemade
- 1 egg
- 1/4 to 1/2 cups whole milk or cream
- 3 to 5 ounces soft chevre style goat cheese, room temperature
- Salt, pepper, and nutmeg to taste

Direction

- Remove the greens from the beets, wash, and set aside.
- Scrub the beets. Most recipes have you roast and then peel your beets, but I peel mine first and then roast them. It's easier to handle them when they aren't slippery, and I lose less of their delicious flesh. But use your preferred method.
- Place each beet on a small square of aluminum foil, drizzle with olive oil, and wrap in the foil. Bake at 400 degrees anywhere from 30 minutes to an hour, depending on the size of your beets. They're done when they are knife tender and can be pierced with the tip of a paring knife with ease.
- Once the beets are knife tender, remove them from the oven and set aside to cool.
- While the beets cool, roll the puff pastry out until you have a rough 10-inch square. Transfer the square to a parchment-lined baking sheet.
- Roll in the edges of the pastry about an inch on all 4 sides so that you have a delicious pastry wall. Use a little water to seal the edges. You want to make sure that the custard doesn't leak out when poured into the "shell".
- Combine the egg and the goat cheese with salt, pepper and nutmeg. Slowly add the milk or cream, stirring until you have a thick but pourable consistency. It should be no thinner than pancake batter.
- Slice the beets into rounds. You should get 5 or 6 rounds from each beet.
- Pour the custard into the pastry shell, then lay the beets on top, being careful not to overflow the pastry shell.
- Bake at 400 until the pastry is golden, the custard is set, and the top is just a little brown.
- About 5 minutes before you pull the tart out of the oven, heat a small amount of oil in a large sauté pan. Roughly chop the beet greens and sauté them until wilted, adding salt and pepper to taste. (We liked these served on top of the tart, but you can also serve them as a simple side dish.)

268. Rustic Pear, Serrano Ham And Goat Cheese Tartlets

Serving: Serves 4 | Prep: | Cook: |Ready in:

Ingredients

- For the crust:
- 2 1/2 cups all purpose flour
- 1/2 cup unsalted butter, cubed and softened
- 1/4 teaspoon baking powder
- 2 egg yolks
- 2 teaspoons fresh rosemary, minced
- 1 1/2 teaspoons fresh ground black pepper
- 1/4 cup plus 2 or 3 tablespoons cold water
- for the tartlets:
- 3 thin slices of serrano ham, torn into strips
- 4 ounces goat cheese, at room temperature
- 3 ounces heavy cream
- 3 bosc pears, firm and just beginning to be ripe, you want them sweet but firm
- a handful of arugula
- extra virgin olive oil
- balsamic vinegar
- sea salt and fresh ground pepper

Direction

- For the crust combine the flour, baking powder, pepper and rosemary with the butter in a mixing bowl. Stir the butter into the flour with a wooden spoon then using your hands cup the flour lightly and rub it back and forth until you have a light mixture with no big butter chunks.
- Mix the egg yolks with a 1/4 cup of cold water and add it to the flour. Using your fingertips stir the dough and then start kneading it until it holds together but is a little crumbly. Add water by the tablespoon as necessary.
- Dust your work surface and turn the dough out onto the flour. It should be moist but with some crumbles. Start with a 4 inch round disk and then take your rolling pin and beat the crap out of the dough until it is about 8 inches round. Fold the dough into thirds letter style and beat the crap out of it again. Repeat the folding and beat the crap out of it two or three more times, whatever makes you feel good. Last night's dinner just think of it as the transit authority.
- Roll the dough out to about a 3/8 inch thickness and then cut it into four 4 x 6 inch squares. Place the squares onto a parchment lined sheet tray. Roll about a 1/4 inch of each side of each crust up and over onto itself a pinch the corners to hold them in place. This creates a lip.
- For the filling: Preheat the oven to 425 degrees. Take two of the pears and cutting lengthwise, cut two 3/8 inch pieces from the center portion of the pear. Usually you can get two pieces from one pear so the third pear is just in case. Core the pears as necessary. Now combine the goat cheese and the cream and mix it till it is creamy and spreadable. Season it with a touch of salt and some fresh ground white pepper. Remember the serrano is salty so not too much salt.
- Lay strips of serrano ham onto the tart crusts and then spread the cheese over it. Lay a pear slice on top of each tartlet, brush the pears with olive oil and season them with salt and

pepper and then slide the sheet tray into the hot oven. Set a time for 15 minutes.
- Toss the arugula with a sprinkle of balsamic vinegar and olive oil. Season the arugula with a pinch of salt.
- When your timer goes off top each tartlet with some of the arugula and then bake the tartlets for another 11 minutes or until browned nicely.
- Let the tarts cool and then serve at room temperature.

269. Rustic Root Vegetable Salad With Citrus And Thyme

Serving: Serves 1-2 | Prep: | Cook: | Ready in:

Ingredients

- 3 parsnips
- 1 medium sized butternut squash
- 2 tablespoons olive oil
- 2 tablespoons unsalted butter, melted
- 1 tablespoon honey
- 1 orange (zested and then halved)
- several sprigs of fresh thyme
- about 1/8 of a cup of toasted pine nuts
- a handful of dried cranberries
- goat cheese

Direction

- Peel the parsnips with a vegetable peeler, cut them in half and cut diagonally (they should sort of resemble French fries).
- Peel the butternut squash with a big, sharp knife and cut into cube sized pieces.
- Put the parsnips and squash in one bowl. In another bowl, combine the melted butter, olive oil and honey and whisk together. Then pour over the vegetables and toss with a big spoon or spatula until they are evenly coated.
- Place them on a baking sheet, sprinkle with kosher salt and several fresh thyme leaves. Give a little squeeze of half of the orange, for a

little juice. Place in the 400 degree oven for about 20 minutes, checking a few times in between to toss the vegetables and shake the pan a little.

- Put the vegetables in a large bowl, add the toasted pine nuts (these can be toasted at 350 degrees for about 5-10 minutes - make sure you shake the pan), the dried cranberries and the orange zest. Toss together. Add a few little dollops of goat cheese on top and serve!

270.   Rustic Zucchini Tart

Serving: Makes one 11- to 12-inch tart | Prep: | Cook: | Ready in:

Ingredients

- 1 cup organic spelt flour
- 1 teaspoon chopped fresh rosemary
- 1/2 teaspoon fine sea salt
- 1/4 cup extra-virgin olive oil
- 2 tablespoons unsalted butter at room temperature
- 3 tablespoons white wine
- 1 zucchini, thinly sliced
- 1/2 teaspoon plus a pinch of flaky sea salt
- 8 ounces goat cheese
- 1 tablespoon finely chopped fresh chives
- 1/8 teaspoon finely grated lemon zest
- 1 teaspoon fresh lemon juice
- 1 teaspoon chopped fresh rosemary
- 1/4 cup grated Parmesan cheese
- Freshly ground black pepper
- Extra-Virgin Olive oil

Direction

- Combine the flour, rosemary, and salt in a large bowl. Add the olive oil and butter and mix together by hand until the dough has the consistency of wet sand. Add the wine and mix together. If the dough is too dry and does not come together, add a little water.

- Knead the dough by hand inside the bowl for a few minutes until it comes together as a ball. Cover with plastic and refrigerate for at least 30 minutes or overnight.
- Place the zucchini slices in a strainer and sprinkle them evenly with the ½ teaspoon salt. Let drain for 30 minutes, then spread them out on paper towels to drain for another 30 minutes.
- When the zucchini has almost finished draining, preheat the oven to 350°F.
- Transfer the tart dough to a baking sheet.
- Using a potato masher, mash together the goat cheese, chives, lemon zest, lemon juice, rosemary, Parmesan, a pinch of salt, and pepper to taste in a small bowl.
- Flour your hands and gently pull and stretch the dough into a 13- to 14-inch circle on the baking sheet.
- Spread the cheese mixture over the base of the crust, leaving a 2-inch border all around. Starting at the outside edge, layer the zucchini in overlapping shingles over the cheese mixture. Drizzle with olive oil.
- Fold the border of the dough over the filling. Bake until the crust is golden brown, 40 to 45 minutes.

271.   SAFFRON PUMPKIN PASTA BAKE WITH PISTACHIOS & GOAT CHEESE

Serving: Serves 4-5 | Prep: | Cook: | Ready in:

Ingredients

- 750 grams kabocha squash, peeled and chopped into cubes
- 400 grams whole grain sea shell pasta
- 200 grams grated parmesan cheese
- 150 grams grated hard goat cheese (or percorino)

- 1 tablespoon coarse sea salt + more for seasing the pasta water
- 3-4 tablespoons tbsp EVO oil + more for greasing the pant
- 50 grams pistachios, crushed
- 20 high quality saffron threads
- Juice of 1/2 large lemon (or one entire)
- 2 mandarins, cut in half*
- 1 red onion, with skin and root, cut into 6 wedges
- 3 whole cloves garlic

Direction

- Preheat the oven at 180° C/350° F/ Gas mark four.
- In a large bowl, mix the chopped pumpkin, the garlic cloves and the onions with the lemon juice, 2 tbsp. EVO oil and salt. Move the seasoned pumpkin to an oven tray covered with baking sheets, add the mandarin halves and put the tray in top-center of the oven. After roasting for about 10 minutes, check the pumpkins, if you see it's browning super quickly while it's still raw inside, turn down the heat, put the tray on top level and let roast until the pumpkin is the soft when you put a fork in it and the edges have slightly browned. Should take about 20 to 40 minutes.
- In a large pan, bring water to boil for cooking the pasta. When the water comes to boils, in a small espresso cup make saffron infusion by adding the (finally crushed) saffron threads to about 2-2 tbsp. of hot water. Cover the cup and let it rest.
- In a blender, mix roasted pumpkin with 2 tbsp. of EVO oil (or more if you prefer), with about 1 cup of hot water. Add the water gradually. This mixture can be very thick in the beginning and by adding hot water. At the end, add the saffron infusion. Adjust the salt and add more water if needed.
- Preheat the oven at 180° C/350° F/ Gas mark four. Season the pasta water with salt (35g for each liter of water). Cook the pasta using the instruction on the package and drain it very al

dente (2 minutes less than indicated). Before draining save about a cup of pasta water.
- Mix the drained pasta with the pumpkin sauce and if needed, add some pasta water to loosen the mixture. Add 1/4 of the goat cheese and 1/4 of the parmesan and mix well.
- Brush a large baking pan with EVO olive, add half of the pasta to the pan. Sprinkle half of the remaining parmesan and goat cheese and half the pistachios.
- Add the remaining pasta, sprinkle the rest of the pistachios on top, cover with the rest of the cheese and add a little EVO oil on top.
- Bake in the oven until the top crust is golden and the pasta is browned in the edges (about 20 minutes).
- You can serve the pasta hot from the oven or even at room temperature.

---

272. Salad With Caramelized Fennel And Apples

Serving: Serves 2, quite generously (or 3-4 less generously) | Prep: | Cook: |Ready in:

Ingredients

- 1 large fennel bulb
- 1 sweet-tart apple, such as Braeburn
- 1 tablespoon (or so) butter
- 2 tablespoons olive oil, divided, plus another dash
- 1 teaspoon raw sugar
- 1/2 teaspoon fennel seeds
- salt and pepper
- 1 garlic clove, crushed
- 1/2 raddichio
- 4-5 leaves of butter lettuce
- 1 teaspoon lemon juice
- 2 tablespoons toasted pine nuts
- 3 ounces or so, soft goat cheese

Direction

- Trim the stalks off of the fennel bulb - reserving some of the fronds for garnish - and trim off any of the bottom bulb that is brown or gross. Remove the outer layers as well, if they are brown. Thinly slice the fennel bulb lengthwise (about 1/4 inch thick pieces), making thin, flat, feathery tear drop shaped pieces. It's okay, however, if the pieces fall apart.
- Cut the apple in half, core it, and slice half of it into thin slices.
- In a large sauté pan, heat 1/2 Tbs. butter and 1/2 Tbs. olive oil over high heat until foaming. Add as much of the fennel as you can fit in a single layer, cook until the undersides have turned a golden brown (a couple of minutes), then flip and cook the other sides until golden. Transfer to a bowl or tray. Repeat, adding more olive oil and butter as needed, until you have browned all of the fennel, and the sliced apple.
- Turn down the heat to medium-low, add another dash of olive oil, sprinkle in the sugar and the fennel seeds and let the sugar just begin to melt (this only takes seconds). Then, stir in the browned fennel and apple, sprinkle well with salt and pepper and stir to get them coated with a bit of caramelizing sugar. Just cook for another minute or so, then transfer back to the bowl. Toss with the crushed garlic.
- Wash, then cut or tear the radicchio and butter lettuce into bite sized pieces. Cut the remaining apple half into small cubes. Toss the lettuces and apple cubes with 1 tsp. lemon juice, 1 Tbs. olive oil and a little sprinkling of salt and pepper, until coated.
- Divide the dressed lettuce and apple between two plates. Mound half of the caramelized apple and fennel on top of the bed of lettuce on each plate. Scatter the toasted pine nuts over the salads, crumble the goat cheese on top, and then finally garnish each salad with a few pieces of fennel fronds. Enjoy!

273.   Sarasin Galettes With Goat Cheese And Smoked Duck Meat

Serving: Serves 4 | Prep: | Cook: | Ready in:

Ingredients

- 250g Sarasin flour
- 350 milliliters milk
- 350 milliliters water
- 1 teaspoon salt
- 1 log of goat cheese
- 20   slices of smoked duck meat
- 4   small of spinach or arugula
- 4 tablespoons honey
- Olive oil

Direction

- For the galettes, combine flour, milk, water, salt and two tbsp olive oil. Add water if necessary. The dough must be thicker than crêpe dough.
- Cut several slices of goat cheese.
- Make your galettes: pour one ladle of dough in a pan. Once one side is cooked, turn over. They should be thin, not like pancakes
- Place five slices of dick meat on each galette than add slices of goat cheese. Cook until the galette is ready and cheese starts to melt.
- Just before serving, add 1 tsp of honey on each Galette and a handful of arugula. Serve warm

274.   Sausage And Sweet Potato Pizza With Goat Cheese

Serving: Makes 8 slices | Prep: | Cook: | Ready in:

Ingredients

- Pizza Crust
- 2 1/2 - 3 cups all purpose flour
- 1 cup very hot water
- 3/4 ounce active dry yeast

- 1 pinch sugar
- 1 tablespoon extra virgin olive oil
- 1 teaspoon salt
- Pizza
- 1 small sweet potato
- 1/2 pound sausage
- 1/2 cup goat cheese
- 1 cup tomato or pizza sauce
- 1 - 1 1/2 cups shredded cheese (mozzarella or your choice)
- salt
- pepper
- cinnamon

Direction

- Pizza Crust
- In small bowl, combine yeast, sugar and 1 teaspoon of flour with water. Stir until dissolved. Cover and set aside for about 15 minutes until mixture is frothy and bubbly. In large bowl, combine 1 cup flour, salt, oil. Add yeast mixture and stir well.
- Add flour 1/2 cup at a time, mixing well until dough begins to form and pulls away from the side of the bowl. The amount of flour can vary. But it generally takes me 2-2 1/2 cups to get a nice dough, then I will use another 1/2 cup to coat the countertop for kneading.
- Once dough has formed, remove from bowl onto a flour covered surface. Dust hands with flour and knead dough thoroughly for about 5 minutes. One technique is to continually flatten dough, fold once or twice and flatten again. You'll develop your own technique. The important thing is to work the dough well.
- Form dough into ball and place in a large, bowl that has been coated with olive oil. Turn dough ball once to lightly coat surface with oil. Cover bowl with a towel and set aside for about 1 hour or until dough has risen enough to double in size.
- This recipe will provide enough dough for two pizzas. After dough has risen, cut in half. The other half can be used for a second pizza or it can be frozen for later use. If you freeze the

dough, remove from freezer and set out until it warms to room temperature.
- Pizza
- Heat oven to 350. Peel sweet potato and dice into medium chunks. In small baking dish, drizzle a bit of olive oil, toss in diced sweet potato and season with salt, pepper, and cinnamon. Bake for 20-25 minutes, or until not quite cooked all the way through. Set aside.
- In skillet, brown sausage slightly over medium heat. Drain and set aside.
- Heat oven to 425. On a pizza stone or coated cookie sheet, roll out pizza dough. Work from middle and stretch outward toward edges, using a rolling pin to evenly distribute the dough.
- Spread sauce on dough with a large spoon.
- Sprinkle shredded cheese, sausage, sweet potatoes, and goat cheese pieces onto pizza.
- Bake for about 20-25 minutes or until cheese begins to brown around outer edge.

---

275.   Savoring Summer Tartine, With Cherry Tomato And Strawberry

Serving: Serves 3 or more depending on appetite | Prep: | Cook: | Ready in:

Ingredients

- 6 ounces of the sweetest yellow cherry tomatoes you can find, preferably locally grown (about 20 tomatoes)
- 3 ounces ripe strawberries, preferably locally grown (about 4-5 strawberries)
- 4-5 tender leaves of curly endive or frisée, washed, thoroughly dried
- 4 ounces soft goat cheese (such as Montrachet) set in a large metal mixing bowl at room temperature to soften
- 4 ounces Fourme d'Ambert (or another mild, soft, crumbly blue cheese), at room temperature

- 1/4 cup plus 3 T heavy whipping cream, divided
- 6 slices whole grain country bread
- Tarragon infused olive oil (see recipe below)
- Tarragon-Cherry Tomato vinaigrette (see step 6)
- Fleur de sel

Direction

- Prep fruits and frisée: Set a fine meshed sieve over a small bowl. Slice each cherry tomato in half, then cut each half into quarters, and carefully place in sieve. Repeat until you have cut all the tomatoes. Using a light hand and a spoon, gently fluff tomatoes, pulling from the bottom up so that excess juice drips through the sieve into the bowl. Set aside to allow juices to continue to drain.
- Hull strawberries and thinly slice lengthwise. Place slices in a bowl and set aside.
- Chop frisée and place in a bowl. You should have a heaping cup of greens.
- Prep cheese: Add 3 T heavy whipping cream to goat cheese. With an electric mixer, whip until mixture is soft and light, about a minute. Use spatula to scrape out all the cheese and transfer mixture to a small bowl (at this point, you can wash out your mixing bowl if desired or just continue with the blue cheese, as I did). Add room temperature Fourme d'Ambert to mixing bowl along with ¼ cup of heavy whipping cream. Whip until mixture is soft and light, about two minutes, and transfer mixture to a small bowl. **Cheese can be whipped and refrigerated, covered tightly, a day in advance.
- Prep bread: Brush one side of each slice with tarragon infused olive oil. Heat grill pan over medium high heat.
- Make Vinaigrette: Fluff tomatoes one last time over bowl. Transfer tomatoes to another bowl. Depending on the juiciness of your tomatoes, you should have between 1-2 tablespoons of accumulated juice. Add 1 Tablespoon Tarragon infused olive oil and 1 teaspoon white wine vinegar to cherry tomato juice. Whisk to emulsify. Set aside.
- When grill pan is hot, place each slice of bread, oiled side down, for two minutes. Flip bread and toast for two minutes more. Remove from pan and allow bread to cool for a minute or two (you do not want your cheese to be runny). Depending on the size of your bread and grill pan, you may be able to do all six slices at once. If not, grill in batches. Alternatively, you could also toast on a pan in a 350-degree oven for 3-4 minutes.
- Make your tartines: Spread three pieces of bread (oiled side) with whipped goat cheese, and three with whipped blue cheese. For each tartine, add a thin layer of sliced strawberries, followed by a small heap of chopped frisée and generous spoonful of cherry tomatoes. Top with about a teaspoon of vinaigrette and finally a sprinkling of fleur de sel. Slice each in half, if desired, as a starter for an al fresco supper. Make sure each person gets both versions. Enjoy, outside, with loved ones and a glass of your favorite white, and let summer last a little longer.
- FOR TARRAGON INFUSED OLIVE OIL:1 ½ cups extra virgin olive oil1 large sprig fresh tarragon (mine was a 7 inch piece), washed and thoroughly dried. In a small, heavy bottomed saucepan, pour extra virgin olive oil over tarragon. Most of the tarragon should be submerged in the oil (press down gently on any leaves that are sticking above the surface). Gently bring up the heat – you do not want your oil to boil, but rather evenly simmer and bubble ever so slightly. Cook for 30 minutes. Strain oil into a glass jar with a lid, discarding solids. Allow oil to cool, enough to touch the jar comfortably. Close the jar and store oil in the refrigerator until needed. Oil should keep at least a week. Use leftover oil for a lovely anise scented vinaigrette.

276. Savory Fennel Hazelnut Tart With Carmelized Onions

Serving: Serves 6 | Prep: | Cook: | Ready in:

Ingredients

- tart crust
- 3/4 cup finely processed, toasted hazelnuts
- 2 cups flour
- 1 teaspoon salt
- 1 teaspoon sugar
- 5 tablespoons cold butter, cut in pieces
- tart topping
- 2 bulbs of fennel, trimmed of fronds and cut into thin slices
- 1 medium onion, thinly sliced
- 1/2 cup dry white wine
- 1/4 cup heavy cream
- 3/4 cup crumbled goats cheese
- salt and pepper to taste
- extra virgin olive oil

Direction

- Preheat oven to 375.
- Add the tart crust ingredients to your food processor. Pulse for about three minutes. Add COLD water a tsp at a time and pulse until the mixture resembles crumbs that you can form into a ball. Roll out the dough into a circle about 1/4 of an inch thick and press into a tart tin. Pop into the oven for five minutes.
- For the topping, begin by sautéing the onions in olive oil on medium-low heat for about 20 minutes, until they are caramelized. Add the fennel and cook until tender, about seven more minutes. Add wine and reduce until mixture is almost dry. Add cream, salt and pepper to taste; stir. Remove from heat and let cool to room temperature. .
- When the topping is cooled to room temp, pour into the tart crust. Sprinkle on the crumbled goat cheese. Bake for about 15 more minutes, until the cheese is golden brown.

277. Savory Lemon Herb Cheesecake

Serving: Makes 8 servings | Prep: | Cook: | Ready in:

Ingredients

- 12 whole grain or gluten free crackers
- 1/4 cup walnut halves, toasted
- 1 tablespoon olive oil
- 4 ounces Neufchatel cheese
- 1/2 cup part skim ricotta
- 1/4 cup softened goat cheese
- 1 egg
- 1 tablespoon sugar
- 1 pinch of salt
- 1 tablespoon fresh lemon zest
- 1 tablespoon minced chives
- 1 tablespoon minced parsley
- 1 tablespoon fresh thyme leaves

Direction

- Preheat oven to 350 degrees and wrap the outside of a 4 1/2-inch springform pan with heavy duty foil. Spray the inside of the pan with cooking spray.
- In the bowl of a food processor fitted with the chopping blade, process crackers and walnuts until they are crumbs. Add olive oil and pulse a few more times to combine.
- Press the crumb mixture into the bottom of the springform pan.
- Bake the crust until golden, about 5-8 minutes.
- Wipe down the bowl of the food processor, and process the Neufchatel, ricotta, and goat cheese. Add egg, sugar, salt and lemon, and process until smooth.
- Mix in the herbs by hand.
- Pour cheese mixture into the prepared crust.
- Place the springform pan into a larger roasting pan, and pour hot water in to the pan to come halfway up the sides of the springform pan.
- Bake the cheesecake for 40 minutes, or until the edges are golden. The center will move

slightly when gently shaken, but it will firm up as it cools.

- Transfer the cake to a wire rack and let cool for one hour. Refrigerate until cold, at least 3 hours, and up to 2 days.
- Before, serving, gently remove the cheesecake from the springform pan by sliding a thin spatula under the crust, and transfer to a serving plate. Serve cold or at room temperature, with crackers, and fruit, if desired.

278. Savory Mushroom Bread Blintzes

Serving: Makes 50 blintzes | Prep: | Cook: |Ready in:

Ingredients

- 2 pounds baby bella mushrooms chopped
- 1 large onion diced
- 4 cloves garlic chopped
- 2 stalks celery diced
- 4 tablespoons olive oil
- 1/4 cup fresh herbs(you can use rosemary, thyme, sage or whatever you like)
- 1 teaspoon kosher salt or more to taste
- 1/4 teaspoon freshly ground pepper or more to taste
- 1/4 cup goat cheese
- 1 loaf sliced white bread
- 2 sticks butter melted

Direction

- To prepare the mushroom filling, sauté the onion and garlic in the olive oil for 2-3 minutes, then add the celery and cook another 2 minutes. Add the mushrooms and cook 5 minutes or till mushrooms release their juices. Continue cooking a few minutes longer until the juices have mostly evaporated. Add the herbs, salt and pepper.
- Put the mushroom mixture in a colander and drain (save the mushroom juices....delicious in

soup or pasta). Add the goat cheese to mushroom mixture and mix well. Transfer mixture to food processor and pulse for 30-40 seconds.

- Cut the crusts off of the white bread. Place a slice of bread between two pieces of wax paper and using a rolling pin flatten out the bread. Using a pastry brush, brush the bread with the melted butter, put a teaspoon of the mushroom filling along the edge of the bread and roll up. Place on a tray with the seam side down. Brush the outside of blintz with melted butter. Continue this process with the rest of the bread. Refrigerate the tray for 2 hours. Then cut the blintzes in half. At this point you can place them back on the tray and when frozen store in a plastic bag. To bake the bread blintzes, simply assemble on baking tray and bake in 350 oven for 10-15 minutes or till golden brown.

279. Savory, Salty, Sweet, Crunchy, Warm Cabbage Salad

Serving: Serves 4-6 | Prep: | Cook: |Ready in:

Ingredients

- 1/2 medium head green cabbage cut into thin 1/4 inch thin strips
- 1 cup crimini or white button mushrooms sliced thin
- 2 teaspoons chopped sage leaves
- 3 slices thick cut bacon
- 1/2 cup slivered almonds toasted
- 6 dried black mission figs sliced thinly
- 3 ounces goat cheese
- 1-2 pinches sea salt
- cracked black pepper to taste
- drizzles of black truffle oil
- drizzles of maple syrup
- optional poached egg

Direction

- Put 5 quarts of water to boil and blanch green cabbage for 6 minutes, drain and put aside.
- Cut Bacon into 1 inch strips and fry in large non-stick skillet until crispy, remove from pan and drain excess fat. Put aside.
- In same skillet that bacon was cooked in, without adding anything else to pan, fry mushrooms until well browned on medium - high flame. When mushrooms are almost done, add sage, lower flame.
- Add drained cabbage and bacon into skillet and toss on low flame for 1-2 minutes then add almonds and figs, sea salt and a few grinds of cracked black pepper to taste. Lightly drizzle Maple Syrup and some Truffle Oil. Toss and remove from flame.
- Serve on plate or in bowl, drizzle additional truffle oil and maple syrup to taste, topped with crumbles of goat cheese.
- Make a great side for a simple pasta dish or have a heartier serving and a meal served with a poached egg on top and some polenta or crusty bread.

280.   Savoury Goat Cheese Oats Biscuits

Serving: Makes 12-15 biscuits | Prep: | Cook: | Ready in:

Ingredients

- 1 cup flour
- 1/2 cup oats
- 3 tablespoons olive oil
- 3 tablespoons single cream
- 1/4   log fresh goat cheese
- 3-4   sun dried tomatoes, cut into very thin diced
- 1 teaspoon dried thyme
- 1 pinch salt and pepper

Direction

- Preheat oven on 350F

- Combine flour, oats, a little bit of salt and pepper. Add the olive oil and rub the very quickly between your fingers until the mixture resembles fine breadcrumbs.
- Add the sundried tomatoes, thyme and crumbled goat cheese. Rub again between your fingers to incorporate the cheese
- Add the cream gradually and form a ball of dough
- Make little balls of dough and flatten them in your hand. Place them on oven plate covered with greaseproof paper. Bake for 10 minutes and let cool

281.   Scallion Omelet

Serving: Serves 1 | Prep: | Cook: | Ready in:

Ingredients

- 2 Eggs
- 3 tablespoons Goat Cheese
- 2 tablespoons Shaved Parmesan
- 1 Scallion, sliced
- 1 tablespoon Butter

Direction

- Heat a small pan over low heat. Add the butter and swirl it around the pan.
- Whisk together the eggs in a small bowl and pour into the pan.
- This is the most important step! Allow the eggs to mostly cook, swirling the pan and lifting up the cooked egg so that when you tilt the pan none of the egg migrates.
- Add the goat cheese, parmesan and scallion to one side of the pan, and fold the other half of the egg on top of the other.
- Allow the cheeses to melt, for 1-2 more minutes, and devour.

282. Scallops & Beet Risotto Chris Hodgson Style

Serving: Makes 10 scallops | Prep: | Cook: | Ready in:

Ingredients

- 8.5 ounces Vegetable Stock
- 6 ounces Risotto Base
- 2 pinches Kosher Salt
- 1.5 ounces Golden Beets (Diced)
- 1.5 ounces Butternut Squash
- 1 ounce Caramelized Apples
- 2 teaspoons Goat Cheese
- 7 ounces U10 Sea Scallops
- 2 tablespoons Blended Oil
- 1 tablespoon Brown Butter
- 3 pieces Beet Chips (3 Per Scallop)
- 2 teaspoons Fried Sage (Per Scallop)

Direction

- Pour 8 oz. of stock into saucepan on medium heat. Add risotto, heat through.
- Stir in veg stock
- Add beets, butternut squash, caramelized onion and goat cheese.
- Make final adjustment to risotto with stock then plate into risotto bowl.
- Sear scallops on one side over medium high heat until golden brown.
- Rest scallops on risotto and garnish with sage and brown butter

283. Scones With Herbed Goat Cheese And Prosciutto

Serving: Makes 14 | Prep: | Cook: | Ready in:

Ingredients

- 2 cups all-purpose flour
- 3 teaspoons baking powder
- 1 teaspoon salt
- 1/4 cup sugar
- 1 cup half and half
- 4 ounces butter
- 3 ounces proscuitto
- 8 ounces goat cheese
- 1 1/2 teaspoons Herbes de Provence

Direction

- Preheat oven to 400 degrees.
- Mix flour, baking powder, salt and sugar in a large bowl and whisk together.
- Cut butter into ½ squares and knead into dry ingredients until butter is about the size of little peas.
- Add ¾ cup half and half and mix with a fork until a slightly sticky dough develops. Add more half and half if the mixture looks dry or crumbly.
- Put your dough on a floured work surface and roll out until ½ an inch thick.
- Cut dough into circles (or whatever shape you want) and brush tops with the leftover half and half. Bake for 20 minutes on a parchment paper-covered baking sheet.
- While the scones are baking, mix goat cheese and Herbes de Provence with a spoon.
- When scones are finished, let cool on cooling rack for 5 minutes, then top with goat cheese and a small slice of prosciutto.

284. Semolina Crackers With Baked On Goat Cheese

Serving: Makes makes about 2 dozen crackers | Prep: | Cook: | Ready in:

Ingredients

- 1 cup (163 g) semolina flour
- 1 cup (120 g) all purpose flour
- 3/4 teaspoon (3 g) fine sea salt
- 2 tablespoons (24 g) extra virgin oil, plus more for finishing
- 1/2 cup plus 1 tablespoon (127 g) cool water
- 4 ounces (113 g) goat cheese

- 2 shallots, peeled and very thinly sliced
- freshly ground black pepper

Direction

- In the bowl of an electric mixer fitted with the dough hook attachment, mix the semolina, all-purpose flour, salt, olive oil, and water for 2 minutes on low speed.
- Raise speed to medium and mix for 1 minute more. Wrap the dough tightly in plastic wrap and let rest at room temperature for 15-20 minutes.
- Preheat the oven to 450°F. Line two baking sheets with parchment paper.
- On a lightly floured surface, roll out the dough to ¼ inch thick. Use a pastry wheel to cut into 2 x 2 inch squares.
- Transfer the squares to the prepared baking sheets (they won't spread so they can be relatively close together). Dock each square 1 or 2 times with the tines of a fork.
- Top each cracker with some goat cheese (about 1 heaping teaspoon per cracker), and a few slices of shallot. Drizzle a little olive oil over the shallots and top with pepper.
- Bake the crackers until they're golden at the edges and very crisp, 10-12 minutes. Let cool at least 5 minutes before serving warm, or cool completely.

285.   Shrimp Pasta In A Goat Cheese And Pine Nut Sauce

Serving: Serves 4 | Prep: | Cook: | Ready in:

Ingredients

- 1 pound Fresh Medium Shrimp, Peeled, Deveined and Tails Removed
- 1 pound Bow Tie Pasta
- 4 ounces Goat Cheese, Firm and Crumbled
- 1 Leek, Washed and Sliced Thinly
- 1 1/2 cups Half and Half
- 3/4 teaspoon Red Pepper Flakes

- 1 tablespoon Unsalted Butter
- 1/3 cup Pine Nuts or Slivered Almonds
- 3 Fresh Garlic Cloves, Thinly Sliced
- Juice and Zest of One Lemon
- 1 teaspoon Sea Salt
- 1 teaspoon Cracked Black Pepper
- 1 Lemon, cut into 4 wedges

Direction

- Boil Bow Ties in a heavily salted pot of boiling water. Cook until al dente. Drain, saving 1/2 cup pasta water, and place back in large pot and toss with olive oil.
- Melt unsalted butter on medium high heat in a large skillet, fry pine nuts until they are beginning to turn brown, about 2 minutes. Add the garlic, shrimp and sliced leeks, fry for a few more minutes until shrimp begins to turn pink.
- To the skillet at the half and half, lemon juice, lemon zest, goat cheese, red pepper flakes and salt and pepper. Stir for 3-5 minutes until cream is bubbling, cheese is melting and shrimp is cooked all the way through.
- Toss skillet mixture with warm bow tie pasta, add pasta water if needed. Sprinkle with fresh chopped parsley and lemon wedge. Serve immediately with warm bread and nice green salad.

286.   Simple Arugula And Goat Cheese Pasta

Serving: Serves 4 | Prep: | Cook: | Ready in:

Ingredients

- 1 pound linguine
- 1 jar of your favorite marinara (mine is Rao's)
- 2 chicken breasts
- 2 tablespoons olive oil
- salt and pepper
- 1 bunch arugula, chopped
- 6 ounces goat cheese

Direction

- Preheat oven to 375. Season chicken breasts with salt and pepper, rub with olive oil. Bake until cooked through but still moist (about 15 minutes on each side, depending on the thickness of the breast). Cut chicken breasts into bite sized pieces.
- Boil water and add linguine. Cook to desired chewiness.
- Heat up marinara sauce on the stove.
- When everything is ready, put hot noodles, sauce and chicken in your bowl. Add a few good chunks of goat cheese (be liberal) and a handful of arugula on top. Mix it all together. Season with lots of pepper.

287. Sliced Apple And Goat Cheese Sandwich With Pesto And Honey

Serving: Serves 2 | Prep: | Cook: |Ready in:

Ingredients

- Basil and Walnut Pesto
- 1/2 cup Fresh Walnuts
- 1 bunch Fresh Basil
- 1 cup Extra Virgin Olive Oil
- 1 teaspoon Salt (or to taste)
- For the Sandwich
- 2-3 tablespoons Soft Goat Cheese (or as much as you like)
- 2 teaspoons Local Honey
- 1 cup Fresh Organic Arugula
- 1 Sliced Tart and Sweet Apple (Fuji, Pink Lady or Granny Smith)
- 2-3 tablespoons Walnut Pesto
- 1 Rustic French Baguette

Direction

- For the walnut pesto, wash the basil and pat dry. Place basil in a hand mixer or blender along with 1/2 cup of extra virgin olive oil.

Blend until a smooth texture is reached (about 30 seconds). Gradually add the rest of the olive oil blending continuously. Add the walnuts and blend again. Finally add salt to taste. If you prefer a thinner pesto, you can add more olive oil, remembering that the pesto should spread easily on the bread without running or soaking the bread.

- Once the pesto has been prepared slice the baguette in half and then slice each half lengthwise. Remove some of the soft center, preserving the crust, to allow space for the filling. On the base of the sandwich spread a thin (or thick) layer of goat cheese. Add a layer of arugula and top with thinly sliced apple. Drizzle with honey. Coat the top half of the baguette with the walnut pesto and assemble. Slice in half and enjoy this delicious summer treat!

288. Slightly Smoky Mixed Bean Chili

Serving: Serves 6 to 8 | Prep: 0hours30mins | Cook: 2hours45mins |Ready in:

Ingredients

- For the beans
- 5 cups assorted dried beans, such as Anasazi, pinto, black, adzuki, pink and red, sorted and rinsed well, soaked in ample salted water for 3 or 4 hours or overnight
- 1 small whole onion
- 3 fresh bay leaves, twisted along their spines to crack them slightly
- For the chili
- 1 large (or 3 small) Spanish onion, chopped
- 4 tablespoons olive oil
- 5 cloves garlic, minced
- 1 tablespoon plus 1 teaspoon ground chili, or to taste
- 1/2 teaspoon chipotle chili powder, or to taste
- 1 teaspoon ground cumin

- 1 teaspoon cumin seeds, lightly toasted and then pounded in a mortar and pestle
- 1 tablespoon dried oregano
- 1 large can fire-roasted tomatoes. (I use Muir Glen). Otherwise, you could use whole, diced, or petite-diced, according to your preference
- 1/2 naval orange, skin and pith removed, coarsely chopped
- 1 teaspoon salt or to taste
- Rice as an accompaniment (see my brown-rice pilaf within my recipe for Sephardic Megedarra -- if you start it at the same time you saute the aromatics here, it will be done just about when the chili is done)
- Guacamole (see my recipe for Plain and Simple Guacamole and maybe increase by 1 avocado + extra lime juice and garlic)
- Plain or goat's milk yogurt
- Sliced scallions or minced white onions
- Shredded cheddar
- Fresh mild goat cheese, crumbled
- Lemon or lime wedges
- Refrigerated-type salsa (or homemade: chopped tomatoes, fresh jalapeno, seeded & minced, diced onion, minced garlic and a squeeze of lime)
- Chopped fresh tomatoes (optional)
- Shredded iceberg lettuce (optional)

Direction

- For the beans
- Drain beans of their soaking liquid and place in a large kettle with whole onion, and bay leaf. Fill pot with fresh filtered water to more than cover the beans — 1 to 2 inches above the surface of the beans should do. Season cooking water with salt — enough that you can taste it. Bring the water gently to the boil, stirring occasionally. When water boils, turn heat to medium low and simmer beans until tender, about 1 1/2 to 2 hours. Older beans will take longer. You will probably have to top off the beans with more water as they cook. You can remove a few beans from the pot and cut through the center with a sharp knife to test for doneness.

- For the chili
- In a heavy-bottomed pan, sauté onions until slightly softened; make an opening in the sautéing onions and add a little more oil and the minced garlic, allowing it to sizzle a bit before stirring into the onions. Sauté mixture until onions are translucent. Quickly add the spices and herbs and stir once or twice into the onion mix to bring out the fragrance then remove from heat before they scorch. Add to the pot of beans along with the canned tomatoes (squeeze over the pot to break them up before adding if they are whole), and orange pieces. Simmer mixture for 1/2 hour or so until flavors blend. Taste for salt and seasoning and adjust. May be made a day ahead for best flavor.
- Serve over rice with choice of garnishes: guacamole, yogurt, scallions, minced onions, shredded cheddar or creamy goat cheese, lemon or lime wedges, chopped tomatoes and lettuce.

289. Slow Roasted Tomato, Caramelized Onion And Goats Cheese Tart

Serving: Serves 6 | Prep: | Cook: | Ready in:

Ingredients

- For the Pastry Shell
- 1 1/3 cups plain flour or whole wheat pastry flour
- 1/2 teaspoon kosher salt
- 8 tablespoons unsalted butter
- 1 egg, lightly beaten
- 1-2 teaspoons ice water
- For the Tart Filling
- 10 on the vine tomatoes, cut in half horizontally
- 5 sprigs fresh thyme
- 1 tablespoon olive oil
- 1 large onion, thinly sliced

- 1 garlic clove, finely chopped
- 8 ounces soft rindless goats cheese
- a few basil leaves, to garnish
- Extra virgin olive oil, to serve

Direction

- For the Pastry Shell
- Place the flour, salt and butter in a small food processor and pulse to blend the flour and butter together- it will resemble breadcrumbs.
- Add half of the egg and pulse again for a few seconds until it forms nuggets of dough. At this point you want to feel the dough. If it is soft, without too many dry bits then you can remove it from the processor at this point. If it still looks very dry and had not formed soft nuggets, add the remaining egg and pulse again for a few seconds, check again and if it still seems dry, add a teaspoon of ice water. If you add too much egg/water add more flour in the processor- do not try to add by hand. The less you work the pastry the more tender and pliable it will be. I found that I only needed 1/2 and egg and no water but all flour is different.
- Once you have a soft dough, bring it together gently into a round disk on a flat surface- ideally with cold, dry hands! Wrap in cling film and chill in the fridge for at least 30 minutes.
- On a lightly floured surface roll the dough out into a 10-11 inch circle. The best way to do this is to bash the dough with the rolling pin evenly in one direction, turn it a quarter turn and bash it again the other way, repeat- this helps for a more evenly rolled dough, helps keep the circular shape, stops it from getting to warm and prevents you from over-working the dough.
- Place on a baking tray, cover and chill for 10 minutes or until you are ready to assemble the tart.
- For the Tart Filling
- Firstly, slow roast the tomatoes by setting your oven to 110C/225F/Gas 1. Lay your sliced tomatoes cut side up on a large tray, sprinkle

with sea salt, freshly ground black pepper and strew with thyme leaves. Place in the oven until the tomatoes have shriveled up and are mostly dried-up in the center. You still want them to have a bit of juice. Ideally you would leave the tomatoes in the oven for 5-8 hours (if it's a convection/fan oven it will be faster) but you can get away with 2-3 hours if you are really pressed for time- just turn the oven up a notch and keep an eye on them.

- Meanwhile, prepare the onions, in a large frying pan (non-stick is fine) heat the oil over a medium-low heat and toss in the onions. Cover the pan and let the onions steam, stirring occasionally until soft (about 10 minutes).
- Remove the cover and turn the heat up to medium-high, stir with a wooden spoon every minute or so, scraping the bottom of the pan to release any areas that are sticking. Every so often add a tablespoon or so of water to help prevent too much sticking (which will cause the onions to burn). You want to cook the onions until they have gone a lovely golden color and appear sticky. You can speed up the process by adding a teaspoon of sugar but it will still take about 20 minutes (longer if you have more onions in the pan). Add the garlic if you are using a minute before you take the onions off the heat. Season to taste with salt and pepper.
- Now for the assembly and cooking. Heat the oven to 200C/400F/Gas 6. Brush your tart tin with oil. Lay the tomatoes cut side down evenly in the bottom of the pan in one layer. Top with your caramelized onions in an even layer.
- Beat your goat cheese until soft (if you are using ricotta you will need to season it or add some grated parmesan for extra flavor). Carefully spread the cheese over the onions as evenly as possible.
- Lay your pastry over the top of the tart and tuck the edges into the tart tin- if you have more than a couple of centimeters (one inch) of dough around the sides, trim it off with a paring knife before tucking in the edges. Brush

with the lightly beaten egg, using a pastry brush and bake in the oven for about 30 minutes, or until the pastry is golden and appears crispy (it should feel sandy when you touch it). Remove from the oven and allow to stand for 10 minutes before turning it out upside down on a large plate. Garnish with the basil leaves and a drizzle of olive oil.

290. Smoked Salmon Salad With Cayenne Almonds, Dried Cranberries, And Goat Cheese.

Serving: Serves one! | Prep: | Cook: |Ready in:

Ingredients

- a handful of almonds
- a pinch or two of cayenne
- a pinch of salt
- mixed greens
- a handful of dried and sweetened cranberries
- a pearl red onion, sliced into thin slivers
- 2 ounces or so of smoked salmon
- 1 1/2 ounces goat cheese crumbles
- olive oil
- balsamic vinegar
- honey

Direction

- Put your almonds in a bag with the cayenne and salt and shake.
- Put the mixed greens in a bowl and add the almonds, dried cranberries, red onion slices, and goat cheese crumbles. Break up the smoked salmon into flakes and add them to the salad. Drizzle a little olive oil and balsamic onto the salad to taste, along with a little bit of honey. Toss gently and eat!

291. Socca Pizza With Goat Cheese

Serving: Makes 1 individual socca pizza | Prep: | Cook: |Ready in:

Ingredients

- 1/3 cup Garbanzo bean flour
- 3/4 cup luke warm water
- 1 tablespoon extra virgin olive oil
- large pinches cumin
- 1/2 teaspoon basil
- 1/4 teaspoon sea salt
- ground black pepper
- Sprig fresh rosemary
- desired amount of goat cheese
- 4 baby bella mushroom caps
- 2 tablespoons white onion
- Handful baby spinach

Direction

- Pre-heat oven to 420 degrees, allow a cast iron skillet or pizza pan, to heat in the oven. While oven is pre-heating, combine flour, water, the olive oil, spices, salt/pepper in a bowl, whisk very well. If able let sit for an hour in the fridge. Sauté sliced baby bella mushrooms, thinly sliced white onion in a pan with a bit of oil.
- Once oven reaches heat, take out Skillet or Pan, Add a bit more Olive oil to pan, allow to heat, and pour batter.
- Cook in oven for 10-15 minutes. Or until slightly brown. Take out of oven, spread goat cheese and add vegetables, mushrooms, caramelized onions, and wilted spinach.

292. Spelt Crusted Heirloom Tomato Tart With Basil Aioli And Goat Cheese

Serving: Serves 6 | Prep: | Cook: |Ready in:

Ingredients

- Spelt Tart Crust
- 1 cup spelt flour
- 4 tablespoons unsalted butter
- 2 tablespoons cold water
- 1/2 teaspoon salt
- Tart Filling
- 1 large heirloom tomato, sliced 1/4 inch
- 1 small sweet onion, sliced very thin
- 1/2 cup roughly chopped fresh basil
- 1/4 cup extra-virgin olive oil
- 2 egg yolks
- 2 teaspoons lemon juice
- 1 clove garlic, minced
- 1/4 cup panko bread crumbs
- 1/4 cup crumbled chevre or favorite aged goat cheese
- 1/4 teaspoon pepper
- 1/4 teaspoon salt

Direction

- For aioli, in blender or food processor, blend egg yolks, lemon juice, garlic, 1/4 cup basil and a pinch of salt.
- Slowly stream in olive oil and when thoroughly blended, set aioli in the fridge for a few minutes.
- Preheat oven to 350 degrees. In small bowl, mix flour and salt.
- Work in butter with your fingers, taking care to not warm it up too much.
- Mix in cold water with a fork.
- Press incorporated dough into a tart pan.
- Push a piece of foil on top of dough and blind bake the tart crust at 350 degrees for 10 minutes.
- Remove foil and bake another 5 minutes.
- After crust has cooled, spread with aioli and top with onions.
- Then, top with an even layer of tomatoes.
- Finally sprinkle the bread crumbs, goat cheese, remaining salt and pepper and remaining basil.

- Bake in 350-degree oven for 10 minutes and then broil until cheese and bread crumbs are golden.

293. Spiced Walnut Goat Cheese Spread

Serving: Makes 1 cup | Prep: | Cook: | Ready in:

Ingredients

- 2 handfuls Walnuts
- 4 ounces Goat cheese
- 1/2 teaspoon Ground ginger
- 1/2 teaspoon Ground cinnamon
- 1/2 teaspoon Ground nutmeg
- 1 tablespoon Almond oil
- 1 pinch Salt
- 2 tablespoons Honey

Direction

- Whisk together honey and goat cheese in a small bowl until smooth and creamy.
- Heat skillet and add almond oil and walnuts. Add cinnamon, nutmeg, ginger, and salt. Continue to stir until walnuts are toasted to a light brown.
- Finely chop walnuts and combine with the goat cheese mixture.
- Enjoy with sliced apples or crisp crackers.

294. Spicy Chicken Posole

Serving: Serves 8 | Prep: | Cook: | Ready in:

Ingredients

- For the posole:
- 1 yellow onion, chopped
- 2 Poblano peppers, seeded and chopped
- 1 bunch Lacinato kale, stemmed and chopped
- 1 jalapeño pepper, seeded and diced

- 10 garlic cloves, crushed and minced
- 8 Cremini mushrooms, quartered
- 4 tablespoons olive oil
- 2 tablespoons fresh oregano, chopped
- 2 tablespoons ground cumin
- 1 teaspoon ground cinnamon
- 1 large orange, zested and juiced
- 1/2 teaspoon freshly ground pepper
- 2 chipotle chiles in adobo sauce, chopped
- 2 tablespoons adobo sauce
- 15.5 ounces can chickpeas, drained
- 28 ounces can fire roasted chopped tomatoes with juice
- 28 ounces can crushed tomatoes
- 7 cups chicken stock
- 2 - 3 pounds chicken, roasted and shredded (or store-bought rotisserie)
- 4 scallions, chopped
- To garnish:
- 1 cup fresh cilantro leaves
- 2 limes, quartered
- 1 cup goat cheese, crumbled
- 1 cup pepitas, lightly salted and roasted

Direction

- Heat the olive oil in a large Dutch oven over medium-high heat.
- Add the onion, poblano peppers, kale, jalapeño pepper, garlic and mushrooms and sauté until softened, about 10 minutes.
- Add the oregano, cumin, cinnamon, orange zest, ground pepper, chipotle chiles and adobo sauce to the vegetable mixture and cook, stirring, for 2 minutes.
- Add the orange juice, chickpeas, tomatoes, and chicken stock. Stir to combine.
- Bring to a boil and reduce heat to low.
- Add the shredded chicken and stir to combine.
- Cover and maintain a very low simmer for 1 to 3 hours, stirring occasionally.
- When ready to serve, stir in the scallions.
- Ladle the pozole into bowls and garnish with fresh cilantro, a squeeze of fresh lime juice, goat cheese and pepitas.

295. Spicy Deviled Eggs

Serving: Serves 8-10 | Prep: | Cook: | Ready in:

Ingredients

- 10 large eggs
- 1/4 cup mayonnaise
- 1 tablespoon Sriracha Sauce
- 3 cornichons, minced
- 4 ounces goat cheese, at room temperature
- 2 teaspoons Dijon Mustard
- 1 1/2 teaspoons shallot, minced
- 2 teaspoons chives, snipped
- 1 dash kosher salt and pepper to taste
- 1 ounce prosciutto, torn into 20 pieces

Direction

- In a large saucepan, cover the eggs with cold water and bring to a boil over high heat. Remove from the heat and let the eggs stand in the hot water for 12 minutes. Transfer the eggs to an ice water bath until chilled, about 5 minutes.
- In a medium bowl, mix the mayonnaise, Sriracha sauce, cornichons, goat cheese, mustard, shallot and 1 teaspoon of the chives. Peel the eggs and halve them lengthwise. Add the yolks to the bowl, mix until smooth and season with salt and pepper.
- Set the egg whites on a serving platter. Scrape the egg yolk mixture into a pastry bag fitted with a large round tip and pipe the filling into the whites; alternatively, use a plastic ziplock bag with a corner snipped off or spoon in the filling with a teaspoon. Top each egg with a piece of prosciutto, sprinkle with the remaining 1 teaspoon of chives and serve.

296.   Spicy Sausage Italian Wonderpot

Serving: Serves 4 | Prep: | Cook: |Ready in:

Ingredients

- 4 cups Low sodium Chicken Broth
- 2 tablespoons Extra virgin Olive Oil
- 12 ounces fettuccine or angel hair pasta
- 28 ounces Diced tomatoes
- 1 cup Thinly Sliced onion
- 4   Cloves of Garlic- Thinly sliced
- 1/2 tablespoon Fresh Basil
- 1/2 tablespoon Fresh Parsley
- 1/2 tablespoon Fresh Oregano
- 1/2 teaspoon Crushed Red Pepper
- 1/2 tablespoon Salt
- Fresh Cracked Pepper to Taste
- 4 ounces Crumbled Goat cheese
- 6 ounces Chopped Fresh Spinach
- 12 ounces Ground Hot Italian Sausage

Direction

- In a large pot over medium high heat, drizzle olive oil and add in Hot Italian sausage and season with a pinch of salt and pepper. Brown meat thoroughly.
- Once meat is browned, drain off excess juice and combine all remaining ingredients into a large pot, be sure all the ingredients are submerged under the liquid
- Turn the heat on high and cover the pot. Allow it to come to a full boil and then remove the top and reduce the heat to medium
- Continue cooking over medium heat for 12-15 minutes, or until pasta is cooked and the majority of the liquid has been absorbed. Continue to stir the pot to avoid pasta sticking.
- Once pasta is cooked, crumble goat cheese over top and serve immediately.

297.   Spicy Shakshuka With Goat Cheese

Serving: Serves 2 | Prep: | Cook: |Ready in:

Ingredients

- 2 tablespoons olive oil
- 1/2   large red bell pepper
- 1/2   large yellow onion, diced
- 1   carrot, peeled and sliced in circles
- 1   clove crushed fresh garlic
- 14 ounces crushed canned tomatoes
- 3   large eggs
- 1/2 cup goat cheese
- 1/4 cup chopped fresh basil
- 2 tablespoons chopped fresh tarragon
- 1 teaspoon red pepper flakes
- 1/2 teaspoon black ground pepper
- 1/2 teaspoon smoked paprika
- 1/2 teaspoon salt

Direction

- Preheat oven to 375 degrees F. and in a medium cast iron skillet, heat oil and garlic on low. Add in onion, bell pepper, and carrot until tender. Add in red pepper, black pepper, paprika, salt, and stir.
- Pour in crushed tomatoes and stir. Add in fresh basil (reserve a bit for garnish) and all of chopped tarragon. Cook until the mixture is bubbling.
- Carefully crack eggs over the top of the mixture. Sprinkle goat cheese on top.
- Bake in oven for about 8-10 minutes, until the eggs have set but the yolks are still runny. Remove from oven and sprinkle with fresh basil. Enjoy!

298.   Spinach And Ricotta Teacakes

Serving: Serves 15 teacakes | Prep: | Cook: |Ready in:

Ingredients

- 2 bags of baby spinach (6 oz each)
- 1 bunch dino kale, ends trimmed, cut in bite size pieces (or substitute with a 3rd bag of spinach)
- 16 ounces part skim ricotta
- 3 ounces spreadable goat cheese (we like Chavrie goat cheese with basil and roasted garlic)
- 2 eggs, lightly beaten
- Freshly ground black pepper
- 1/4 teaspoon crushed red pepper flakes
- 1 pinch salt (we like smoked salt)
- 1 pinch grated nutmeg
- 1 tablespoon each of freshly chopped chervil, dill, parsley
- 1/4 cup toasted pine nuts
- 1/2 cup grated pecorino romano (Parmesan would be great too)

Direction

- Preheat the oven to 325F. Place ricotta and goat cheese in a bowl and mix until smooth and combined. Add the eggs, salt, pepper, red pepper flakes, nutmeg and herbs and mix well.
- Place the spinach in a saucepan of boiling water for 5 to 10 seconds, then drain, squeezing any excess water and chop. If using the kale repeat the previous step with the kale, leaving the kale to blanch for 1 minute before draining.
- Add the spinach, kale, pine nuts & pecorino to the ricotta mixture, mix until well combined. Spoon the mixture into greased muffin tins - if very lazy line with baking cups. Place in the oven for 40-45 minutes or until the teacakes are firm and golden.

---

299. Spring Garlic And Chickpea Tartine

Serving: Makes 4 long toasts | Prep: | Cook: |Ready in:

Ingredients

- 3 heads of spring garlic
- sea salt
- 2 tablespoons olive oil, divided
- 1 14-ounce can of chickpeas
- freshly ground black pepper
- 4 long slices pain de seigle
- goat cheese
- 4 slices prosciutto

Direction

- Preheat the oven to 400F.
- Remove the long stalk from the garlic, so you are left with just the heads. In a bowl, toss them with 1 tablespoon of the olive oil, as well as a pinch of sea salt. Wrap the garlic in aluminum foil, and roast for about 30 minutes.
- Meanwhile, drain and wash the can of chickpeas. Heat the remaining olive oil in a shallow pan over medium-high heat, and add the chickpeas. Toss in a liberal sprinkling of black pepper and sea salt. Using tongs, toss the chickpeas around. Let them cook for about 5 minutes, until they are almost splitting, and quite hot. Remove them to a bowl.
- When the garlic is ready, squeeze the cloves into the chickpea bowl. Use a fork to mash everything together. Give it a taste; add more pepper and sea salt, if necessary.
- Toast your bread. Spread each one with some goat cheese. Pile the smashed chickpeas/garlic on top of that, and then layer with 1 slice of prosciutto. Repeat.
- I like to cut each slice of toast into fingers. They are good for lunch, or as finger food at a party.

300.   Spring Onion Soup En Croute

Serving: Serves 4-6 servings | Prep: | Cook: | Ready in:

Ingredients

- 4   bunches spring onions or scallions (about 28)
- 1 tablespoon Olive Oil
- 3   cloves Garlic
- 1/2 cup White Wine
- 6 cups Vegetable Broth
- 1 cup Buttermilk
- 2 ounces Goat Cheese
- 2 tablespoons Flour
- 1/2 cup Sour Cream (light)
- 1 teaspoon Horseradish
- 1/4 teaspoon Salt
- 1/4 teaspoon Pepper

Direction

- (NOTE: Follow the instructions for the puff pastry, and thaw overnight in the refrigerator.) Rough chop 2/3 of the onions into 1 inch pieces. Separate the white parts from the green parts. Dice 3 cloves of Garlic.
- Heat up 1 TBLS Olive Oil in a soup pot. Sauté the chopped onion whites for about 4 minutes. Add the Garlic, and sauté for another minute.
- Pour in the Vegetable Broth, and add in the Green Onion tops. Bring to a simmer for about 3 minutes, then turn off the heat.
- Working in batches, ladle about 1 1/2 - 2 cups of the onions and broth at a time into a blender. Hold a towel over the lid, and start on a slow speed, then work up to a faster speed to puree. Pour into a separate bowl until all the soup is blended.
- Pour the blended soup back into the soup pot. Turn heat on to medium. Next, add the Buttermilk, Goat Cheese, Flour, Horseradish and Sour Cream into the blender, and blend until smooth.
- Temper the buttermilk mixture by adding a ladle of the broth mixture and stirring. Slowly stir the buttermilk mixture into the soup pot until mixed.
- Chop the last bunch of Spring Onions, and add to the soup. Bring to a low simmer over medium heat, and simmer for 3 minutes, then turn off the heat.
- Preheat oven to 400 degrees. Roll out the thawed Puff Pastry according to the package, and cut to size for your serving container. Ladle the soup into the serving bowl/cup, and then cover with the puff pastry. Brush the top with an egg wash, and bake for 12 minutes.

301.   Spring Onion And Herb Tart

Serving: Makes 1, 13-inch tart, or 6-8 individual ones | Prep: | Cook: | Ready in:

Ingredients

- Dough
- 1.5 cups flour, plus extra for dusting
- 3/4 teaspoon kosher salt, divided
- 1.5 sticks (170 grams), plus 1 tablespoon, chilled unsalted butter
- 1/4 cup ice water
- 1 teaspoon fresh thyme leaves (optional)
- Filling
- 3 leeks
- 9 spring onions or scallions
- 2/3 cup minced chives
- 6 ounces soft goat cheese
- 1 teaspoon lemon zest
- 1/4 cup crème fraîche
- 1/4 cup heavy cream
- 2 teaspoons minced fresh tarragon
- 3 eggs
- 1 cup finely grated aged gruyère
- freshly ground black pepper

Direction

- Dough

- Add the flour and the salt to the bowl of a food processor. (The thyme too, if you're using it.) Cut 1.5 sticks of the butter into slices, and add that too–the butter should be cold, frozen even–keeping everything as cold as possible will yield a flaky crust. Turn the machine on low, and slowly add the ice water, just until the dough comes together.
- Form the dough into a disk. Scatter a fine dusting of flour onto some plastic wrap, and wrap up the dough. Move it to the coldest part of the fridge for at least 30 minutes. (You can also do this the night before.)
- Roll out the dough; you want it about 1/4-inch thick. I like to roll my dough between two, floured sheets of plastic wrap; I find it's easy, and it minimizes mess. Now ease the dough into a 13-inch tart pan. Move the pan to the freezer for about 20 minutes.
- Heat oven to 375F. Blind bake the tart for 20 minutes (I use dried beans). With a fork, poke holes into the base of the tart (this will help prevent bubbles in the dough), and move the tart back into the oven for another 15 minutes, or until the edges are golden.
- Filling
- Quarter the leeks, slice up the white and light green bits, and wash well. Warm the remaining 1 tablespoon of butter in a pan over medium heat, until it is bubbling gently. Add the sliced leeks, and sauté until they are wilty, about 7 minutes. Set the leeks aside.
- Prep the spring onions: cut away and discard the whiskery bottoms. Wash the stalks well, and then slice.
- Wash your chives. I use kitchen shears to mince them. Don't worry about making them perfectly uniform.
- Add the: goat cheese, lemon zest, crème fraîche, heavy cream, and tarragon to a large mixing bowl. Use a whisk to blend everything together. Add the eggs, and the remaining 1/2 teaspoon of salt, and mix to incorporate. Lastly, whisk in the minced chives.
- Now put the tart together: scatter the leeks, the spring onions, and the aged gruyère across the bottom of the tart. Pour in the cream mixture.

Grate some black pepper across the top. Move the tart to the oven, and cook for 22 more minutes, until the cream mixture is just set. Let the tart cool slightly. Serve warm or at room temperature.

---

302. Spring Pea, Mint And Goats Cheese Bruschetta

Serving: Makes 8 | Prep: | Cook: | Ready in:

Ingredients

- 1/2 french baguette, 1 cm slices
- 150 grams soft goats cheese, preferably a light & lemony one
- 200 grams frozen peas, or fresh if you have them
- 10 mint leaves, finely shredded
- 1 lemon, all the zest and half the juice
- generous pinches pepper & salt

Direction

- Start by making the whipped goat cheese. Place the goat cheese, with a little reserved separately for sprinkling, in a large bowl and add a generous pinch of pepper and half the lemon zest. Whip all together till light and smooth. Place in the fridge to chill.
- Place a griddle pan on a medium heat and leave to heat up, or if you have a BBQ fire it up. Once the pan/BBQ is hot, place the sliced bread in a single layer and leave till nicely griddled on one side. Once toasted on one side, flip over and cook on the other side.
- While the bread is cooking place the peas in a small pan and pour over a kettle of boiling water to cover the peas. Turn on the heat and simmer for 3 minutes until the peas are hot but not too soft. Drain the peas.
- Place the drained peas in a pestle and mortar, or a processor, add the remaining lemon zest, the lemon juice, chopped mint, generous pinch of pepper and a pinch of salt. Bash the

ingredients to release all the flavors but not till a paste is created - you still want some texture left.

- Place the bread on a board with the bowl of goat cheese and the mortar of pea mix. If you don't have a mortar just put the mixture into a small serving dish. Let people help themselves by spreading a slice of toast with a thick layer of cheese and piling high the pea mixture on top. Sprinkle each slice with a little reserved goat cheese and some fresh lemon zest.

303. Springtime Asparagus Pizza

Serving: Serves 2 | Prep: | Cook: | Ready in:

Ingredients

- 1 ball pizza dough, ~12 oz
- 3/4 pound pencil thin asparagus spears, cut or broken in half and tossed with a drizzle of olive oil and salt
- 1 cup shredded mozzarella, loosely packed
- 4 ounces goat cheese
- zest of 1 lemon
- 1/4 teaspoon chili flakes
- 8 oil-packed anchovies (can be increased or omitted, as desired)

Direction

- Preheat your oven (with a stone, if you have) to 500 degrees for 2 hours.
- Place the pizza dough on a lightly-floured counter top, and press outward into a thick disk (leaving a 1" unpressed area along the edge). Pick up the disk and let it drape over the backs of your hands, letting gravity help you stretch it into a 12-14" disk. Place the dough on a peel (or overturned cookie sheet or cutting board) that's lightly dusted with semolina or other type of flour.
- Scatter the mozzarella on top of the dough, then the asparagus and clumps of the goat

cheese in whatever artful pattern you desire. Side the pizza onto the preheated stone in your oven, and bake ~7-10 minutes, until the crust browns and the cheese melts.

- Remove the pizza from the oven, and scatter the lemon zest and chili flakes on top. Add anchovies, if desired. Slice and serve.

304. Squash And Goat Cheese Lasagna

Serving: Serves 9 small portions, 6 large portions | Prep: | Cook: | Ready in:

Ingredients

- 3 pounds summer squash (any type)
- 1 cup yellow onion - diced
- 2 leeks - sliced
- 8 ounces ricotta cheese
- 8 ounces goat cheese (at room temperature)
- 1 egg
- 2 tablespoons fresh parsley - finely chopped
- 3 cups marinara sauce
- bechamel sauce - see below
- 1/2 cup butter
- 1/3 cup flour
- 1/4 cup cream or half & half
- 8 ounces whole wheat lasagna noodles - cooked

Direction

- To prepare béchamel sauce: melt butter in sauce pan over medium heat, gradually add flour to melted butter, stirring constantly to blend flour into butter. Once all flour has been blended, cook on low for 2-3 minutes. Slowly add cream or half & half to the butter/flour mixture, and cook on low for 3-5 minutes. Remove from heat, blend with marinara.
- To prepare squash: in 1 tablespoon butter, sauté diced onion over medium heat until glistening. Add squash, salt & pepper. Sauté for 3-5 minutes (do not overcook).

- To prepare cheese mixture: blend ricotta and goat cheese together in a large mixing bowl. Add parsley and egg; mix well.
- Layer lasagna: in a 2 quart (8x11") glass baking dish, spread a thin layer of the marinara/béchamel sauce mixture on the bottom of the pan and top with a layer of lasagna noodles. Then layer: sauce, leeks and squash, and cheese mixture. Top with noodles and repeat layering process until you reach the top of the casserole dish. Top the casserole with cheese sauce. Bake at 350 degrees for 45 minutes to an hour. Let cool for approximately 15 minutes before slicing.

305.   Strawberries & Cheese Bites

Serving: Serves 4 | Prep: | Cook: |Ready in:

Ingredients

- 1 cup strawberries - chopped
- 1 tablespoon mint - chopped
- 1 tablespoon honey or agave nectar
- 1 teaspoon crushed black pepper
- 1/2 cup Goat cheese spread
- puff pastry sheets - thawed (If you use the 8"x8" sheets, then you will need 3. If you use the regular pepperidge farm sheets, then you will need 1 & 1/3. You could also you the puff pastry shells.)

Direction

- Pre-heat the oven at 350º F.
- Mix in strawberries, mint, honey or agave nectar and black pepper in a bowl and refrigerate.
- Coat the muffin pan with cooking spray.
- Cut the puff pastry sheets into 2"x2" squares and place one in each muffin cup.
- Bake for 15-20 minutes or until the puff pastries are golden brown.

- Spread a spoonful of goat cheese on each puff pastry and a spoonful of strawberry mixture.
- Eat while the puff pastries are still a bit warm.

306.   Strawberry Goat Cheese Oat Pie With Whipped Goat Cheese

Serving: Serves 8 | Prep: | Cook: |Ready in:

Ingredients

- Strawberry Goat Cheese Oat Pie
- 2 cups rolled oats, certified gluten-free
- 3 tablespoons olive oil
- 2 tablespoons honey
- 2 tablespoons dark brown sugar
- 1/4 cup yogurt
- 1/4 cup heavy cream
- 3 ounces goat cheese
- 3 eggs
- 1/2 teaspoon vanilla extract
- 1 1/4 teaspoons baking powder
- 1/4 teaspoon baking soda
- 1/4 teaspoon kosher salt
- 1 handful fresh strawberries
- Whipped Goat Cheese
- 4 ounces heavy cream
- 2 ounces goat cheese
- 1 dash honey

Direction

- Strawberry Goat Cheese Oat Pie
- Preheat oven to 375° F. While oven is preheating, toast your oats (for a nuttier flavor). Spread oats out on large, parchment-lined pan. Let toast for 15 minutes, stirring every 5 minutes.
- In the bowl of your food processor or a medium bowl, combine olive oil, honey, dark brown sugar, yogurt, heavy cream, goat cheese, eggs and vanilla. Process or whisk thoroughly, until creamy.

- In a large bowl, whisk together oats, baking powder, baking soda and salt.
- Stir the wet ingredients into the dry ingredients and mix well.
- Pour into a greased 9" pie pan. [The pan should be at least 2" deep or there will be overflow.]
- Place sliced strawberries in three concentric circles on the oat mixture.
- Bake for 20 minutes or until a toothpick tester comes out clean.
- Let fully cool [at least 4 hours] before slicing. Top with whipped goat cheese and fresh strawberries.
- Whipped Goat Cheese
- Combine heavy cream and goat cheese in a medium bowl and whip with an electric mixer [or large whisk] until airy and doubled in size.
- Add the dash of honey [a small drizzle to cut the goaty tang] and mix thoroughly. Chill until serving.

---

307. Strawberry Macaroon Tart

Serving: Serves 8 (i used a 5x14 inch rectangluar tart pan with removable bottom) | Prep: | Cook: |Ready in:

Ingredients

- 1 egg white
- 1 teaspoon maple syrup
- 1/4 teaspoon kosher salt
- 1 1/2 cups unsweetened shredded coconut
- 9 ounces organic fresh strawberries, diced
- 2 tablespoons organic coconut palm sugar
- 1 teaspoon fresh lemon juice
- 2 ounces soft goat cheese, room temperature
- 4 ounces cream cheese, room temperature
- 1 teaspoon vanilla
- Additional fresh strawberries to garnish

Direction

- Preheat the oven to 350 degrees. Cut a piece of parchment paper to fit the bottom of your tart pan and set aside.
- In a small mixing bowl, lightly whisk the egg white, maple syrup and salt together for a few seconds. Add the shredded coconut and gently stir to mix and coat the coconut. Spread the mixture in the prepared tart pan and gently press to evenly cover the sides and bottom of the pan. Bake for 14-15 minutes, until the edges are golden and the crust is set. Remove and let cool completely.
- In a medium sized mixing bowl, stir together the strawberries, coconut sugar and lemon juice and set aside to macerate for about half an hour.
- In another bowl, combine the goat cheese, cream cheese and vanilla and beat with an electric mixer until smooth. Using a spatula, fold in the strawberries and collected juices and gently stir and mash until well blended. Spoon the strawberry-cheese mixture into the cooled crust and spread evenly. Pop it into the fridge and let it chill for at least 1-2 hours. It will firm up as it chills.
- When ready to serve, take the tart from the fridge and remove the bottom of the tart pan. Slide the tart onto a cutting board or serving platter and garnish with sliced strawberries or a few shavings of dark chocolate (or both!). Using a serrated knife, slice into wedges and serve. It is best eaten on the day it is prepared, and can be made in the morning to be served in the evening.

---

308. Strawberry And Quinoa Salad With Tarragon, Soft Goat's Cheese And Poached Egg

Serving: Serves 4 | Prep: 0hours0mins | Cook: 0hours0mins |Ready in:

Ingredients

- 150 grams (5½ oz) quinoa
- 500 grams (1 lb 2 oz) strawberries
- 3 to 4 mint sprigs
- 3 to 4 tarragon sprigs
- 2 tablespoons olive oil
- 60 milliliters (2 fl oz/ 1/4 cup) white-wine vinegar
- Pinch of finely grated orange zest
- 1 orange, juice of
- 4 small eggs
- 1 handful rocket (arugula), red sorrel, or mizuna
- 1 pinch salt and freshly ground black pepper, to taste
- 100 grams (3½ oz) soft goat's cheese

Direction

- Rinse the quinoa under cold water, to wash away any bitterness. Combine 300 ml (10 fl oz.) water and ½ teaspoon salt in a saucepan, then cover and bring to the boil. Rain in the quinoa and simmer gently over very low heat for 5 minutes. Remove from the heat and leave, covered, for about 15 minutes to swell up.
- Meanwhile, slice the strawberries or chop into wedges. Pick the mint and tarragon leaves and roughly chop. In a bowl, combine the quinoa, olive oil, 1 tablespoon of the white-wine vinegar, and the orange zest and juice.
- Fill a saucepan with 2 liters (68 fl oz./8 cups) water and add the remaining vinegar. Bring to the boil. Break the eggs, one at a time, into a cup, taking care not to break the yolk. Carefully slide the eggs, one at a time, into the bubbling water and spoon the white over the yolk. Reduce the heat – the water should be just under boiling. Cook the eggs for 3–4 minutes then, using a skimmer or slotted spoon, remove the poached eggs from the water and drain on paper towel.
- Toss the herbs, salad leaves and strawberries with the quinoa and transfer to a serving plate. Season with salt and pepper, crumble over the goat's cheese and top with the poached eggs.

309.   Stuffed Chicken Boats (Bateaux Aux Poulets)

Serving: Serves 4 | Prep: 0hours20mins | Cook: 1hours0mins | Ready in:

Ingredients

- Boats:
- 4 large boneless, skinless chicken breasts
- 3/4 cup chicken broth
- Dash Salt
- Dash Pepper
- Dash Old Bay
- Dash Oregano
- Stuffing:
- 2 Large yellow onions
- 2 Generous handfuls of spinach
- 4 ounces Goat cheese
- 1/3 cup Panko breadcrumbs
- Dash Salt
- Dash Pepper
- 2 tablespoons Olive oil
- 2-3 cloves Garlic

Direction

- In a large frying pan, heat the olive oil on medium heat. Meanwhile, slice the onions thinly; add the garlic and onions to the pan and cook until the onions are significantly softened, 8-10 minutes.
- While the onions are cooking down, wash and dry the spinach. When the onions are soft, add the spinach, salt, and pepper. Cook until the spinach is fully wilted, 3-5 minutes.
- Make the chicken boats: slice into each breast with a large knife as though you were going to open the breast up like a book (you will in a moment). Stop halfway through the breast; using the tip of the knife, cut deeper into the middle of the breast, making sure the ends remain only half-fileted. Pull the cut edges open into the boat shape and place opening-down in a large baking dish. Sprinkle liberally

with salt, pepper, oregano, and Old Bay. Flip over again. Preheat oven to 400° F (205° C).

- Once the spinach is wilted, remove pan from heat and crumble goat cheese into the pan. Mix until the contents have coalesced. N.B.: It's better to have to add more goat cheese than to have too much, so you may want to crumble it into the pan in batches, mixing in between to achieve the right ratio.
- Spoon the mixture into the chicken boats; you'll probably have a fair amount of extra, don't be afraid to pile it on the breasts. Top with panko and a dusting of Old Bay. Add the chicken broth to the baking dish (don't pour it directly on the chicken, you don't want soggy panko!) and put into the oven for 40 minutes, covered with aluminum foil.
- Check the temperature with a meat thermometer; if it's sufficiently high, remove the foil and cook for another 5-10 minutes. Serve hot with a crisp salad and potatoes au gratin.

310. Stuffed Peppadew Peppers

Serving: Serves 24 stuffed peppers | Prep: | Cook: | Ready in:

Ingredients

- 24   peppadew peppers
- 4 ounces soft goat cheese- at room temperature
- 2 tablespoons finely crumbled feta cheese
- 1 tablespoon chopped herbs of your choice- good additions are basil, flat leaf parsley, tarragon, mint, chives, or a mix

Direction

- Briskly mix goat cheese, feta, and herbs together. If mixture appears too stiff to pipe from a pastry bag or a large zip lock bag, mix in a touch of water to loosen mixture.

- Add mixture to a pastry bag or a large zip lock bag and snip one corner off to allow for piping.
- Pipe mixture into each pepper and place on a serving platter.
- If you wish, reserve some extra herbs when preparing the stuffing and sprinkle around the plate.

311. Stuffed Conchiglioni: Pumpkin And Goat Cheese

Serving: Serves 4 | Prep: | Cook: | Ready in:

Ingredients

- 40   conchiglioni
- 2 teaspoons flat parsley
- 1   small onion
- 550   gr butternut
- 50 milliliters dry white wine
- 4 tablespoons ricotta
- 30 milliliters milk
- 3-4 tablespoons cooked chestnut, hacked
- 300 milliliters liquid cream
- 1 teaspoon nutmeg powder
- 1/2 cup goat cheese
- 4 tablespoons grated cheese (cheddar, swiss etc)
- 3 tablespoons almonds

Direction

- Peel the onion. For the butternut, remove the skin and the seeds, and cut into small dices.
- Cook the onion is a pan with a little bit of olive oil. Add the wine and stir well. Bring down the heat and add the butternut. Cook on low heat for 10 minutes. Season to taste. Add the flat parsley, nutmeg, cooked chestnut, milk and ricotta. Keep warm.
- In a small sauce pan, heat the cream with the goat cheese but do not boil. Season to taste and set aside.
- Preheat oven to 450°F.

- Cook the pasta in a large sauce. Drain and sprinkle with olive oil.
- Pour the goat cheese sauce in an oven dish
- Fill each conchiglioni with butternut farce and place on top of the sauce. Sprinkle almonds and cheese on top. Bake in the oven for 10 minutes.

312.   Summer Cucumber Rolls

Serving: Serves 10 | Prep: | Cook: |Ready in:

Ingredients

- 2 Large Cucumbers
- 4 Asian Pears
- 8 ounces Fresh Goat cheese
- 1/2 pound Thinly sliced Prosciutto
- 1/2 cup Honey

Direction

- Wash and peel the cucumbers and Asian pears.
- Using a mandolin slicer or veggie peeler with a wide blade, slice thin long slices of the cucumber and Asian pear. Depending on the length of your cucumber, you may use two pieces of Asian pear per slice.
- Lay out all slices of cucumber. Spread goat cheese on each slice of cucumber.
- Lay a slice of Asian pear on top of the goat cheese.
- Lay a slice of Prosciutto on top of the Asian pear.
- Drizzle each stack with honey.
- Roll up the cucumber and secure with a toothpick or party pick.
- Serve to your guests on a large platter!

313.   Summer's Sweet Heat Salad

Serving: Serves 4-6 | Prep: | Cook: |Ready in:

Ingredients

- Jalapeno cilantro pesto
- 2 cups cilantro
- 2-4   garlic cloves, depending on taste
- 1-2 jalapenos, depending on the amount of heat you want
- 1/4 cup toasted pine nuts
- 1/2 cup olive oil
- squeeze of lemon
- salt to taste
- Veggie medley
- 2   cobs of corn
- 1-2 cups green beans, cut into 2 inch pieces
- 2-4 tablespoons olive oil
- 1   vidalia onion, chopped
- 1   clove garlic, chopped or crushed
- 1-2 cups cherry tomatoes
- 2   small/med zucchinis or summer squash, sliced
- 1/4-1/2 cups jalapeno cilantro pesto (to taste)
- (OPTIONAL: 2 cups Farro)
- (OPTIONAL: 1/2 c. goat cheese)

Direction

- Jalapeno cilantro pesto
- Blend ingredients together in food processor. Start with a little oil and add as necessary. Add salt to taste.
- Veggie medley
- Bring pot of salted water to boil. Heat oil in a sauté pan. Add onions and garlic and sauté until translucent.
- Once water comes to boil, put corn in the pot for 2-3 minutes - no longer. Remove from water rinse in cool water and put to side.
- Once onions are translucent, add beans and cover pan partially so beans can steam a bit. After a few minutes with the beans in the pan, add squash and cover partially again. Add

more oil if veggies seem to need it. Add salt at this point as well.

- As squash, beans, onions are sautéing, chop tomatoes in half or quarters, and cut corn off the cob.
- When squash and beans are cooked to your liking (sometimes I make them more caramelized, sometimes I make them more steamed with a little crunch, both are good), turn the heat on low and toss in the corn and tomatoes. Add the pesto and toss through once or twice and turn the heat off. (The heat from the veggies will help the pesto mix thoroughly and distribute in a balanced way).
- Put veggies in a serving bowl, add salt and pepper to taste. Dish can be served warm or room temperature. Great for a picnic or a weeknight meal along with some grilled meat.
- (Optional: adding crumbled goat cheese will make the dish a bit creamy and adds a nice mellow flavor; additionally, including farro at the end turns a vegetable side dish into a main course. The meaty/nutty quality of farro stands up perfectly to texture/flavors of the vegetables. Delicious for a fresh summer meal!)

314. Sweet Potato Fries With Goat Cheese And Raspberry Sauce

Serving: Serves 2-4 | Prep: | Cook: | Ready in:

Ingredients

- 3 Medium to Large Sweet Potatoes
- 1/10-1/4 pounds Semi-firm Goat Cheese
- 1/4 cup Raspberry Jam
- 2 tablespoons Olive oil
- 1 pinch Chili Powder *Optional but excellent
- Salt to taste

Direction

- Preheat your oven to 400F.

- Cut the sweet potatoes into even sized strips. I cut them by hand and prefer not to peel them as it gives some of the fries an extra crispy edge.
- Place the strips in a bowl and drizzle with olive oil. Sprinkle salt over the sweet potato strips and toss until lightly coated.
- Line a cookie sheet with parchment or aluminum foil. Pour out the fries onto the sheet and spread evenly over the cookie sheet.
- Bake in the oven for 30mins. Remove cookie sheet from the oven and mvd/flip the fries using a sharp spatula, some may stick a bit depending on how thick the fries are cut. For thinner fries, they may only take 15-20mins at this temperature.
- Place the fries back in the oven and bake for an additional 15-20 mins depending on thickness. Remove when they have crispy brown edges and are browning on the bottoms.
- While the fries are baking, place the raspberry jam in a small sauce pot and heat over a low flame until it begins to liquefy. Do not melt it completely, it should still be partially gelled. Add the chili powder at this point if desired and stir it into the sauce. The chili flavor should not be readily perceivable, but just enough to give the raspberry sauce a "kick". Turn off the flame and allow the sauce to cool a bit.
- When the fries are ready, plate them and crumble the goat cheese over the fries. It will soften with the heat of the fries and even melt a little.
- Spoon the desired amount of raspberry sauce over the fries. If it looks strange then you have done it perfectly!

315. Sweet Potato, Goat Cheese Gratin

Serving: Serves 3 | Prep: | Cook: | Ready in:

Ingredients

- 2 medium sweet potatoes
- 2 big carrots
- 5 garlic cloves
- 1 tablespoon dried sage
- 1/2 cup goat milk
- 1 pound soft goats cheese
- peper and salt
- drizzle of olive oil

Direction

- Preheat the oven on 200C / 390F.
- Wash the sweet potato, leave the skin on. Cut the potato in slices of 5mm and cut the carrot in slices of 3mm. The carrot needs some more time in the oven but by making the slices thinner, the cooking time will be the same. Cut the carrot diagonal so they become taller, preferably as wide as the potato slices. Put everything in an oven dish.
- Cut the garlic cloves small and add to the potato, now add the sage, pepper, salt, olive oil and toss everything together well. Arrange the potato and carrot one by one like roof tiles so you will only see the upper edge of the slices when done.
- Cover with aluminum foil and put in the oven for 45 minutes.
- Mix the goat milk with 3/4 of the soft goat cheese until smooth.
- After 45 minutes, take the oven dish out of the oven, cover the potatoes with the creamy goats cheese, put the rest of the goats cheese over it in small chunks and return for another 25 minutes to the oven, uncovered. Ready when all the slices are very soft.

316.   Sweet Potato, Goat Cheese, & Sage Pasta Pile Up

Serving: Serves 8 | Prep: 0hours0mins | Cook: 0hours40mins | Ready in:

Ingredients

- 2 sweet potatoes
- 1/2 pound lasagna noodles
- 8 ounces goat cheese
- 1/4 cup butter
- 1 bunch sage
- salt and pepper to taste

Direction

- Bring two pots of water to boil, meanwhile scrub the potatoes and stab them with a knife. Once the water is boiling toss in the potatoes and cook until easily impaled. This should take around 20 minutes.
- Once the potatoes are done remove them from the heat, for a quick cool down run cold water over them. Put the lasagna noodles in the other pot of boiling water and set the time for about 10 minutes
- Once the potatoes are cooled pinch off their skin. Cut them into small pieces and mash them up with the goat cheese. (Note if you want them creamy heat them up a little while you are doing this). Salt to taste.
- In a sauce pan heat the butter on medium-low. Add the sage and cook until browned, about 4-5 minutes.
- Drain the lasagna noodles. Place a few noodles on a plate and scoop some of the sweet potato mixture around them. Repeat this until all the noodles and mix are used up.
- Crack some pepper on top and devour!

317.   Sweet Potato, Spinach & Goat Cheese Frittata

Serving: Serves 4-6 | Prep: | Cook: | Ready in:

Ingredients

- 12 eggs
- 1/2 - 1 cups milk or half n' half
- 4-6 ounces goat cheese
- 1 shallot finely chopped
- 1 large sweet potato or yam

- 4 tablespoons butter or olive oil
- 1 bunch spinach - washed & destemmed
- 1 teaspoon salt (or less depending on taste)
- 1 dash black pepper

Direction

- Peel sweet potato and slice into quarter inch thick rounds.
- Melt 2 tablespoons of butter or olive oil in the bottom of a large cast iron skillet. Once oil/butter is warm cover bottom of skillet with one layer of sweet potato rounds. Let cook for 4-5 min.
- Meanwhile chop shallot and sauté in remaining 2 tablespoons of butter/olive oil in separate pan.
- Turn off sweet potatoes (no need to turn - they cook fast).
- Whisk eggs together and then whisk in milk or half n' half, salt and pepper. Set aside.
- Wash and de-stem one bunch of spinach or one package of baby spinach. Make sure to remove the stems to avoid stringiness.
- Pour egg mixture into pan with sweet potatoes, add shallots next, spinach and finally chunks of goat cheese evenly distributed. Cook for two minutes on the stove-top on medium heat.
- Transfer to broiler and cook for another 2 - 2 1/2 minutes or until eggs puff. Remove from oven, let cool 5 minutes and serve.

318. Sweet Potatoes With Orange Bitters

Serving: Serves 4 | Prep: | Cook: | Ready in:

Ingredients

- 1 1/2 cups freshly squeezed orange juice (the juice of 4 to 5 oranges)
- 1/3 cup brown sugar
- 1/4 cup red wine vinegar
- 1/4 cup Angostura bitters
- 1 1/2 tablespoons olive oil
- 4 to 5 sweet potatoes, unpeeled, halved crosswise, each half cut into 1-inch-wide wedges
- 2 red chiles, split open along the center
- 3 sage sprigs
- 10 thyme sprigs
- 2 heads garlic, unpeeled and halved horizontally
- 3 ounces goat cheese log, broken into pieces
- Salt

Direction

- Preheat the oven to 425° F.
- Place the orange juice in a saucepan with the sugar and vinegar. Bring to a boil over high heat, then turn down the heat to medium-high and simmer fairly rapidly for about 20 minutes, until the liquid has thickened and reduced to scant 1 cup (about the amount in a large glass of wine). Add the bitters, olive oil, and 1 1/2 teaspoons salt.
- Place the potatoes in a large bowl, add the chiles, sage, thyme, and garlic, and then pour in the reduced sauce. Toss well so that everything is coated and then spread the mixture out in a single layer on a baking sheet on which it fits snugly, about 12 by 16 inches.
- Place in the oven and roast for 50 to 60 minutes, turning and basting the potatoes every 15 minutes or so. They need to remain coated in the liquid in order to caramelize, so add more orange juice if the pan is drying out.
- At the end, the potatoes should be dark and sticky. Remove from the oven and leave to cool slightly before arranging on a platter and dotting with the goat cheese. Serve warm or at room temperature.

319. Sweet And Savory Burger With Fig Jam, Goat Cheese, And Arugula

Serving: Makes 2 burgers | Prep: | Cook: |Ready in:

Ingredients

- 2 burger buns
- 1/2 pound ground beef
- 1/2 to 1 teaspoons crushed red pepper flakes
- 1/4 teaspoon onion powder
- 1/4 teaspoon garlic powder
- Salt and freshly ground black pepper
- 2 to 3 tablespoons fig jam (I like Trader Joe's)
- 2 ounces goat cheese
- 1 handful arugula
- 1 teaspoon olive oil

Direction

- Preheat oven to 350° F. Place buns on a baking sheet, and toast in oven for about 10 minutes.
- In a small bowl, drizzle olive oil over arugula, and season with salt and pepper. Give it a toss.
- In a mixing bowl, combine ground beef with salt, pepper, crushed red pepper, onion powder, and garlic powder. Mix with your hands. (NOTE: Any time you handle raw meat, wash your hands thoroughly with soap and water before touching anything else.) Form beef into two patties.
- Heat your cast iron skillet over medium heat. Melt butter or oil in skillet, and carefully place patties in pan. Always lay meat away from you to avoid splattering hot oil on yourself. Let patties cook for about 2 to 3 minutes before flipping (cooking time will depend on how thick your patties are). Once flipped, place goat cheese on each patty to warm and soften cheese. Cook second side for 2 to 3 minutes.
- Assemble! Spread fig jam on the bottom bun. Place patty on top of fig jam. Top patty with arugula. Top arugula with top bun.

320. Sweet Potato, Goat's Cheese And Bacon Frittata

Serving: Serves 4 to 6 | Prep: | Cook: |Ready in:

Ingredients

- 1 medium sweet potato, peeled and cut into chunks
- 8 ounces goat's cheese
- 3 shallots, finely chopped
- 6 pieces bacon, preferably maple or hickory
- 10 eggs
- 1/3 cup freshly grated Parmesan
- salt and freshly ground black pepper
- 1 tablespoon olive oil

Direction

- Place the sweet potato chunks in a saucepan. Cover with cold water and bring to a boil. Lower the heat and simmer until tender, about 10 to 15 minutes. Drain and transfer to a large bowl.
- While the sweet potato is still warm, crumble the goat's cheese and shallots into the bowl.
- Meanwhile, cook the bacon in a skillet. Set aside to drain on a plate lined with a paper towel. When cool, chop into bite-sized pieces. Add to the sweet potato and goat's cheese mixture.
- Beat the eggs in a large bowl and add in the Parmesan, mixing well to combine. Season with salt and pepper.
- Place an 8- or 9-inch nonstick frying pan over a medium heat and add the olive oil. Add the sweet potato mixture, distributing it evenly over the base of the pan. Pour in the beaten egg mixture, making sure it evenly coats the sweet potato mixture. Reduce the heat to low and cook for 8 to 10 minutes, or until the eggs on top are almost set.
- Put the pan under a hot broiler for a few minutes to finish the frittata, until it's golden brown on top. (Remember to be careful when taking the pan out of the oven and for some time afterward, as the handle will be hot!)

Don't worry if it's still a little soft or runny in the center, as it will continue to cook as it cools.

- Loosen the frittata with a knife or spatula until it moves freely in the pan, then slide it out onto a platter or place a platter over the pan and invert. Cut the frittata into wedges to serve. This is best served at room temperature.

321. Sweetbreads Crostini With On Hand Chimichurri

Serving: Serves 6-10 | Prep: | Cook: | Ready in:

Ingredients

- Chimichurri
- 1 cup Parsley
- 1 cup Cilantro
- 1 cup basil/oregano mix (or whatever floats your boat)
- 1/4 cup extra virgin olive oil
- 1/4 cup white wine vinegar
- 1 pinch ground cayenne pepper
- salt and pepper to taste
- 1 clove garlic, smashed
- Veal Sweetbreads
- 1 pound large veal sweetbreads, roughly 3
- 1 lemon
- 1/2 cup flour
- 1 cup heavy cream (optional)
- 1 baguette or quality bread, sliced and lightly toasted
- salt and pepper to taste.
- 4 tablespoons butter
- 1/4 pound fresh goat cheese or brie.

Direction

- Put the sweetbreads in a ziplock bag with ice and cold water. Let sit overnight.
- Take the sweetbreads out, put into a high-rimmed pan. Cover with water, and add the juice of the 1 lemon.

- Bring the water to a boil, turn the heat down to a simmer, cover, and let it go for 5 minutes
- Remove from heat and let the sweetbreads sit in the covered pan for another 45 minutes.
- Turn out the pan into a colander and let some cold water run over the sweetbreads. When cooled, using your best paring knife cut the sweetbreads in half lengthwise (or thick-wise)--roughly a third of an inch; trim of any tough membrane you see and then cut into four crostini-sized pieces per half.
- Put the pieces on a towel-topped plate, put a heavy cast iron skillet and top and weigh it down with whatever is heavy in your pantry. Fridge it and let sit overnight (again).
- Make the chimichurri: put all of the ingredients in a food processor and pulse it into a paste. This is about your taste; if you want it thicker, add herbs (can't over-herb it); if you like thinner, you can add a splash or oil or (if you would like tangier and thinner) vinegar.
- Optional step**: remove the sweetbreads from the weight, put in a zip-lock bag with heavy cream for 1-2 hours.
- Heat a skillet to medium-high heat (I go 8/10 on my electric stovetop but I believe my stovetop is cooler than most). Meanwhile toast your bread (can be done in advance) and bring the sweetbreads & cheese to close to room temp. I brought out the cheese and veal sb's about a half hour before cooking.
- Dredge the sweetbreads in the flour (which you should season liberally with salt) so that it is completely covered; but shake and knock off excess (it'll just burn in the fat).
- Add the butter to the pan. When hot, add the sweetbreads and fry on each side about 2 minutes per (4-5 total) until both sides get good color. The goldening butter in the pan should make your house smell like heaven. Cooking these, by the way, isn't like a burger or steak where you have to go one flip and one flip only; if you flip after 2 minutes and the color ain't there, just flip it back over. No one'll know and I won't tell...

- Assembly: either shmear some goat cheese on each piece of bread or give them a thin slice of the brie. As soon as the sweetbreads come out of the pan, place the pieces onto a respective bread/cheese piece. Spoon a bit of the chimichurri onto the top of each and serve immediately.

---

322. Swiss Chard, Goat Cheese And Winter Squash Phyllo Torte

Serving: Serves 8 | Prep: | Cook: |Ready in:

Ingredients

- Layered Filling
- 1 large yukon gold potato
- 2 cloves garlic, minced
- 1 small onion, minced
- 1 bunch swiss chard, washed
- 2 teaspoons fresh dill, minced
- 1 teaspoon fresh thyme, minced
- 2 tablespoons fresh parsley, minced
- 2 medium butternut squash, neck only (reserve bulb for another use)
- 2 large eggs
- 3 tablespoons heavy cream
- 1/8 teaspoon scant, nutmeg
- 2 ounces fresh goat cheese
- Phyllo Crust
- 8 sheets phyllo
- 4 tablespoons melted butter
- 1/2 cup toasted hazelnuts, ground

Direction

- Wash and peel the potato. Dice in ½" dice. Place in cold water in a saucepan and bring to a boil, cook for about 5 minutes, or until just tender. Drain and set aside.
- Separate the chard leaves and ribs, chopping each finely.
- Heat olive oil in a large skillet. Cook onion and garlic until transparent. Add chard stems and cook 2-3 minutes. Add chard leaves and cook, stirring for 5-7 minutes, until just done and any moisture has cooked off. If there is some 'likker' left in the pot, leave it behind.
- Gently stir potatoes, chard and herbs together. Taste for seasoning. Set aside.
- Peel the squash necks and slice very thinly. I like to use a mandoline for this step. Set aside.
- Assemble the Torte: Cut the phyllo sheets in half and stack one half on top of the other. Keep the stack covered with plastic wrap so it doesn't dry out as you complete the assembly.
- Brush the bottom and side of a 9" springform pan with melted butter. Butter a phyllo sheet and line the pan, allowing the excess to drape over the side. Do not concern yourself with tears, but do try to keep the phyllo from pleating and wrinkling.
- Continue to create the crust, turning the pan a quarter turn between each phyllo sheet. Sprinkle some hazelnuts between a couple of the layers. You'll use eight half-sheets for this step. When you're done, sprinkle a good covering of nuts on the bottom of the torte.
- Put half the chard/potato mixture in the pan. Place half the butternut squash slices in a couple of spiral layers on top of the chard. Grate a little bit of nutmeg over the squash. Salt & pepper generously.
- Pinch off marble sized pieces of goat cheese and scatter over the squash. Add the remaining chard mixture on top of the cheese and pour the egg mixture over everything. Add a double spiral layer of squash; then salt, pepper and a quick grating of nutmeg.
- Make a top crust for the torte with the remaining pieces of phyllo, buttering each sheet before it is placed on the torte, and scattering nuts between a couple of the layers. Gather the edges of the phyllo that are draped over the side of the pan and trim & fold in a decorative way around the edge of the pan. Butter the top. Sprinkle sparingly with nuts.
- Bake in a 425 oven for 45 minutes. Allow to cool for 10 minutes before removing the springform.

323.   Taste Of Summer Orzo Salad

Serving: Serves 6-12 as a side dish | Prep: | Cook: |Ready in:

Ingredients

- 1 packet orzo pasta
- 1/3 cup minced red onion
- 1 1/2 cups chopped fresh tomatoes (not grape or cherry ones, heirloom if possible)
- 1/2 cup minced celery
- 1/3 cup fresh chopped basil
- 1/4 cup sliced Kalamata olives
- 1/4 cup capers, drained and rinsed
- 1 tablespoon coarse grain mustard
- 1/2 teaspoon sugar
- 6 tablespoons olive oil
- 3 tablespoons balsamic vinegar
- 4-6 ounces goat cheese, crumbled

Direction

- Cook the orzo in salted water according to package instructions.
- While the orzo is cooking, cut up the onion, tomatoes, celery, basil, and olives.
- In a small bowl, whisk together the mustard, sugar, pinch of salt, and balsamic vinegar. Slowly whisk in the olive oil until an emulsion forms.
- Drain the orzo and place in a large bowl. Add the onion, tomatoes, celery, basil, olives, and capers. Toss. Pour the vinaigrette over the orzo mixture and toss to coat. Chill well.
- Just before serving, mix in the crumbled goat cheese.

324.   The Fluffiest Scrambled Egg

Serving: Serves 1 | Prep: | Cook: |Ready in:

Ingredients

- The base
- 3 eggs
- 1/4 cup Organic soy cream
- 1 Scallion
- Salt'n'pepper
- Toppings
- 1 tablespoon Goat cheese
- 1 handful Any sprout

Direction

- In a bowl whisk the eggs until they are smooth. Add salt, pepper, goat cheese and about half of the soy cream to start.
- In a well-oiled saucepan heated to medium pour the egg mixture. Use a whisk to stir the eggs. Once your eggs begin to coagulate pour the remaining cream and continue to whisk.
- Continue whisking and cooking until desired consistency. (I personally love when they are wet). Once your eggs are ready, pour into a bowl, put sprouts on top, drizzle with olive oil and you're done!
- Serve with your favorite bread! (I personally love pumpernickel bread)

325.   The Ghostie Sandwich

Serving: Serves 1 | Prep: | Cook: |Ready in:

Ingredients

- For the sandwich
- 2 slices of sourdough bread, buttered on one side
- 5 1/4 ounces (150g) soft goat's cheese
- 1 teaspoon finely chopped chives
- pickled beet (below)
- For the pickled beets
- 3-4 medium, raw beets
- 2 tablespoons olive oil
- 1 cup (200g) caster (superfine) sugar
- 1 1/4 cups (300ml) white wine vinegar

- 2 tablespoons balsamic vinegar
- 1 cup minus 3 tbsp (200ml) water
- 2 bay leaves

Direction

- Preheat the oven to 180°C/350°F/Gas 4. Trim any leaves or stalks off the beetroot (beet), clean and coat in 1 tablespoon of the oil. Wrap in foil and roast in the oven for 1–1 1/2 hours, until the point of a knife can be easily inserted. Remove and leave to cool in the foil, then unwrap and peel off the skin; use gloves or paper towels to stop your hands being stained. Cut into thick slices and place in a sterilized jar.
- For the pickling liquor, put the sugar, both vinegars, water and bay leaves in a saucepan and bring to the boil. Turn down to a simmer and gently stir so that all the sugar is dissolved. Carefully pour enough of the hot liquid into the jar to fully cover the beetroot (depending on the size of the jar, you may not need it all). Leave to cool, uncovered, then spoon the remaining tablespoon of oil into the jar and seal. Leave for at least 24 hours, and store in the refrigerator for up to a month.
- To assemble the sandwich, place the bread slices buttered side down. Spread the goat's cheese onto one slice of the bread. Place some of the pickled beetroot slices on top, then sprinkle on the chives. Close the sandwich and cook using your preferred method (panini press, frying pan, toasted sandwich machine, oven).

326.   The One Egg Dilemma

Serving: Serves 1 | Prep: | Cook: |Ready in:

Ingredients

- 1 Medium Hass Avocado
- 1 Farm Egg
- 1 bunch Spinach
- 0.5 cups Goat Cheese
- 0.25 cups Bacon Bits
- 1 piece Radish
- 1 teaspoon Chopped Chives
- 1 pinch Sea Salt
- 1 pinch Fresh Ground Black Pepper
- 1 tablespoon Best Quality Olive Oil
- 1 splash Red Wine Vinegar

Direction

- For the radishes, thinly slice a radish (Easter egg radishes, French breakfast radishes, any kind works) and place in a shallow dish. Splash with red wine vinegar and set aside. I normally do this the night before, but you flash pickling it works fine too.
- Fry a piece of bacon over low heat until most of the fat renders out and the bacon is crispy. Let it rest over a paper towel.
- For the soft-boiled egg, I like using David Chang's 5:10 method: bring a pot of water to boil; place egg in pot and time for around 5 minutes and 10 seconds; using a slotted spoon transfer the eggs into an ice bath. Once completely cooled, crack and peel the egg under cold running water. Set aside.
- Scoop the avocado out into a shallow dish. Using a fork mash the avocado with a small pinch of salt until creamy. Spread creamed avocado on a plate.
- Heat a pan to medium/medium-low heat with a little olive oil. Sauté spinach with a pinch of salt until wilted. Spoon spinach over the avocado cream on the plate. Place soft-boiled egg on top.
- Crumble the bacon bits. Roughly spread crumbled bacon bits and crumbled goat cheese over the plate. Garnish with the quick-pickled radishes and chopped chives. Finish with sea salt and fresh ground pepper if you feel like it (you should!) I like to splash some good quality olive oil on the plate; the interplay between avocado and olive oil is a thing of beauty.
- And there you have it! One egg turned into a substantial, beautiful breakfast. Enjoy!

327. Toasted Goat Cheese Crostini With Basil And Red Onion Jam

Serving: Serves about 30 crostini | Prep: | Cook: | Ready in:

Ingredients

- For the red onion jam
- 2 medium red onions, thinly sliced
- 2 tablespoons unsalted butter
- 1/4 cup sugar
- 1/4 teaspoon salt
- freshly ground black pepper
- 1/3 cup red wine
- 1 tablespoon sherry vinegar or red wine vinegar
- For the crostini
- 1 baguette
- 1 log fresh goat cheese
- 30-40 small basil leaves, rinsed and dried

Direction

- To make the jam, cook the onions, butter, sugar, salt and pepper in a covered saucepan over low heat, stirring occasionally, until the onions are soft and slightly caramelized, about 30 minutes. Add the wine and vinegar and simmer uncovered, stirring occasionally, until thick, about 20 minutes. Cool to room temperature before using. The jam may be prepared as much as two weeks in advance and refrigerated. (Makes about 2 cups jam.)
- Preheat the oven to 450°F. Slice the baguette thinly on the diagonal and arrange on a baking sheet. Cut the goat cheese into 1/4-inch slices (unwaxed dental floss works well for this) and top each baguette slice with a basil leaf, followed by a slice of cheese. Bake the crostini for about 5 minutes, or until the cheese starts to brown lightly. Top each toast with a small dollop of red onion jam and serve warm.

328. Tomato Galette With Goat Cheese, Caramelized Onions, And Bacon

Serving: Serves 4 | Prep: | Cook: | Ready in:

Ingredients

- Tart Crust
- 1 1/4 cups all purpose flour
- 1/2 teaspoon salt
- 8 tablespoons cold butter, cubed
- 3 tablespoons ice water, or more as needed
- Galette
- 5 strips bacon, diced
- 1 onion, thinly sliced
- 1 cup goat cheese, crumbled
- 1 large heirloom tomato, thinly sliced
- salt and freshly ground pepper
- egg wash, as needed

Direction

- To make the crust, process the flour and salt in a food processor until combined. Add the butter and continue to process until the butter is pea-sized.
- Add the water gradually and continue to process until it forms a smooth dough. Wrap in plastic wrap, and refrigerate until chilled.
- In a sauté pan, cook the bacon over highly heat until the fat renders. Add the onion and continue to cook until the onions caramelize and the bacon crisps. Set aside.
- Roll out the dough into a rectangle or several small circles about ¼" thick. Sprinkle/spread half of the goat cheese over the base of the dough, leaving about ½" border around the outside. Top with the bacon and onion mixture, and top with tomato slices.
- Crumble remaining goat cheese on top, and season with pepper. Fold the edges over the

middle, pressing lightly to seal. Brush the outer crust with egg wash.

- Bake in a 375 degree oven until the filling is bubbly and the crust is golden brown, about 15-20 minutes. Let cool slightly (or completely) before serving.

329. Tomato Tart With Goat Cheese, Quark, Prosciutto, And Gremolata

Serving: Serves 4 to 6 | Prep: | Cook: | Ready in:

Ingredients

- 1 recipe for your favorite tart or pie dough
- 9 small heirloom tomatoes (preferably Early Girl and even better if they are dry-farmed)
- 4 to 6 anchovies packed in oil, finely chopped
- 1 tablespoon drained capers, finely chopped
- 4 tablespoons finely chopped parsley (or any combination of tarragon, parsley, basil, mint, sage, arugula, or cilantro)
- 2 cloves garlic, peeled and microplaned
- 1 tablespoon lemon juice
- 1 teaspoon lemon zest
- 4 tablespoons finely grated Parmesan (like snow)
- 1 tablespoon extra-virgin olive oil (or just enough to bring the mixture together)
- pinch kosher salt (optional)
- 1 egg yolk, room temperature
- 3/4 cup creamy fresh goat cheese, room temperature
- 2 to 3 tablespoons heavy cream or half and half, room temperature
- 1 teaspoon lemon zest
- 1/4 teaspoon kosher salt, plus additional for tomatoes
- 1/2 cup quark cheese, room temperature
- 9 slices prosciutto (as thinly sliced as possible)

Direction

- Roll out your dough and press into your tart pan. Keep in the fridge until you're ready to assemble the tart.
- Heat the oven to 375° F.
- Core the tomatoes (1-inch wide). One at a time, turn the tomatoes upside-down over a bowl and use your fingers to scoop out as much of the liquid, pulp, and seeds as possible. Really tuck your fingers up into the cavities to release almost everything. Reserve liquid for another use (soup? tomato water?). Place tomatoes cored-side down on a cooling rack over a plate to let excess liquid drip out.
- Mix together the anchovies, capers, herbs, garlic, lemon juice, lemon zest, Parmesan, and olive oil. Taste it. Only add salt if it needs it. Set aside.
- In a standing mixer or by hand, mix together the egg yolk, goat cheese, cream, lemon zest, and salt until smooth (about 30 seconds). You want it spreadable but not runny (almost pourable but not quite). If it's too thick, add a splash more of cream. If too thin, add a bit more goat cheese. (It might be a bit lumpy if you do this: Don't stress). Set aside.
- Spread goat cheese mixture all over the bottom of the tart. On top of this mixture add a thin layer of quark.
- Sprinkle a small pinch of salt into each tomato cavity, and then evenly distribute the caper anchovy mixture between the 9 tomatoes. It's quite intense. A little bit goes a long way. So don't worry if it doesn't reach the tomato's brim. Wrap each tomato in a piece of prosciutto (sort of like a wide belt). It's fine to tear the slices up a bit in order to wrap the tomatoes nicely. Don't cover the tops or bottoms, and you might not need all of the prosciutto. Gently press the tomatoes down into the cheese bed. Bake for 40 to 50 minutes. About 25 minutes in, you can use a spatula to smash the cooking tomatoes down a bit. Be gentle—you don't want the tomato juice to squirt out on the cheese—it's just a tiny nudge downward. If the tart shell starts to brown too much, cover it with aluminum foil while the tomatoes cook. Remove the tart from the oven

when the cheese is starting to brown and the tomatoes are starting to shrivel and darken. Cool for 30 minutes. Carefully remove the outer ring of the tart pan. Slide the tart off of the metal bottom and onto a cutting board. Cut into 9 squares. Serve right away with a crunchy green salad. It will keep in the fridge for a few days, or you can freeze it for a few months.

---

330. Tomato Vegetable Sauce

Serving: Serves 6 | Prep: | Cook: | Ready in:

Ingredients

- 3 pounds plum tomatoes, peeled, seeded and chopped
- 26 ounces boxed or canned chopped tomatoes
- 1 1/2 cups carrots, diced
- 1 cup bell peppers or small sweet peppers, diced
- 4 cloves garlic, diced
- 2 teaspoons oregano
- 1/4 - 1/2 teaspoons crushed red pepper
- 1/2 cup red wine
- 2 teaspoons sugar, if needed
- 3 - 4 handfuls spinach
- basil, fresh
- salt & pepper
- 2 tablespoons olive oil
- goat cheese, for serving

Direction

- Heat the olive oil in a large, heavy pot and add the onion. Sauté the onion for a few minutes, until it starts to soften, and then add the carrots, peppers, garlic and oregano. Season with some salt and pepper and sauté for approximately 10 minutes.
- Add the fresh and boxed/tinned tomatoes, as well as the crushed red pepper. If you're sensitive to spiciness, go easy on the red pepper. If you like things with a little more

heat, go for the 1/2 teaspoons. Stir in the wine and then cover and cook for about 45 minutes - until the tomatoes are breaking down and everything is cooked through.

- Remove the lid and taste the sauce. If the flavor seems a little flat, add the sugar a little bit at a time until the flavor has rounded out.
- Stir in the spinach and basil. This will mute the beautiful, red color of the sauce, but all that veg is super good and one must make certain sacrifices in life.
- Remove the pot from the heat and either transfer to a blender (be careful when blending hot things! Steam hurts!) or use an immersion blender to blend to a consistency you like. Taste and adjust the seasoning with salt/pepper or any of the other herbs. If, for some reason, the sauce appears to thing, put it back on the heat and reduce until it's more to your liking.
- Toss with pasta for super deliciousness. If you really want a treat, serve with a little goat cheese crumbled over the top.

---

331. Tomato, Corn And Goat Cheese Pie

Serving: Serves 6 | Prep: 0hours20mins | Cook: 0hours55mins | Ready in:

Ingredients

- 3 Eggs
- 1 cup Half & Half
- 4 ounces Goat Cheese
- 1 teaspoon Salt
- 1 tablespoon Chopped Chives
- 2 cups Grilled Corn
- 1/2 cup Tomatillos, thinly sliced
- 1 cup Sliced Roma Tomatoes
- 1 9" Cooked Pie Crust

Direction

- Preheat oven to 375 degrees.

- In a food processor, add eggs, chives, half & half, goat cheese and salt and process until combined. Transfer to a medium bowl and stir in corn and tomatillos and then fold in tomatoes.
- Pour into prepared crust. Bake in oven 45-55 minutes until it passes the knife test.

---

332. Tomatoes, Goats Cheese And Herb Salad

Serving: Serves 4 | Prep: | Cook: | Ready in:

Ingredients

- 6-8 Large ripe tomatoes (Yellow, Orange and Green are all in season so experiment and mix it up a bit)– Slice into quarters
- generous pinches Salt and white and freshly ground black pepper
- 2 Cloves of garlic – Crushed and finely chopped
- 100 grams Capers (add a glug of the vinegar from the jar too)
- 1 handful Parsley- Finely sliced
- 1 handful Basil leaves – Roughly torn
- 250-300 grams Goats cheese (vegetarian) – Roughly broken up
- big splashes White wine vinegar
- generous Gglug of extra virgin olive oil

Direction

- Slice the fresh ripe tomatoes and place in a large serving bowl or plate and season.
- Throw in the chopped garlic, capers, vinegar from the capers, parsley and basil followed by the crumbled goat's cheese. Add a big glug of white wine vinegar and roughly mix so all flavours combine and then drizzle over the extra virgin olive oil and a little extra seasoning.
- Serve straight away- mop up left over oil and vinegar with a big hunk of sourdough. No part of this dish should go to waste.

---

333. Tri Cheese And Arak Dip

Serving: Serves 4 | Prep: | Cook: | Ready in:

Ingredients

- 3 ounces Blue cheese
- 6 ounces labneh (yogurt cheese)
- 2 ounces goat cheese
- 2 pieces garlic cloves
- 1 tablespoon chopped fresh parsley
- 3 ounces toasted pecans
- 2 tablespoons arak

Direction

- Drain the yogurt to make labneh for a few hours or overnight
- Chop the pecans in a mini-processor
- Mash the garlic with a pinch of salt
- Place the blue cheese, labneh, goat cheese, garlic, pecans, parsley and arak in the mini-processor and mix to a smooth purée for two minutes
- Taste and adjust seasoning; serve with French fries or veggies

---

334. Tri Colored Carrot Salad With Goat Cheese, Mint And Peas Tendrils

Serving: Serves 2 | Prep: | Cook: | Ready in:

Ingredients

- 6 carrots
- 4 sprigs mint
- goat cheese
- extra virgin olive oil
- balsamic vinegar
- Handful pea tendrils

- cracked black pepper
- salt
- 2 pieces Loaf of fresh baked bread

Direction

- 1. With a vegetable peeler, peel all carrots in long strips from bottom to top and from dark to light in color. Be forewarned if your purple carrots are as fresh and juicy as mine were, the purple juices will splatter, so it's best to use a large bowl.
- 2. Break off leaves of mint from your sprigs and break into smaller pieces, then add on top of carrots. Dress the carrots and mint with your extra virgin olive oil and just a touch of balsamic vinegar. Using your pepper mill crack some black pepper on top and add salt to taste. Then toss all ingredients in bowl together.
- 3. Plate the carrot salad separately. On top of the salad break up pieces of goat cheese, mine was a goat cheese from Spain I found at the Food Coop. Then to finish it off add about 5 or 6 pea tendrils on top and eat with a piece of your favorite loaf of bread. Don't forget to save a piece of bread at the end to soak up all those delicious flavors at the bottom of the plate. This recipe serves two.

335.   Two Bean Turkey Chili

Serving: Serves a crowd | Prep: | Cook: | Ready in:

Ingredients

- 2 tablespoons olive oil
- 2 onions, chopped
- 2 garlic cloves, smashed and minced
- 1 jalapeno chili, minced
- 2 28 oz. cans chopped plum tomatoes or two boxes Pomi chopped tomatoes
- 1/2 cup tomato paste
- 1 tablespoon ground cumin
- 3/4 teaspoon salt

- 1/2 teaspoon cayenne pepper
- 1/4 teaspoon ground cloves
- 1/4 teaspoon ground cinnamon
- 2 15 oz. cans black beans, drained
- 2 15 oz. cans kidney beans, drained
- 1/2 cup raisins
- goat cheese
- cilantro
- 1 pound ground turkey
- 1/2 cup red wine (optional)

Direction

- Heat the olive oil over medium heat. Add the onions and saute until translucent (about five minutes).
- Add the garlic and jalapeno and saute one to two minutes being careful not to let the garlic burn.
- Add the turkey, breaking up and cooking until no longer pink.
- Add the tomatoes, tomato paste, wine (if using), cumin, salt, cayenne, cloves, cinnamon. Reduce heat to low and simmer for about 20 minutes, stirring frequently.
- Add the beans and continue to cook for another 15 minutes, stirring occasionally.
- Add the raisins and cook for the last five minutes.
- Serve, topping with goat cheese and cilantro (or sour cream, shredded cheddar, and whatever else screams "chili" to you).

336.   Two Pot Penne With Chicken Sausage

Serving: Serves 6 | Prep: | Cook: | Ready in:

Ingredients

- 1 Bag or box of penne
- 3 Chicken Sausage links (I used Trader Joe's Chicken with Sundried Tomato)
- 1 Can fire roasted diced tomato
- 1 Small fennel bulb, sliced thin

- 1 Small yellow onion, diced
- 2 Celery stalks, diced
- 2 Garlic cloves, minced
- 1/4 cup Goat cheese
- Parsley for serving
- Salt, pepper, and smoked paprika to taste

Direction

- Brown the chicken sausage in a large saucepan over medium heat. Scoop out the sausage and set aside.
- In the remaining fat, sauté the onion, fennel, and celery for about ten minutes until soft and translucent. Season with salt, pepper, and smoked paprika. Then add in the garlic and cook for thirty more seconds or so.
- Pour in the can of tomatoes and add the sausage back in. Mix all of the ingredients together. Let simmer for 20 Minutes to an hour, depending on how much time you've got.
- Meanwhile, cook the penne to just almost al dente. Drain and set aside.
- When you're just about ready to serve, add the penne to the sauce pan, along with the goat cheese. Mix well and let simmer for a few minutes so the flavors meld a bit.
- Sprinkle with parsley and serve!

337.　　Vegetable Tacos With Goat Cheese And Truffle Oil

Serving: Makes 8 tacos | Prep: | Cook: | Ready in:

Ingredients

- 2 tablespoons olive oil
- 1 leek, chopped (white part only)
- 2 cups chopped mushrooms
- 1 1/4 cups corn
- 2 zucchini, chopped
- 1 1/2 cups lacinato kale, sliced thinly
- 1 1/2 teaspoons fresh thyme leaves
- 1/2 teaspoon salt

- freshly ground black pepper
- 1 tablespoon champaigne vinaigrette
- 8 soft corn tortillas {5" size}
- 4 ounces crumbled goat cheese
- truffle oil

Direction

- Heat olive oil in a sauté pan or skillet over medium high heat. Add the vegetables, thyme, salt and 1/2 t freshly ground pepper. Sauté until vegetables are tender, stirring occasionally, about 8 minutes.
- Add the vinegar, stir and sauté for 1 minute. Taste and adjust seasoning {salt} if you like.
- Warm the tortillas in the microwave. If they are dry, place them between 2 damp paper towels and warm for 30 - 40 seconds.
- To serve, divide the vegetable filling among tortillas. Top with crumbled goat cheese. Drizzle a little truffle oil on top. Dust with freshly ground black pepper.

338.　　Vegetable And Goat Cheese Lasagna

Serving: Serves 6-8 | Prep: | Cook: | Ready in:

Ingredients

- 12 ounces lasagna noodles (about 15 noodles)
- Boiling water for soaking the noodles
- 2 tablespoons olive oil
- 1 large yellow onion, diced
- 1 pound white (button) or brown (cremini) mushrooms, diced
- 4-6 garlic cloves, minced
- 1/2 teaspoon crushed red chile flakes, or to taste
- 1/2 teaspoon dried oregano
- 1 large red bell pepper, diced
- 2 medium zucchini, diced
- 1 medium carrot, finely diced
- 1 pound broccoli florets (from about 1 bunch), cut or broken into small pieces

- 1   28-oz can whole peeled tomatoes
- 16 ounces whole-milk ricotta cheese, at room temperature
- 8 ounces goat cheese, at room temperature
- 1 large egg
- Salt to taste
- Freshly ground black pepper to taste
- 1/2 cup finely grated Parmesan cheese

Direction

- Lay the lasagna noodles flat in a deep-sided dish. Pour over boiling water to cover, and let the noodles soak for 15-30 minutes, or until they're pliable. (You may want to move the noodles around every few minutes to make sure they're not sticking together.) Drain the noodles, cover with cold water, and set aside.
- In a large deep-sided skillet or sauté pan, heat olive oil over medium heat. Add onion and a pinch of salt, and sweat for 8-10 minutes, or until the onions are translucent and starting to color. Add mushrooms and another pinch of salt and cook, stirring occasionally, for 10-15 minutes, or until the mushrooms have given up their liquid and started to brown around the edges. Add garlic, chile flakes, and oregano, and cook for another 30 seconds to a minute, or until fragrant.
- Add bell pepper, zucchini, carrot, and broccoli to the pan, and cook, stirring frequently, for 2-3 minutes, or until the vegetables are just starting to soften. Add tomatoes and use a woodenly spoon or potato masher to break them up into small chunks. Bring the mixture to a boil, then reduce the heat to keep it at a steady simmer. Simmer for 20-30 minutes, or until the mixture is saucy, the vegetables are tender, and most of the liquid has evaporated. Remove from the heat and season with salt and pepper to taste.
- While the vegetables cook, combine ricotta, goat cheese, and egg in a medium mixing bowl, and mix until smooth. Season generously with salt and pepper, and set aside.

- Preheat the oven to 350º F, and place a rack in the top third of the oven. Spread a small amount of the vegetable mixture over the bottom of a 9 x 13 baking dish. Place a layer of noodles over the vegetables, tearing the noodles into pieces as needed to cover the bottom of the dish. Spread half of the cheese mixture over the noodles, then top with about 1/3 of the remaining vegetables. Add another layer of noodles, the rest of the cheese mixture, and another 1/3 of the vegetables. Lay down a final layer of noodles, and spoon over the rest of the vegetables. Sprinkle the top evenly with Parmesan.
- Lightly grease the shiny side of a sheet of aluminum foil. Cover the pan tightly with the foil, greased side down. Bake on the top rack for 20-25 minutes, or until the lasagna is warm all the way through. Remove the foil, increase the oven temperature to 400º F, and bake for another 10-15 minutes, or until the sauce is bubbling and the cheese on top is starting to brown.
- Remove the lasagna from the oven and let it rest for about 10 minutes before slicing. Serve warm. If there are leftovers, cut them into squares, wrap each square tightly in a double layer of plastic wrap, and freeze for up to 2 months.

339.   Vegetarian Lasagna

Serving: Serves 8 | Prep: | Cook: |Ready in:

Ingredients

- For the sauce
- 2 tablespoons olive oil
- 1 yellow onion, diced
- 1 large carrot, diced
- 1/4 cup white wine
- 28 ounces canned whole tomatoes
- 28 ounces canned tomato purée
- 1 teaspoon dried thyme
- 1 tablespoon salt

- Freshly ground pepper
- For the lasagna
- 4 to 6 tablespoons olive oil
- 3 to 4 medium zucchini, sliced 1/3 inch thick (they'll shrink when cooked)
- 2 Italian eggplants, sliced 1/3 inch thick
- 1 egg
- 15 ounces ricotta cheese
- 9 ounces no-boil or oven-ready lasagna noodles
- 4 ounces goat cheese (I love the Vermont Creamery brand)
- 1 pound fresh mozzarella, sliced (you should have enough slices to cover the whole top of the lasagna)
- 4 tablespoons grated Parmesan cheese
- Salt and pepper

Direction

- To make the sauce: Heat the olive oil in a Dutch oven on medium-high heat. When the oil is shimmering, add onions and carrots. Sautée for 2 to 3 minutes, until the vegetables are beginning to soften.
- Add the white wine and deglaze the pan. Stir the liquid and wait for it to reduce by half. Next, add the tomatoes, the tomato purée, and the thyme. Bring the mixture to a boil, then reduce to a simmer, cover partially, and cook while you prepare the other ingredients.
- After about 20 minutes, the vegetables should be soft enough to puree with a handheld immersion blender. If you don't have one, break up the whole tomatoes using a wooden spoon. Taste again for seasoning -- it should taste a little on the salty side, but this will work to flavor the noodles.
- To make the vegetables: Preheat your grill (or grill pan) to medium-high heat. Rub olive oil into the sliced vegetables, and season with salt and pepper. Grill the vegetables for a few minutes on each side, until the grill lines are pronounced. Transfer the vegetables to a plate, and turn off the grill (or grill pan).
- To assemble the lasagna: Preheat the oven to 350° F. In a medium bowl, crack the egg into

the ricotta, season with 1 1/2 teaspoons salt, and mix well. Set aside. Then, set up your lasagna assembly station. You should have at the ready: tomato sauce, noodles, vegetables, and goat cheese.

- In a large casserole dish, start your layering. Start with the tomato sauce, spreading enough to cover the bottom of the dish (about 1/2 cup). Next, layer your noodles, overlapping them slightly. (My pan usually fits 4 noodles across.) Spread 1/3 of your ricotta mixture over the noodles.
- Top with a layer of zucchini (you're aiming for 2 total layers of zucchini). Crumble half the goat cheese on top of the zucchini. Add more sauce to cover the vegetables and cheese.
- Repeat with the noodles and ricotta, and then layer your eggplant (you only need one layer of eggplant, so feel free to use it all). Cover the eggplant with sauce, and repeat the next layer: noodles, ricotta, and zucchini. Crumble the remaining half of the goat cheese on top of your zucchini. Add more sauce to cover the vegetables and cheese, then top with a final layer of noodles, and cover with the remaining sauce.
- Add the mozzarella slices and sprinkle the Parmesan. If you'd like, drizzle a little olive oil over the whole lasagna, and season once more with salt and pepper.
- Cover with foil, and bake in the oven, covered, for 30 minutes. Remove the foil and bake for another 30 minutes. If the mozzarella isn't fully melted at this point, turn on the broiler. Watch the lasagna carefully so that it doesn't burn.
- Most importantly, rest your lasagna for 5 minutes before slicing so that the pieces stay intact. Serve and enjoy!

340.   Very Easy Vegetarian Tapas

Serving: Serves 2 | Prep: | Cook: | Ready in:

Ingredients

- 200 grams Chickpeas
- 1 Tomato
- 1 Onion
- 2 Figs
- 1 Goat cheese
- 1 tablespoon Cutter peppermint
- 4 Artichokes (hearts)
- 1 Juice of a lemon
- 2 Green Peppers
- Chilies
- Black Pepper
- Sea salt
- Olive Oil
- Balsamic vinegar creamy

Direction

- Cut the pepper in small pieces. Sauté peppers spicy in olive oil and chili and sea-salt
- Chickpeas Prepare as usual or buy finished in tin. Onions chop. Tomatoes also chop. Mix everything. Prepare dressing in which one vinegar and virgin olive oil, pepper and a Little bit lemon. Give it to the salad. Wait 10minutes. Also delicious with green beans.
- Goat cheese with figs. In this case I have the figs picked fresh from the tree. Then they taste particularly delicious. Unfortunately, this is often not possible in Germany yes -what a pity. Simply the goat cheese cut and figs together with a little sea-salt and good Balsamic Vinegar.
- Artichokes buy canned or fresh. Canned artichokes are delicious as well and much easier to handle. Wash artichokes. Marinate them with a little bit lemon juice, good olive oil, salt and pepper. Add peppermint

---

341.   **WARM GOAT CHEESE AMUSE BOUCHE**

Serving: Serves 6 | Prep: | Cook: |Ready in:

Ingredients

- 1 piece Goat Cheese - Montrachet Style Log
- 12 pieces Bite Sized Toasts
- 1 bunch Pine Nuts
- 3 tablespoons Honey
- 2 teaspoons Argan Oil

Direction

- You could either start with a pre-made toasts to save you some time, or you could make your own. Take your bread of choice, cut it into a circular bite size, drip Argan Oil on it for added taste and toast in the oven until lightly golden. They will continue to crisp in step 3.
- Chill the goat cheese in the freezer for 10 minutes. Cut the goat cheese into a 1/2 inch slice.
- Place the extra cold cheese over the toast and return to the oven. Remove when the cheese will start to caramelize on the outside and lightly soften on the inside.
- Finally, drizzle with honey and Argan oil. The combination of sweet and deliciously nutty will complement the creamy cheese to perfection.
- Top it off with toasted pine nuts. We also added some dried figs for good measure.

---

342.   **Walnut , Date & Chevre Cups**

Serving: Makes 24 | Prep: | Cook: |Ready in:

Ingredients

- 5 large pitted dates chopped fine
- 1/2 cup walnut pieces, toasted
- 1 packet puff pastry cups (1 packet has 24 shells)
- Hawaij spice blend to taste
- 2 ounces goat cheese
- fresh cracked peppercorn to taste.

Direction

- Combine the walnuts and dates in a food processor and pulse to make the mix into a coarse crumbly mixture. Transfer into a bowl and combine with the goat cheese and the hawaij & pepper.
- Preheat oven to 400 F. Place the individual puff pastry cups on a baking sheet lined with parchment paper. Place the sheet in the oven and bake for 10 minutes. Remove from the oven and allow to cool slightly. Press down the centers (the centers are scored and so it can be worked with easily) with a small melon ball scoop. Spoon about a teaspoon of the walnut date mixture into the depression of the puff pastry cups. Return the baking sheet to the oven and bake for 10 minutes more until the tops of the puff pastry cups turn a golden brown.

343.   Warm Roasted Beet Orange Salad With Goat Cheese

Serving: Serves 2 | Prep: | Cook: | Ready in:

Ingredients

- 3 medium or 2 large red beets
- 1 orange plus one teaspoon zest
- 1 splash sesame oil
- Handful chopped curly parsley
- 2 tablespoons goat cheese
- Dash coriander seeds

Direction

- Preheat the oven to 400F. Peel and slice beets into 1/2 centimeter pieces. Chop in half and place in baking dish or roasting pan. Squeeze the juice of half of the orange onto the beets. Add a splash of sesame oil and one tablespoon of julienned orange zest. Season with salt and fresh ground pepper. Roast in oven for about 30 minutes, until the beets are to your liking.

- Divide the beets into two bowls and to each add a tablespoon of the goat cheese, the rest of the orange (diced with the sections removed), chopped parsley, and coriander seeds. Share and enjoy!

344.   Warm Caramelized Onion, Eggplant And Roasted Pepper Pasta Salad

Serving: Serves 8 | Prep: | Cook: | Ready in:

Ingredients

- On the Grill
- 2 eggplants
- 1/2 cup Balsamic vinaigrette
- 1 sweet, yellow pepper
- 1 sweet, red pepper
- 2 Poblano peppers
- On the Stove
- 3 pounds onions, peeled and sliced thinly
- 3 tablespoons olive oil
- 3 cloves garlic , minced
- 2 tablespoons balsamic vinaigrette
- 1 pound pasta (penne or your choice)
- 12 basil leaves, cut in ribbons
- 1/2 cup balsamic vinaigrette
- 4 ounces goat cheese
- 1/2 cup pine nuts
- fresh ground black pepper to taste

Direction

- On the Grill
- Wash the eggplants. You may peel them if you like. I prefer them unpeeled. Slice them crosswise in 1 1/2 inch rounds.
- Salt the rounds and allow to weep for 30 min. to 1 hr. (your convenience).
- Wash off the salt, pat dry and place in a large zip lock bag with the vinaigrette. Marinate 1-2 hrs.
- Heat a grill to high.

- Roast the peppers until the skins blister and blacken. Place the peppers in a paper bag and sweat for 10 min.
- Turn the grill down to medium-high.
- Drain the eggplant slices and grill 3-5 minutes (depending on the heat of your grill) on one side. You want a bit of charring. Flip the slices and grill the other side. The eggplant is done when the center is pierced and the flesh is as tender as fresh baked bread. Undercooked it will be tough and rubbery.
- Cut the eggplant into 1 inch cubes. Keep warm.
- Peel and seed the peppers. Cut them into bite size pieces. Keep warm.
- On the Stove
- Heat the olive oil in a very large pan on the stove. The onions may nearly overfill the pan but will cook down to almost nothing.
- Sauté the onions with frequent stirring until caramelized. If the onions begin to stick add a tablespoon of water and stir to loosen and continue to sauté.
- When the onions are well browned add the garlic and sauté until soft.
- Add two Tbsp. of the vinaigrette to deglaze the pan and combine with the onions. Keep warm.
- Boil the pasta in a large pot of salted boiling water until al dente.
- Drain the pasta and combine with the vegetables, basil and 1/2 cup of vinaigrette.
- Serve warm with 1/2 ounce of goat cheese, a sprinkle of pine nuts, a grind of black pepper and additional vinaigrette to taste.

> ### 345.   Watermelon And Arugula Salad

Serving: Serves 4 | Prep: | Cook: | Ready in:

Ingredients

- Honey Roasted Walnuts

- 1 cup walnut halves
- 1 tablespoon honey
- 3 tablespoons sugar
- 1/2 teaspoon kosher salt
- 1/4 teaspoon chili powder
- Citrus Dressing
- 4 tablespoons olive oil
- 1/4 cup fresh mint leaves
- 1 tablespoon fresh lime juice
- 2 teaspoons honey
- 1/2 teaspoon kosher salt
- 1/2 teaspoon freshly group black pepper
- 1 tablespoon fresh lemon juice
- Watermelon Salad:
- 3 cups watermelon, cut into 3/4-inch cubes
- 1/4 cup fresh mint leaves, thinly sliced
- 5 cups baby arugula
- 1 cup crumbled goat cheese

Direction

- 1) For the walnuts, preheat oven to 350°F. Line a baking sheet with parchment paper and set aside.
- 2) In a medium bowl, combine walnuts and honey, tossing well to coat. In a small bowl, combine sugar, salt and chili powder. Pour over walnuts and mix well. Place on prepared baking sheet and bake 8 minutes. Stir nuts and continue baking 6-8 minutes more until lightly toasted. Remove from oven and let cool before adding to salad.
- 3) For the dressing, in a blender, combine olive oil, mint, lemon juice, lime juice, honey, salt and pepper. Process until smooth.
- 4) To serve, place watermelon cubes, mint, arugula and honey-roasted walnuts in a large serving bowl. Toss with dressing and gently toss in crumbled goat cheese. Serve immediately.

346. When The Temperature Hits 100 . . . . Go For Beets

Serving: Serves 3-4 | Prep: | Cook: |Ready in:

Ingredients

- 3 tablespoons Olive Oil
- 3/4 pound Hot sausage, cut up into small chunks
- 1 bunch Beets with greens attached
- 1/2 Chopped onion
- Salt and Pepper
- 3/4 cup Crumbled Goat Cheese
- 1/2 cup White wine
- 1/4 teaspoon Hot pepper flakes (if you're sausage isn't that hot)
- Grated Parmesan
- 1/2 pound Fusili or other pasta

Direction

- Trim beets and save the greens. Clean the beats but if they are small don't even bother to peel them. Roast the beets in 350 oven till done. (Salt and pepper them with a bit of olive oil) About 3/4 of an hour. Rinse and chop the greens and throw away the red stems - although you could probably use those as well. Set aside.
- Sauté sausage in a large pan in olive oil till brown. Remove from pan. Add onion and sauté till translucent. Add S&P. Deglaze with wine. Add Beet greens till wilted. Put sausage back in pan.
- Boil Pasta. When done, add to pan along with roasted beets and goat cheese. Toss all together and serve with Parmesan. You're going to have pinkish pasta but it will be good.

347. White Asparagus Salad With Goat Cheese And Pickled Rhubarb

Serving: Serves 4 | Prep: | Cook: |Ready in:

Ingredients

- Pickled Rhubarb
- 4 rhubarb stalks, sliced thinly (about 1/3 inch)
- 1 cup sugar
- 1 cup apple cider vinegar
- 1 teaspoon salt
- Asparagus Salad
- 1 1/2 pounds very thick white asparagus
- 1 1/2 cups chicken stock, approximately
- 2 tablespoons unsalted butter
- 1 bay leaf
- walnut oil, to taste
- 4 cups butter or Bibb lettuce, washed and torn into bite size pieces
- 5 ounces goat cheese, crumbled
- some of the pickled rhubarb (as much as you can handle)
- black pepper, to taste

Direction

- Pickled Rhubarb
- Bring the sugar, vinegar, and salt to a boil. As soon as all of the sugar is dissolved, pour over the sliced rhubarb. Let stand for at least 3 hours. Then put them in the refrigerator until well chilled. These will keep covered a couple of weeks in the refrigerator. They are a bit addicting so make plenty.
- Asparagus Salad
- You may peel or not peel the asparagus. I leave that for you to decide. Once you have made up your mind, place the asparagus into a heavy saucepan. Choose a pan large enough to hold all the spears in a single layer. Otherwise work in batches.
- Add enough stock to come about halfway up sides of the spears. Add 2 tablespoons butter, and the bay leaf, and cook uncovered over

medium heat about 8 minutes. Roll the spears around until spears are very tender and glazed.

- Remove the spears from the braising liquid and set aside on a plate. One of the joys of white asparagus is that it does not quickly discolor from cooking so there is no need to plunge into ice water as with green asparagus. But you can if you want to. If you have an audience in the kitchen (and well, who doesn't??) then please plunge away as dramatically as you can!
- Once the asparagus has cooled completely cover it and place it in the refrigerator until well chilled.
- When you are ready to plate this, toss a mild-tasting lettuce such as butter or Bibb with just enough walnut oil to make them glisten. Use the oil sparingly. It does not need to be mixed with vinegar or lemon juice. This salad has plenty of zip on its own! Mound the dressed lettuce in the center of each salad plate.
- Stack a pile of 4 or 5 spears of white asparagus around or on top of the lettuce. Sprinkle a generous amount of crumbled goat cheese on top followed by plenty of the pickled rhubarb.
- Drizzle with some more of the walnut oil, just a few drops here and there for sparkle. Then add a good grind of black pepper over everything. Pucker up and enjoy!

---

348. Whole Wheat Pizza With Sundried Tomato Puree, Red Onions, Asparagus, And Goat Cheese

Serving: Serves 4-6 | Prep: | Cook: |Ready in:

Ingredients

- Sundried Tomato Paste
- 3/4 cup packed sundried tomatoes (not packed in oil)
- 1 cup water

- 2 garlic cloves
- 1 pinch salt
- 2 tablespoons olive oil
- Pizza Assembly
- 1 pound asparagus, tough ends snapped off
- 1/2 red onion, sliced into half moons
- 2 cloves of garlic, finely chopped
- 1 small log of goat cheese, crumbled
- 1 handful fresh basil, chopped

Direction

- Sundried Tomato Paste
- Bring the water to a boil in a small saucepan. Add the tomatoes, cover, lower heat to low, and simmer for about 15 minutes. In a blender or food processor puree the sundried tomatoes, garlic cloves, salt, and then stir the olive oil in.
- Pizza Assembly
- Preheat oven to 450F. Stretch your pizza crust onto your pan that has been greased with some olive oil. Brush the top of your crust with olive oil and bake for 10 minutes. Take crust out the oven and spread with a layer of the sundried tomato paste. Layer on the red onion and then arrange the asparagus on top. Crumble the goat cheese on top. Return to the oven and bake for 15 minutes. The veggies will still be crispy and the cheese will have just started to melt and the freshness of the asparagus really comes out.

---

349. Wild Piedmont Mushroom & Goat Cheese Strudel Served Over Spring Arugula With Toasted Pine Nuts

Serving: Makes 2 whole strudel | Prep: | Cook: |Ready in:

Ingredients

- 1/4 cup Chicken or Vegetable Stock

- 1 shallot
- 1 clove Garlic
- 1 pound Wild Mushroom Blend
- 1/2 cup Dry White Wine
- 6 ounces Goat Cheese, crumbled
- 6 whole Phyllo Sheets (3 per strudel)
- 6 tablespoons Butter, melted
- 1/4 cup Pine Nuts, lightly toasted
- 1 bunch Wild Greens

Direction

- Feel free to use a nice mix of store bought mushrooms if you're not in the mood to hunt. Toast pine nuts and set aside. In a large sauté pan heat the stock and half of the butter. Add the shallots and garlic and sweat until the shallots are translucent. Add the mushrooms and sauté until cooked and juices are reduced. Add the wine and reduce until almost dry.
- Spread the mushroom mixture on a sheet pan to cool. When cool, add the crumbled goat cheese and pine nuts.
- To prepare one (1) strudel. On sheet pan, stack 3 sheets of phyllo. Brush the top sheet thoroughly with the melted butter. Mound ½ the mushroom mixture along the long edge of the dough. Roll the strudel tightly, completely enclosing the mushroom mixture. Brush the entire outside with the melted butter.
- Repeat above to assemble 2nd strudel. Score the tops of the strudels; 5 portions per strudel. Bake at 350 for 15 minutes or until golden brown. Serve on a bed of greens with a drizzle of good balsamic vinegar and some olive oil.

350. Wild Rice & Goat Cheese Stuffing

Serving: Serves 6-8 | Prep: | Cook: |Ready in:

Ingredients

- 2 cups wild rice
- 6 cups water

- 3/4th pounds Kialbasa or chorizo, diced
- 5 tablespoons unsalted butter, plus extra for greasing
- 1/2 cup diced Spanish onion
- 1/2 cup diced carrots
- 1 leek, diced
- 3 cloves garlic, finely chopped
- 2 tablespoons fresh thyme, diced
- 1 (day old) loaf country bread, cubed
- 2-4 cups stock
- 12 ounces goat cheese
- 1/2 cup fresh parsley, chopped
- S&P

Direction

- Preheat the oven to 375 degrees F.
- Combine rice, water and 1 tablespoon of salt in a large saucepan, bring to a boil over high heat and cook fully about 1 hour 30 minutes. Drain and set aside.
- Heat butter in a high-sided sauté pan over medium-high heat. Add the meat, onions, carrots and leeks and cook until soft. Add garlic and thyme and cook for 1 minute.
- Add this mixture, bread, goat cheese, parsley and 2 cups stock to the rice. Mix to combine. The mixture should be quite wet; add more stock, if needed. Season with salt and pepper to taste.
- Transfer to a large buttered baking dish and bake, uncovered, until heated through and golden brown, about 30 minutes. Rest 10 minutes before serving.

351. Winter Couscous And Bulgur Salad

Serving: Serves 2 | Prep: | Cook: |Ready in:

Ingredients

- 1 small winter squash (i.e., 1 lb delicata) peeled, seeded and cut into cubes
- 3 shallots, cut into quarters or eights

- 1 tablespoon olive oil
- salt and pepper to season
- 3/4 cup whole wheat couscous
- 1/4 cup bulgur
- 1 1/4 cups water
- Splash of olive oil
- Dash of salt
- 1 tablespoon dijon mustard
- 2 tablespoons champagne vinegar
- 4 tablespoons olive oil
- 1/2 teaspoon salt
- 1/4 teaspoon pepper
- 2 ounces goat cheese, crumbled
- fresh herbs, like parsley, scallions or chives to garnish (if they aren't frozen in your garden)

Direction

- Preheat oven to 425. Toss squash and shallots with olive oil, salt and pepper. My preferred method is to roast in my non-stick skillet, but a baking sheet would probably be the standard. Roast for 25-30 minutes, stirring once. When done, remove from pan and allow to cool.
- In the meantime, add water, oil and salt to saucepan. Bring to a boil, remove from heat and add couscous and bulgur. Cover and sit for 10 minutes. Fluff with fork and allow to cool.
- Mix mustard, vinegar, remaining olive oil, salt and pepper in large bowl for vinaigrette. Stir in squash and shallots, couscous and bulgur, crumbled goat cheese and fresh herbs if available. Adjust seasoning if necessary. Serve at room temperature or refrigerate prior to serving.

---

352. Winter Greens Gremolata And Pesto

Serving: Makes 2 cups winter greens gremolata (half of which you can extend into winter greens pesto) | Prep: | Cook: | Ready in:

Ingredients

- Winter Greens Gremolata
- 1 bunch arugula
- 1 bunch Italian parsley
- 1 bunch dinosaur kale
- 1 tablespoon kosher salt, for the blanching water
- 6 anchovy fillets
- 6 garlic cloves, peeled
- 3 tablespoons lemon juice
- 1 tablespoon lemon zest
- 2 tablespoons capers (drained of brine)
- 2 teaspoons white wine or champagne vinegar
- 1/2 cup extra virgin olive oil
- Kosher salt, to taste
- Winter Greens Pesto
- 1 cup Winter Greens Gremolata
- 1/2 cup blanched almonds, lightly toasted
- 1/2 cup goat cheese (fresh, not aged)
- 1/2 cup parmesan, finely grated
- 1/2 cup extra virgin olive oil
- Kosher salt, to taste
- Lemon juice. to taste
- White wine vinegar, to taste

Direction

- Winter Greens Gremolata
- Bring a large pot of water to the boil. Wash arugula, parsley, and kale (no need to dry them). Trim off any large stems. Add salt to water and turn down to a simmer. Toss in the kale. Blanch for five minutes, stirring occasionally. Remove kale with tongs and place in a colander over a large bowl. Using the same water, blanch parsley and arugula for only one minute. With tongs, remove second batch of greens and add to draining kale. Allow all greens to cool for a few minutes. Form greens into a ball and squeeze out most of the liquid. Place in food processor.
- With a mortar and pestle, bash anchovy and garlic to a paste. Into the food processor, add anchovy/garlic paste, lemon juice/zest, capers, vinegar, and olive oil. Pulverize the

heck out of it for 30 seconds. Taste for balance and texture. Add salt, more lemon juice, or vinegar as needed. Pulverize more if texture is too coarse.

- You can keep it in a jar in the fridge with a thin layer of olive oil on top (just know that it won't be vibrant green by the next day). Or you can freeze it in a jar or in an ice cube tray. It stays green and beautiful when you freeze it. Thaw for an hour or so at room temperature before using.
- Winter Greens Pesto
- If you're extending some of the Gremolata into pesto, leave 1 cup of Gremolata in the food processor. Add warm nuts, goat cheese, parmesan, and olive oil. Taste. It will probably need more salt. Maybe a bit more acid like lemon or vinegar.
- Keeps for a few days in the fridge in a jar with a thin layer of olive oil on top of the pesto. Alternatively, you can freeze it in a jar or in an ice cube tray for easy access. Thaw by leaving it out room at temperature for an hour or so.

---

353.   Zucchini & Cucumber 'Beat The Heat' Carpaccio

Serving: Serves 4-6 | Prep: | Cook: |Ready in:

Ingredients

- 2 Medium Zucchini, Sliced Paper Thin
- 2 Cucumbers,Sliced Paper Thin
- 3 tablespoons Fresh Lemon Juice
- 1/4 cup Extra-Virgin Olive Oil
- 1/4 teaspoon Lemon Zest
- 1 tablespoon Rice Wine Vinegar
- 1/2 cup Goat Cheese, Crumbled
- 1 tablespoon Fresh Dill, Finely Chopped
- 2 tablespoons Fresh Basil, Finely Chopped
- 1 tablespoon Fresh Italian Parsley, Finely Chopped
- 1/2 Kosher Salt
- Fresh Cracked Black Pepper to Taste

- Pinch of Red Pepper Flakes

Direction

- In a small bowl, whisk together the lemon juice, lemon zest, olive oil and vinegar.
- On a large platter, arrange zucchini and cucumber au gratin style, overlapping the zucchini and cucumber.
- When ready to serve, drizzle with 3 tablespoons of the dressing. Top with goat cheese, basil, dill, parsley salt, cracked pepper and red pepper flakes. Serve immediately.

---

354.   Zucchini & Goat Cheese Frittatas With Smoked Trout

Serving: Serves 12 | Prep: | Cook: |Ready in:

Ingredients

- 5 eggs
- 1/2 cup milk
- 4 ounces of goat cheese (can be pre-seasoned: roasted garlic & herbs) at room temperature
- 1/2 cup grated parmesan (plus more to top)
- 1/2 cup chopped parsley
- 1 tablespoon olive oil
- 1 large glove of garlic, minced
- 2 zucchinis, finely diced
- 1 small white onion, chopped
- Fresh ground salt & pepper
- 4 ounces of wild smoked trout

Direction

- In a large skillet set to medium high, heat the olive oil. When the pan is hot add the garlic and cook for 1 minute then add the onion, stirring gently until slightly translucent, about 3 minutes. Add the chopped zucchini and cook until slightly browned, stirring occasionally about 5 minutes. Set aside.
- Preheat the oven to 350F. In a large mixing bowl beat the eggs vigorously, add the milk

and keep mixing. Incorporate the goat cheese & the parmesan cheese. Season generously with salt and pepper. Add the parsley and mix to combine then add the zucchini & onion mixture.

- Pour the frittata mixture into a nonstick or greased muffin tray (make sure the muffin tray is a 1/2 cup capacity) Sprinkle with extra parmesan cheese. Cook for 30 to 35 minutes or until the frittata is set and golden.
- Place mini frittatas on a serving platter and top with smoked trout & a dollop of goat cheese.

355.   Zucchini Flowers Stuffed With Goat Cheese And Basil

Serving: Serves 2-6 | Prep: | Cook: |Ready in:

Ingredients

- 1 egg
- 4 ounces goat cheese
- ¼ teaspoon pepper
- ¼ teaspoon sea salt
- 6-8 basil leaves chopped
- about 6 medium zucchini flowers
- olive oil
- extra salt for sprinkling

Direction

- Preheat the oven to 425 degrees.
- Mix the egg, goat cheese, pepper, salt and basil together.
- Stuff flowers with this mixture and place on a parchment-lined baking sheet that has been brushed with a little olive oil. Brush the stuffed flowers lightly with olive oil and sprinkle a little salt on top.
- Bake for about 12 minutes at 425 degrees, or until flowers are golden and cheese is bubbly and cooked.

356.   Zucchini Frittata With Caramelized Red Onion And Goat Cheese

Serving: Serves 4 | Prep: | Cook: |Ready in:

Ingredients

- 2 zucchini
- 2 small red onions
- 1 tablespoon coconut or olive oil, divided
- 2 tablespoons balsamic vinegar
- 4 zucchini flowers (optional)
- 1 clove garlic, minced
- 4 large eggs
- Leaves from 10 sprigs thyme
- Zest of 1 lemon
- 1/4 cup milk
- Sea salt and freshly ground pepper, to taste
- 130 grams goat cheese

Direction

- Preheat oven to 350° F (175° C).
- Cut zucchini and onion in thin slices.
- Preheat a skillet over high heat. Add half of the oil and sauté the onion for about 6 minutes, until soft. Add the balsamic vinegar and sauté for another 5 minutes. Remove from the pan.
- In the same pan, add the other half of the oil and cook the zucchini until browned and soft, adding the garlic halfway through.
- In a large bowl, whisk together the eggs, thyme, lemon zest, and milk. Season with salt and pepper.
- In an ovenproof skillet, combine the zucchini and onions. Pour the egg mixture on top and then crumble the goat cheese over the whole dish.
- Gently place the zucchini flowers on top, if using, and bake the frittata for about 30 minutes, until set and golden brown. Take out of the oven, sprinkle on some more thyme, and serve with a salad and/or bread.

- Topping it off: Finally, garnish the dish with sun-dried tomatoes and crumbled goat cheese.

357. Zucchini Ribbons With Goat Cheese & Infused Herb Chilli Oil

Serving: Serves 4 | Prep: | Cook: | Ready in:

Ingredients

- 8 Zucchinis
- 1 white onion
- 1 bunch Basil
- 2 sprigs Italian Parsley
- 1 handful Sun-dried tomatoes
- 1 handful Goat Cheese
- 1 teaspoon Cinnamon
- 2 teaspoons Chilli flakes
- 2 teaspoons Cumin
- Olive oil infused with garlic, herbs and chilli

Direction

- Peeling the Zucchinis: I used a regular potato peeler to make the zucchini ribbons (of course, other tools can be used to make zucchini noodles "zoodles" rather than ribbons). Since zucchinis release a lot of water while cooking, make sure to peel until you see the seeds starting to surface – we don't want the core because they have higher water content compared to the rest of the vegetable. This is the most time-consuming step, but I assure you that the rest is just a matter of putting everything into one pan!
- Cooking the Zucchinis: I grilled about half the amount of zucchini ribbons to get those nice lines on the vegetable (this is optional). It adds a smoky flavor to the dish and also makes it look nicer! After they're cooked, set them aside. While doing that, I caramelized the diced shallots and onions in another pan and added a bit of brown sugar along with the chili-infused oil. Add the uncooked zucchini along with the herbs and spices, using tongs to carefully stir without breaking the ribbons.

358. A Very Good Thing Indeed

Serving: Serves me, or 4 | Prep: | Cook: | Ready in:

Ingredients

- 1 large, organic spaghetti squash
- 2 packages organic grape tomatoes
- 1/2 large red onion, finely chopped
- 4 cloves organic garlic
- 1 packet, or handful, organic fresh basil
- coarse sea salt
- lots of fresh cracked black pepper
- 4 splashes white wine
- 1 packet soft goat's cheese
- hunk, pecorino cheese (I use a variety that has black peppercorns in it! delicious)
- 1/2 organic lemon
- 1/2 clamshell organic baby arugula
- extra virgin olive oil

Direction

- Day One: Prepare the spaghetti squash by cutting it into 4 pieces, roasting in pie plates or baking dishes, insides down. Roast at 350 with skin on, deseeded and rubbed with a little olive oil, sea salt and pepper. I roasted a fairly large one recently for about 30 mins until the insides began to peel away with a fork like spaghetti strands.
- I like to refrigerate my cooked squash overnight, cooled and packed in ziplock bags with the skin and strands intact. I find it has a better texture when it's reheated!
- Day Two: Remove the squash from the fridge. Tear out the strands with a fork, piling them into a large cake pan. Preheat the oven to 370. Once the strands are spread out in the large pan, drizzle with a little oil, salt and pepper.

Bake in the oven for 10-15 minutes while you prepare the sauce.

- Wash the arugula and place in a mixing bowl. Dress with a little olive oil, sea salt and freshly cracked pepper. Squeeze 1/4 of the lemon over it and stir. Set aside.
- The Sauce: Dice your onion and garlic. Sauté in individual little frying pans (the size you would make an omelet in, one per person) in a little olive oil, salt and pepper. Sauté gently until translucent. Chop your tomatoes while the onions cook, if using grape tomatoes, in half is fine.
- Add the tomatoes and sauté, letting them get really juicy in the pan, you can add a touch of water to them. After they've started to form a fresh style sauce, add the white wine over medium high heat and let it reduce a little. Add a little more oil and a little squeeze of lemon to each frying pan. Add in your basil and stir through once slowly. Add a quarter of the goat's cheese packet to each frying pan of sauce. Stir to incorporate into a rose sauce. Remove the pan of squash from the oven. Add 1/4 of the squash to each pan of sauce. Do not stir.
- Drizzle a little oil over each mound of squash. The pan heat should be on medium. Grate roughly 1/4 cup of pecorino over each mound. Allow the cheese enough time to melt slightly. Give each pan of squash and sauce one loose stir that does not evenly incorporate the sauce over the squash. Empty each little pan into its own bowl for eating -- large soup bowls or udon bowls are good size for this.
- Top each bowl of squash/sauce with a big handful of the arugula you set aside earlier. Grate a bit more pecorino on top of it, a little drizzle of oil, and a ton of fresh cracked pepper. Serve immediately. COMPLICATED RECIPE BUT WORTH IT!!! :)

Serving: Serves 4 | Prep: | Cook: |Ready in:

Ingredients

- 8 chicken legs (you can also use breasts with the skin and bone in if you want white meat)
- 1 bunch of fresh thyme
- 2 shallots, finely minced
- 1 1/2 cups goat cheese, at room temp
- 2 lemons, thinly sliced
- 1 scant tablespoon lemon zest
- 2-3 tablespoons olive oil
- salt and pepper

Direction

- Preheat oven to 420 degrees.
- In a bowl mix together the goat cheese, lemon zest, shallots, about two tablespoons of the fresh thyme leaves, and salt and pepper.
- Peel back the skin of the chicken parts to create a small pocket in each part. Stuff each part with about 11/2 tablespoons of the cheese mixture. Sprinkle the parts with salt and pepper and place parts in a roasting pan. Sprinkle about 2 tablespoons of the thyme leaves over the top and place two or three lemon slices on each piece of meat. Drizzle the olive oil over the chicken and place in the oven for about 25 minutes.
- Turn on broiler in your oven and broil the chicken for about 5 minutes more or until the skin and lemon slices are nicely browned.
- Transfer to platter and serve.

360. Fig, Goat Cheese And Prosciutto Tart

Serving: Serves 6 | Prep: | Cook: |Ready in:

Ingredients

- pie crust
- 2 cups all-purpose flour
- 1 1/2 cold sweet butter cut into cubes
- 1/4 teaspoon salt
- 1/3 cup cold water
- 1 egg, beaten with 1 tablespoon of water
- for the filling
- 3/4 pound (about 12) fresh black figs
- 1/3 pound mild prosciutto
- 10 1/2 ounces soft goat cheese
- 1/4 cup pine nuts
- 3 tablespoons fig jam
- 1/4 cup olive oil
- about 6 fresh basil leaves

Direction

- For the crust, put the butter, flour and salt in a food processor and mix until the mixture starts to come together. Slowly add the water until the dough forms a ball. Wrap in plastic and put in the refrigerator for at least an hour before rolling out.
- Heat oven to 400 degrees. Flour a board or flat surface and roll out the dough. Place it in a buttered 9" pie dish and bake blind for 15 minutes. Remove the beans or whatever you have used as weights, prick with a fork and brush the crust with the egg mixture. Bake for another 10 minutes. In the meantime, place the fig jam in a saucepan and heat until it loosens.
- Brush the bottom of the crust with a thin layer of the fig jam. Slice the figs in quarters. Sprinkle about half of the goat cheese on the pie shell, then lay the prosciutto in a fan shape around the whole pie. Sprinkle the figs on top of that and then crumble the rest of the goat cheese around them. Sprinkle the top of the tart with the pine nuts and bake return to the oven for another 15 minutes.
- When the tart is out of the oven drizzle it with the olive oil. Then tear the basil leaves and scatter over the top.

361. Green Goat Dip

Serving: Serves 8-10 people | Prep: | Cook: | Ready in:

Ingredients

- 6 Avocados, peel and pit removed
- 8 ounces Fresh goat cheese
- 2 Garlic cloves
- Bunch of fresh parsley
- Lemon juice
- Salt and pepper
- Glug of good olive oil

Direction

- Combine avocado, goat cheese, parsley and garlic into a food processor. Blend until smooth and creamy. Add salt, pepper and lemon juice to taste and a nice Glug of olive oil right at the end. Mix well.
- Serve dip with pita chips or crostini. The dip can also be used on sandwiches and as a pasta filling.

362. Pecan Crusted Goat Cheese Salad With Blood Orange Tahini Dressing

Serving: Makes 4 main course servings | Prep: | Cook: | Ready in:

Ingredients

- For the Dressing
- 1/2 cup sunflower seed oil
- 1/4 cup champagne vinegar
- Juice from one blood orange
- Juice from one tangerine
- 2 tablespoons dried cherries
- 1 tablespoon tahini
- 1 tablespoon honey
- 1 teaspoon sea salt
- For the Salad
- 1.5 cups forbidden rice, uncooked

- 2 pounds boneless, skinless chicken breasts
- 1 tablespoon Datil Pepper Spice OR 1 teaspoon each sea salt and pepper
- 1 tablespoon olive oil
- 1.5 cups chicken stock
- 3 blood oranges, divided (one for the braise; two for the salad)
- 5 ounces goat cheese
- 1 cup pecans, divided (1/2 cup for the salad, 1/2 cup crushed for the goat cheese)
- 8 cups baby arugula, cleaned and dried
- 1 cup fresh basil leaves, whole
- 1 cup dried tart cherries

Direction

- For the Dressing
- Put the sunflower seed oil, champagne vinegar, juice from both a blood orange and tangerine, dried cherries, tahini, honey and salt in your blender and blend on high speed until the cherries are broken up and the mixture is completely emulsified. Set aside.
- For the Salad
- Preheat the oven to 400 degrees F. Make sure you have a rack in the middle of the oven.
- Cut one blood orange in half. One half will be used to squeeze over the chicken prior to the oven; the other half needs to be thinly sliced.
- Grab two large plates: one for your raw chicken (in which to season it on) and another to rest the chicken after you've browned it.
- Place the chicken on one of the plates and coat with 1 tablespoon Datil spice or 1 teaspoon each sea salt and pepper.
- Heat either a large cast-iron pot (I use a 5.5 QT cocotte) or Dutch oven over medium-high heat. Add 1 tablespoons of olive oil. Once it's shimmering, swirl it around so that it coats the surface.
- Place the chicken in the pot, without crowding it. You may need to brown the chicken in batches depending on the size of your pot. Leave the chicken, undisturbed, for 2-3 minutes or until a nice brown crust forms. Flip and repeat on the other side. Remove from the pan and place on the other clean plate. Repeat

until all breasts are browned, but not cooked through.
- Pour the chicken broth into the pot, scraping the bottom with a wooden spoon to get up any brown bits.
- Add the chicken and accumulated juices to the pot. Squeeze half of one blood orange over the chicken and then place the blood orange slices from the other half in and round the chicken.
- Place the pot on the middle rack of the oven, with the lid on, and cook for 25 minutes or until the chicken is cooked through.
- Set the chicken aside to cool.
- Once cooled, cut the chicken into small, bite-size chunks.
- Cook your rise according to the instructions on the package. Set aside to cool.
- Grab your crushed pecans, goat cheese and a plate to rest the balls on. Make sure your pecans are finely crushed up. Roll about 1 teaspoon of goat cheese into a ball between your palms. Gently roll the goat cheese balls in the crushed pecans and place on the plate. Once all of the goat cheese is coated and rolled, place the plate in the freezer. After 1-2 hours, they should be frozen and you can place them in a resealable plastic bag and put back in the freezer. Take them out of the freezer 2 hours prior to serving the salad.
- Peel and thinly slice crosswise the remaining two blood oranges.
- Put the arugula in a large bowl. Sprinkle the rice, basil leaves, pecans, cherries and chicken. Drizzle with half of the salad dressing and toss a bit. Taste. Do you need all of the dressing? Everyone's taste is different. Add more in small increments until you hit the sweet spot. Place the blood orange slices around the salad and sprinkle with the pecan-crusted goat cheese balls. That's it. You're done.
- This should be eaten within an hour of tossing...arugula + dressing won't last long together once introduced. That's just how some relationships go. Enjoy!

363. Salmon With Caramelized Onion Frittata

Serving: Serves 2 | Prep: | Cook: |Ready in:

Ingredients

- 1 tablespoon olive oil
- 3 large crimini or button mushrooms, sliced
- 1 cup fresh kale
- 1/4 cup caramelized onions
- 4 eggs, whisked
- 1/2 teaspoon kosher salt
- 1/4 teaspoon black pepper
- 1/4 cup crumbled goat cheese or feta
- chopped parsley for garnish

Direction

- Preheat the oven to 375 degrees.
- In a small 7" skillet (preferably cast iron) heat the olive oil over medium heat. Add the mushrooms and sauté for 3-4 minutes until they start to brown and give off some of their liquid.
- Stir in the kale and cook for 2-3 minutes until it begins to wilt. Add the caramelized onions and stir to combine. Add the salmon and gently fold into the kale and onion mixture. Spread the ingredients evenly in the pan.
- Add salt and pepper to the eggs and whisk to combine. Pour the eggs over the salmon mixture. Sprinkle the goat cheese over the top and cook for one minute -- do not stir.
- Transfer the pan to the hot oven and cook for about 6 minutes or until eggs are just set. Turn the temperature gauge to "broil" and continue to cook the eggs for an additional 2 -3 minutes until they start to brown on top.
- Let the frittata rest for about 2 minutes before cutting. Sprinkle with chopped parsley.

364. Spicy Pumpkin + Goat Cheese Shakshuka

Serving: Serves 2-4 | Prep: | Cook: |Ready in:

Ingredients

- 1 small onion, finely diced
- 2 cloves garlic, finely diced
- 1 teaspoon cumin
- 1/4 teaspoon crushed red pepper
- pinch of cayenne
- 4 medium-sized tomatoes, finely chopped
- 1 tablespoon tomato paste
- 8 ounces pumpkin puree
- salt and pepper to taste
- 4 eggs
- 4 ounces goat cheese, crumbled
- cilantro, finely chopped
- pumpkin and sesame seeds
- crunchy bread on the side

Direction

- Set the oven to 375 degrees.
- In the bottom of a heavy Dutch oven or enamel-lined cast iron skillet set over medium-high heat, add a few tablespoons of olive oil. Add the onion and garlic and cook for about a minute. Add the cumin, red pepper, and cayenne and stir to combine.
- Add the tomatoes (plus their juice) and sauté until the tomatoes are soft and the juices slightly evaporated. Make a small well in the middle of the pan and add the tomato paste, frying for a few seconds then stir to combine. Lastly, add the pumpkin puree and stir until fully incorporated. Turn off the heat and salt and pepper to taste.
- Using the back of a spoon, make four little divets in the tomato-pumpkin sauce. Crack each egg individually and carefully pour one into each little divet. Cover the pan and transfer to the oven, cooking for 8 to 10 minutes or until the eggs are set to your liking.
- Remove from oven, sprinkle with the goat cheese, and replace lid for a few minutes to

help the cheese melt. Sprinkle with cilantro and pumpkin and sesame seeds. Serve with crunchy bread on the side.

365.　　Sunblush Tomato Napoleon With Basil Goat Cheese Mousse

Serving: Serves 4 | Prep: | Cook: | Ready in:

Ingredients

- 1　puff pastry sheet
- 1 pound　tomatoes
- 2 teaspoons　fresh basil, chopped
- 2 teaspoons　olive oil
- 1　small garlic clove, minced
- 5 ounces　goat cheese
- 1 cup　heavy whipping cream
- 1/2 cup　storebought tomato chutney or jam

Direction

- On a floured surface, roll out puff pastry sheet to 1/8 inch thick. Using a knife, cut the pastry sheet into 3 equal sized rectangles. Place each pastry rectangle on a baking sheet lined with parchment paper. Bake according to package directions and let cool completely.
- Cut tomatoes into bite sized pieces {if using cherry tomatoes, slice in half}. Place sliced tomatoes in mixing bowl, and add 1 teaspoon chopped basil, add minced garlic, olive oil and salt and pepper to taste. Mix thoroughly to combine. Set aside.
- In mixing bowl, add goat cheese and whipping cream. Mix using handheld mixers for about 1 minute or until light and creamy and the consistency of whipped cream. Add 1 teaspoon basil and stir to combine. Set aside.
- To compile the mielle fueille, cut each puff pastry rectangle in half and fold open like a book until each pastry sheet splits into two pieces. Repeat with each pastry sheet. You will need to use three pastry sheet halves total so save the remainder for other uses.
- Place one half of a pastry sheet on a serving platter. Spread about 2 tablespoons tomato jam onto pastry sheet. Then spread with 2 tablespoons goat cheese mousse. Lightly sprinkle with sea salt. Spoon one third of the tomatoes on top of the goat cheese mousse. Place another pastry sheet on top and repeat process {tomato jam, goat cheese mousse, sea salt, tomatoes} two more times, finishing with the tomatoes. Serve immediately.

Index

225

Conclusion

Thank you again for downloading this book!

I hope you enjoyed reading about my book!

If you enjoyed this book, please take the time to share your thoughts and post a review on Amazon. It'd be greatly appreciated!

Write me an honest review about the book – I truly value your opinion and thoughts and I will incorporate them into my next book, which is already underway.

Thank you!

If you have any questions, **feel free to contact at:** _author@shellfishrecipes.com_

Fannie Sims

shellfishrecipes.com